Shojo Beat

ANONYMOUS NOISE

Ryoko Fukuyama

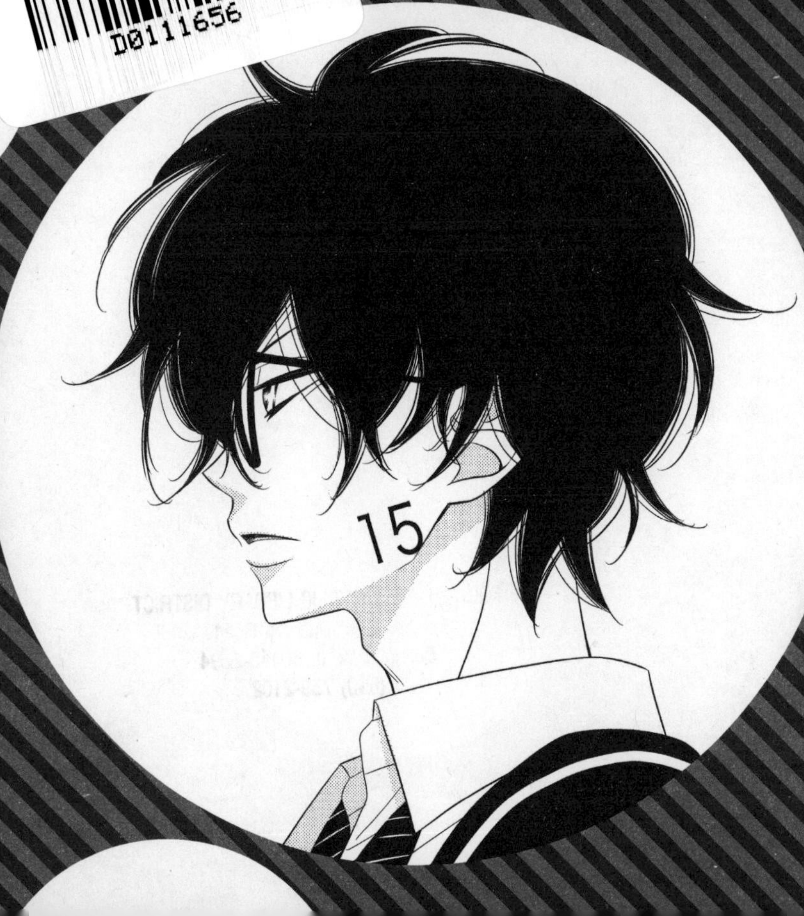

15

Anonymous Noise
Volume 15

CONTENTS

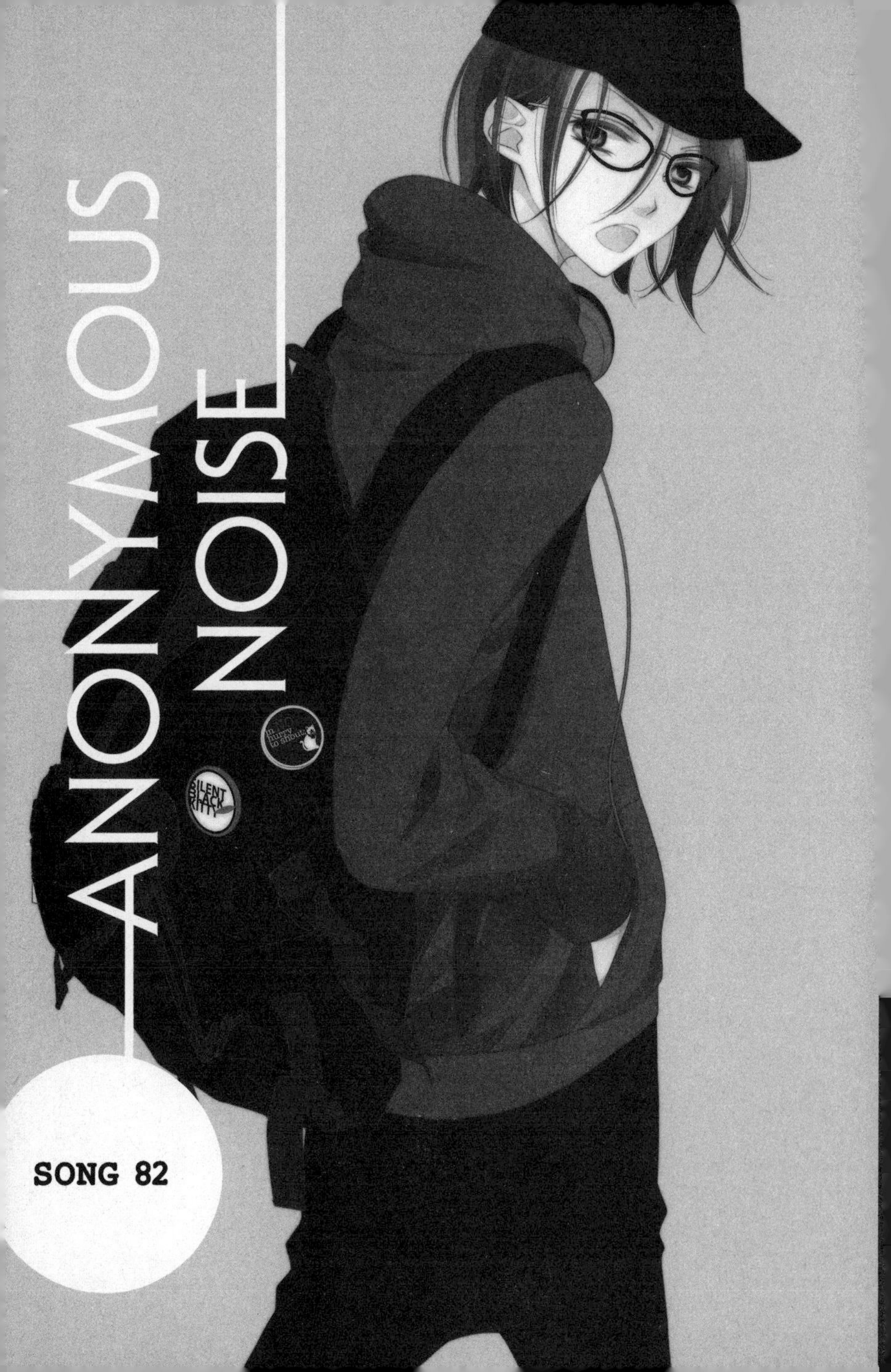
ANONYMOUS
NOISE
SILENT BLACK KITTY
in hurry to shout
SONG 82

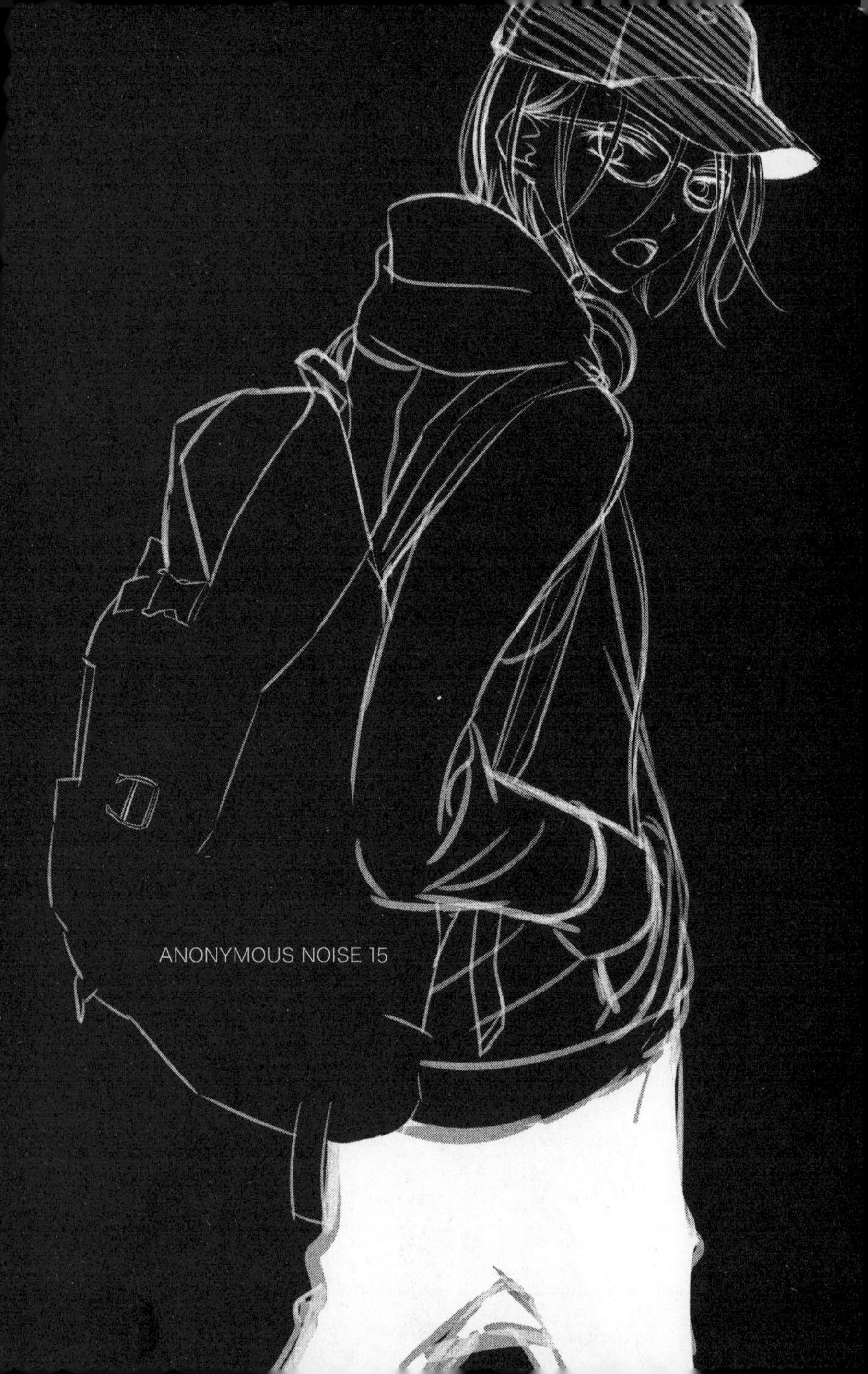
ANONYMOUS NOISE 15

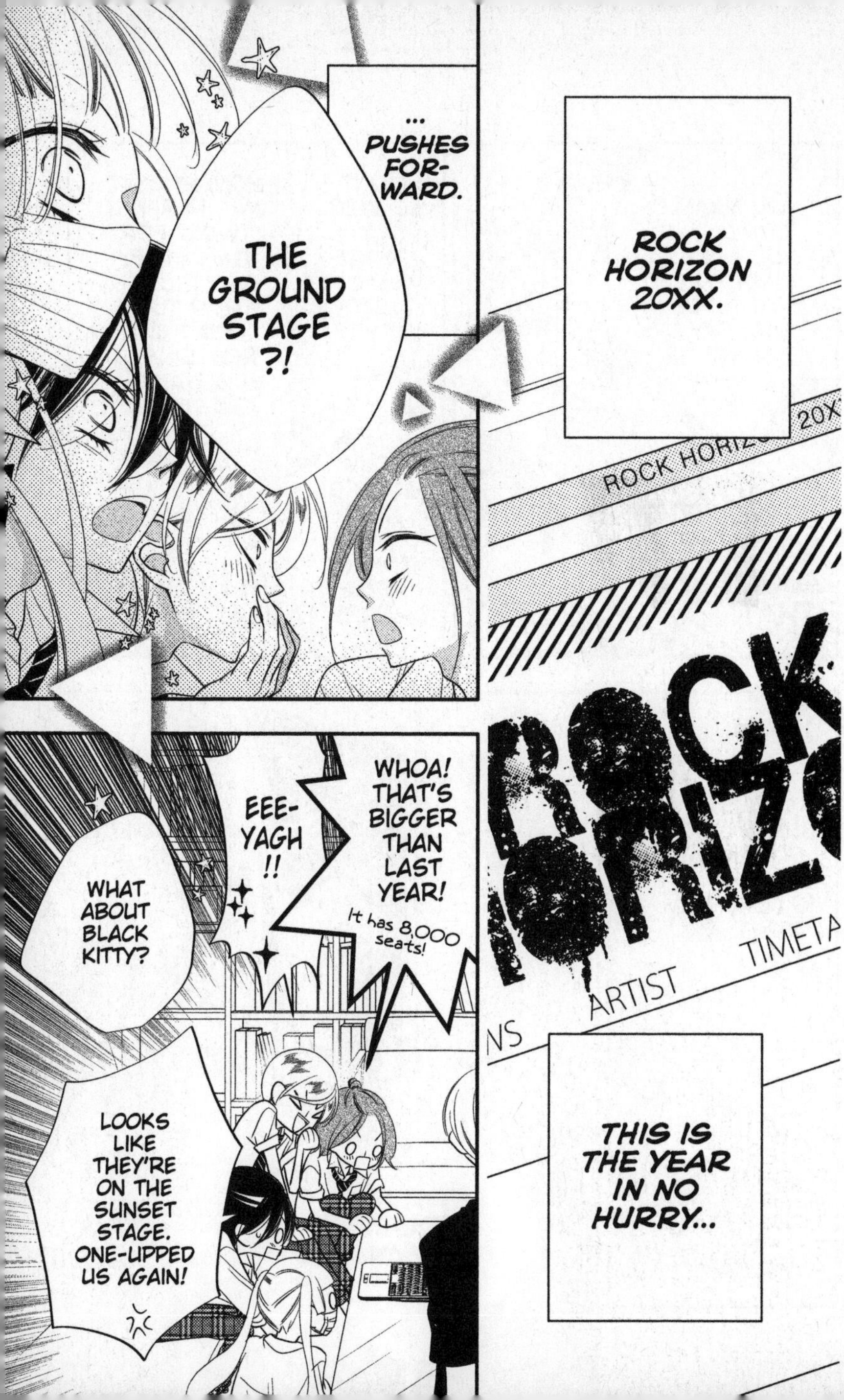
ROCK HORIZON 20XX.
ARTIST
THIS IS THE YEAR IN NO HURRY...
... PUSHES FOR-WARD.
THE GROUND STAGE ?!
WHOA! THAT'S BIGGER THAN LAST YEAR!
It has 8,000 seats!
EEE-YAGH !!
WHAT ABOUT BLACK KITTY?
LOOKS LIKE THEY'RE ON THE SUNSET STAGE. ONE-UPPED US AGAIN!

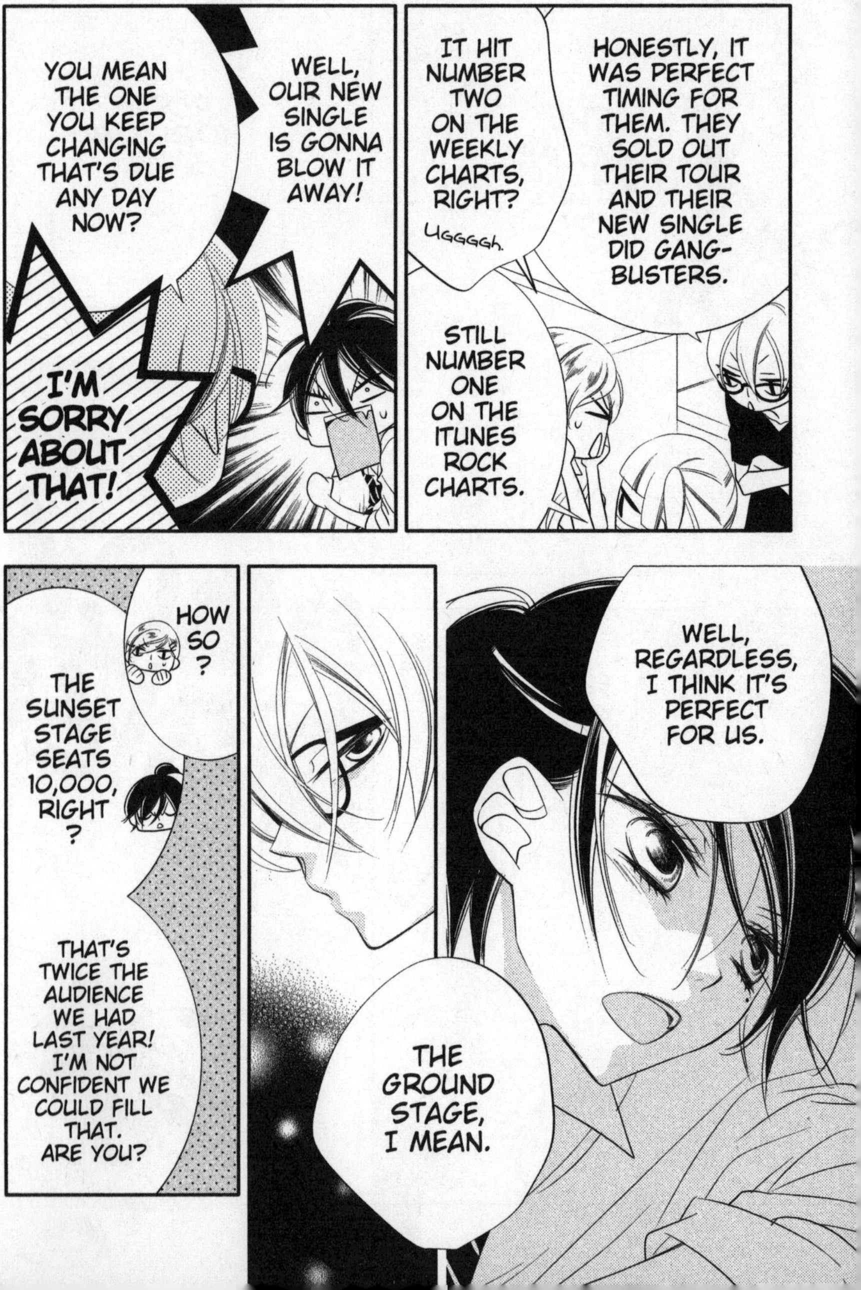
HONESTLY, IT WAS PERFECT TIMING FOR THEM. THEY SOLD OUT THEIR TOUR AND THEIR NEW SINGLE DID GANG-BUSTERS.
IT HIT NUMBER TWO ON THE WEEKLY CHARTS, RIGHT?
Uggggh.
STILL NUMBER ONE ON THE ITUNES ROCK CHARTS.
WELL, OUR NEW SINGLE IS GONNA BLOW IT AWAY!
YOU MEAN THE ONE YOU KEEP CHANGING THAT'S DUE ANY DAY NOW?
I'M SORRY ABOUT THAT!
WELL, REGARDLESS, I THINK IT'S PERFECT FOR US.
THE GROUND STAGE, I MEAN.
HOW SO?
THE SUNSET STAGE SEATS 10,000, RIGHT?
THAT'S TWICE THE AUDIENCE WE HAD LAST YEAR! I'M NOT CONFIDENT WE COULD FILL THAT. ARE YOU?

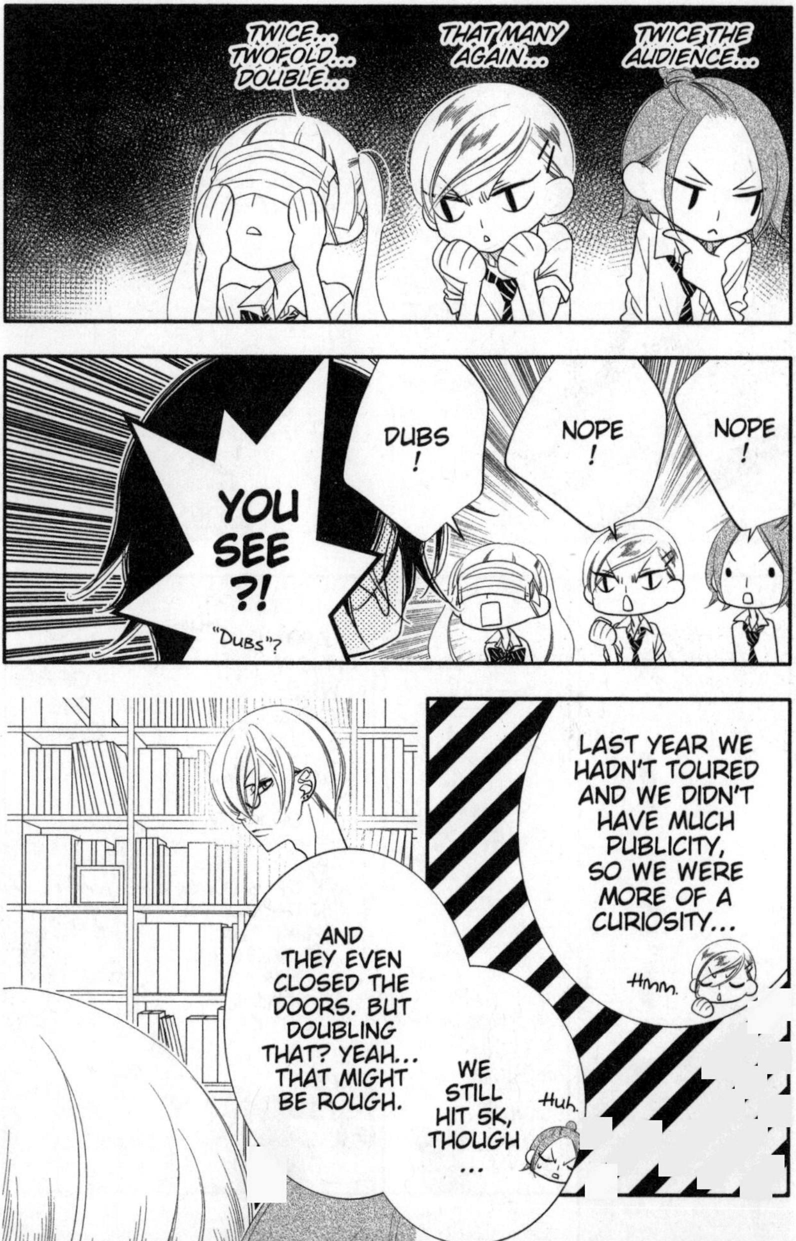
TWICE THE AUDIENCE...
THAT MANY AGAIN...
TWICE... TWOFOLD... DOUBLE...
NOPE!
NOPE!
DUBS!
YOU SEE?!
"Dubs"?
LAST YEAR WE HADN'T TOURED AND WE DIDN'T HAVE MUCH PUBLICITY, SO WE WERE MORE OF A CURIOSITY...
Hmm.
WE STILL HIT 5K, THOUGH...
Huh.
AND THEY EVEN CLOSED THE DOORS. BUT DOUBLING THAT? YEAH... THAT MIGHT BE ROUGH.

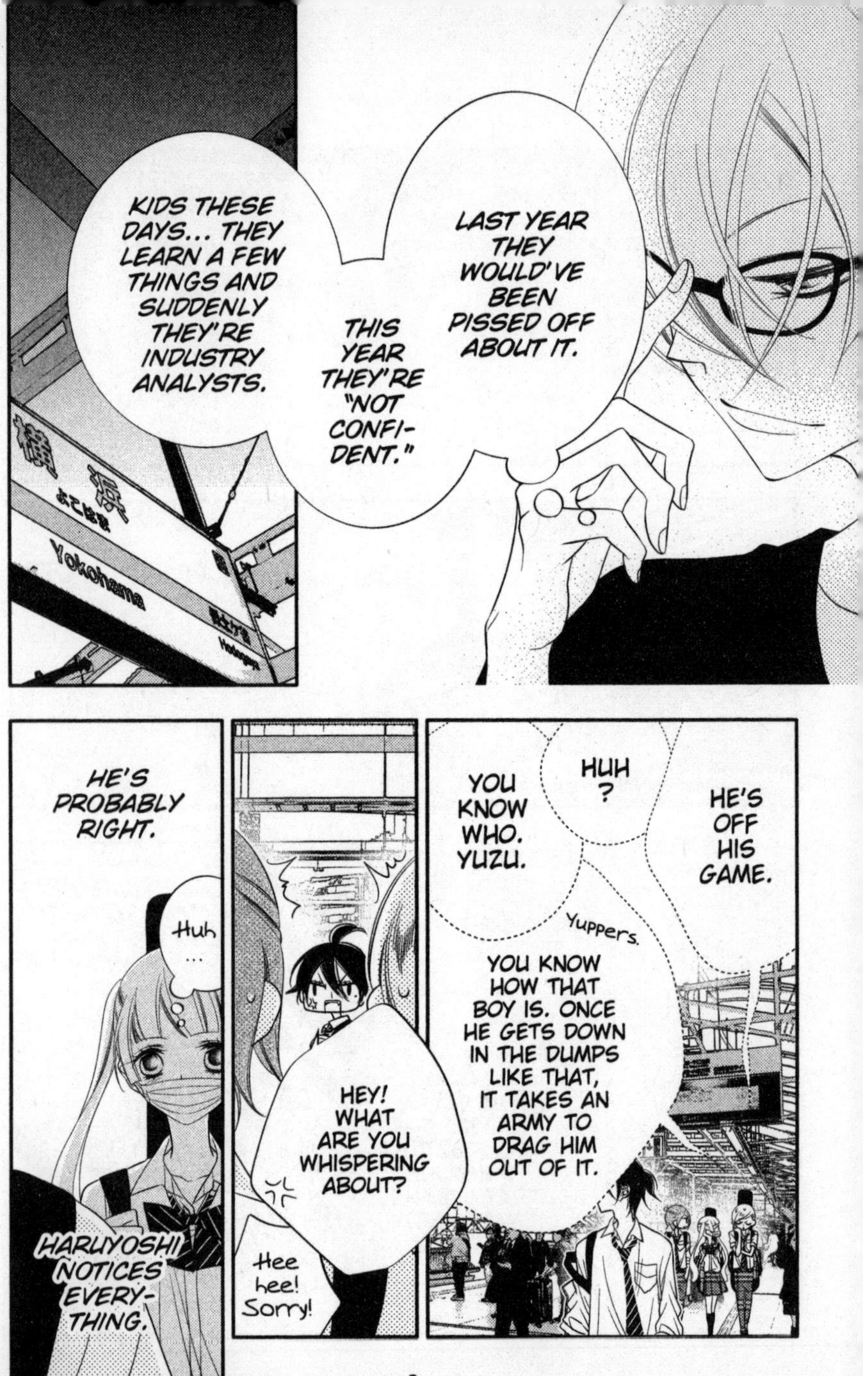
LAST YEAR THEY WOULD'VE BEEN PISSED OFF ABOUT IT.
THIS YEAR THEY'RE "NOT CONFI-DENT."
KIDS THESE DAYS... THEY LEARN A FEW THINGS AND SUDDENLY THEY'RE INDUSTRY ANALYSTS.
Yokohama
HE'S OFF HIS GAME.
HUH?
YOU KNOW WHO. YUZU.
Yuppers.
YOU KNOW HOW THAT BOY IS. ONCE HE GETS DOWN IN THE DUMPS LIKE THAT, IT TAKES AN ARMY TO DRAG HIM OUT OF IT.
HEY! WHAT ARE YOU WHISPERING ABOUT?
Hee hee! Sorry!
HE'S PROBABLY RIGHT.
Huh...
HARUYOSHI NOTICES EVERY-THING.

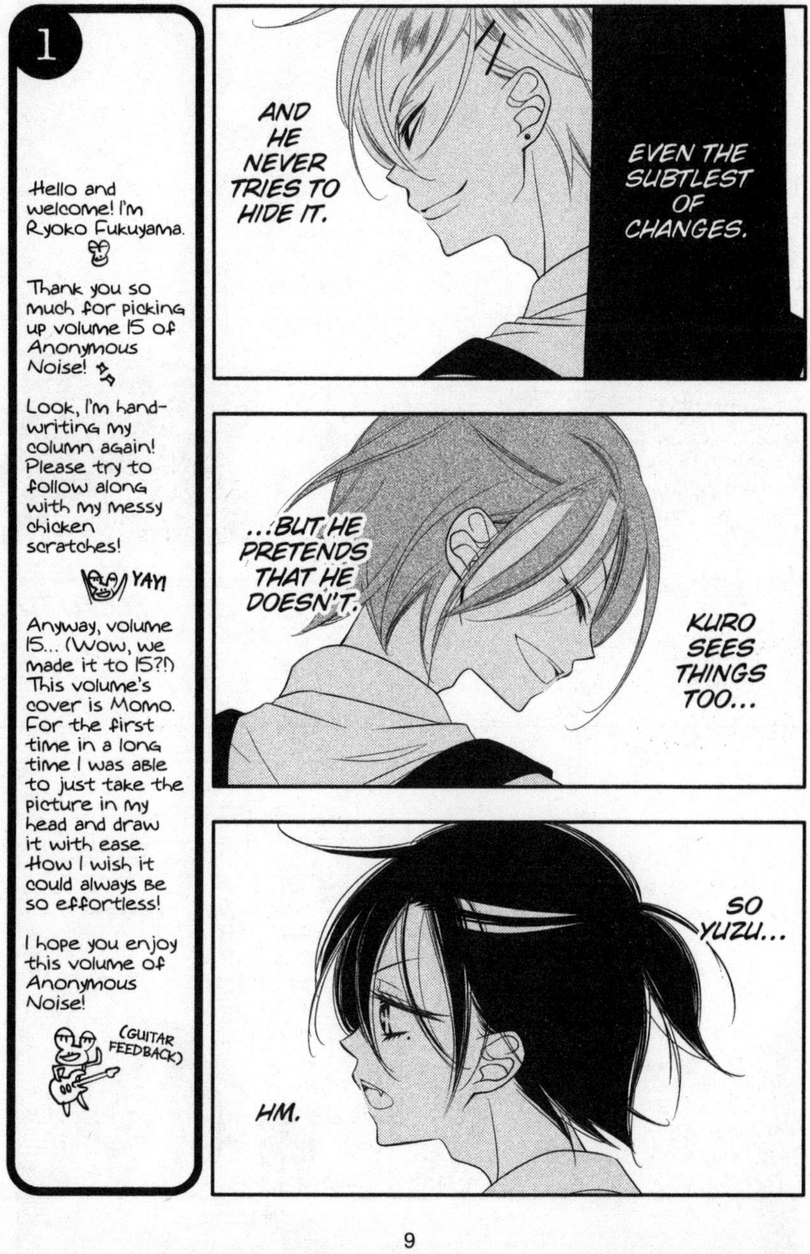
EVEN THE SUBTLEST OF CHANGES.
AND HE NEVER TRIES TO HIDE IT.
KURO SEES THINGS TOO...
...BUT HE PRETENDS THAT HE DOESN'T.
SO YUZU...
HM.

1

Hello and welcome! I'm Ryoko Fukuyama.

Thank you so much for picking up volume 15 of Anonymous Noise!

Look, I'm hand-writing my column again! Please try to follow along with my messy chicken scratches!

YAY!

Anyway, volume 15... (Wow, we made it to 15?!) This volume's cover is Momo. For the first time in a long time I was able to just take the picture in my head and draw it with ease. How I wish it could always be so effortless!

I hope you enjoy this volume of Anonymous Noise!

(GUITAR FEEDBACK)

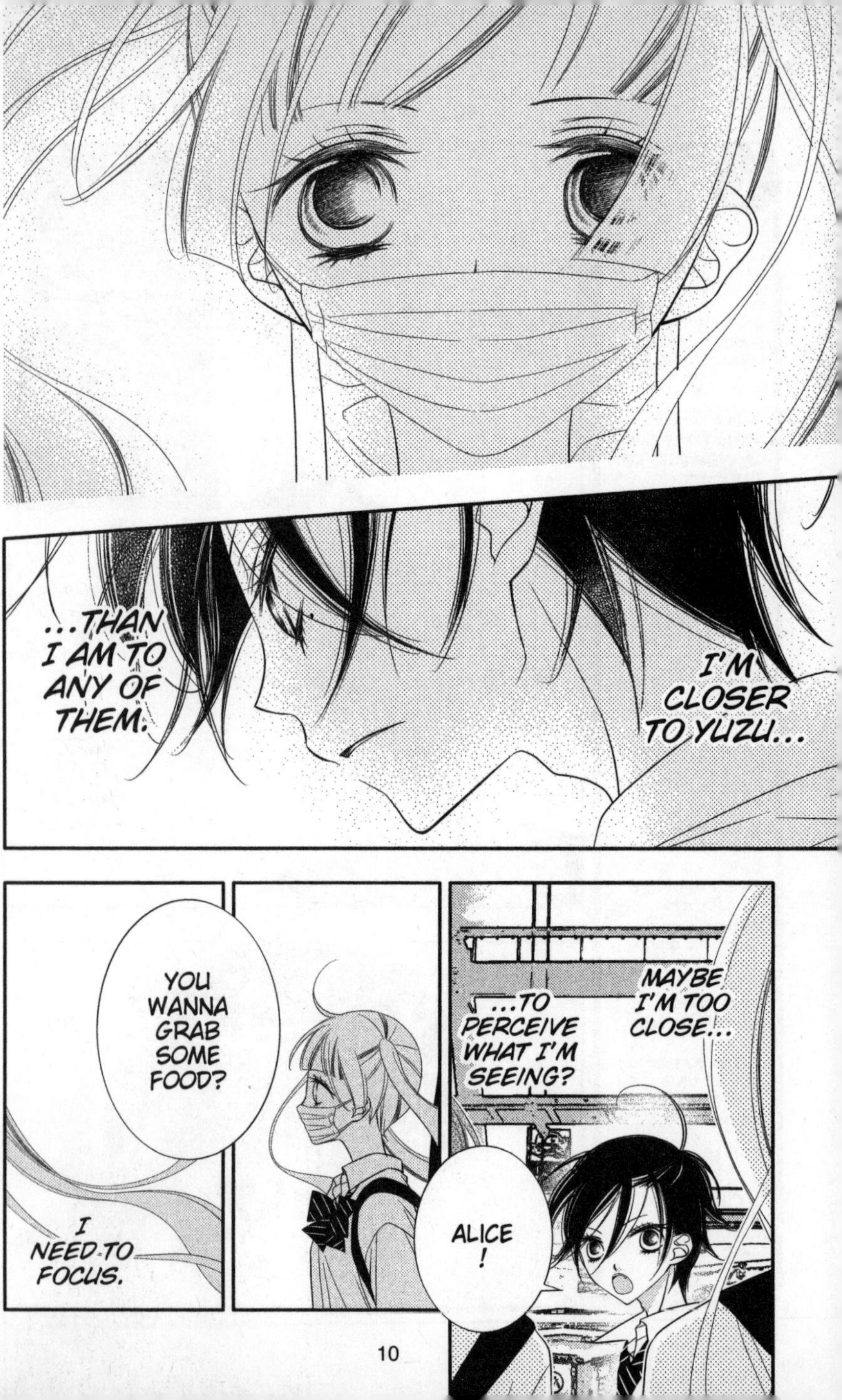
I'M CLOSER TO YUZU...
...THAN I AM TO ANY OF THEM.
MAYBE I'M TOO CLOSE...
...TO PERCEIVE WHAT I'M SEEING?
ALICE!
YOU WANNA GRAB SOME FOOD?
I NEED TO FOCUS.

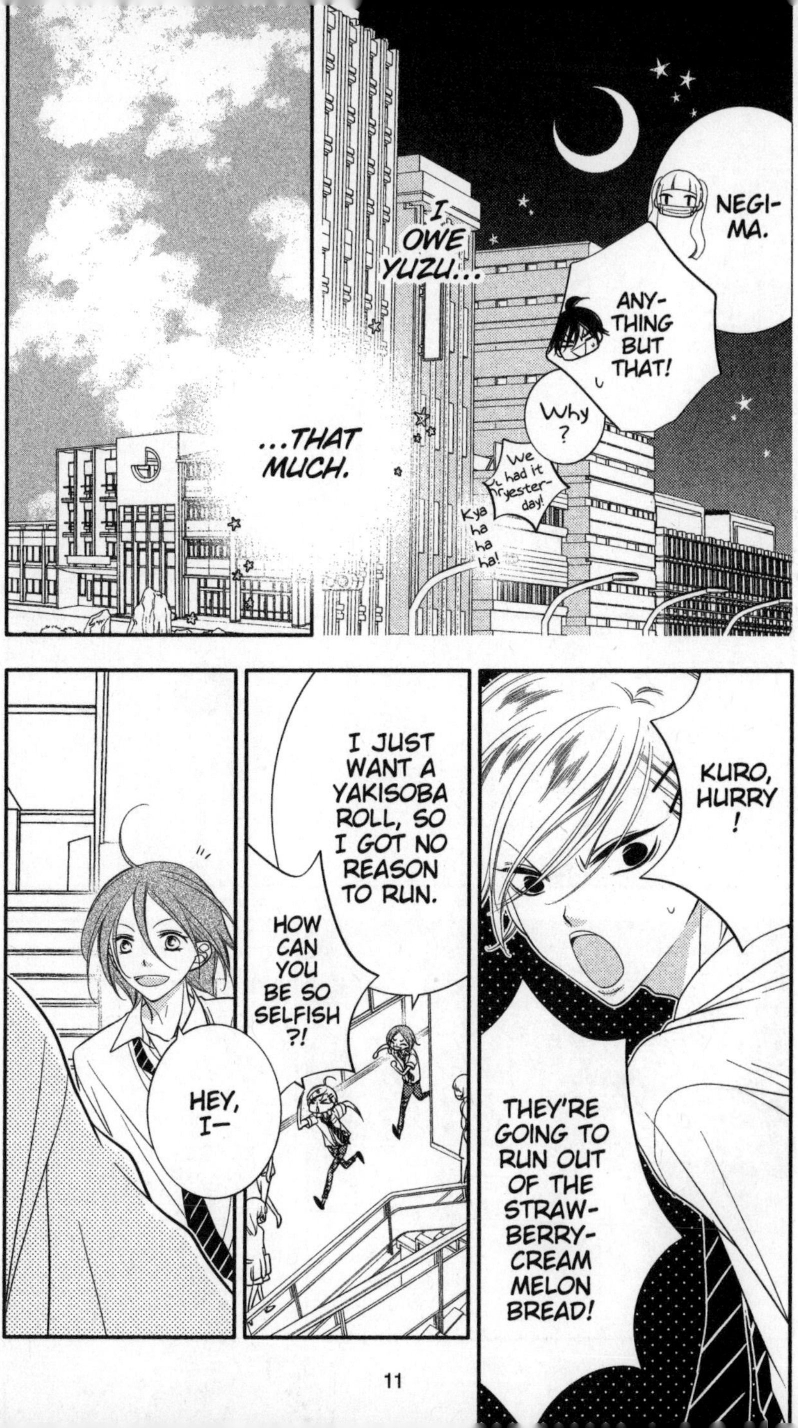
NEGI-MA.
ANYTHING BUT THAT!
Why?
We had it yesterday!
Kya ha ha ha!
I OWE YUZU...
...THAT MUCH.
KURO, HURRY!
THEY'RE GOING TO RUN OUT OF THE STRAWBERRY-CREAM MELON BREAD!
I JUST WANT A YAKISOBA ROLL, SO I GOT NO REASON TO RUN.
HOW CAN YOU BE SO SELFISH?!
HEY, I—

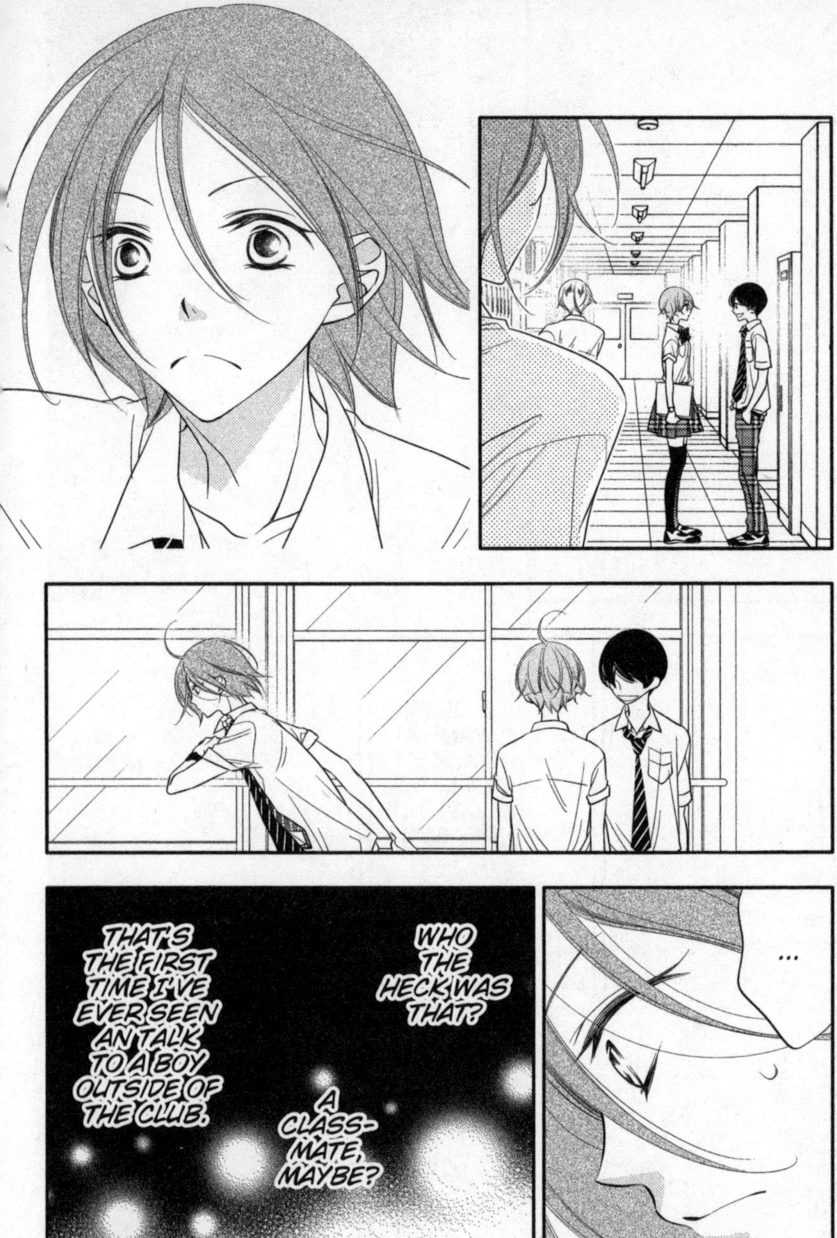
...
WHO THE HECK WAS THAT?
THAT'S THE FIRST TIME I'VE EVER SEEN AN TALK TO A BOY OUTSIDE OF THE CLUB.
A CLASSMATE, MAYBE?

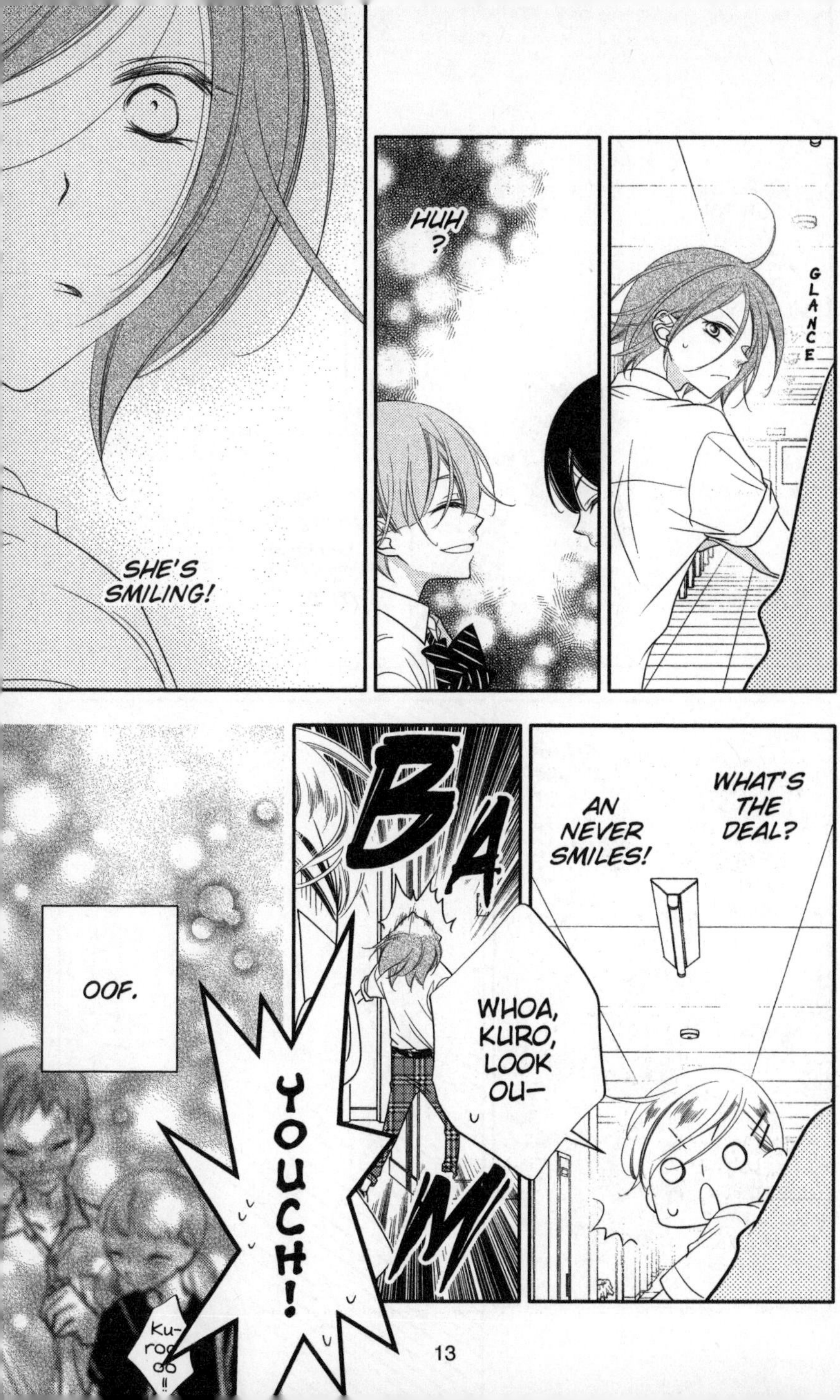
GLANCE
HUH?
SHE'S SMILING!
WHAT'S THE DEAL?
AN NEVER SMILES!
WHOA, KURO, LOOK OU—
BAM
YOUCH!
OOF.
Ku-rooo!!

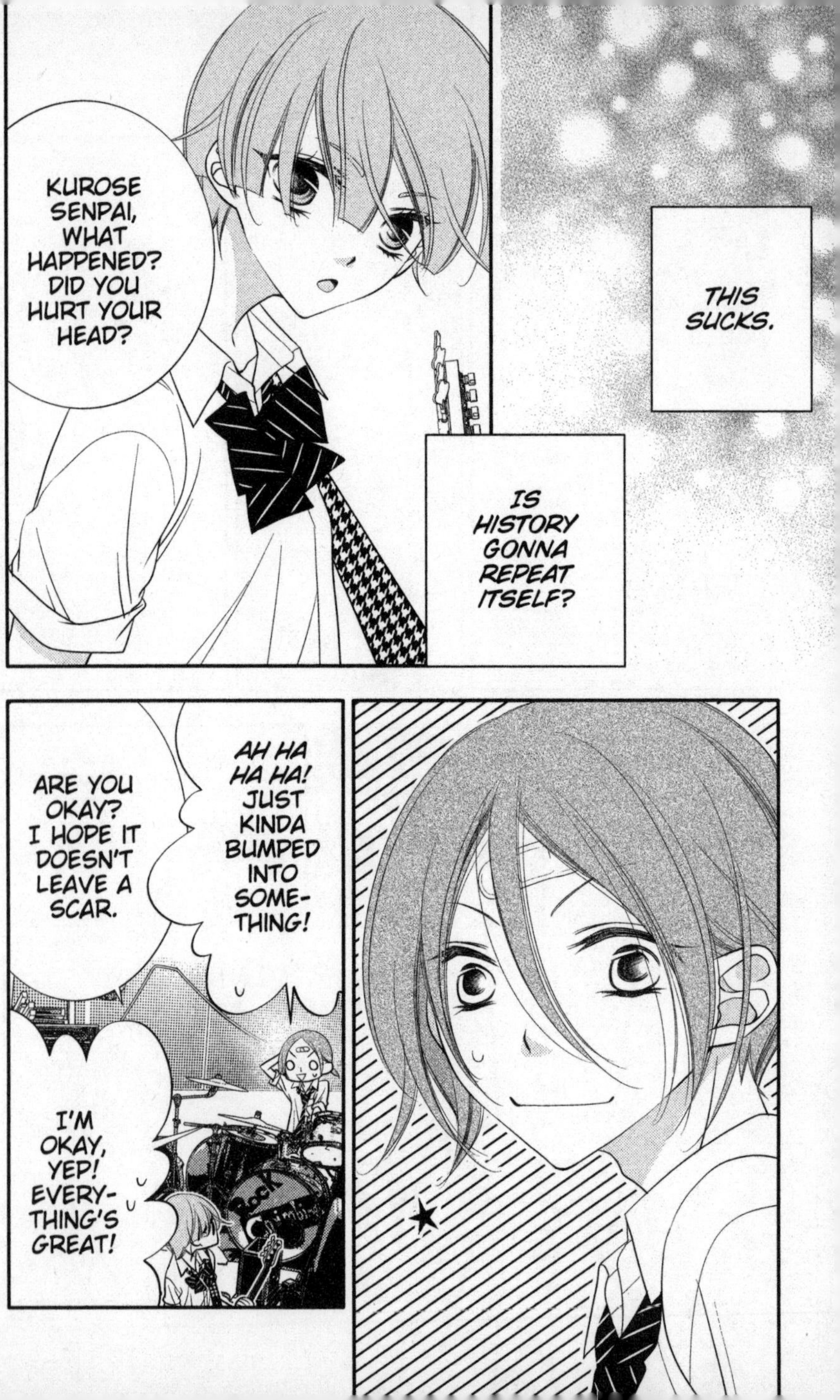
THIS SUCKS.
IS HISTORY GONNA REPEAT ITSELF?
KUROSE SENPAI, WHAT HAPPENED? DID YOU HURT YOUR HEAD?
AH HA HA HA! JUST KINDA BUMPED INTO SOME-THING!
ARE YOU OKAY? I HOPE IT DOESN'T LEAVE A SCAR.
I'M OKAY, YEP! EVERY-THING'S GREAT!

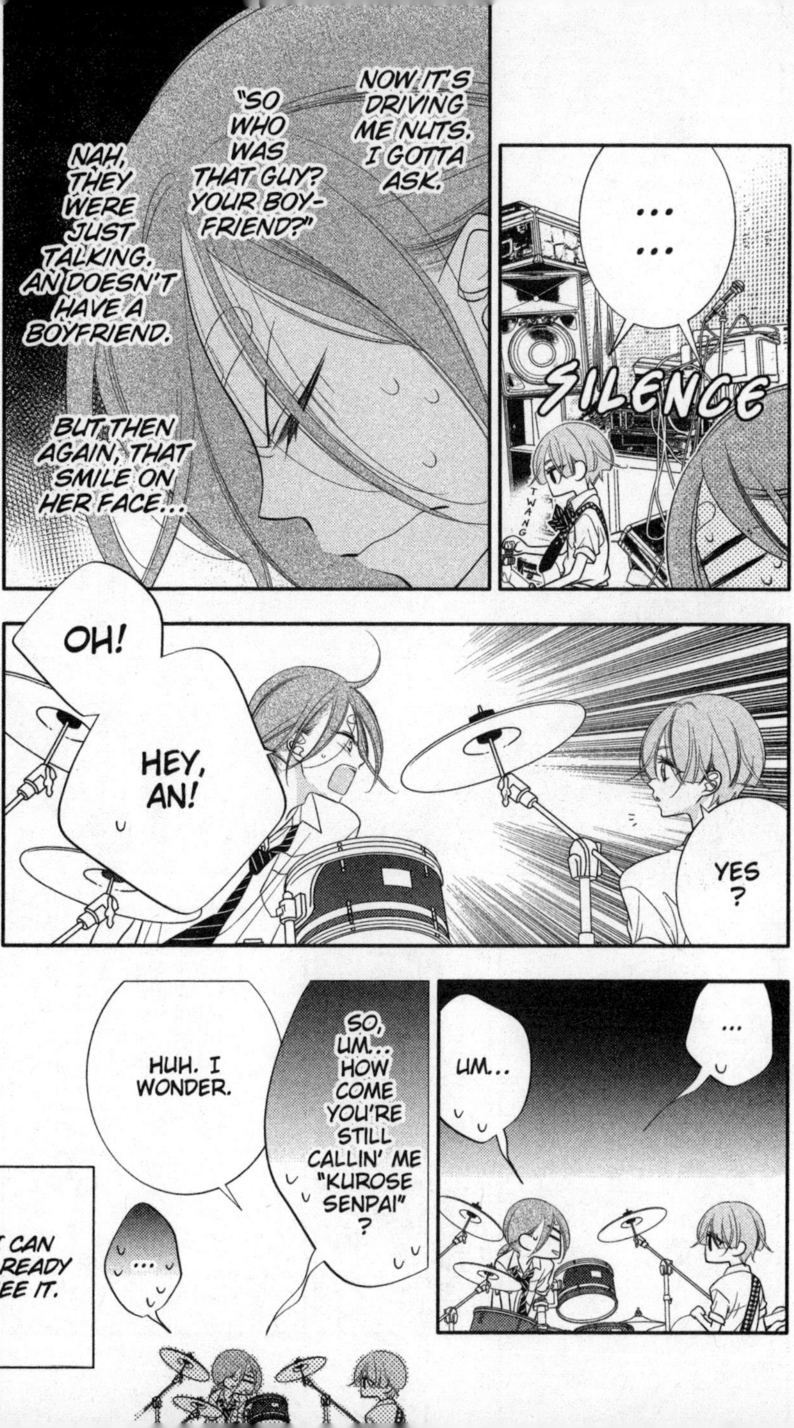

...
...
SILENCE
TWANG
NOW IT'S DRIVING ME NUTS. I GOTTA ASK.
"SO WHO WAS THAT GUY? YOUR BOY-FRIEND?"
NAH, THEY WERE JUST TALKING. AN DOESN'T HAVE A BOYFRIEND.
BUT THEN AGAIN, THAT SMILE ON HER FACE...
OH!
HEY, AN!
YES?
...
UM...
SO, UM... HOW COME YOU'RE STILL CALLIN' ME "KUROSE SENPAI"?
HUH. I WONDER.
...
I CAN ALREADY SEE IT.

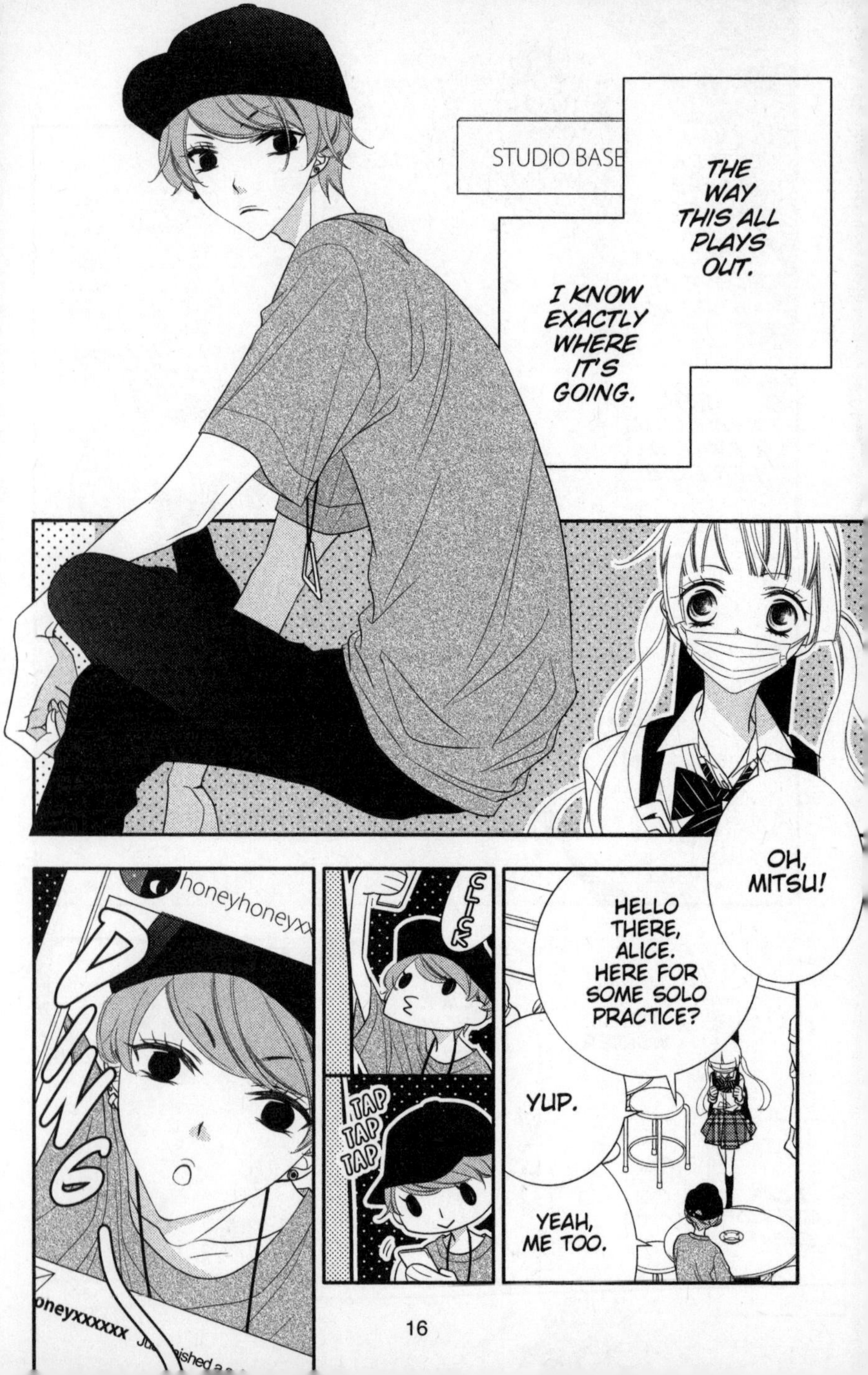
STUDIO BASE
THE WAY THIS ALL PLAYS OUT.
I KNOW EXACTLY WHERE IT'S GOING.
OH, MITSU!
HELLO THERE, ALICE. HERE FOR SOME SOLO PRACTICE?
YUP.
YEAH, ME TOO.
CLICK
TAP TAP TAP
honeyhoneyxx
DING

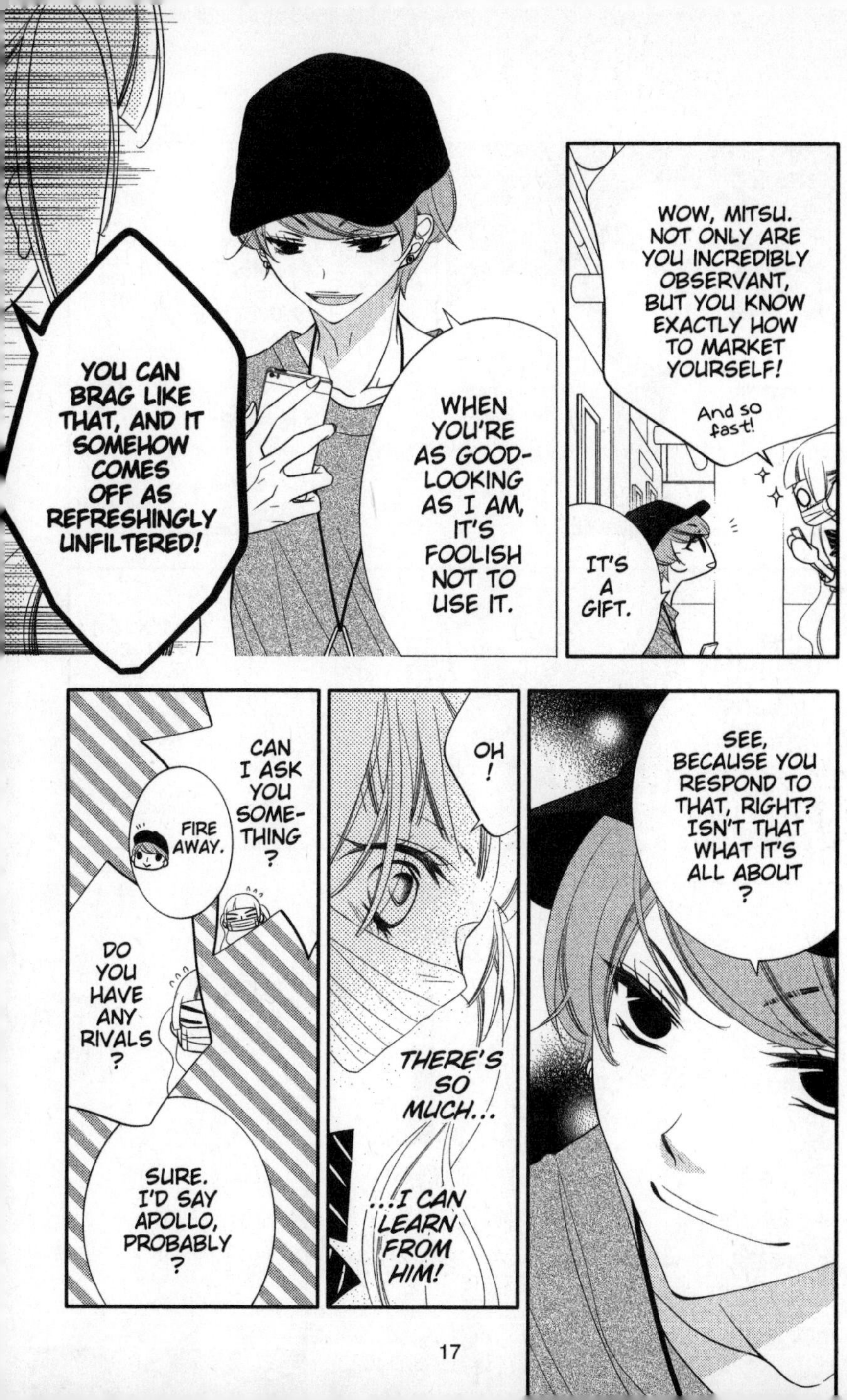
WOW, MITSU. NOT ONLY ARE YOU INCREDIBLY OBSERVANT, BUT YOU KNOW EXACTLY HOW TO MARKET YOURSELF!
And so fast!
IT'S A GIFT.
WHEN YOU'RE AS GOOD-LOOKING AS I AM, IT'S FOOLISH NOT TO USE IT.
YOU CAN BRAG LIKE THAT, AND IT SOMEHOW COMES OFF AS REFRESHINGLY UNFILTERED!
SEE, BECAUSE YOU RESPOND TO THAT, RIGHT? ISN'T THAT WHAT IT'S ALL ABOUT?
OH!
THERE'S SO MUCH...
...I CAN LEARN FROM HIM!
CAN I ASK YOU SOMETHING?
FIRE AWAY.
DO YOU HAVE ANY RIVALS?
SURE. I'D SAY APOLLO, PROBABLY?

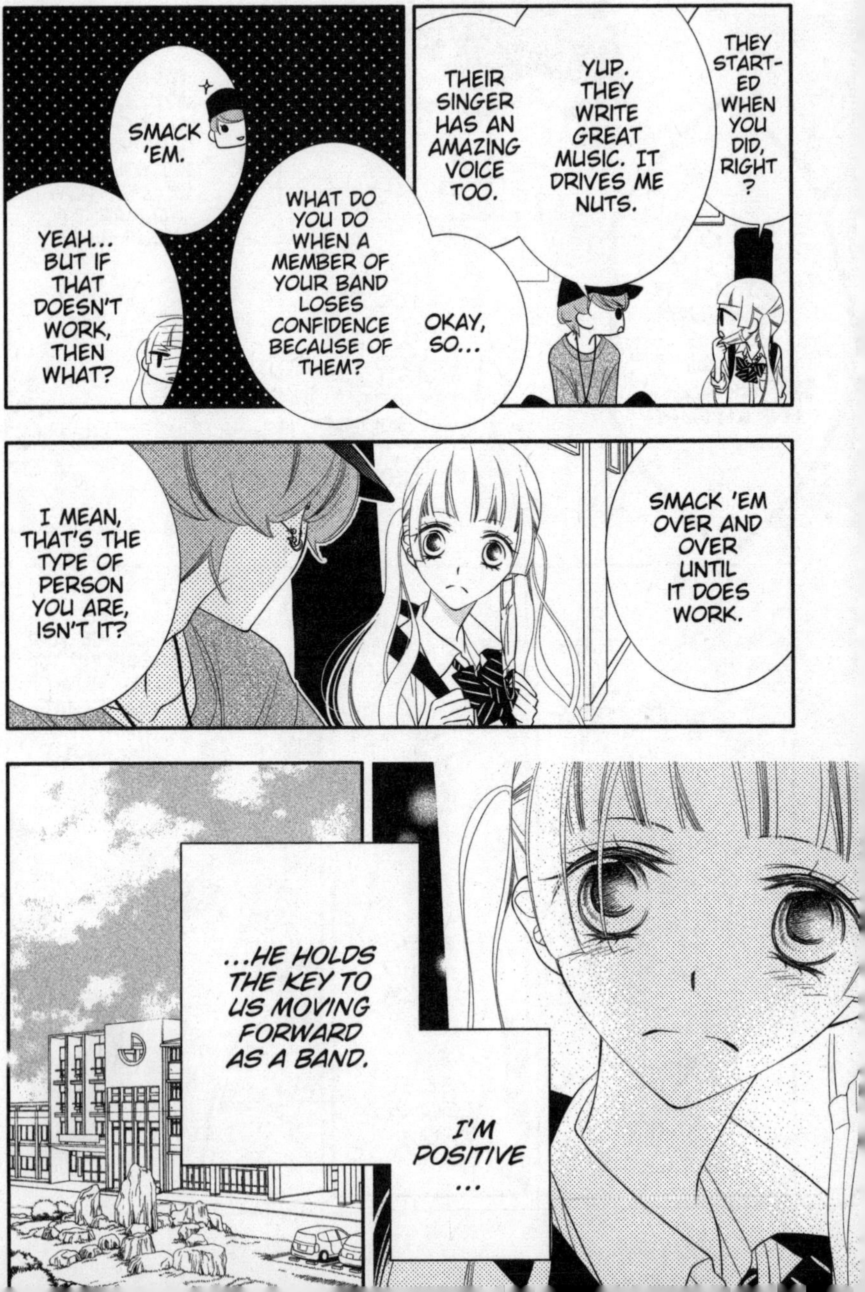
THEY START-ED WHEN YOU DID, RIGHT?
YUP. THEY WRITE GREAT MUSIC. IT DRIVES ME NUTS.
THEIR SINGER HAS AN AMAZING VOICE TOO.
OKAY, SO...
WHAT DO YOU DO WHEN A MEMBER OF YOUR BAND LOSES CONFIDENCE BECAUSE OF THEM?
SMACK 'EM.
YEAH... BUT IF THAT DOESN'T WORK, THEN WHAT?
SMACK 'EM OVER AND OVER UNTIL IT DOES WORK.
I MEAN, THAT'S THE TYPE OF PERSON YOU ARE, ISN'T IT?
I'M POSITIVE ...
...HE HOLDS THE KEY TO US MOVING FORWARD AS A BAND.

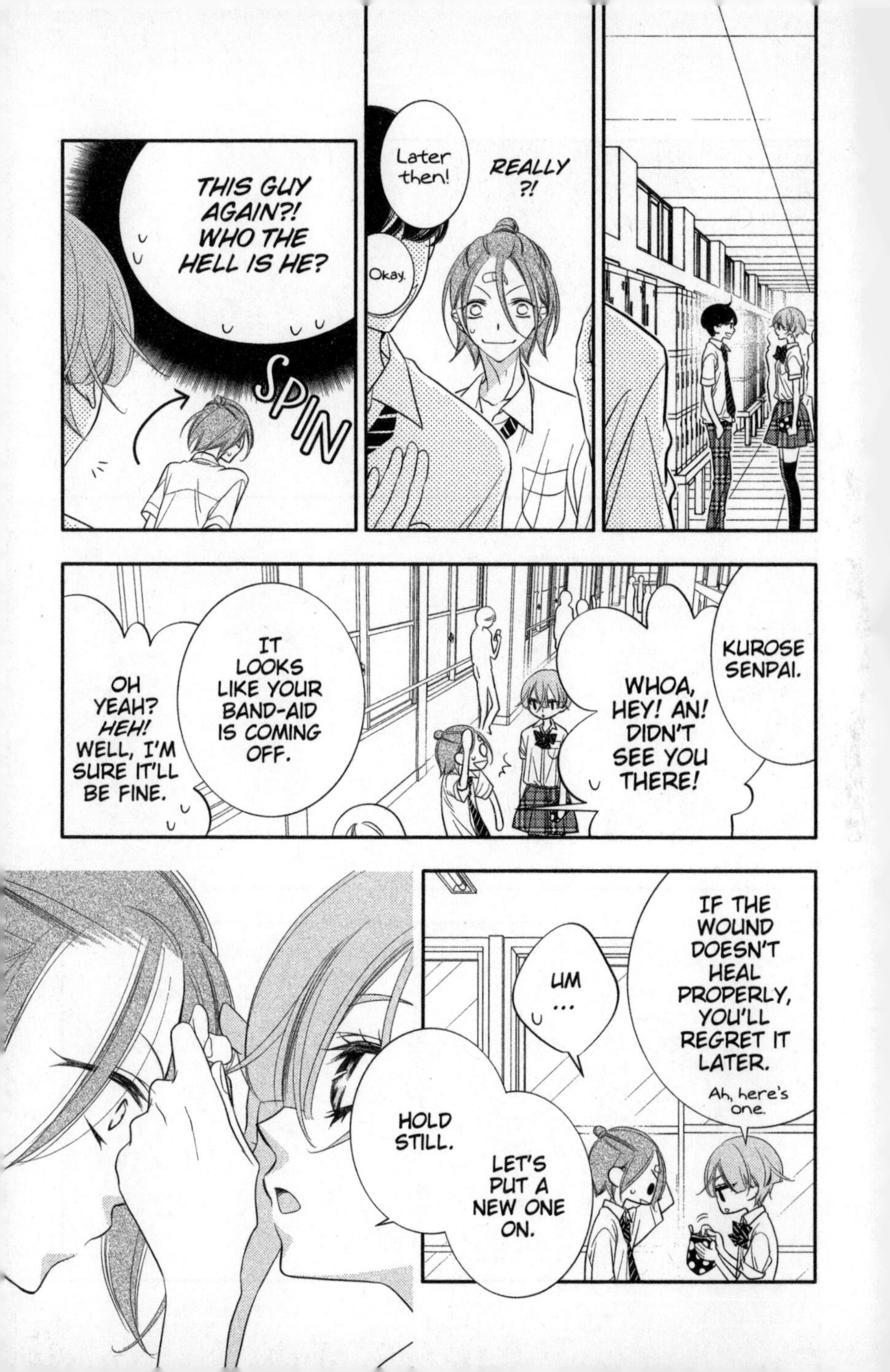
Later then!
Okay.
REALLY ?!
THIS GUY AGAIN?! WHO THE HELL IS HE?
SPIN
KUROSE SENPAI.
WHOA, HEY! AN! DIDN'T SEE YOU THERE!
IT LOOKS LIKE YOUR BAND-AID IS COMING OFF.
OH YEAH? *HEH!* WELL, I'M SURE IT'LL BE FINE.
IF THE WOUND DOESN'T HEAL PROPERLY, YOU'LL REGRET IT LATER.
Ah, here's one.
UM ...
HOLD STILL.
LET'S PUT A NEW ONE ON.

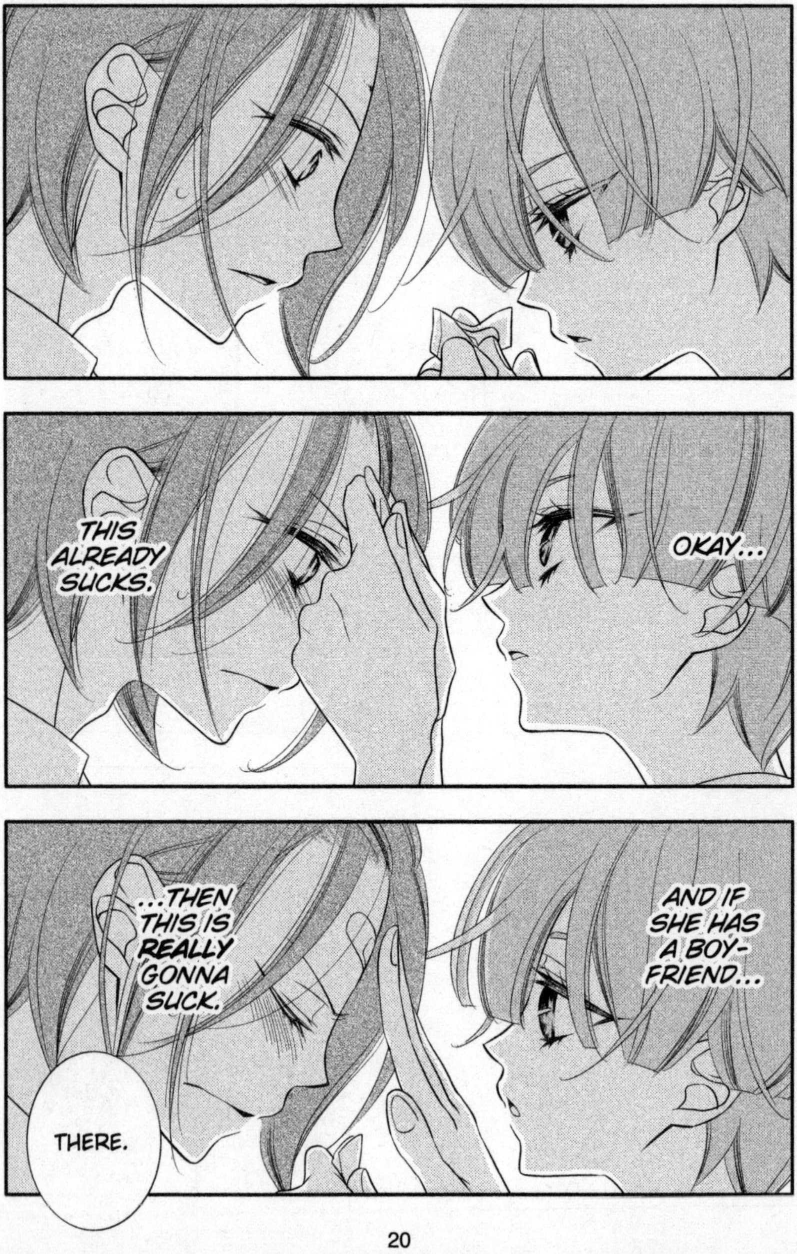
OKAY...
THIS ALREADY SUCKS.
AND IF SHE HAS A BOY-FRIEND...
...THEN THIS IS REALLY GONNA SUCK.
THERE.

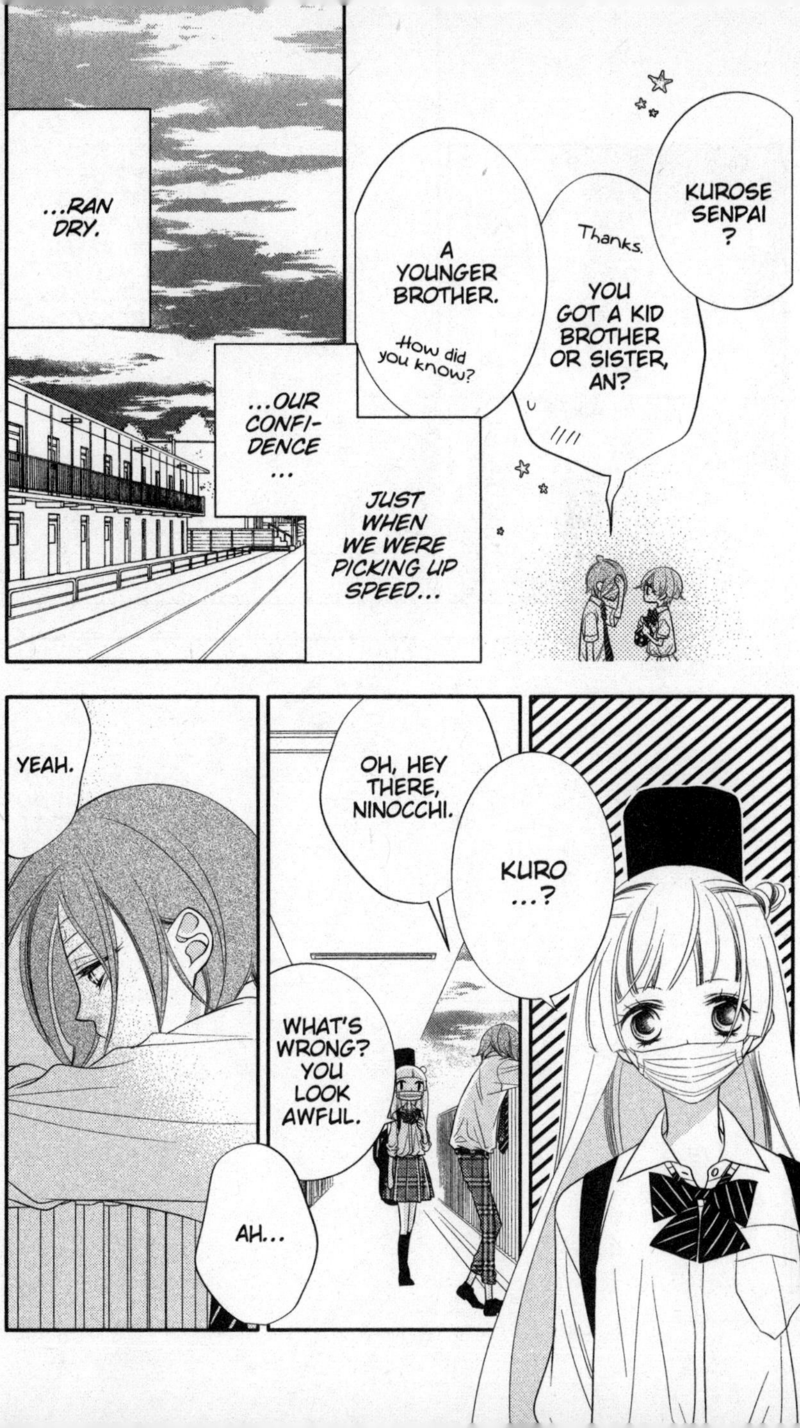
KUROSE SENPAI ?
Thanks.
YOU GOT A KID BROTHER OR SISTER, AN?
A YOUNGER BROTHER.
How did you know?
JUST WHEN WE WERE PICKING UP SPEED...
...OUR CONFIDENCE...
...RAN DRY.
KURO ...?
OH, HEY THERE, NINOCCHI.
WHAT'S WRONG? YOU LOOK AWFUL.
AH...
YEAH.

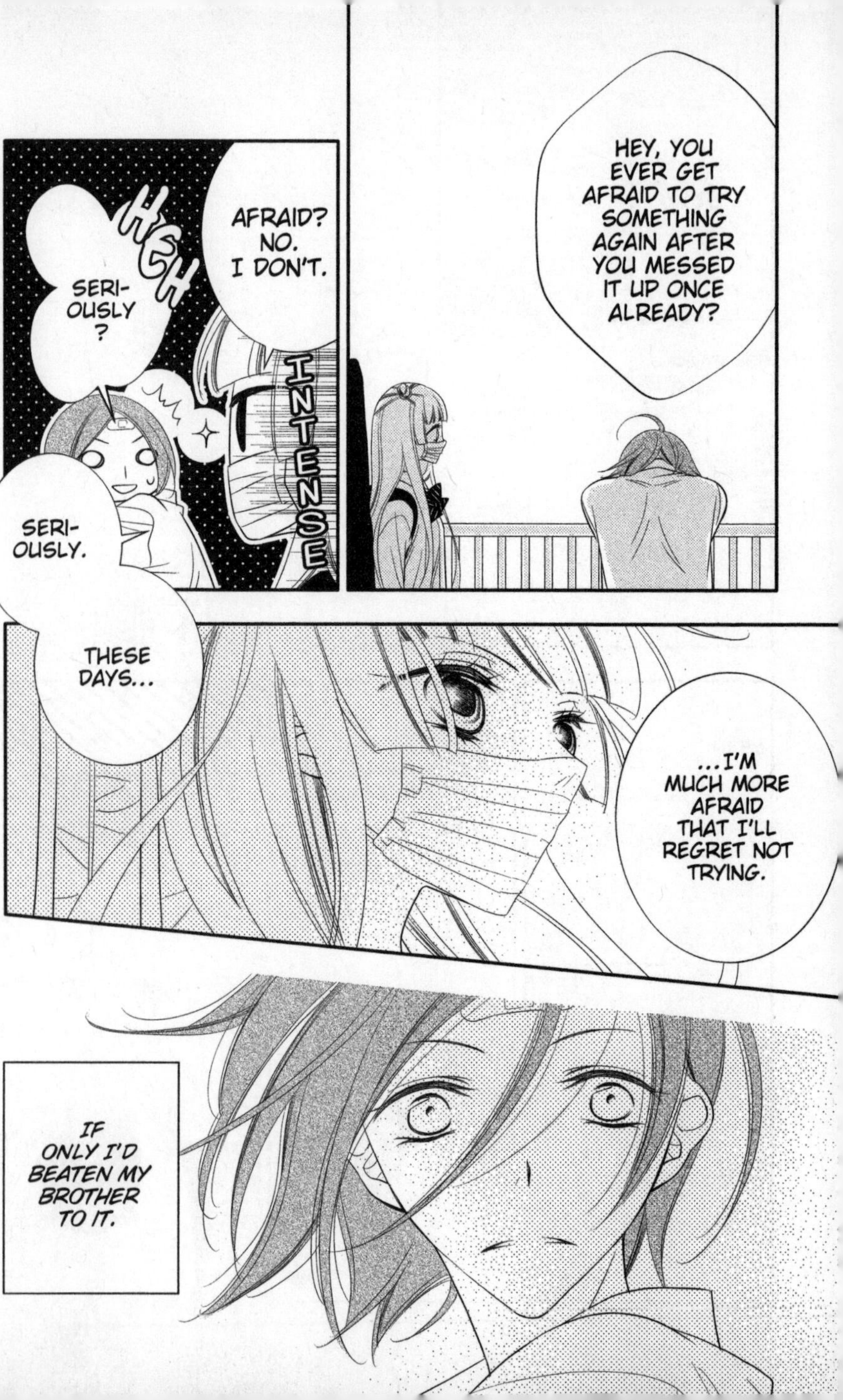
HEY, YOU EVER GET AFRAID TO TRY SOMETHING AGAIN AFTER YOU MESSED IT UP ONCE ALREADY?
AFRAID? NO. I DON'T.
HEH
SERI-OUSLY?
INTENSE
SERI-OUSLY.
THESE DAYS...
...I'M MUCH MORE AFRAID THAT I'LL REGRET NOT TRYING.
IF ONLY I'D BEATEN MY BROTHER TO IT.

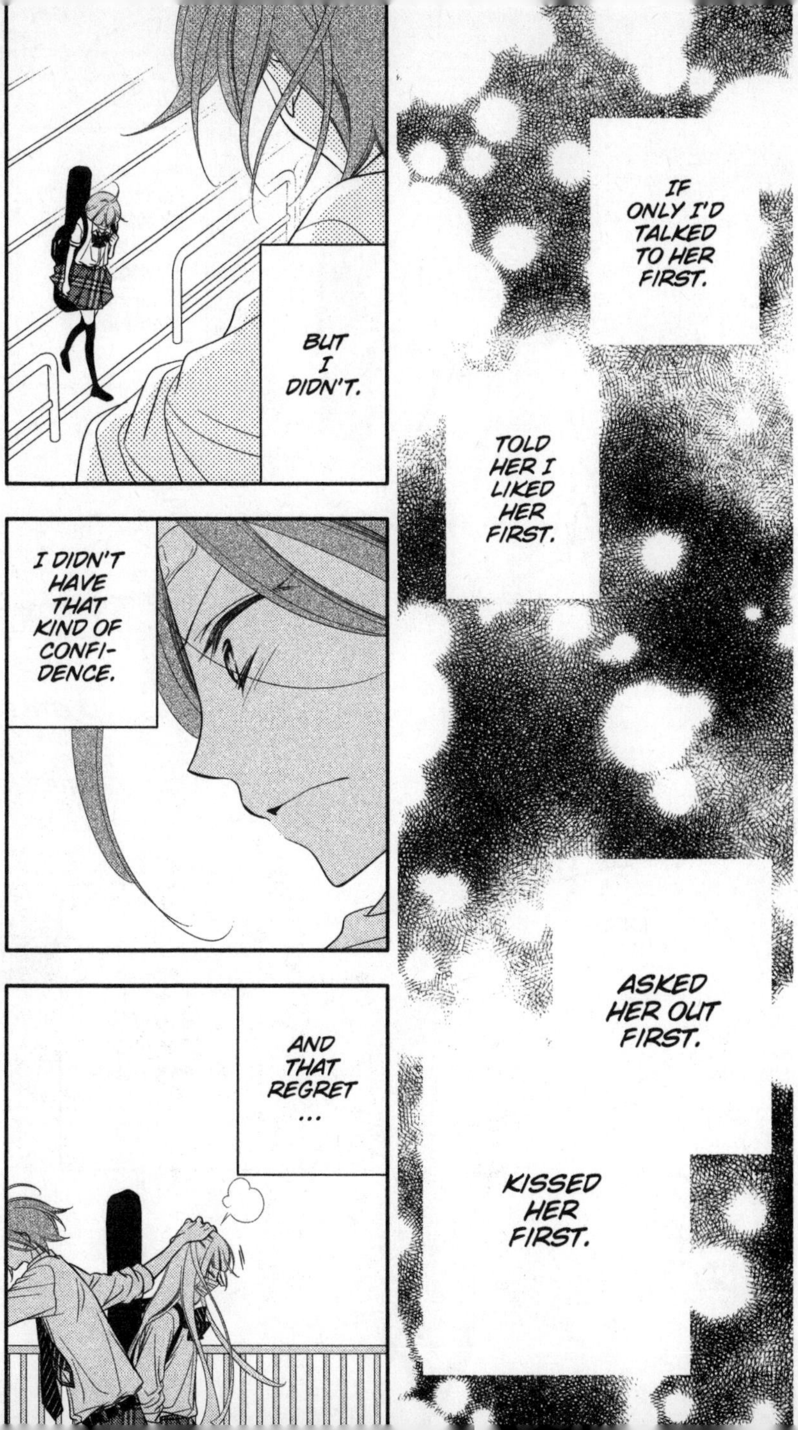
IF ONLY I'D TALKED TO HER FIRST.
TOLD HER I LIKED HER FIRST.
ASKED HER OUT FIRST.
KISSED HER FIRST.
BUT I DIDN'T.
I DIDN'T HAVE THAT KIND OF CONFI-DENCE.
AND THAT REGRET...

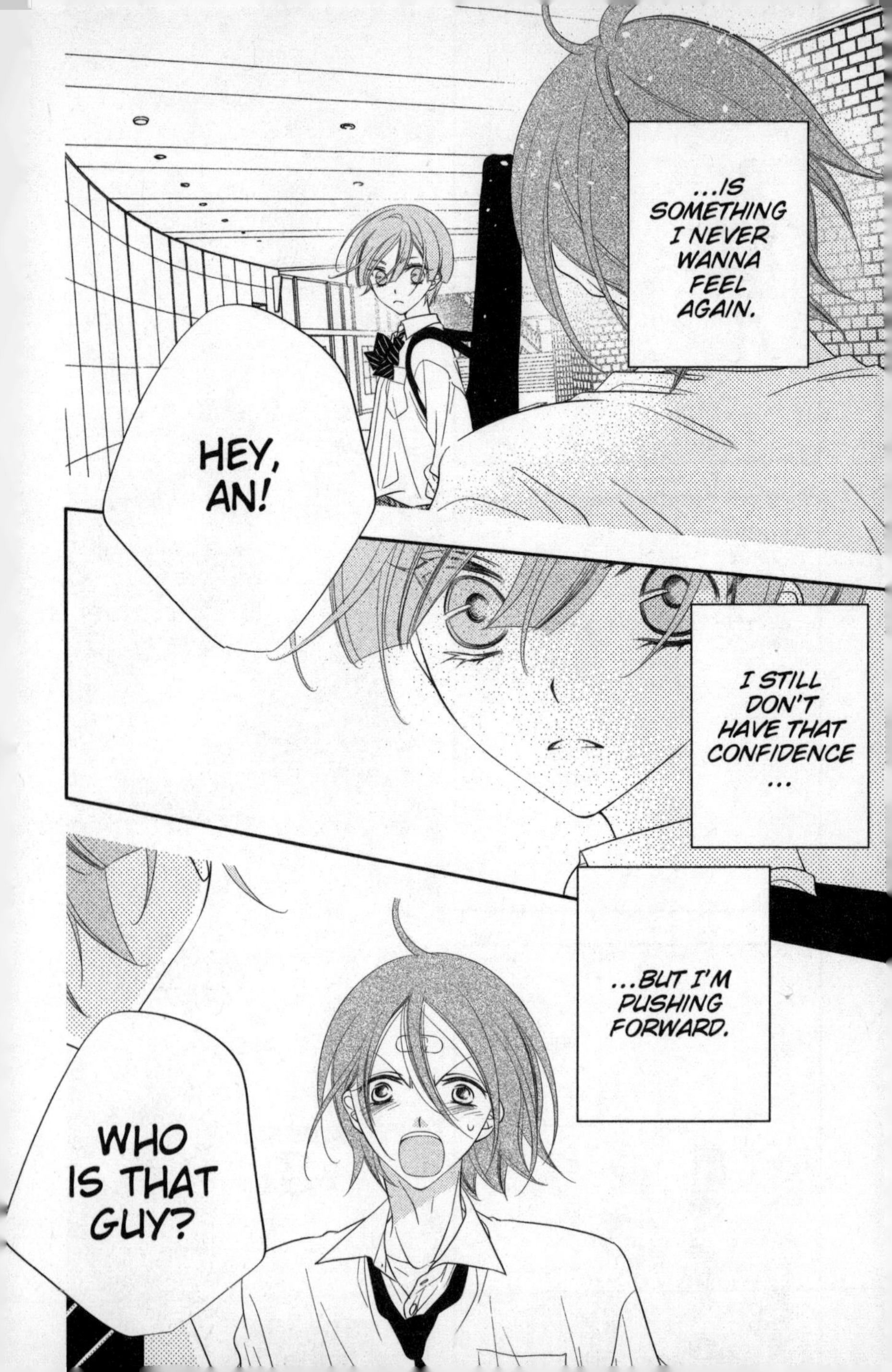
...IS SOMETHING I NEVER WANNA FEEL AGAIN.
HEY, AN!
I STILL DON'T HAVE THAT CONFIDENCE...
...BUT I'M PUSHING FORWARD.
WHO IS THAT GUY?

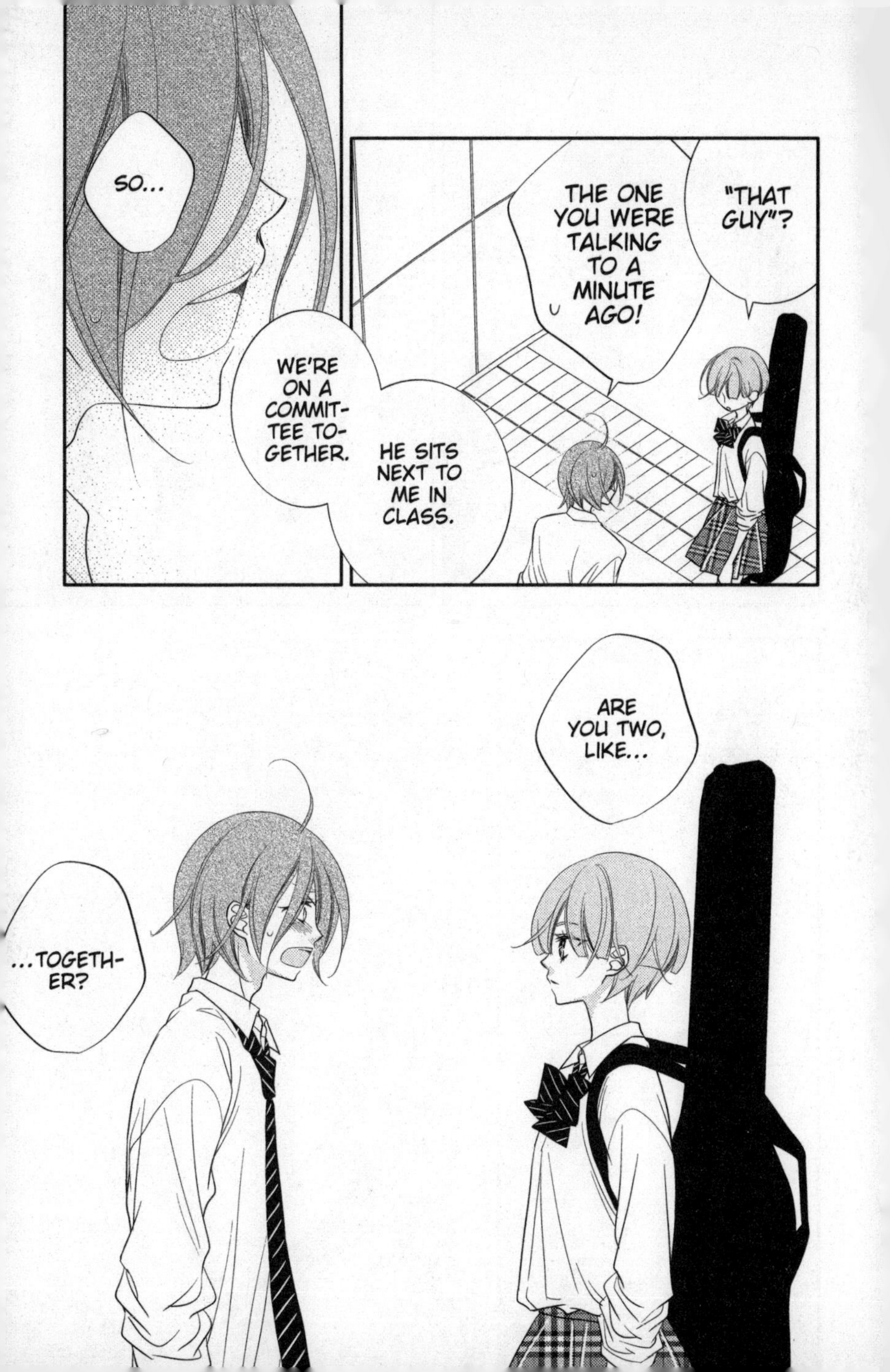
"THAT GUY"?
THE ONE YOU WERE TALKING TO A MINUTE AGO!
SO...
WE'RE ON A COMMIT-TEE TO-GETHER.
HE SITS NEXT TO ME IN CLASS.
ARE YOU TWO, LIKE...
...TOGETH-ER?

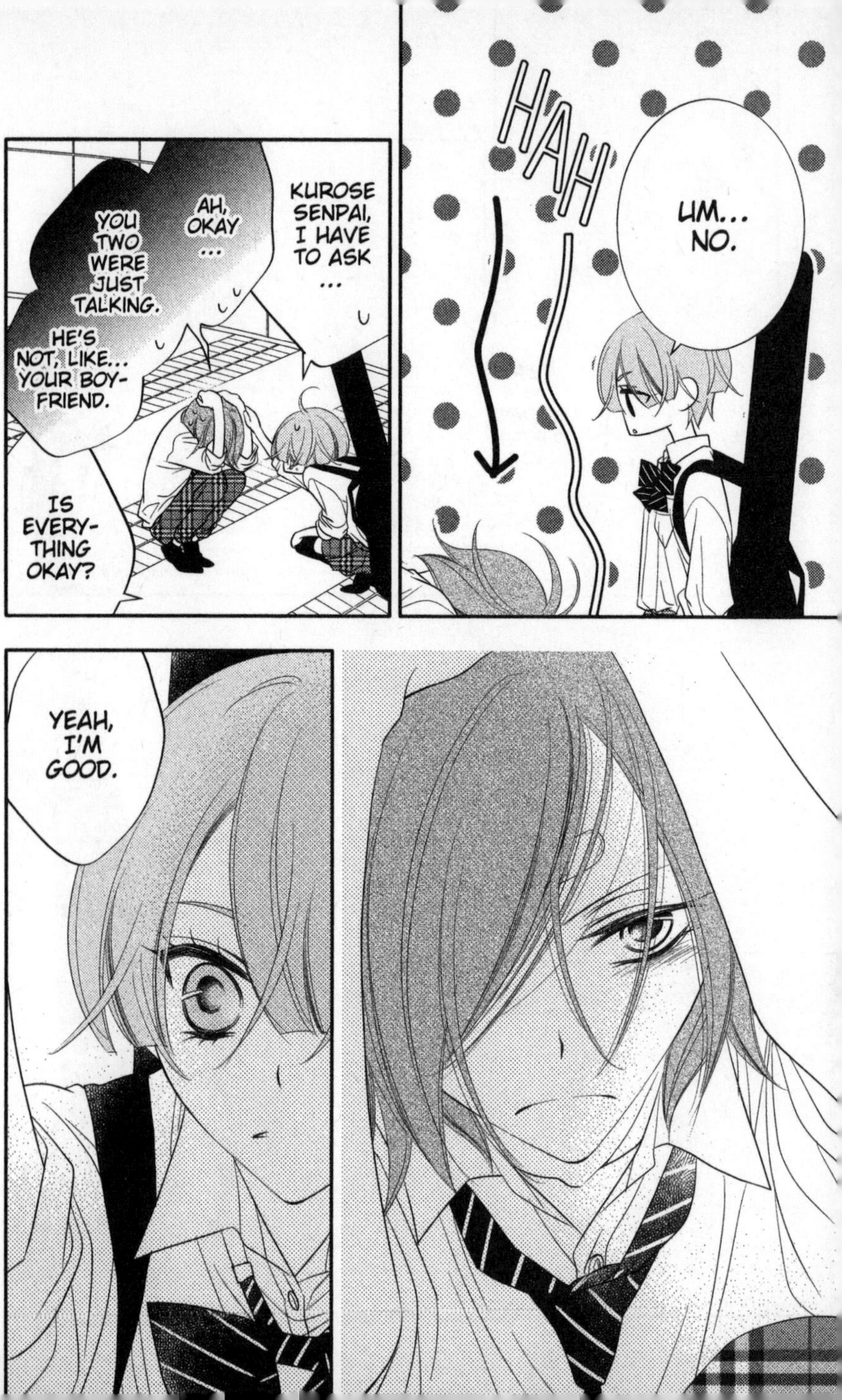
HAH
UM... NO.
KUROSE SENPAI, I HAVE TO ASK...
AH, OKAY...
YOU TWO WERE JUST TALKING.
HE'S NOT, LIKE... YOUR BOY-FRIEND.
IS EVERY-THING OKAY?
YEAH, I'M GOOD.

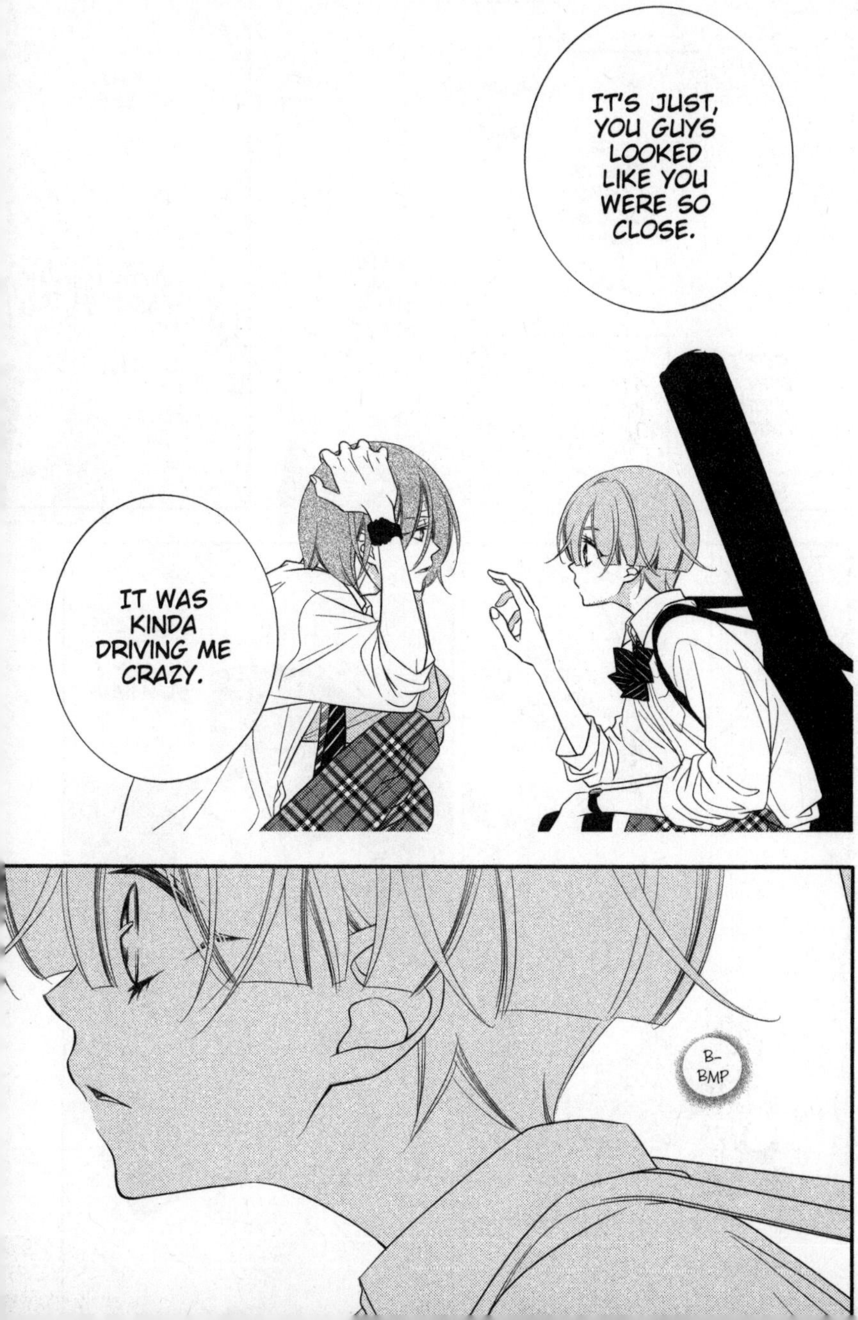
IT'S JUST, YOU GUYS LOOKED LIKE YOU WERE SO CLOSE.
IT WAS KINDA DRIVING ME CRAZY.
B-BMP

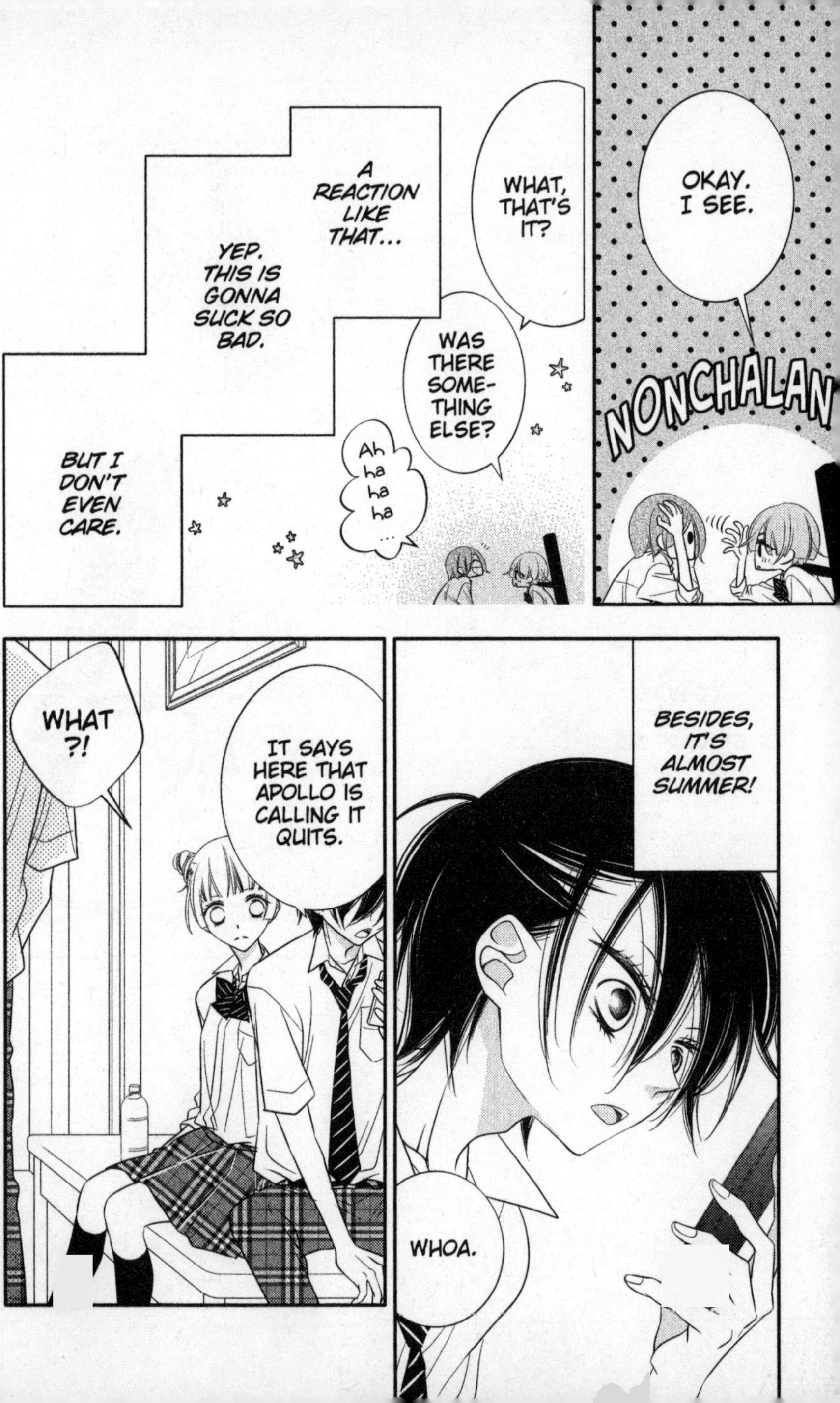
OKAY. I SEE.
NONCHALAN
WHAT, THAT'S IT?
WAS THERE SOMETHING ELSE?
Ah ha ha ha...
A REACTION LIKE THAT...
YEP. THIS IS GONNA SUCK SO BAD.
BUT I DON'T EVEN CARE.
BESIDES, IT'S ALMOST SUMMER!
WHOA.
IT SAYS HERE THAT APOLLO IS CALLING IT QUITS.
WHAT?!

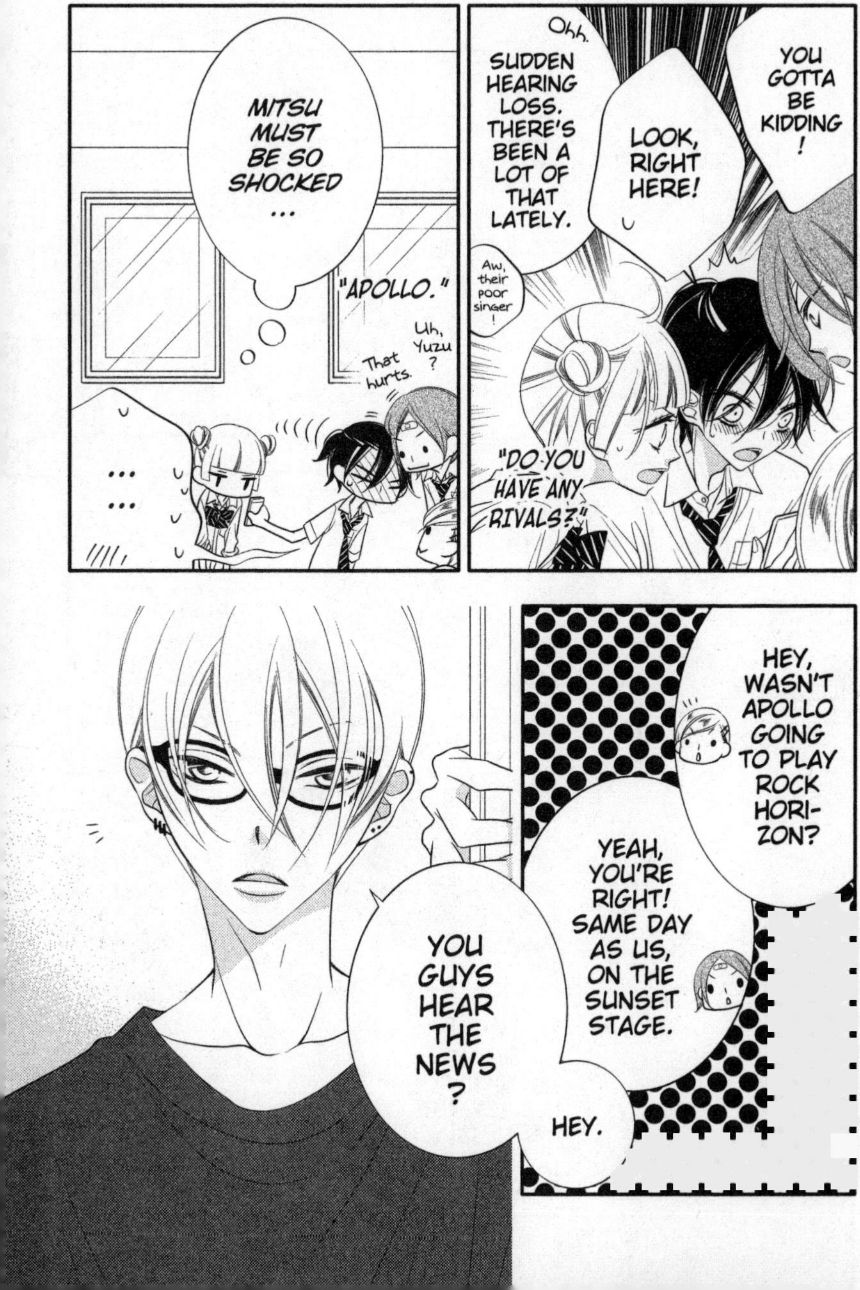
YOU GOTTA BE KIDDING!
LOOK, RIGHT HERE!
Ohh.
SUDDEN HEARING LOSS. THERE'S BEEN A LOT OF THAT LATELY.
Aw, their poor singer!
"DO YOU HAVE ANY RIVALS?"
MITSU MUST BE SO SHOCKED...
"APOLLO."
Uh, Yuzu?
That hurts.
... ...
HEY, WASN'T APOLLO GOING TO PLAY ROCK HORI-ZON?
YEAH, YOU'RE RIGHT! SAME DAY AS US, ON THE SUNSET STAGE.
HEY.
YOU GUYS HEAR THE NEWS?

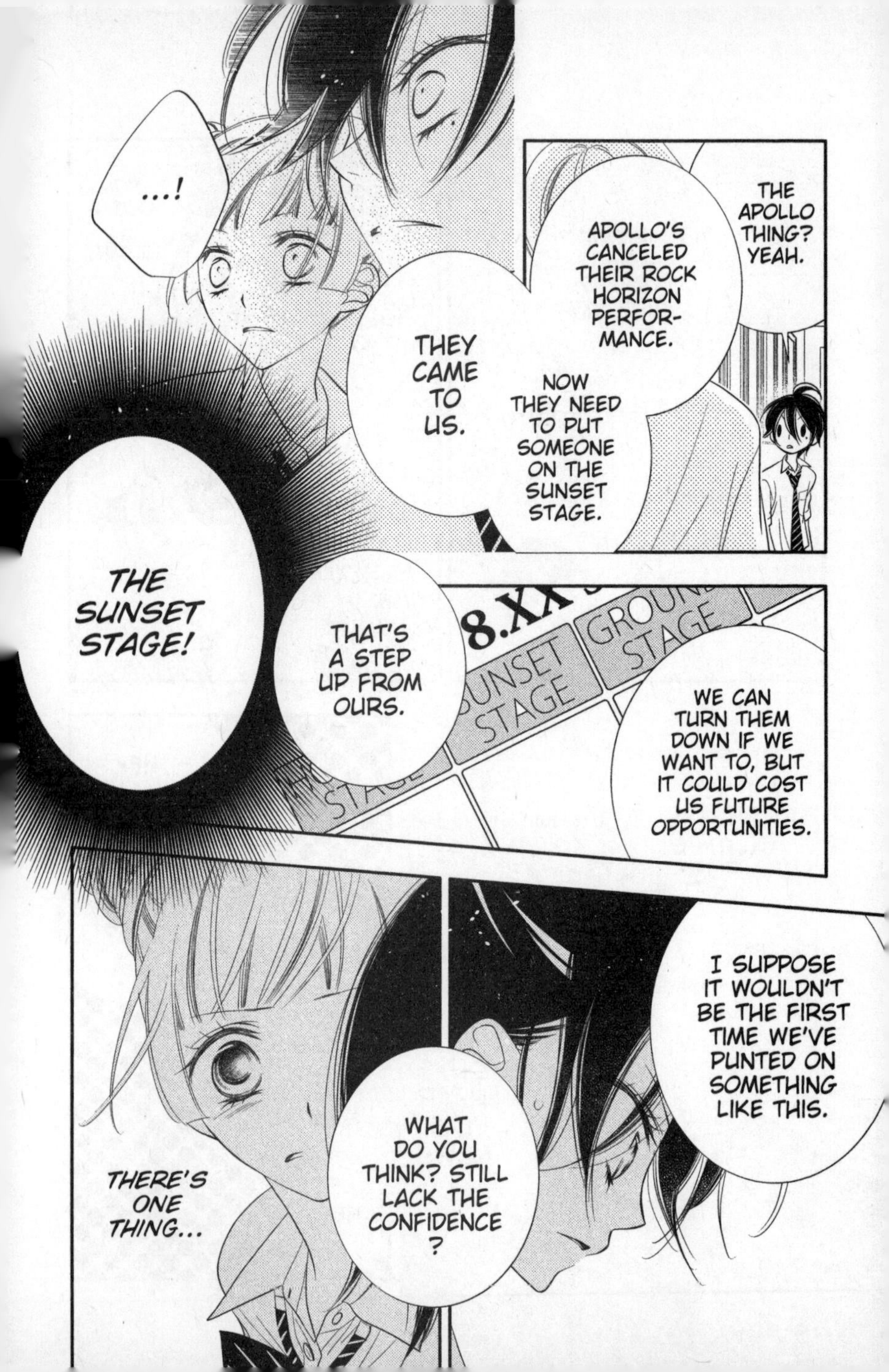
THE APOLLO THING? YEAH.
APOLLO'S CANCELED THEIR ROCK HORIZON PERFORMANCE.
NOW THEY NEED TO PUT SOMEONE ON THE SUNSET STAGE.
THEY CAME TO US.
8.XX
GROUND STAGE
SUNSET STAGE
STAGE
WE CAN TURN THEM DOWN IF WE WANT TO, BUT IT COULD COST US FUTURE OPPORTUNITIES.
THAT'S A STEP UP FROM OURS.
...!
THE SUNSET STAGE!
I SUPPOSE IT WOULDN'T BE THE FIRST TIME WE'VE PUNTED ON SOMETHING LIKE THIS.
WHAT DO YOU THINK? STILL LACK THE CONFIDENCE?
THERE'S ONE THING...

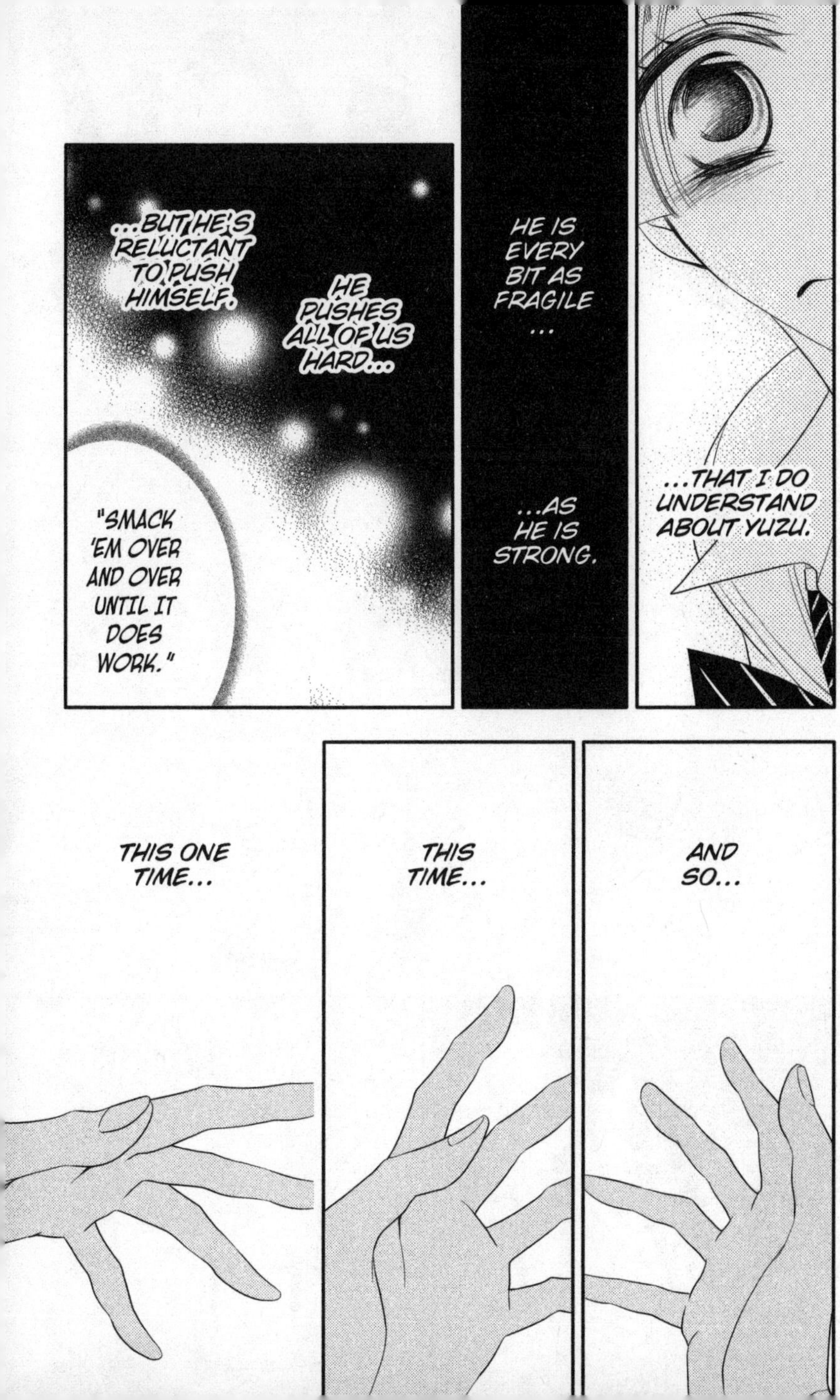
...THAT I DO UNDERSTAND ABOUT YUZU.
HE IS EVERY BIT AS FRAGILE...
...AS HE IS STRONG.
HE PUSHES ALL OF US HARD...
...BUT HE'S RELUCTANT TO PUSH HIMSELF.
"SMACK 'EM OVER AND OVER UNTIL IT DOES WORK."
AND SO...
THIS TIME...
THIS ONE TIME...

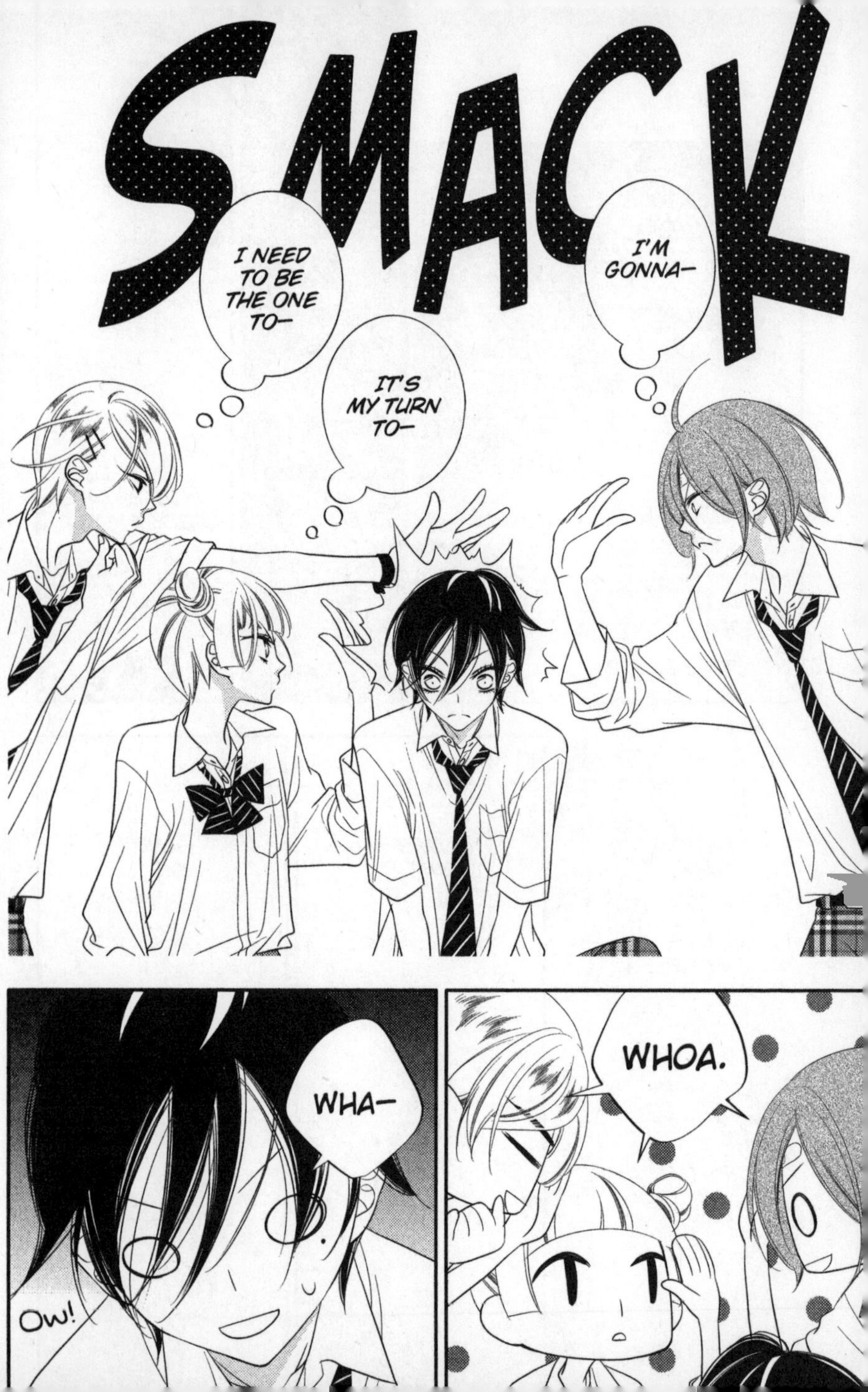
SMACK
I'M GONNA—
IT'S MY TURN TO—
I NEED TO BE THE ONE TO—
WHOA.
WHA—
Ow!

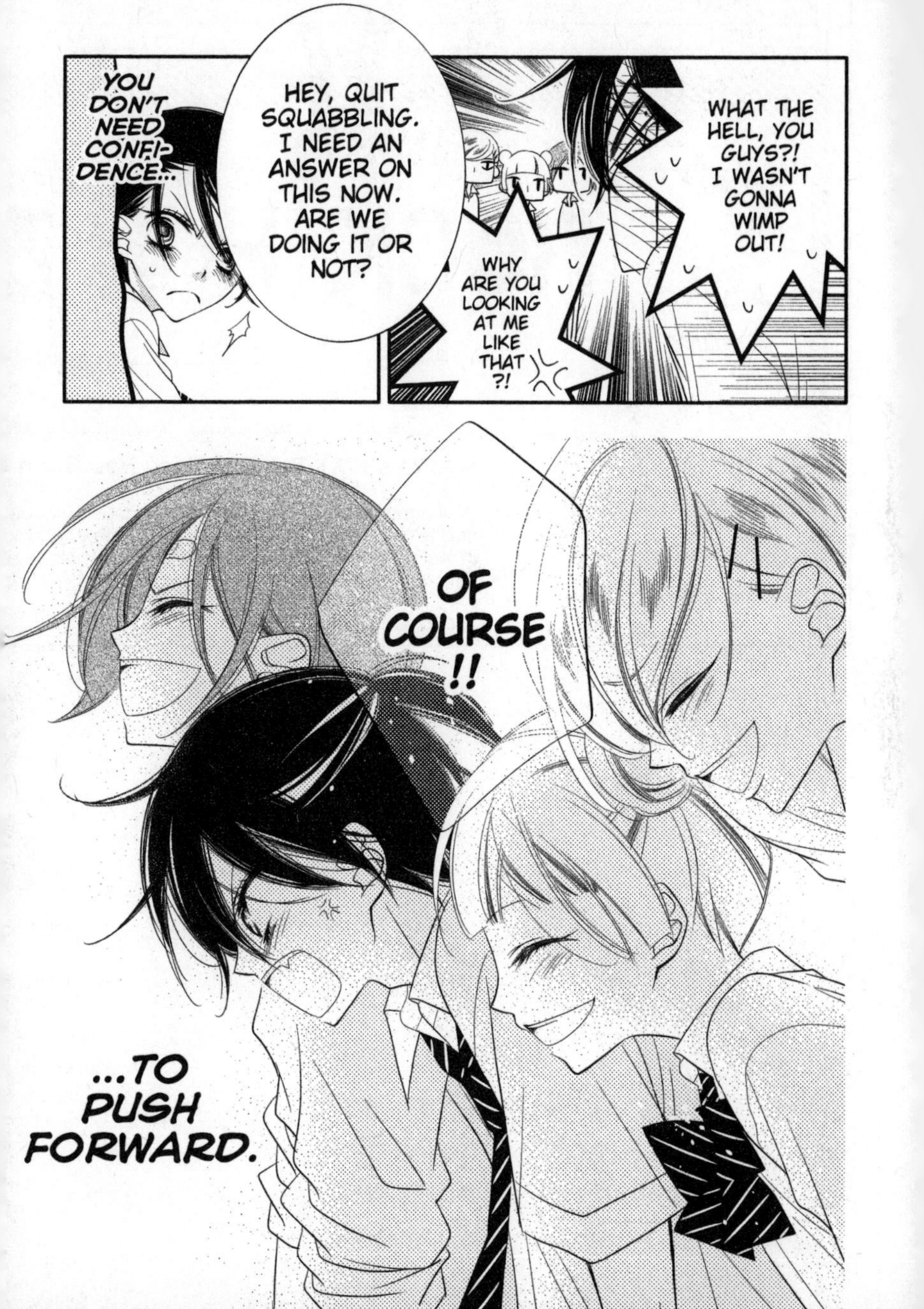
WHAT THE HELL, YOU GUYS?! I WASN'T GONNA WIMP OUT!
WHY ARE YOU LOOKING AT ME LIKE THAT?!
HEY, QUIT SQUABBLING. I NEED AN ANSWER ON THIS NOW. ARE WE DOING IT OR NOT?
YOU DON'T NEED CONFI-DENCE...
OF COURSE!!
...TO PUSH FORWARD.

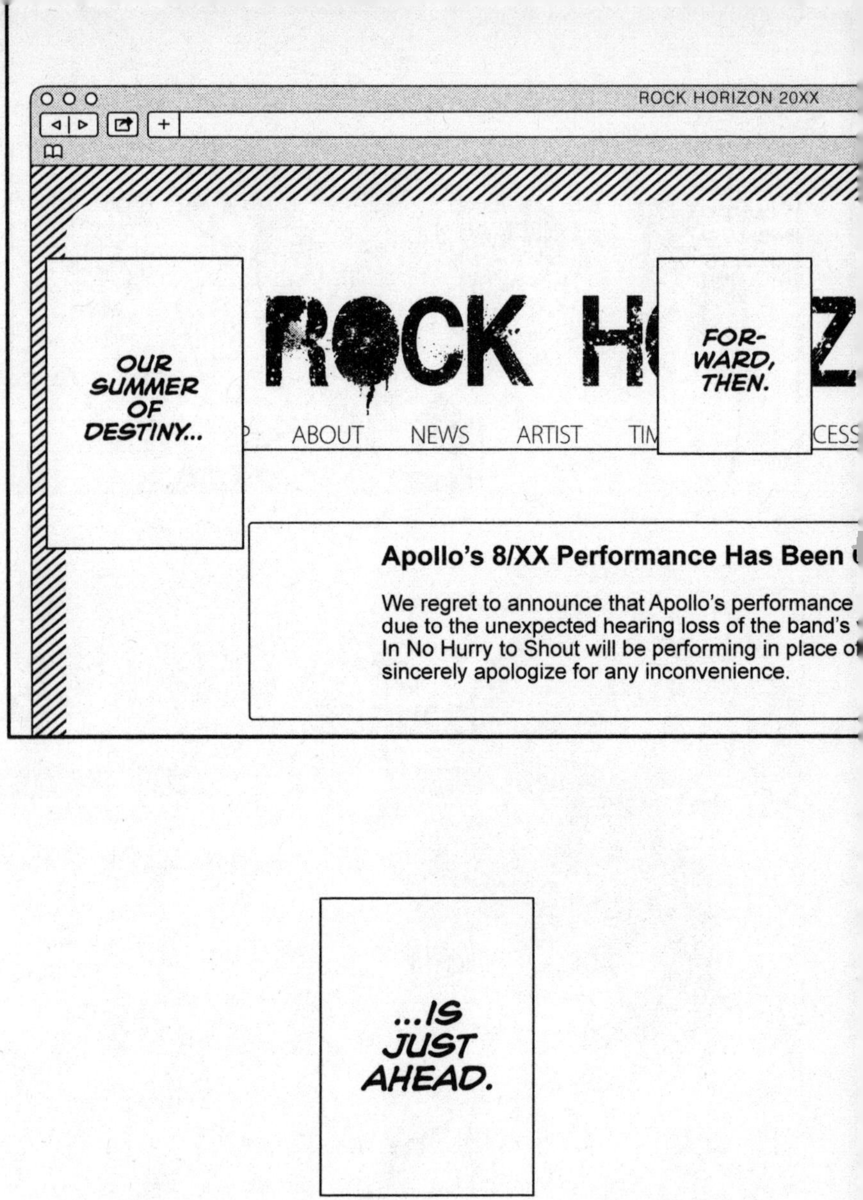
ROCK HORIZON 20XX
FORWARD, THEN.
ROCK H
ABOUT
NEWS
ARTIST
Apollo's 8/XX Performance Has Been
We regret to announce that Apollo's performance
due to the unexpected hearing loss of the band's
In No Hurry to Shout will be performing in place of
sincerely apologize for any inconvenience.
OUR SUMMER OF DESTINY...
...IS JUST AHEAD.

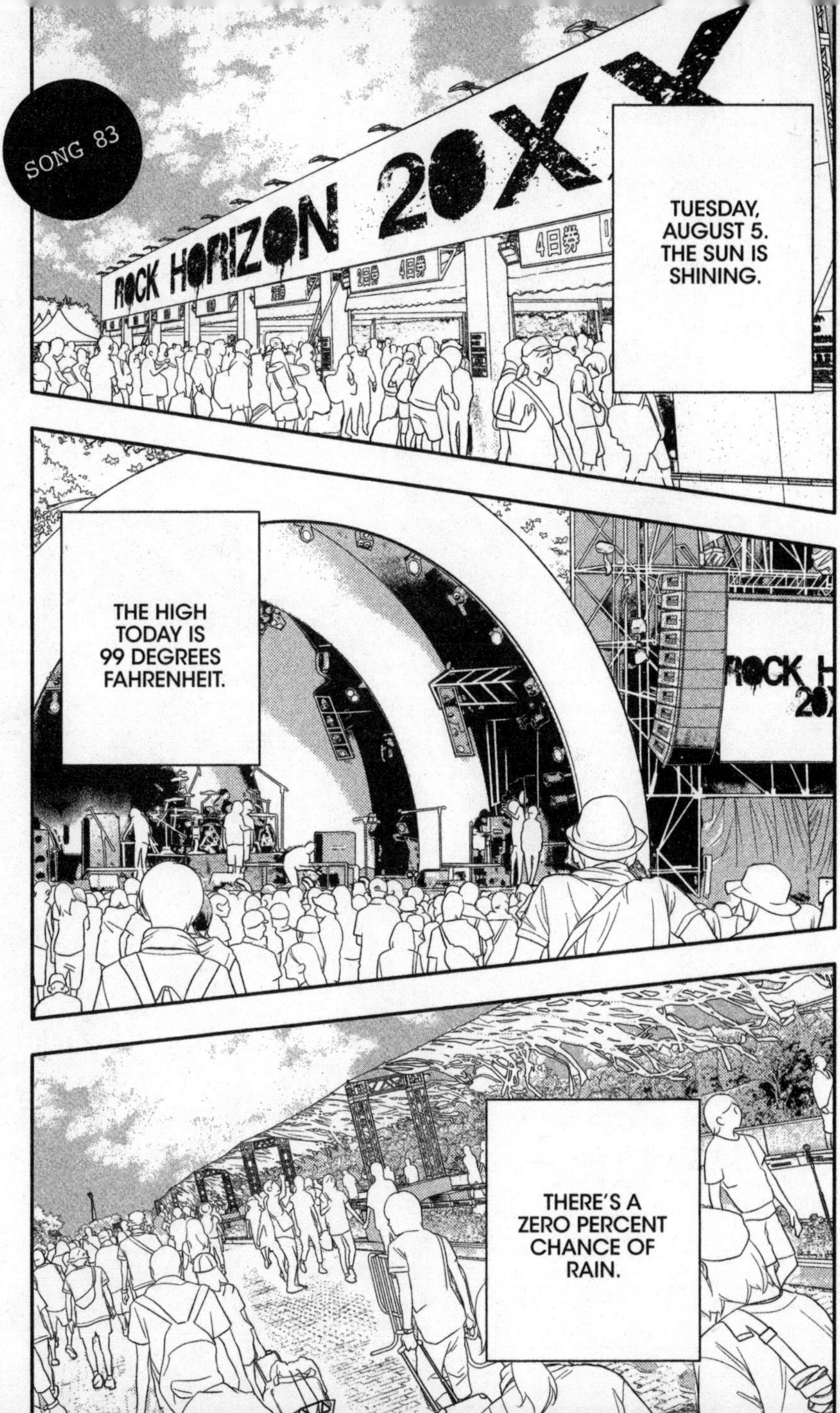
SONG 83
ROCK HORIZON 20XX
4日券
2日券
4日券
TUESDAY, AUGUST 5. THE SUN IS SHINING.
THE HIGH TODAY IS 99 DEGREES FAHRENHEIT.
ROCK H 20X
THERE'S A ZERO PERCENT CHANCE OF RAIN.

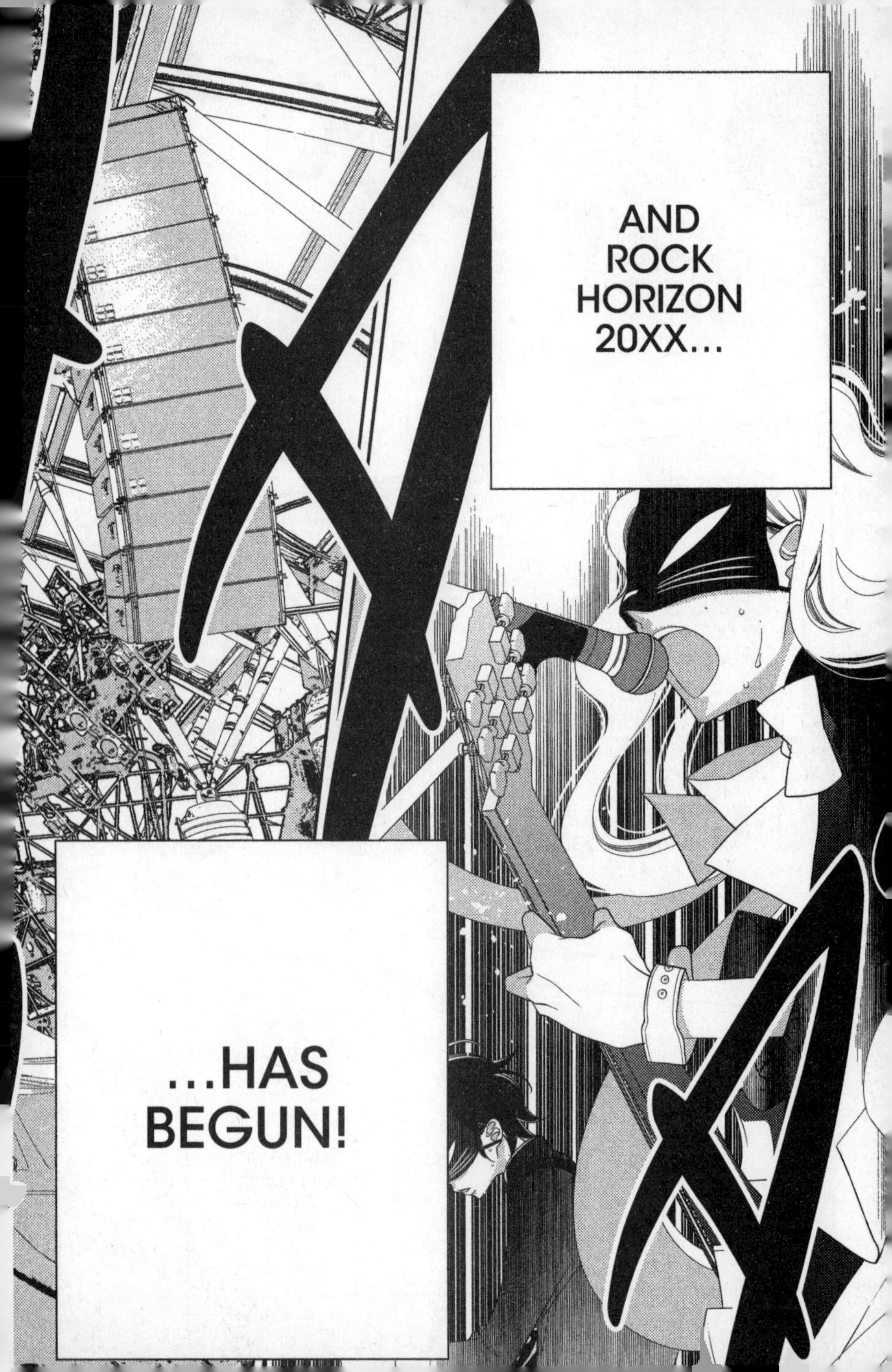
AND ROCK HORIZON 20XX...
...HAS BEGUN!

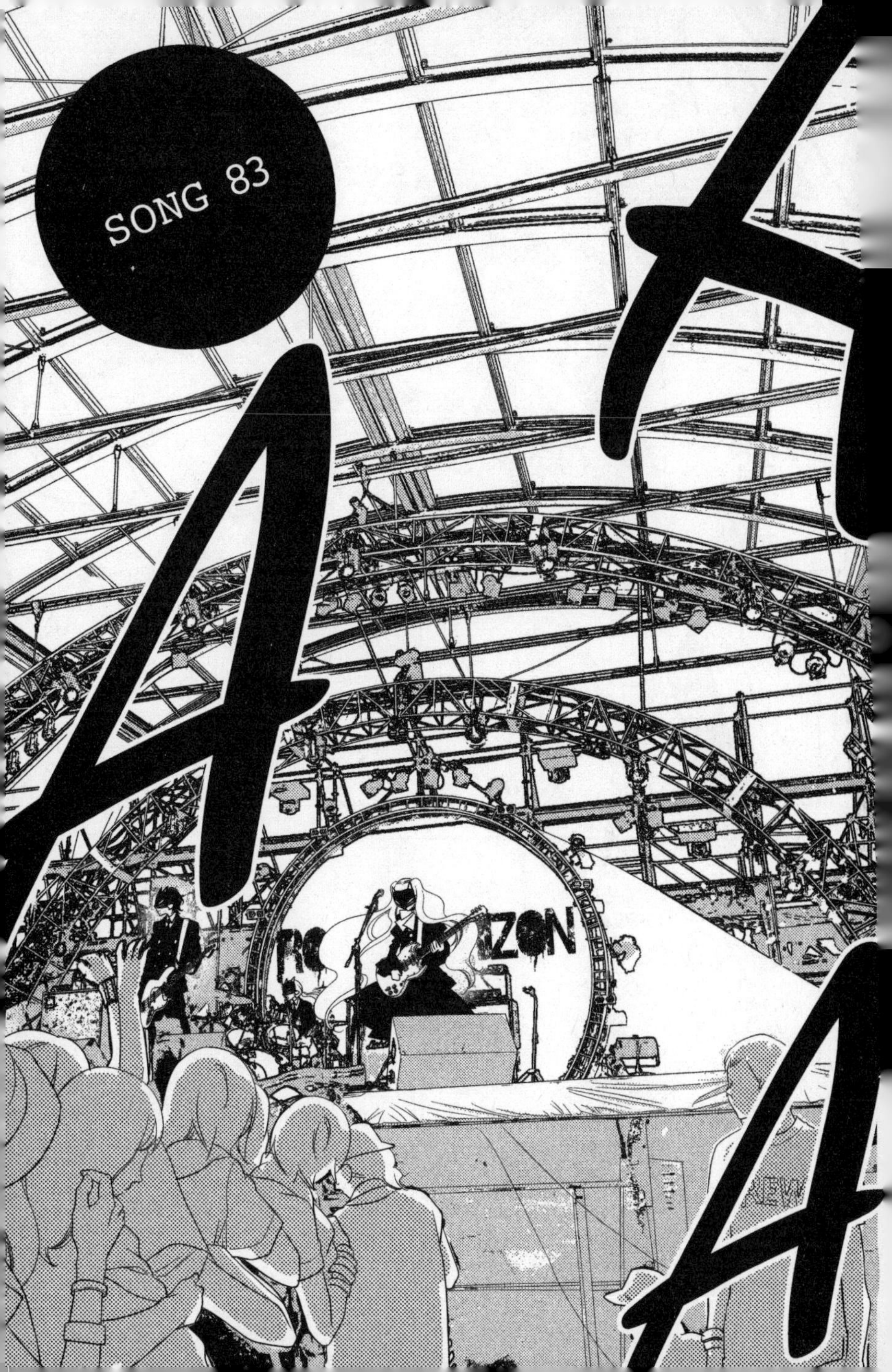
SONG 83

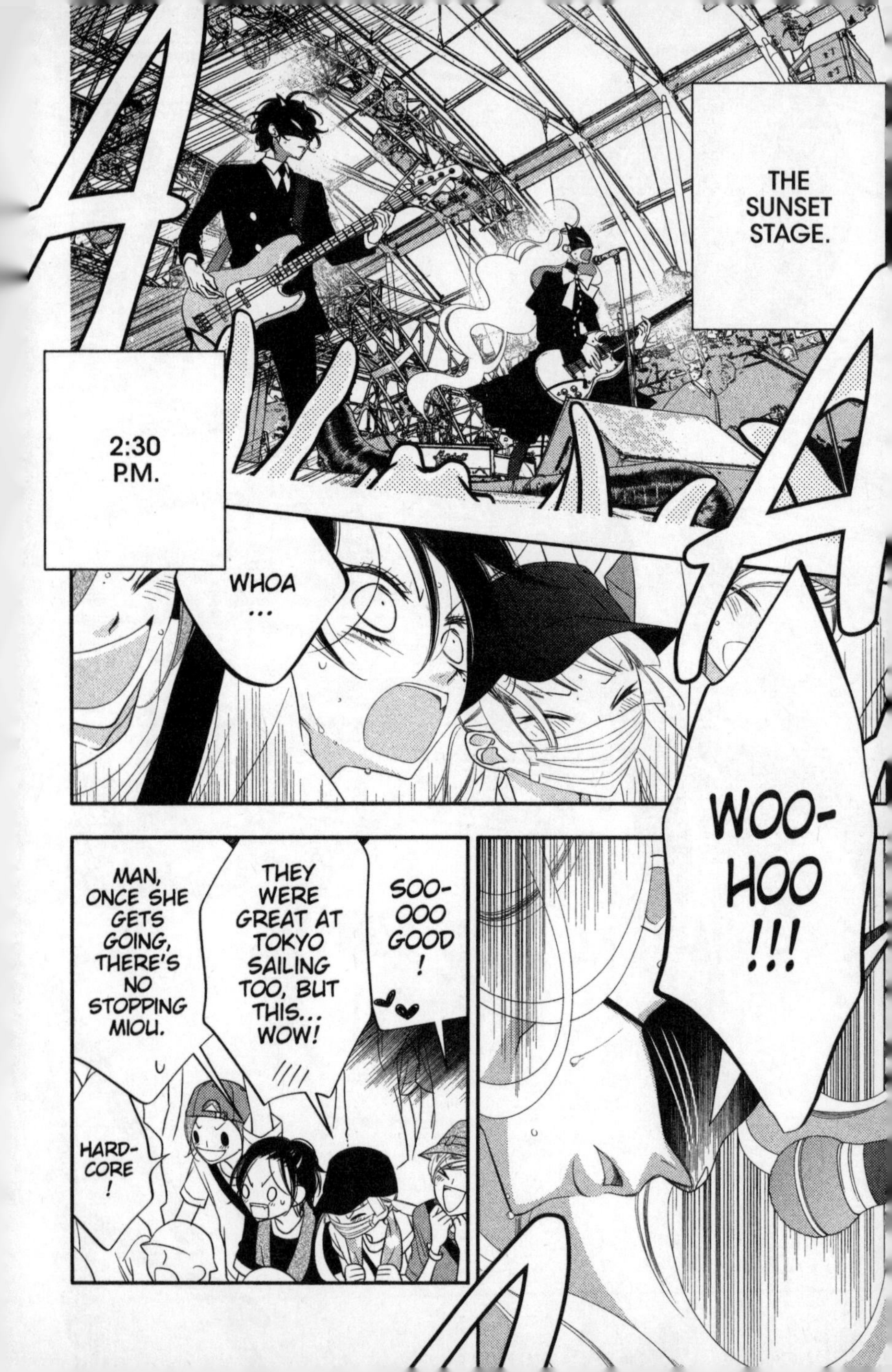
THE SUNSET STAGE.
2:30 P.M.
WHOA...
WOO-HOO!!!
SOO-OOO GOOD!
THEY WERE GREAT AT TOKYO SAILING TOO, BUT THIS... WOW!
MAN, ONCE SHE GETS GOING, THERE'S NO STOPPING MIOU.
HARD-CORE!

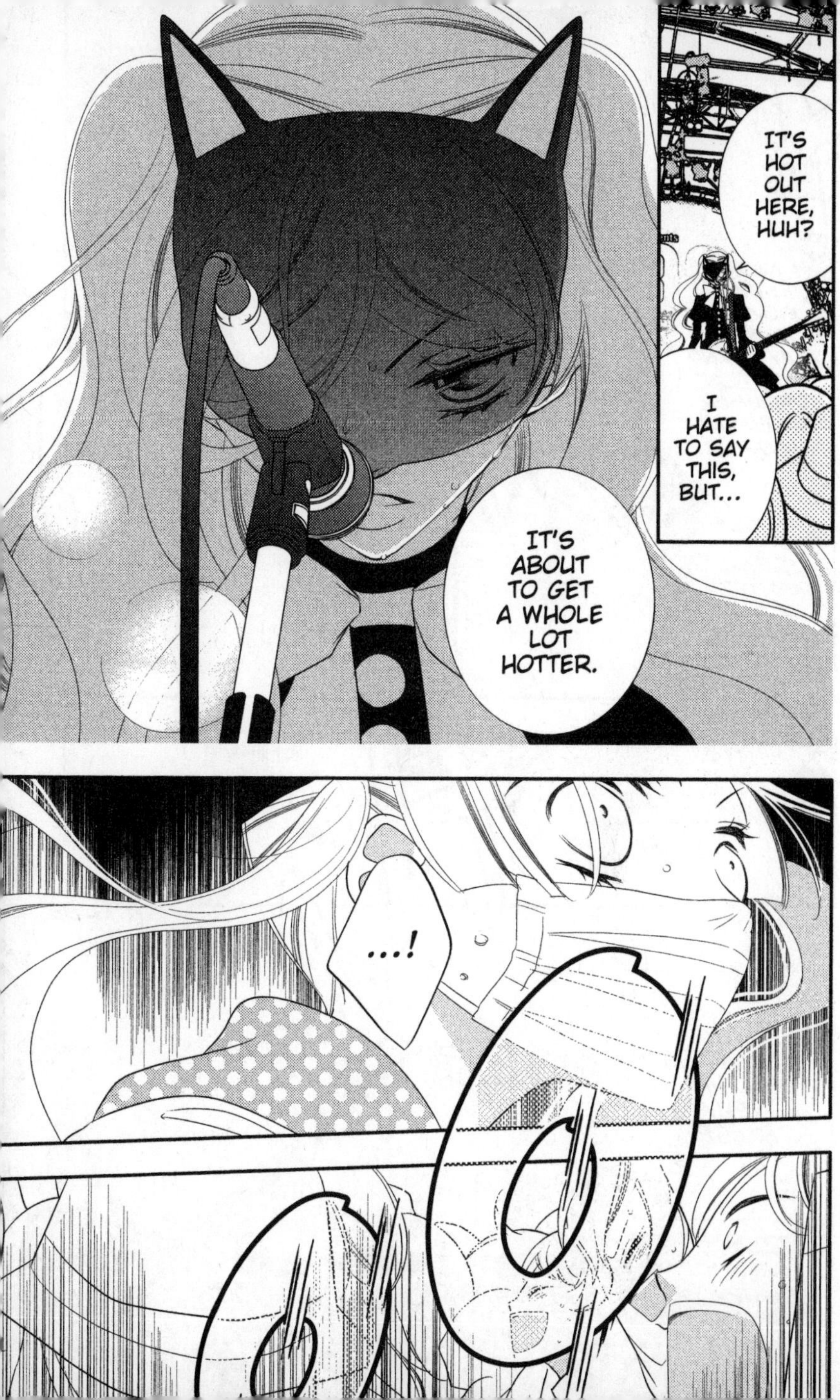
IT'S HOT OUT HERE, HUH?
I HATE TO SAY THIS, BUT...
IT'S ABOUT TO GET A WHOLE LOT HOTTER.
...!

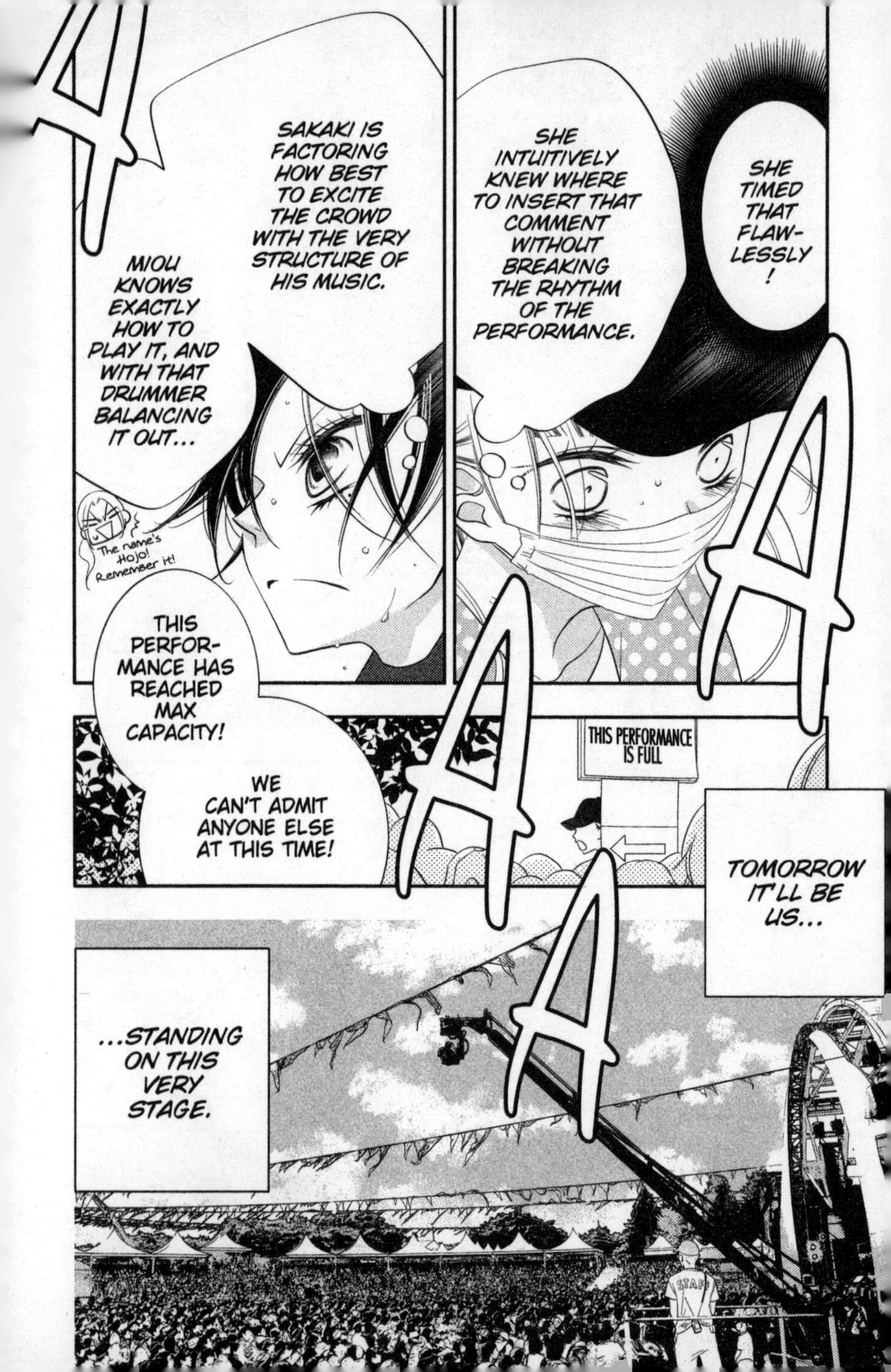
SHE TIMED THAT FLAW-LESSLY!
SHE INTUITIVELY KNEW WHERE TO INSERT THAT COMMENT WITHOUT BREAKING THE RHYTHM OF THE PERFORMANCE.
SAKAKI IS FACTORING HOW BEST TO EXCITE THE CROWD WITH THE VERY STRUCTURE OF HIS MUSIC.
MIOU KNOWS EXACTLY HOW TO PLAY IT, AND WITH THAT DRUMMER BALANCING IT OUT...
The name's Hojo! Remember it!
A
AAAAAA
THIS PERFORMANCE IS FULL
THIS PERFORMANCE HAS REACHED MAX CAPACITY!
WE CAN'T ADMIT ANYONE ELSE AT THIS TIME!
TOMORROW IT'LL BE US...
...STANDING ON THIS VERY STAGE.
STAFF

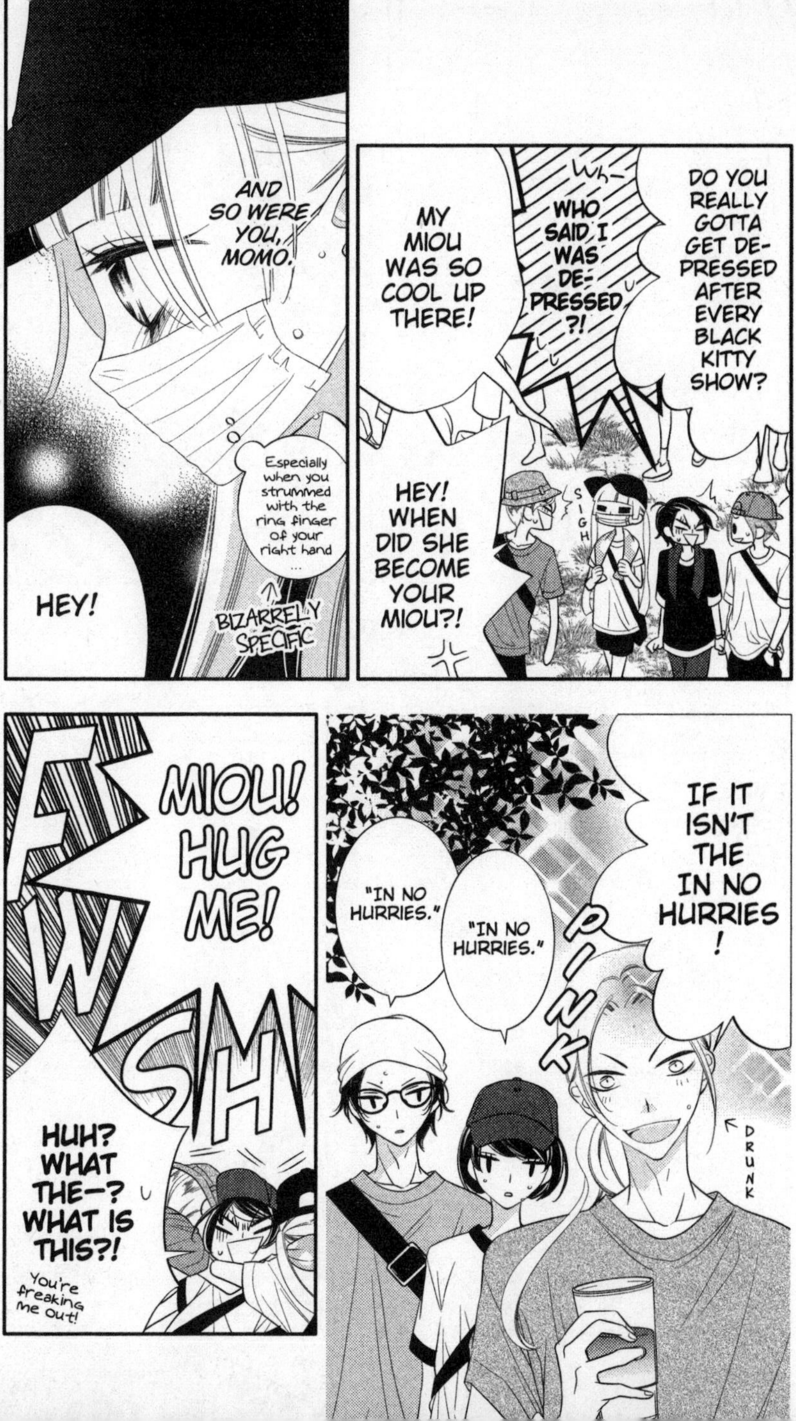
DO YOU REALLY GOTTA GET DE-PRESSED AFTER EVERY BLACK KITTY SHOW?
WHO SAID I WAS DE-PRESSED?!
MY MIOU WAS SO COOL UP THERE!
SIGH
HEY! WHEN DID SHE BECOME YOUR MIOU?!
AND SO WERE YOU, MOMO.
Especially when you strummed with the ring finger of your right hand ...
BIZARRELY SPECIFIC
HEY!
IF IT ISN'T THE IN NO HURRIES!
PINK
"IN NO HURRIES."
"IN NO HURRIES."
DRUNK
MIOU! HUG ME!
FWSH
HUH? WHAT THE—? WHAT IS THIS?!
You're freaking me out!

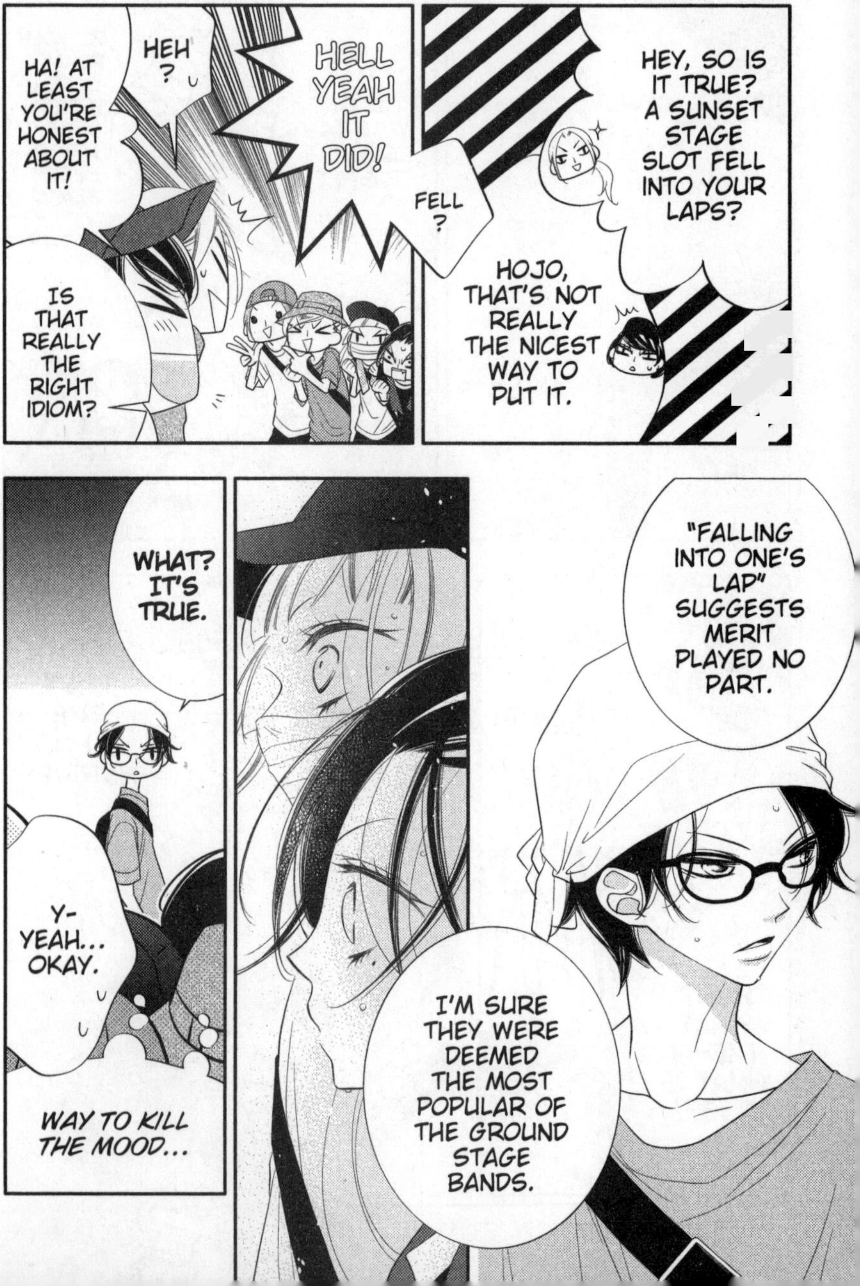
HEY, SO IS IT TRUE? A SUNSET STAGE SLOT FELL INTO YOUR LAPS?
HOJO, THAT'S NOT REALLY THE NICEST WAY TO PUT IT.
FELL?
HELL YEAH IT DID!
HEH?
HA! AT LEAST YOU'RE HONEST ABOUT IT!
IS THAT REALLY THE RIGHT IDIOM?
"FALLING INTO ONE'S LAP" SUGGESTS MERIT PLAYED NO PART.
I'M SURE THEY WERE DEEMED THE MOST POPULAR OF THE GROUND STAGE BANDS.
WHAT? IT'S TRUE.
Y-YEAH... OKAY.
WAY TO KILL THE MOOD...

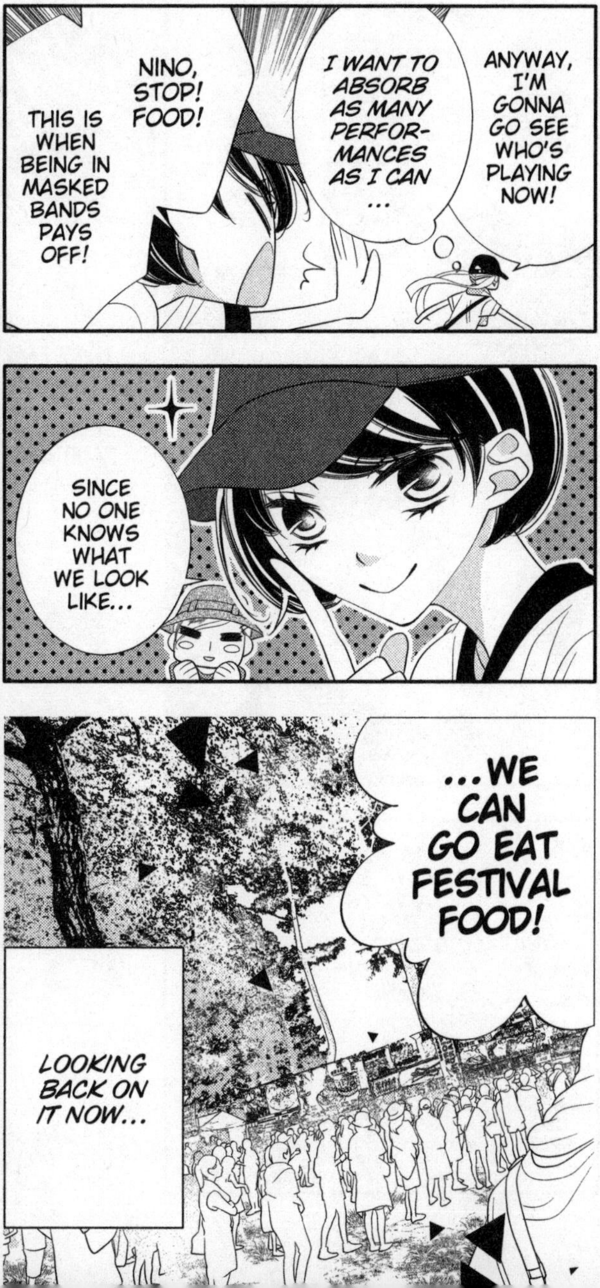
ANYWAY, I'M GONNA GO SEE WHO'S PLAYING NOW!
I WANT TO ABSORB AS MANY PERFOR-MANCES AS I CAN...
NINO, STOP! FOOD!
THIS IS WHEN BEING IN MASKED BANDS PAYS OFF!
SINCE NO ONE KNOWS WHAT WE LOOK LIKE...
...WE CAN GO EAT FESTIVAL FOOD!
LOOKING BACK ON IT NOW...

2

As of this writing, I'm in the middle of my first vacation in a long time—probably not since Anonymous Noise began serialization!

I worked so hard in 2017 that I nearly collapsed, so I really do need a good rest. I get pretty crazy about my manga, so left to my own devices I'll happily write till my hands fall off.

WHEE!

But lately I've finally come to realize how important it is to take some time off now and then. Keeping busy is not, in fact, a virtue, and health and sanity are our most precious assets!

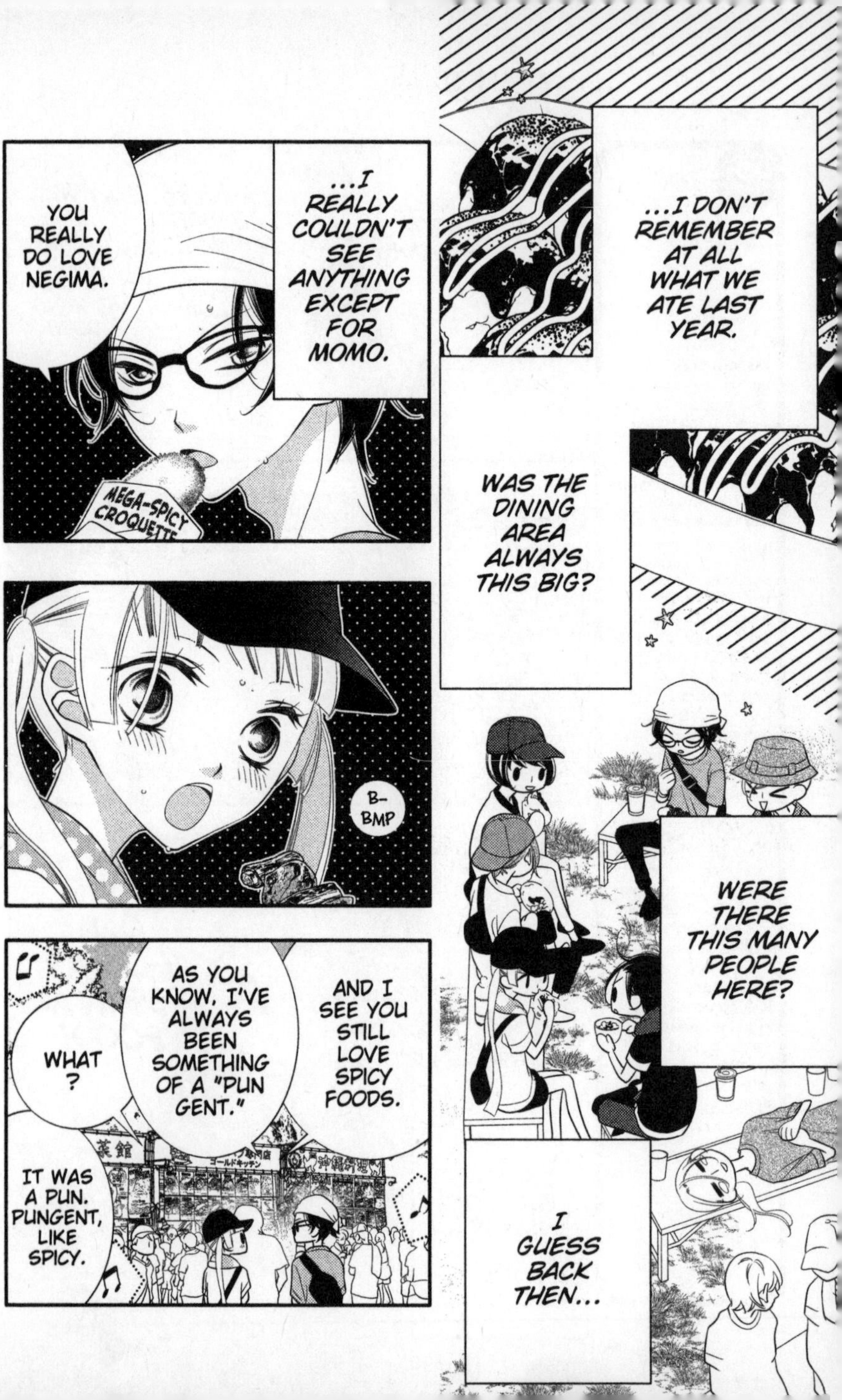
...I DON'T REMEMBER AT ALL WHAT WE ATE LAST YEAR.
WAS THE DINING AREA ALWAYS THIS BIG?
WERE THERE THIS MANY PEOPLE HERE?
I GUESS BACK THEN...
...I REALLY COULDN'T SEE ANYTHING EXCEPT FOR MOMO.
YOU REALLY DO LOVE NEGIMA.
MEGA-SPICY CROQUETTE
B-BMP
AND I SEE YOU STILL LOVE SPICY FOODS.
AS YOU KNOW, I'VE ALWAYS BEEN SOMETHING OF A "PUN GENT."
WHAT?
IT WAS A PUN. PUNGENT, LIKE SPICY.

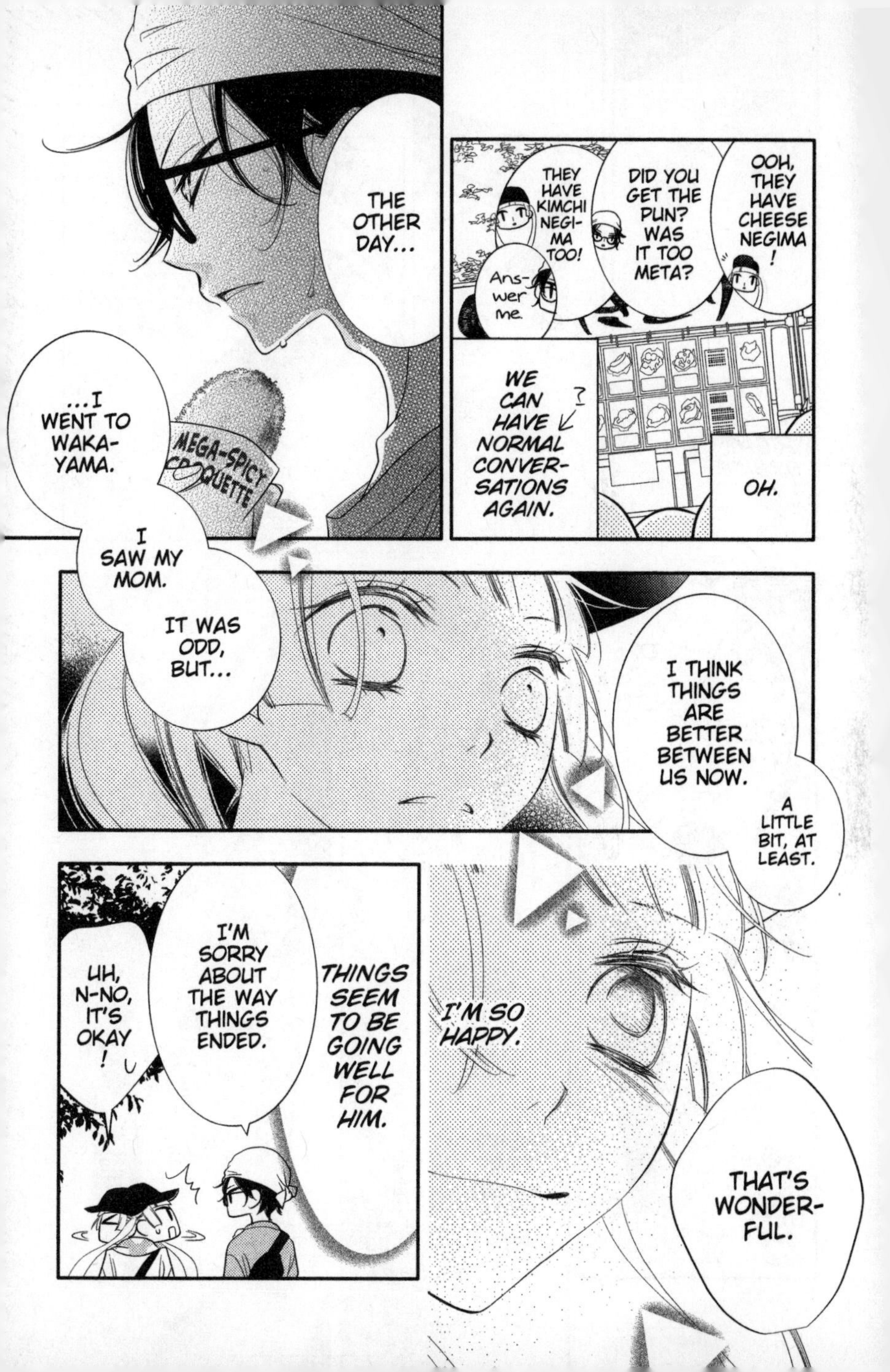
OOH, THEY HAVE CHEESE NEGIMA!
DID YOU GET THE PUN? WAS IT TOO META?
THEY HAVE KIMCHI NEGIMA TOO!
Answer me.
OH.
WE CAN HAVE NORMAL CONVERSATIONS AGAIN.
?
THE OTHER DAY...
...I WENT TO WAKAYAMA.
MEGA-SPICY CROQUETTE
I SAW MY MOM.
IT WAS ODD, BUT...
I THINK THINGS ARE BETTER BETWEEN US NOW.
A LITTLE BIT, AT LEAST.
I'M SO HAPPY.
THAT'S WONDERFUL.
THINGS SEEM TO BE GOING WELL FOR HIM.
I'M SORRY ABOUT THE WAY THINGS ENDED.
UH, N-NO, IT'S OKAY!

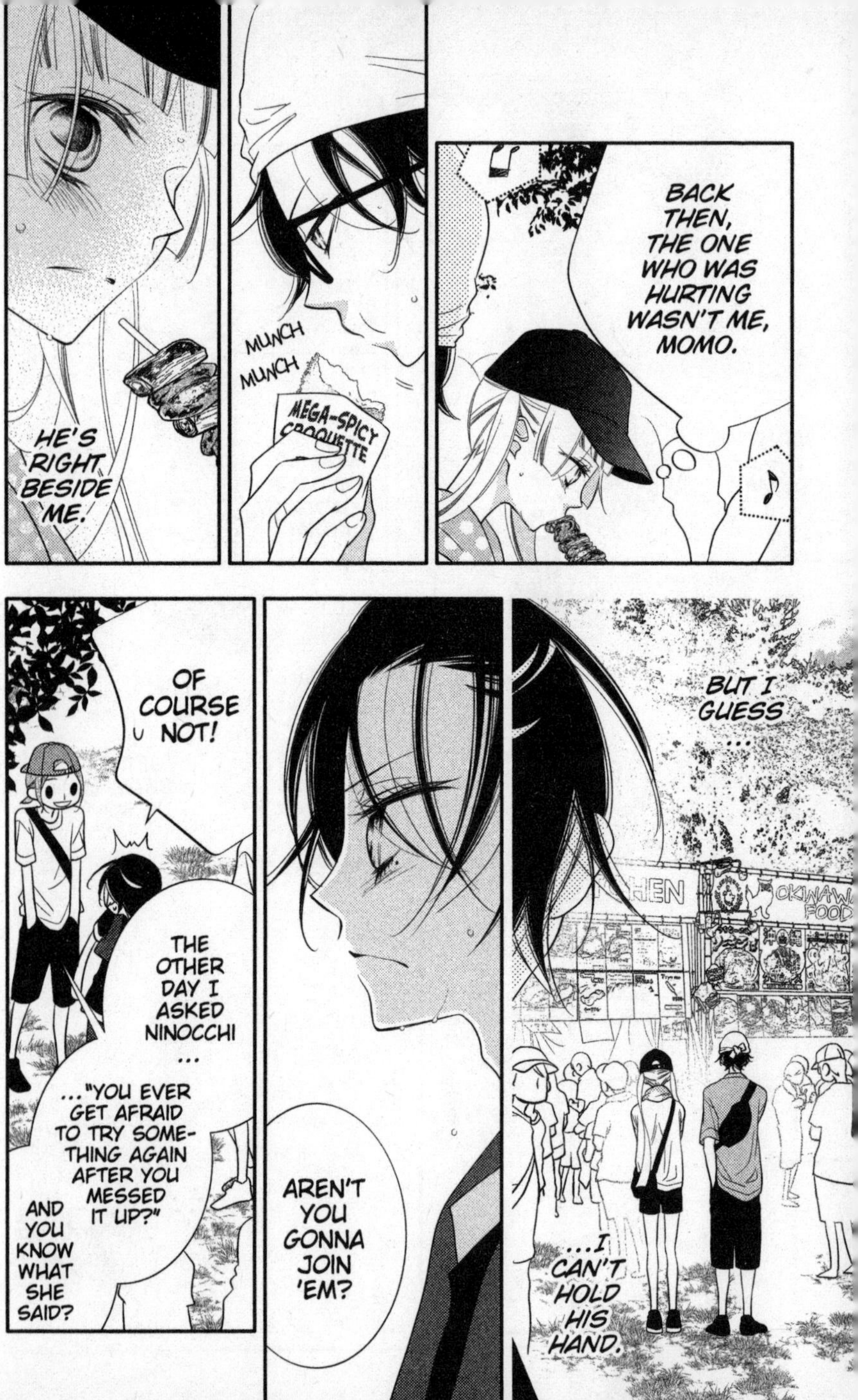
BACK THEN, THE ONE WHO WAS HURTING WASN'T ME, MOMO.
MUNCH
MUNCH
MEGA-SPICY CROQUETTE
HE'S RIGHT BESIDE ME.
BUT I GUESS ...
...I CAN'T HOLD HIS HAND.
AREN'T YOU GONNA JOIN 'EM?
OF COURSE NOT!
THE OTHER DAY I ASKED NINOCCHI ...
..."YOU EVER GET AFRAID TO TRY SOME-THING AGAIN AFTER YOU MESSED IT UP?"
AND YOU KNOW WHAT SHE SAID?

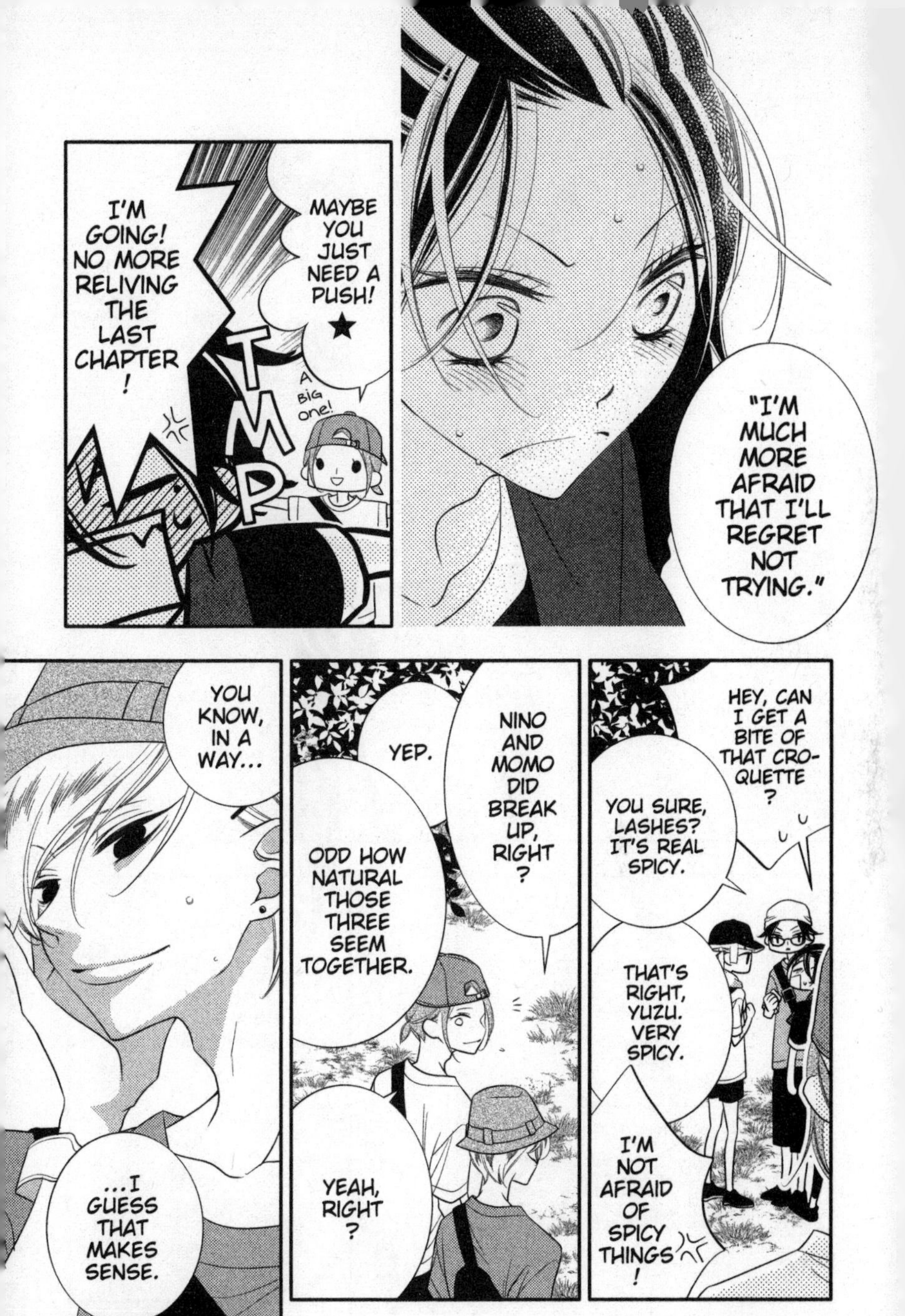
"I'M MUCH MORE AFRAID THAT I'LL REGRET NOT TRYING."
MAYBE YOU JUST NEED A PUSH! ★
I'M GOING! NO MORE RELIVING THE LAST CHAPTER!
A BIG ONE!
TMP
HEY, CAN I GET A BITE OF THAT CROQUETTE?
YOU SURE, LASHES? IT'S REAL SPICY.
THAT'S RIGHT, YUZU. VERY SPICY.
I'M NOT AFRAID OF SPICY THINGS!
NINO AND MOMO DID BREAK UP, RIGHT?
YEP.
ODD HOW NATURAL THOSE THREE SEEM TOGETHER.
YEAH, RIGHT?
YOU KNOW, IN A WAY...
...I GUESS THAT MAKES SENSE.

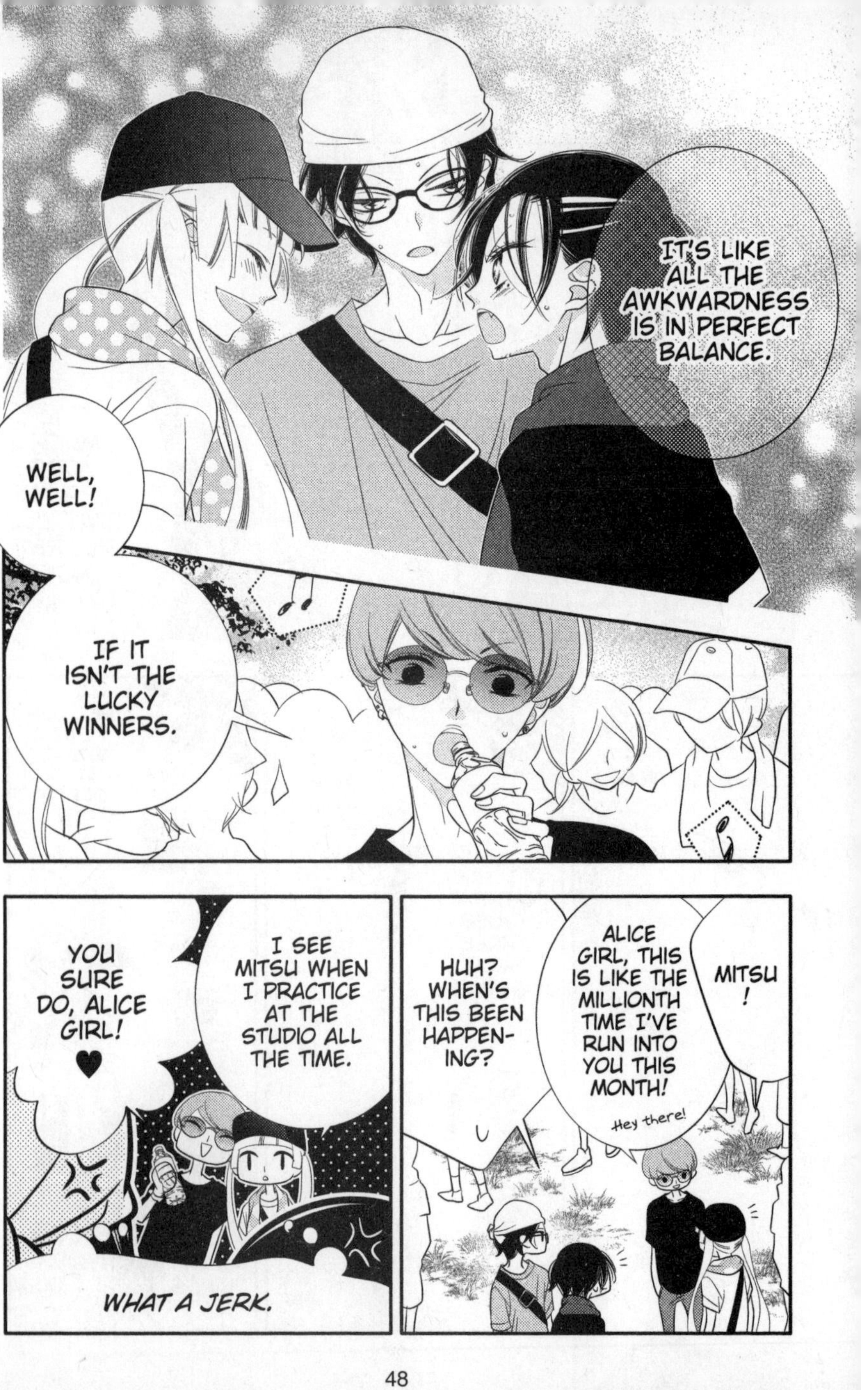

IT'S LIKE ALL THE AWKWARDNESS IS IN PERFECT BALANCE.
WELL, WELL!
IF IT ISN'T THE LUCKY WINNERS.
MITSU!
ALICE GIRL, THIS IS LIKE THE MILLIONTH TIME I'VE RUN INTO YOU THIS MONTH!
Hey there!
HUH? WHEN'S THIS BEEN HAPPEN-ING?
I SEE MITSU WHEN I PRACTICE AT THE STUDIO ALL THE TIME.
YOU SURE DO, ALICE GIRL! ♥
WHAT A JERK.

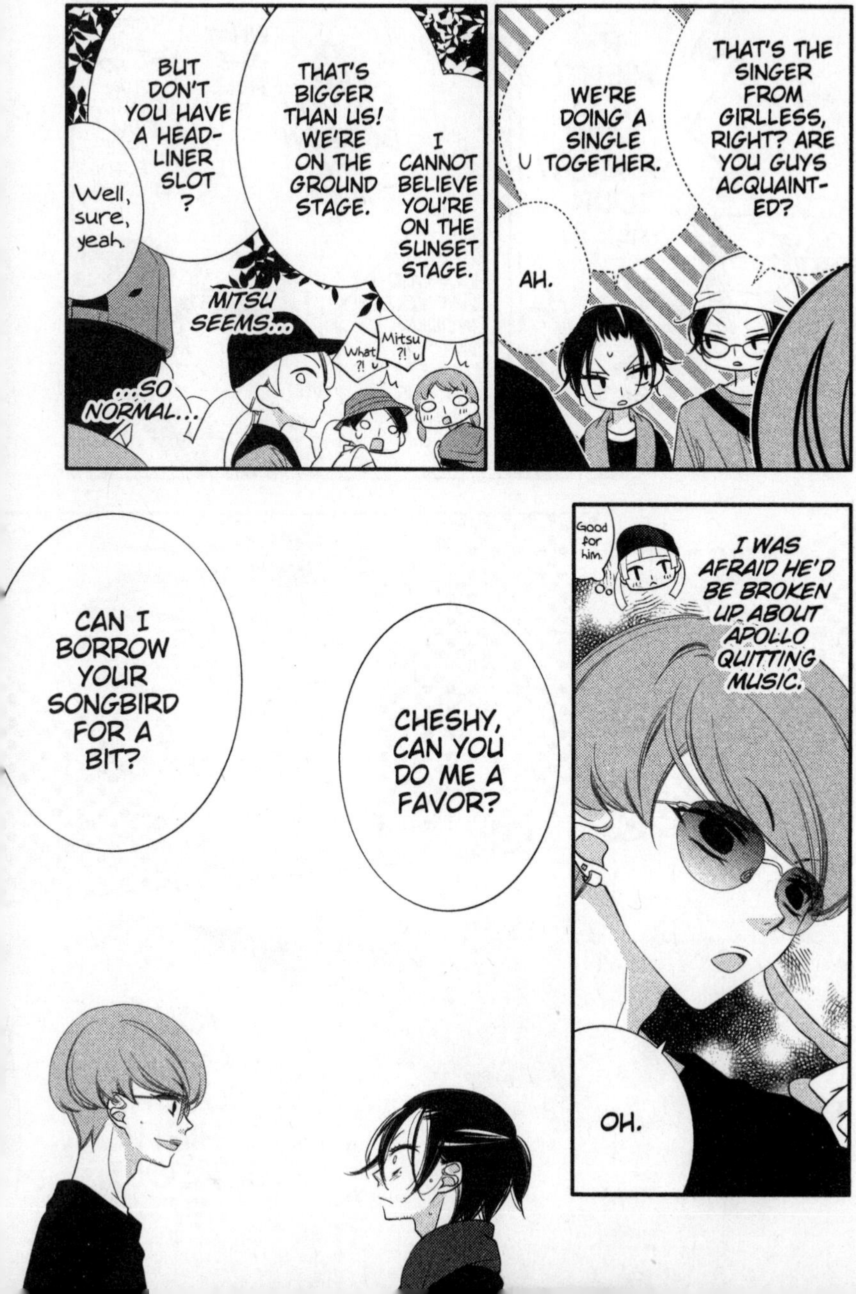
THAT'S THE SINGER FROM GIRLLESS, RIGHT? ARE YOU GUYS ACQUAINT-ED?
WE'RE DOING A SINGLE TOGETHER.
AH.
I CANNOT BELIEVE YOU'RE ON THE SUNSET STAGE.
THAT'S BIGGER THAN US! WE'RE ON THE GROUND STAGE.
BUT DON'T YOU HAVE A HEAD-LINER SLOT?
Well, sure, yeah.
Mitsu?!
What?!
MITSU SEEMS...
...SO NORMAL...
I WAS AFRAID HE'D BE BROKEN UP ABOUT APOLLO QUITTING MUSIC.
Good for him.
OH.
CHESHY, CAN YOU DO ME A FAVOR?
CAN I BORROW YOUR SONGBIRD FOR A BIT?

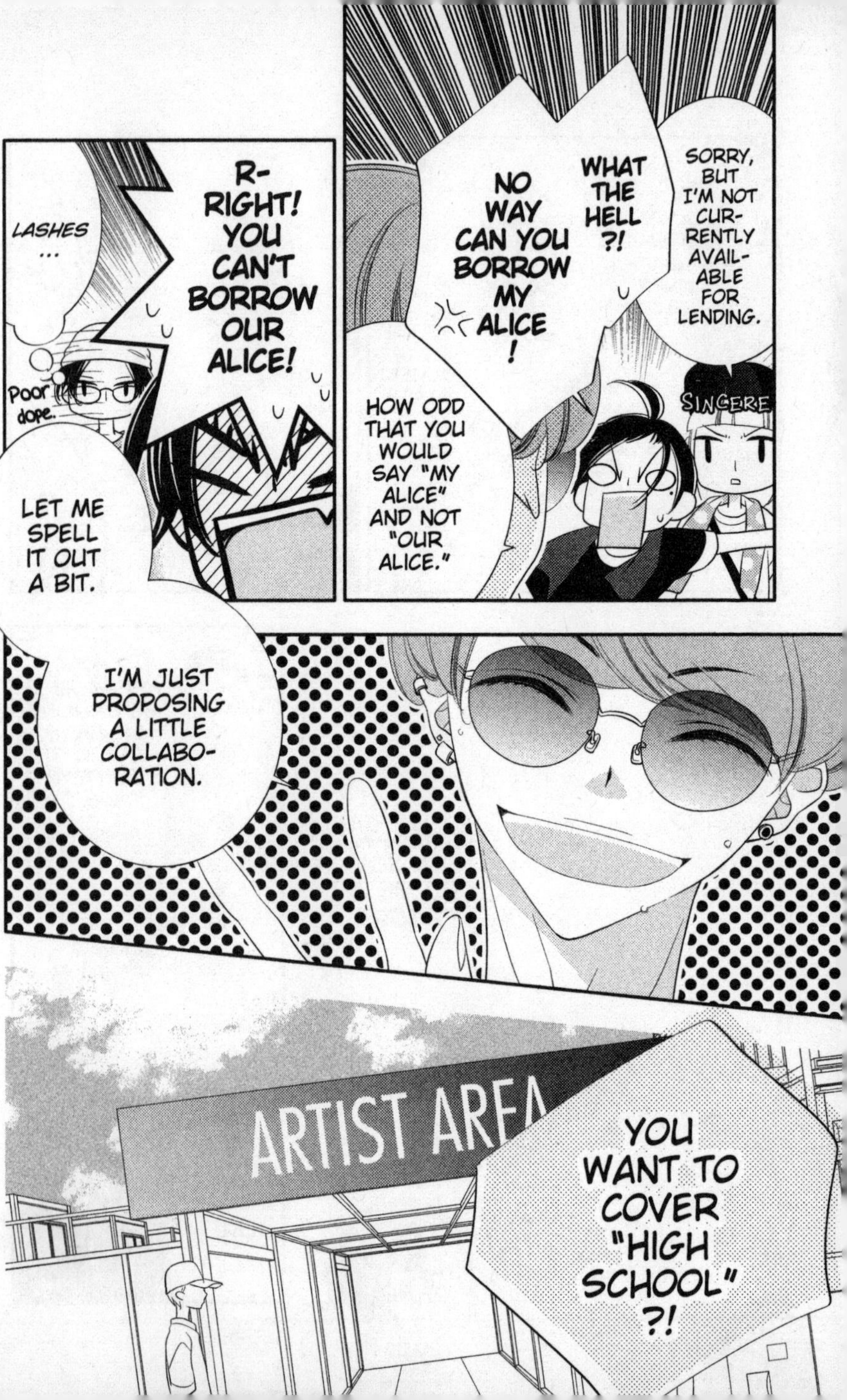
SORRY, BUT I'M NOT CURRENTLY AVAILABLE FOR LENDING.
WHAT THE HELL?!
NO WAY CAN YOU BORROW MY ALICE!
SINCERE
HOW ODD THAT YOU WOULD SAY "MY ALICE" AND NOT "OUR ALICE."
R-RIGHT! YOU CAN'T BORROW OUR ALICE!
LASHES ...
Poor dope.
LET ME SPELL IT OUT A BIT.
I'M JUST PROPOSING A LITTLE COLLABORATION.
ARTIST AREA
YOU WANT TO COVER "HIGH SCHOOL"?!

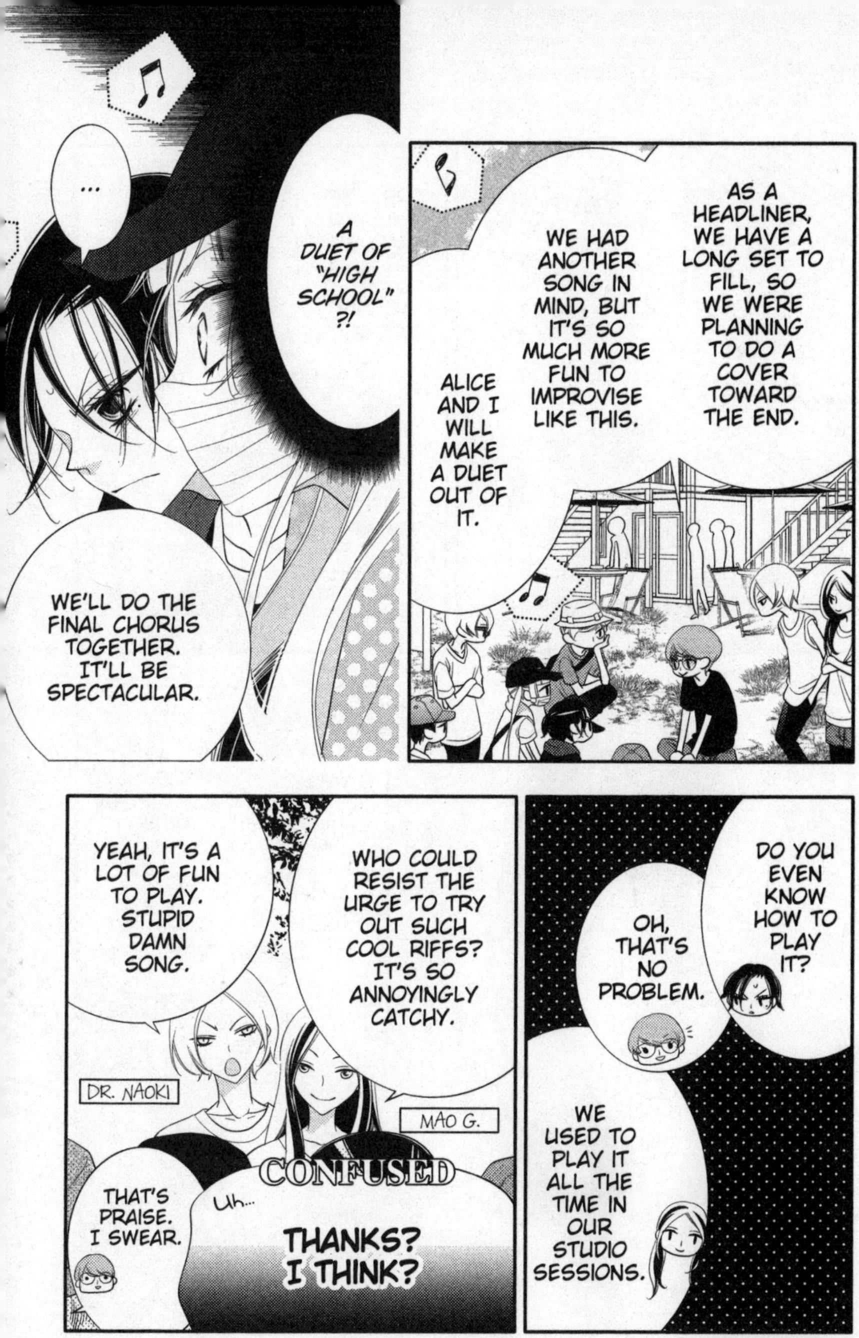
AS A HEADLINER, WE HAVE A LONG SET TO FILL, SO WE WERE PLANNING TO DO A COVER TOWARD THE END.
WE HAD ANOTHER SONG IN MIND, BUT IT'S SO MUCH MORE FUN TO IMPROVISE LIKE THIS.
ALICE AND I WILL MAKE A DUET OUT OF IT.
A DUET OF "HIGH SCHOOL"?!
...
WE'LL DO THE FINAL CHORUS TOGETHER. IT'LL BE SPECTACULAR.
DO YOU EVEN KNOW HOW TO PLAY IT?
OH, THAT'S NO PROBLEM.
WE USED TO PLAY IT ALL THE TIME IN OUR STUDIO SESSIONS.
WHO COULD RESIST THE URGE TO TRY OUT SUCH COOL RIFFS? IT'S SO ANNOYINGLY CATCHY.
YEAH, IT'S A LOT OF FUN TO PLAY. STUPID DAMN SONG.
MAO G.
DR. NAOKI
CONFUSED
Uh...
THANKS? I THINK?
THAT'S PRAISE. I SWEAR.

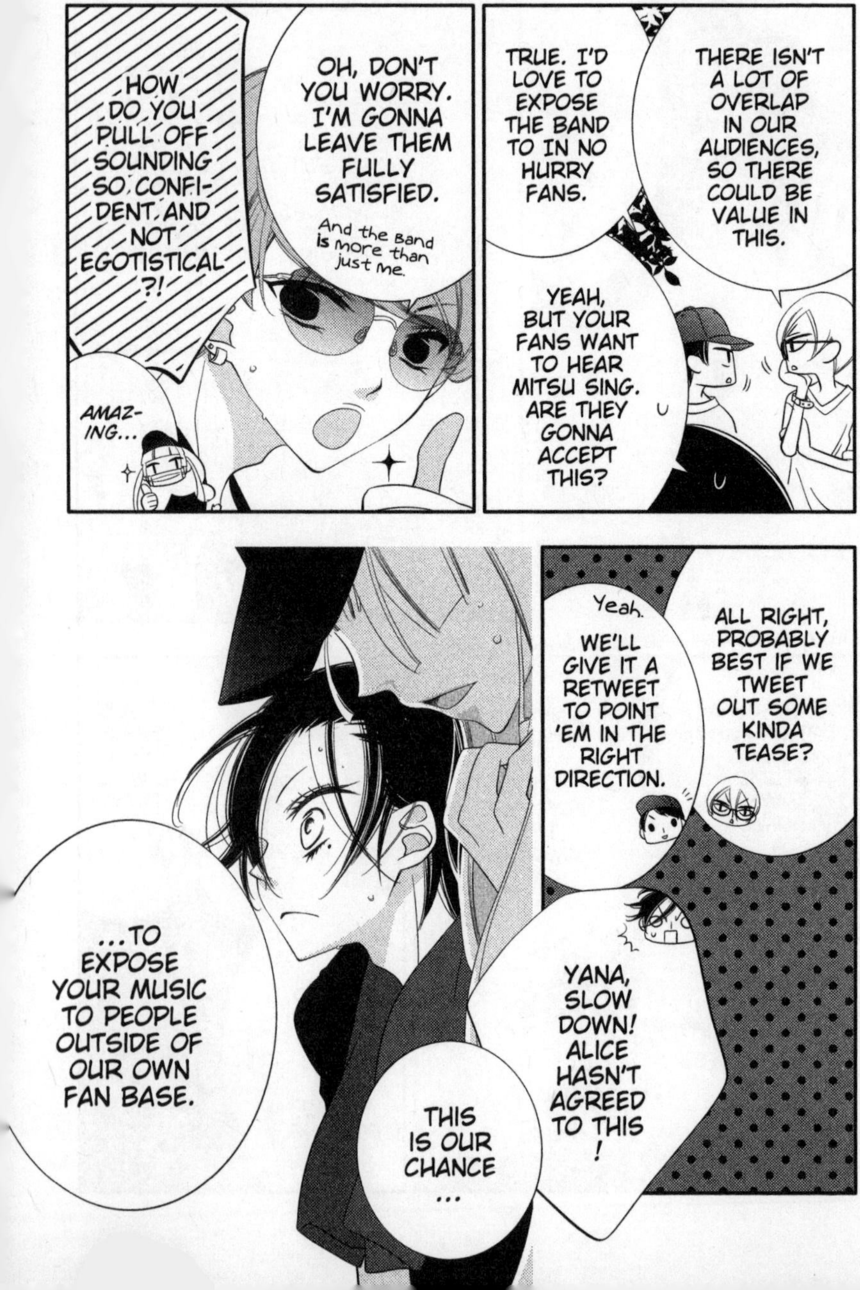
THERE ISN'T A LOT OF OVERLAP IN OUR AUDIENCES, SO THERE COULD BE VALUE IN THIS.
TRUE. I'D LOVE TO EXPOSE THE BAND TO IN NO HURRY FANS.
YEAH, BUT YOUR FANS WANT TO HEAR MITSU SING. ARE THEY GONNA ACCEPT THIS?
OH, DON'T YOU WORRY. I'M GONNA LEAVE THEM FULLY SATISFIED.
And the band is more than just me.
HOW DO YOU PULL OFF SOUNDING SO CONFI-DENT AND NOT EGOTISTICAL?!
AMAZ-ING...
ALL RIGHT, PROBABLY BEST IF WE TWEET OUT SOME KINDA TEASE?
Yeah.
WE'LL GIVE IT A RETWEET TO POINT 'EM IN THE RIGHT DIRECTION.
YANA, SLOW DOWN! ALICE HASN'T AGREED TO THIS!
THIS IS OUR CHANCE...
...TO EXPOSE YOUR MUSIC TO PEOPLE OUTSIDE OF OUR OWN FAN BASE.

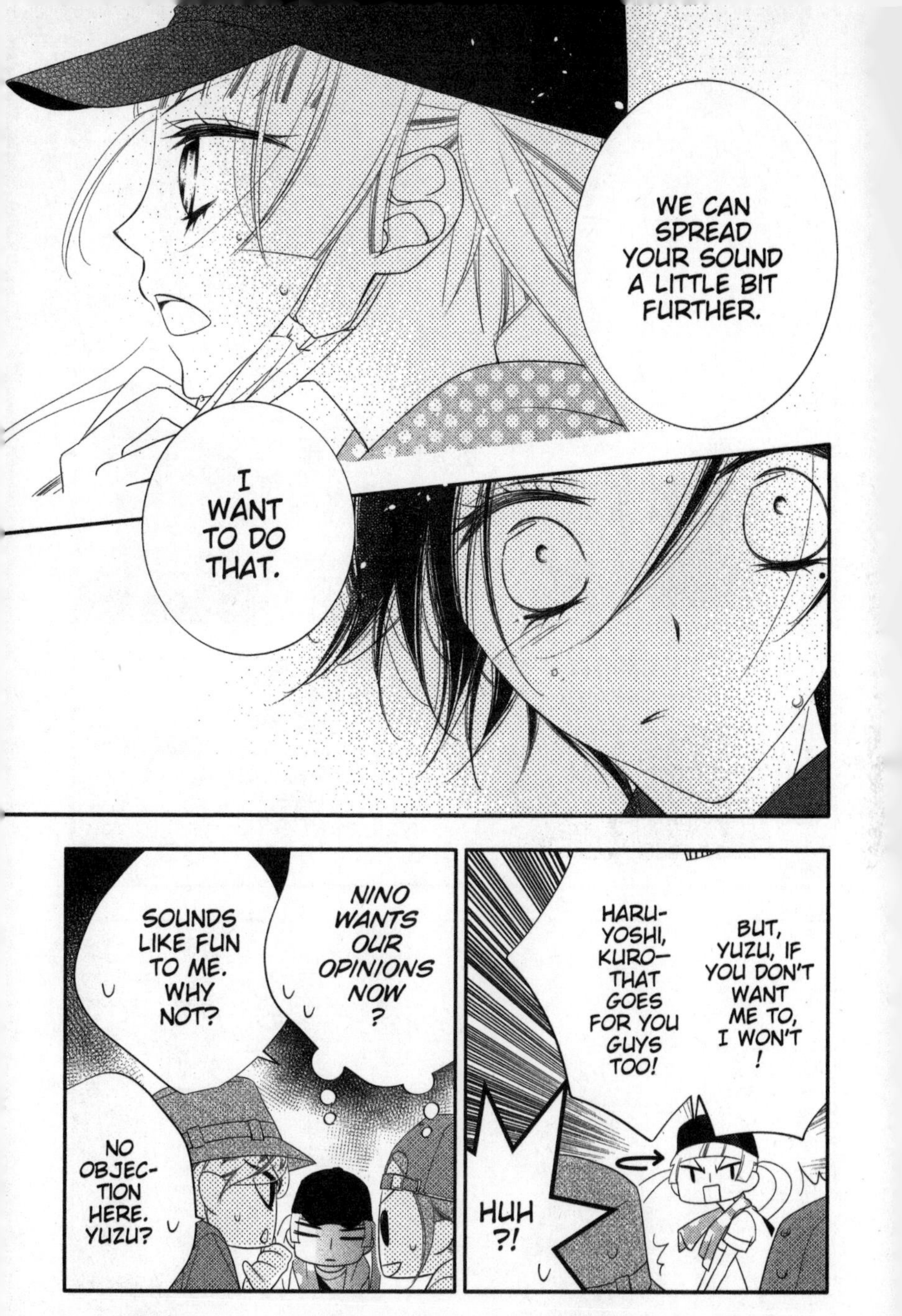
WE CAN SPREAD YOUR SOUND A LITTLE BIT FURTHER.
I WANT TO DO THAT.
BUT, YUZU, IF YOU DON'T WANT ME TO, I WON'T!
HARU-YOSHI, KURO— THAT GOES FOR YOU GUYS TOO!
HUH?!
NINO WANTS OUR OPINIONS NOW?
SOUNDS LIKE FUN TO ME. WHY NOT?
NO OBJECTION HERE. YUZU?

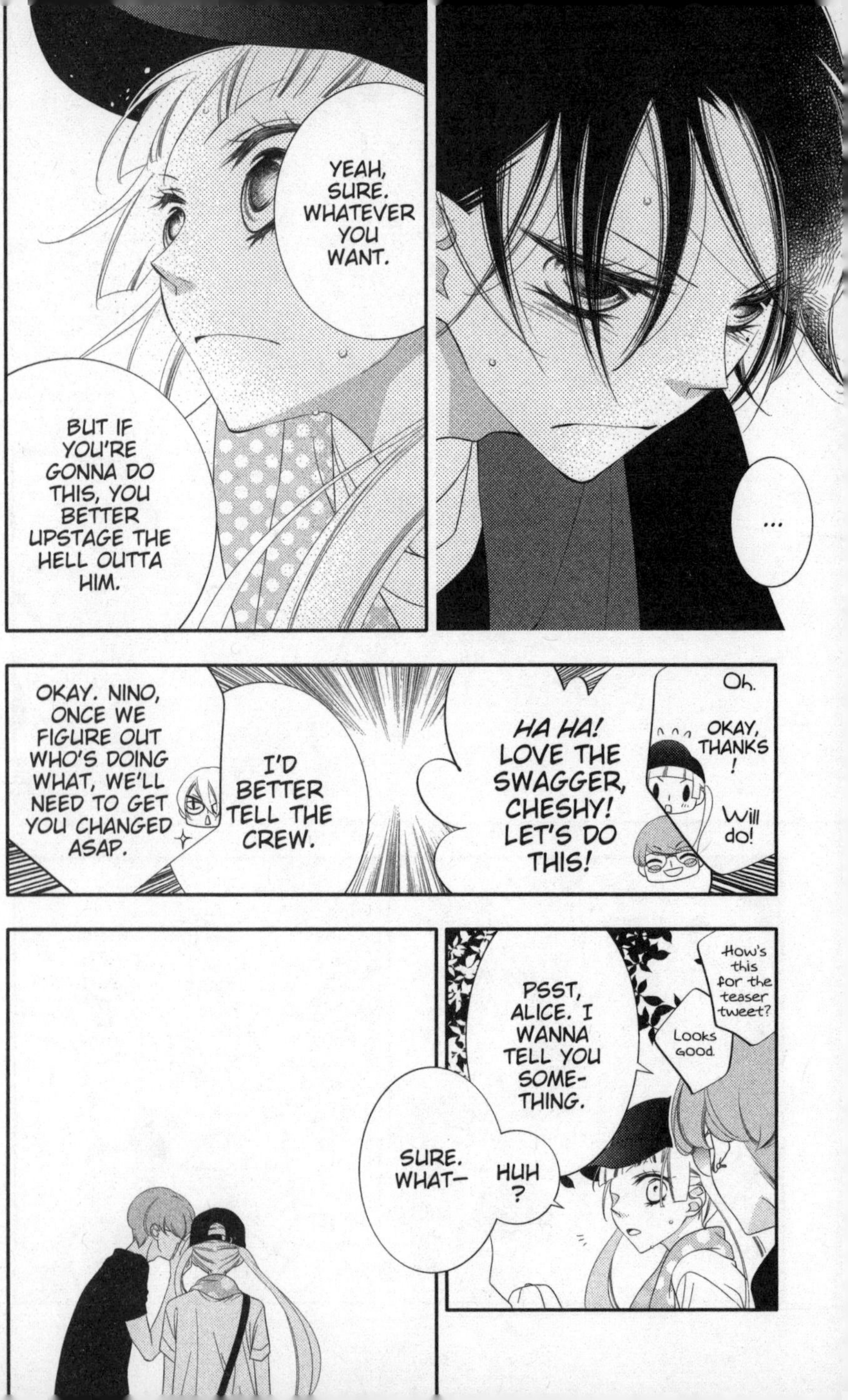
...
YEAH, SURE. WHATEVER YOU WANT.
BUT IF YOU'RE GONNA DO THIS, YOU BETTER UPSTAGE THE HELL OUTTA HIM.
Oh.
OKAY, THANKS!
Will do!
HA HA! LOVE THE SWAGGER, CHESHY! LET'S DO THIS!
I'D BETTER TELL THE CREW.
OKAY. NINO, ONCE WE FIGURE OUT WHO'S DOING WHAT, WE'LL NEED TO GET YOU CHANGED ASAP.
How's this for the teaser tweet?
Looks good.
PSST, ALICE. I WANNA TELL YOU SOME-THING.
HUH?
SURE. WHAT—

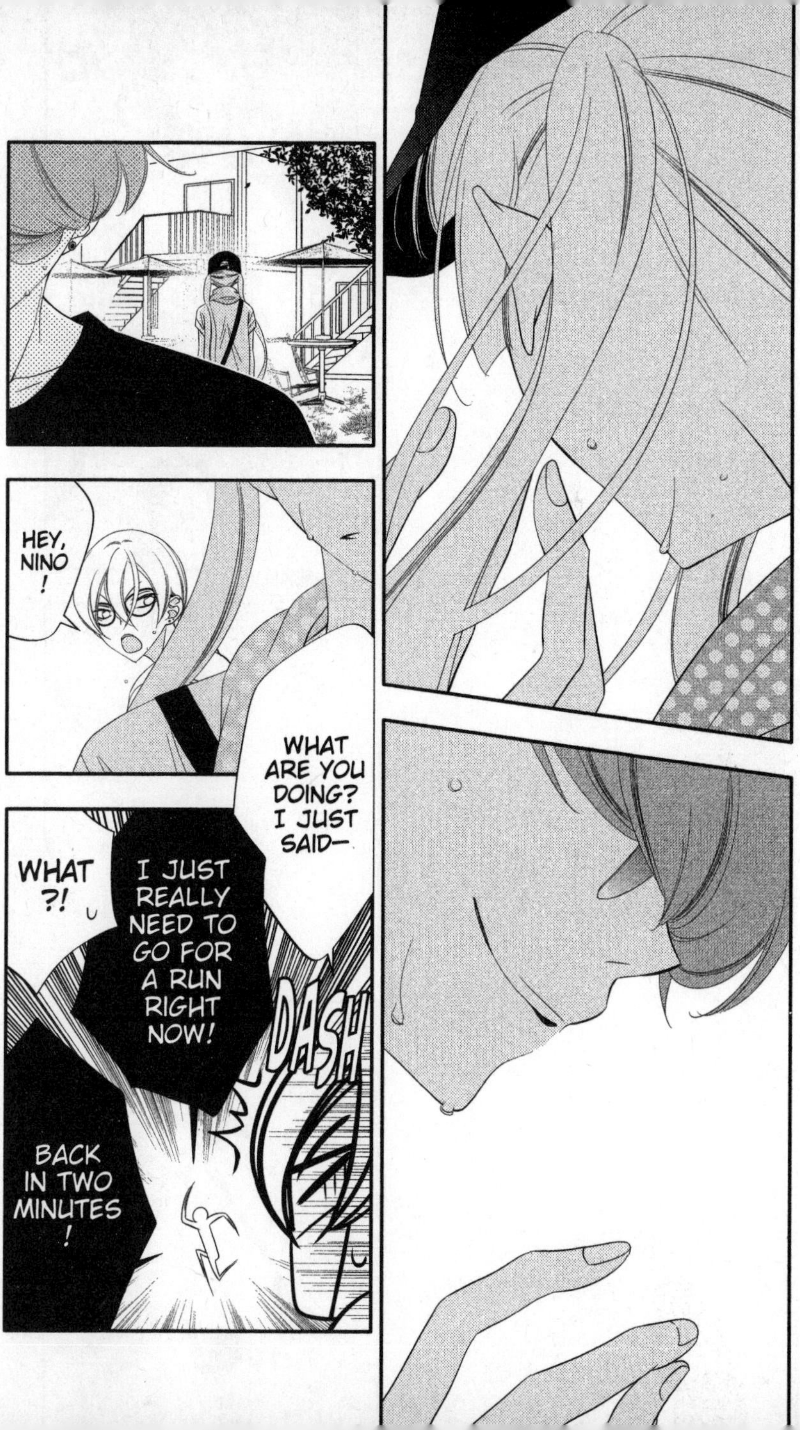
HEY, NINO!
WHAT ARE YOU DOING? I JUST SAID—
I JUST REALLY NEED TO GO FOR A RUN RIGHT NOW!
WHAT?!
DASH
BACK IN TWO MINUTES!

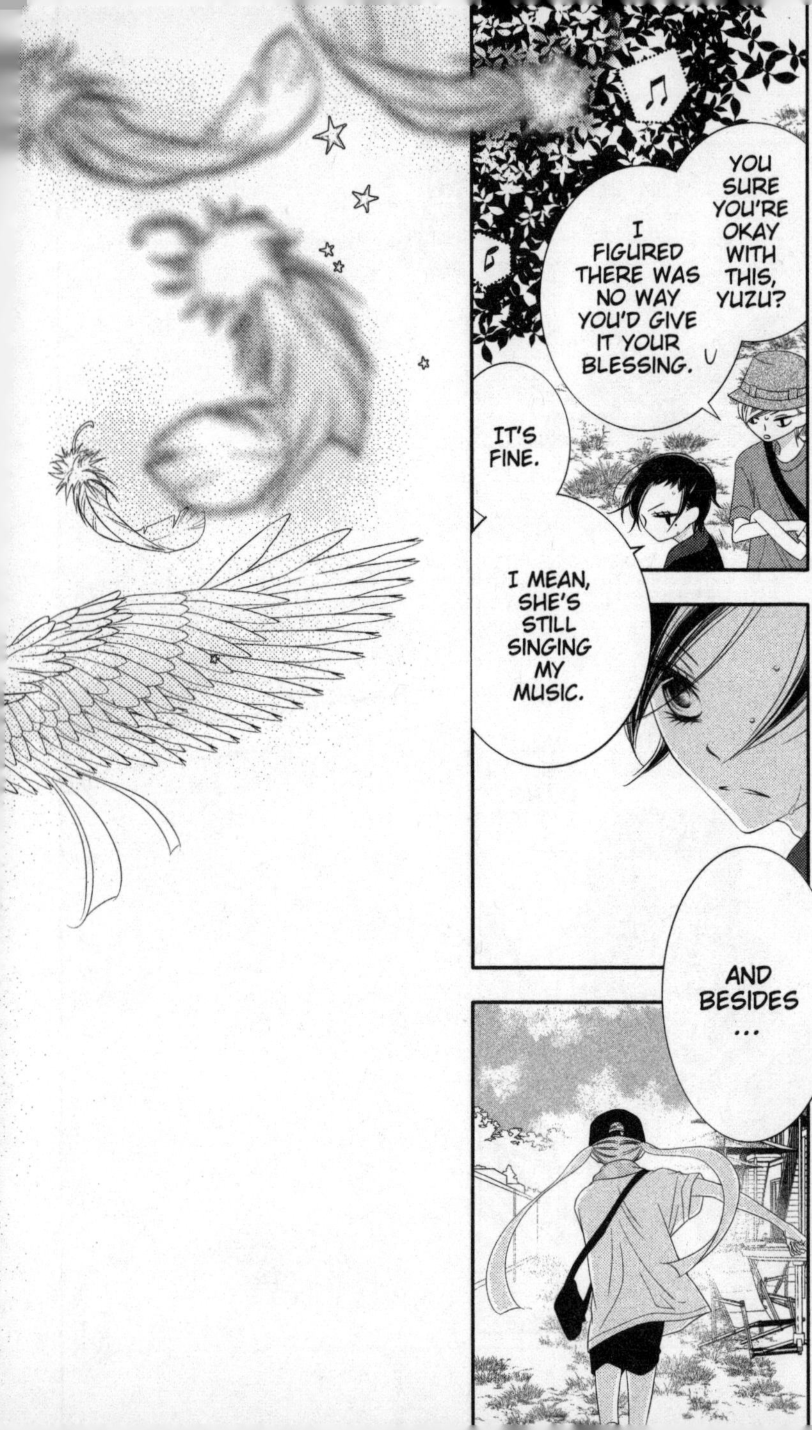
YOU SURE YOU'RE OKAY WITH THIS, YUZU?
I FIGURED THERE WAS NO WAY YOU'D GIVE IT YOUR BLESSING.
IT'S FINE.
I MEAN, SHE'S STILL SINGING MY MUSIC.
AND BESIDES ...

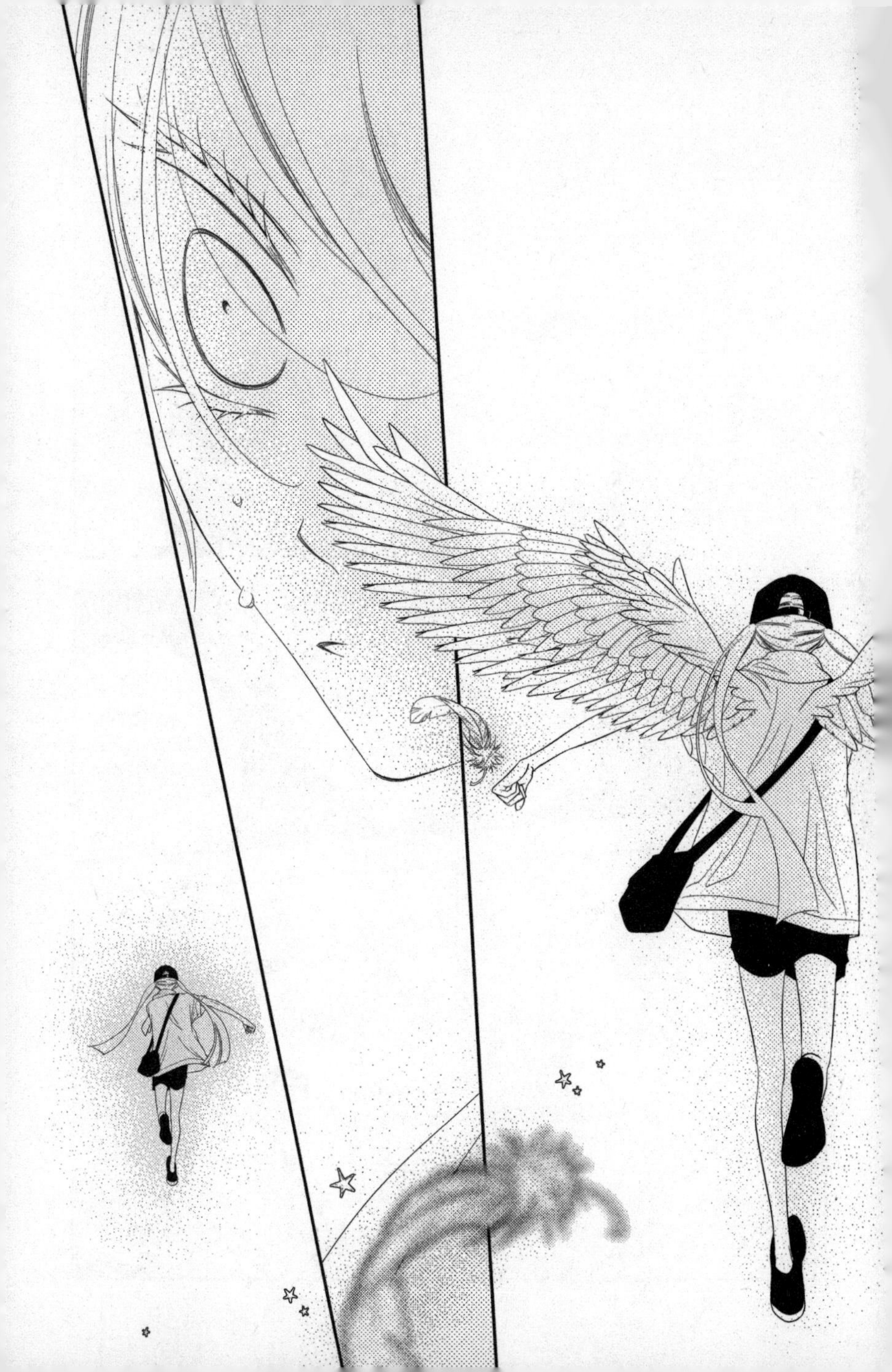

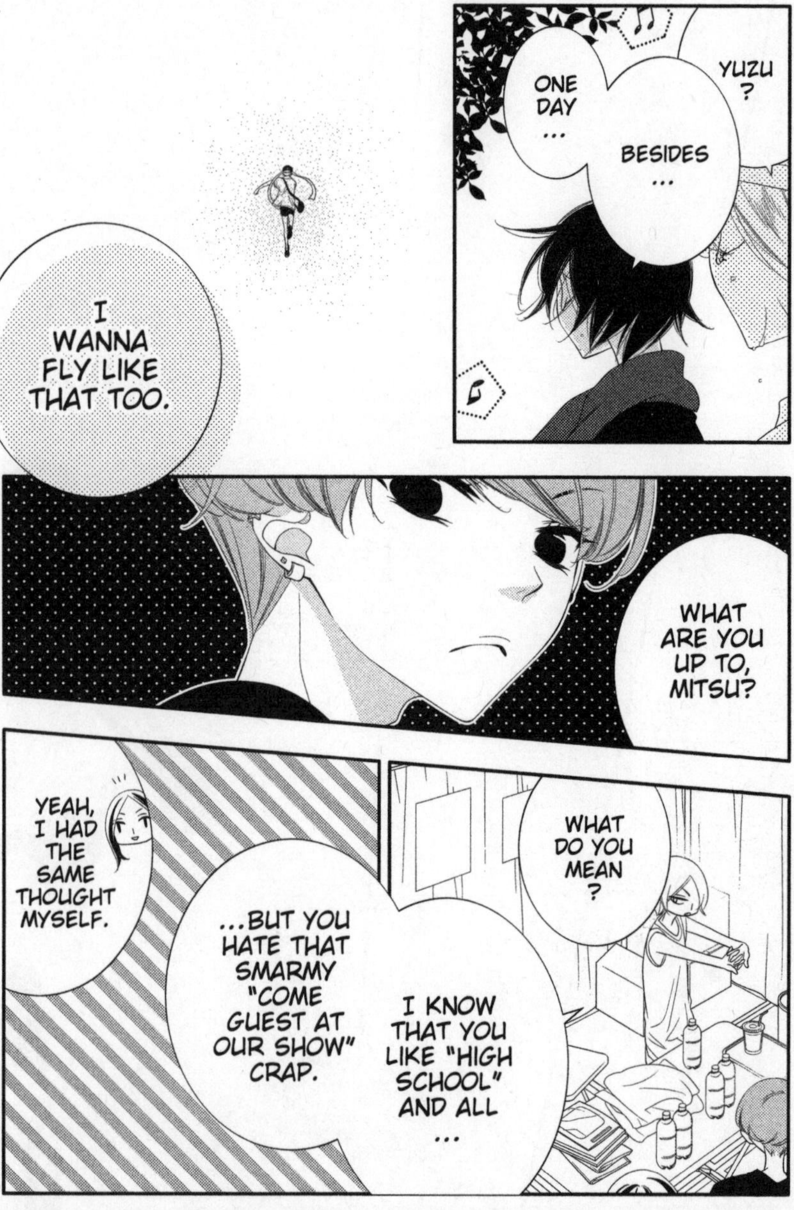
YUZU?
ONE DAY...
BESIDES...
I WANNA FLY LIKE THAT TOO.
WHAT ARE YOU UP TO, MITSU?
WHAT DO YOU MEAN?
I KNOW THAT YOU LIKE "HIGH SCHOOL" AND ALL...
...BUT YOU HATE THAT SMARMY "COME GUEST AT OUR SHOW" CRAP.
YEAH, I HAD THE SAME THOUGHT MYSELF.

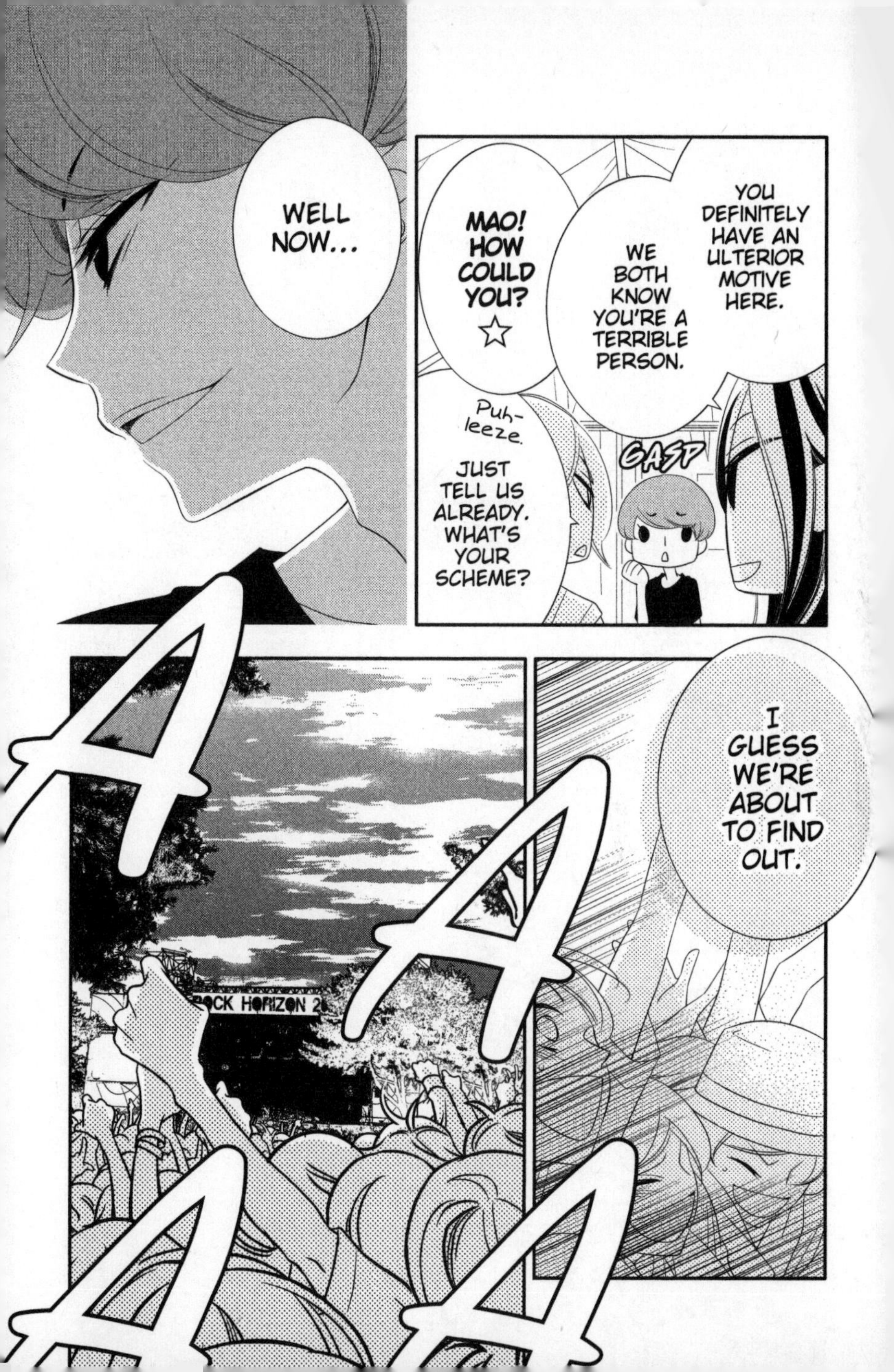

YOU DEFINITELY HAVE AN ULTERIOR MOTIVE HERE.
WE BOTH KNOW YOU'RE A TERRIBLE PERSON.
MAO! HOW COULD YOU? ☆
GASP
Puh-leeze.
JUST TELL US ALREADY. WHAT'S YOUR SCHEME?
WELL NOW...
I GUESS WE'RE ABOUT TO FIND OUT.
OCK HORIZON 2
AAAAA

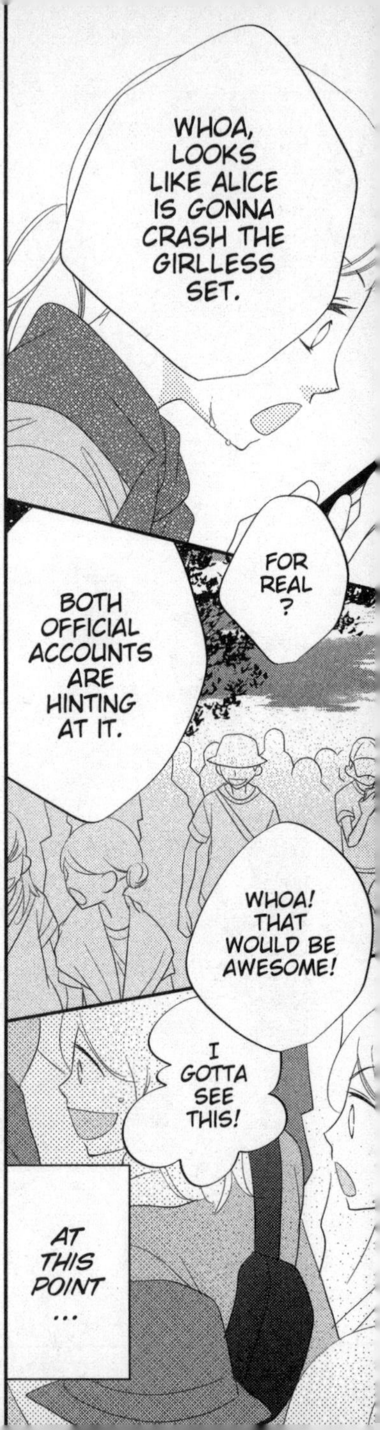
WHOA, LOOKS LIKE ALICE IS GONNA CRASH THE GIRLLESS SET.
FOR REAL?
BOTH OFFICIAL ACCOUNTS ARE HINTING AT IT.
WHOA! THAT WOULD BE AWESOME!
I GOTTA SEE THIS!
AT THIS POINT...

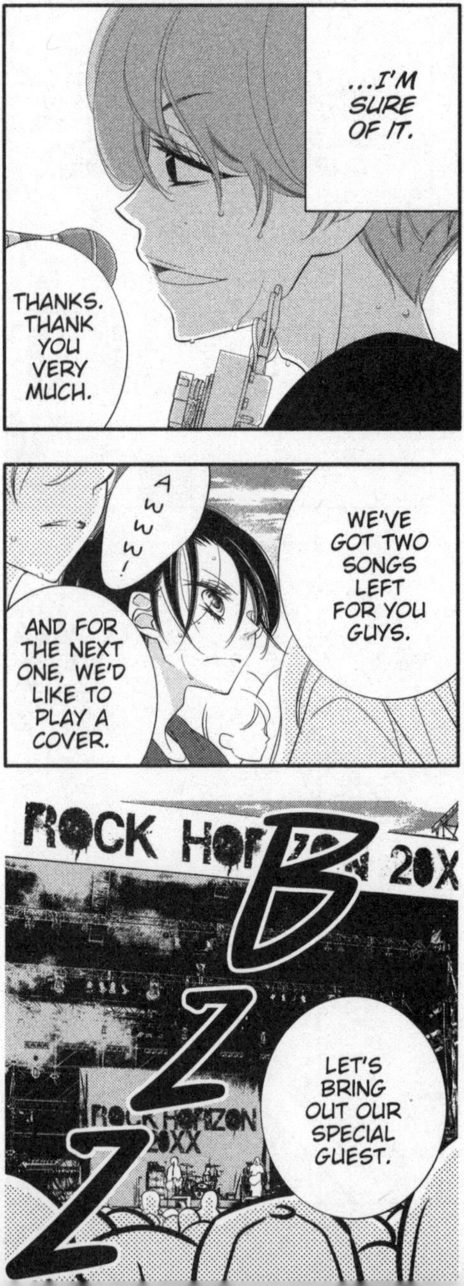
...I'M SURE OF IT.
THANKS. THANK YOU VERY MUCH.
WE'VE GOT TWO SONGS LEFT FOR YOU GUYS.
AWWW!
AND FOR THE NEXT ONE, WE'D LIKE TO PLAY A COVER.
ROCK HORIZON 20XX
BZZ
LET'S BRING OUT OUR SPECIAL GUEST.

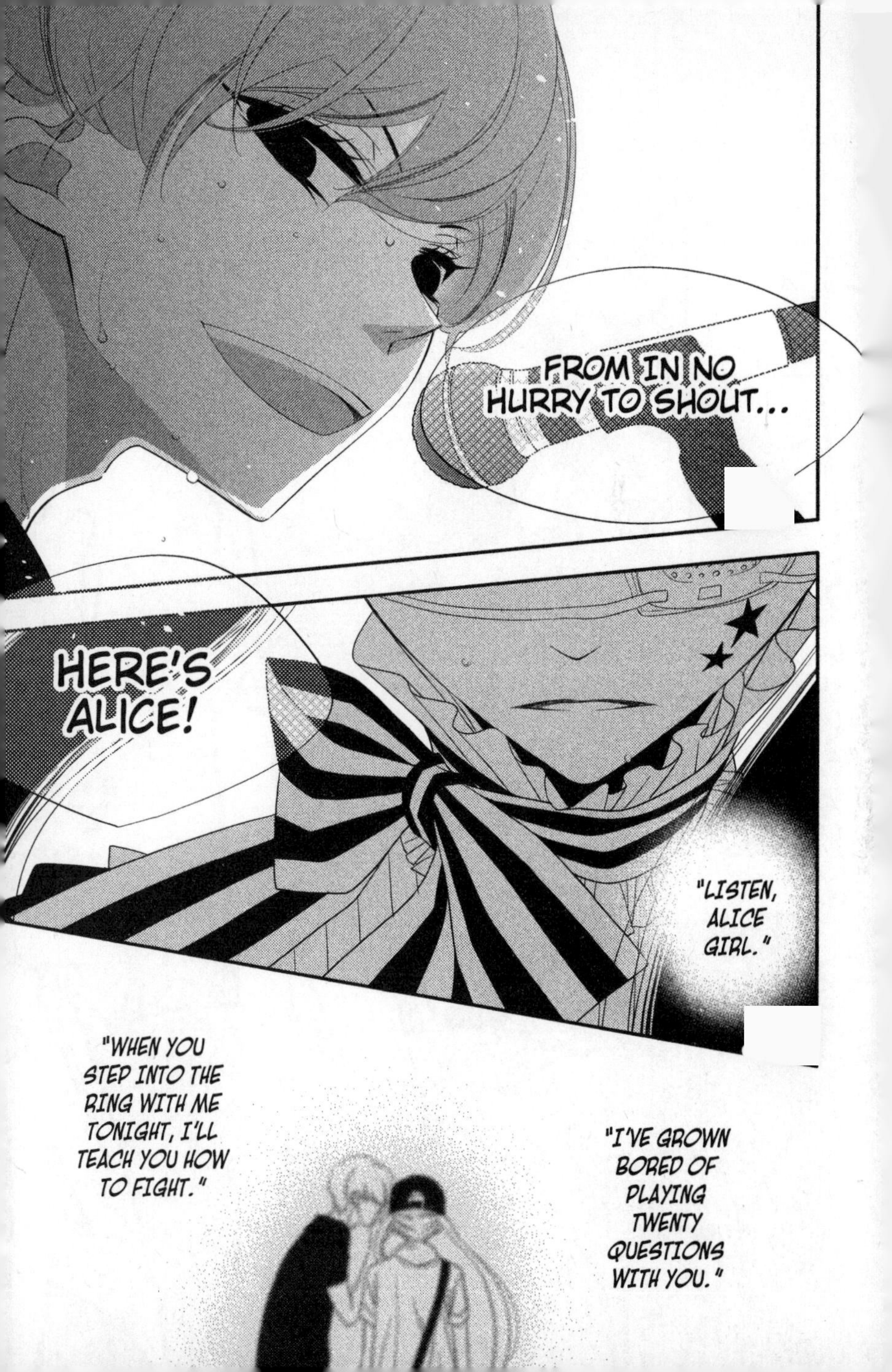
FROM IN NO HURRY TO SHOUT...
HERE'S ALICE!
"LISTEN, ALICE GIRL."
"I'VE GROWN BORED OF PLAYING TWENTY QUESTIONS WITH YOU."
"WHEN YOU STEP INTO THE RING WITH ME TONIGHT, I'LL TEACH YOU HOW TO FIGHT."

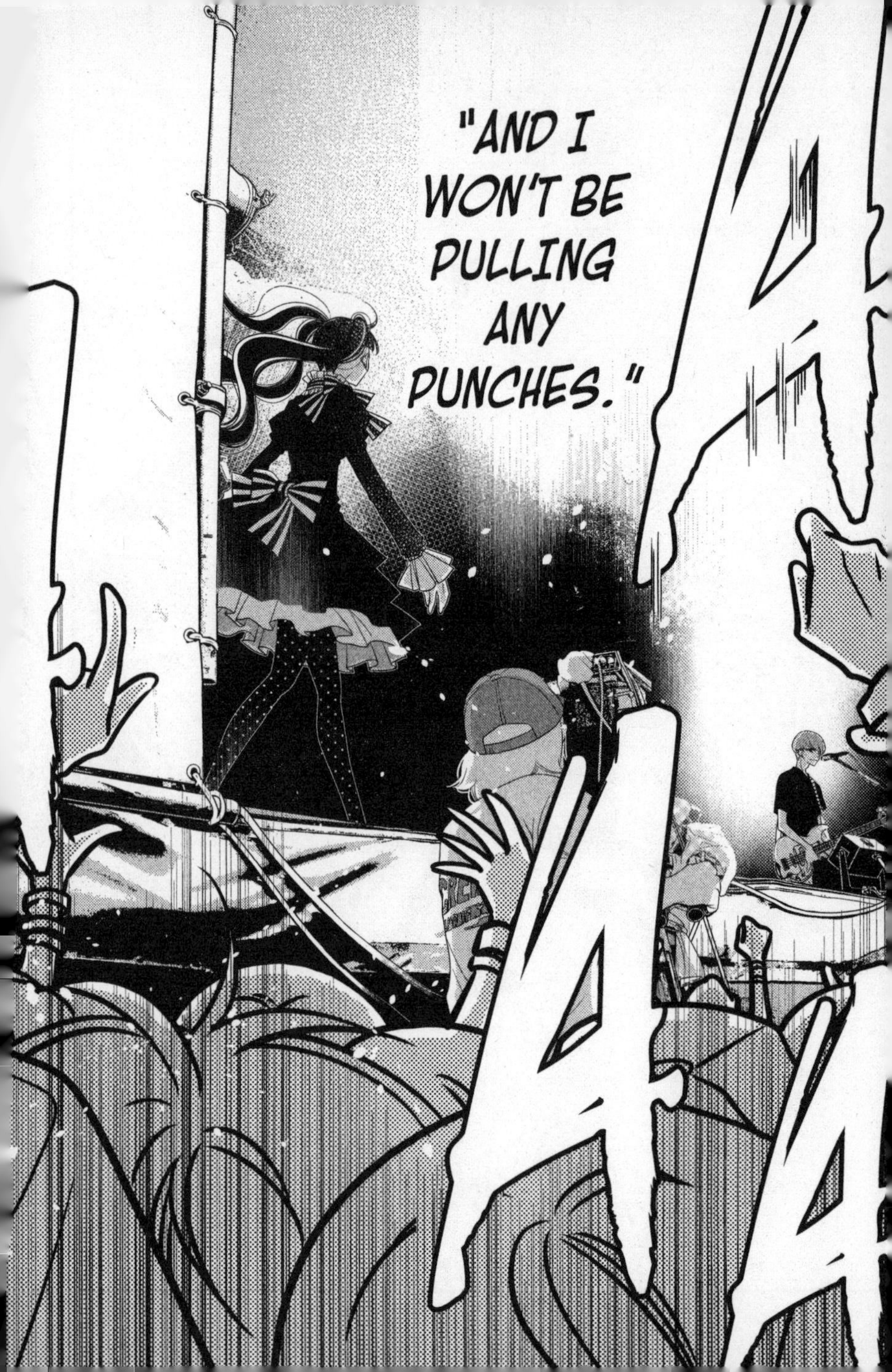
"AND I WON'T BE PULLING ANY PUNCHES."

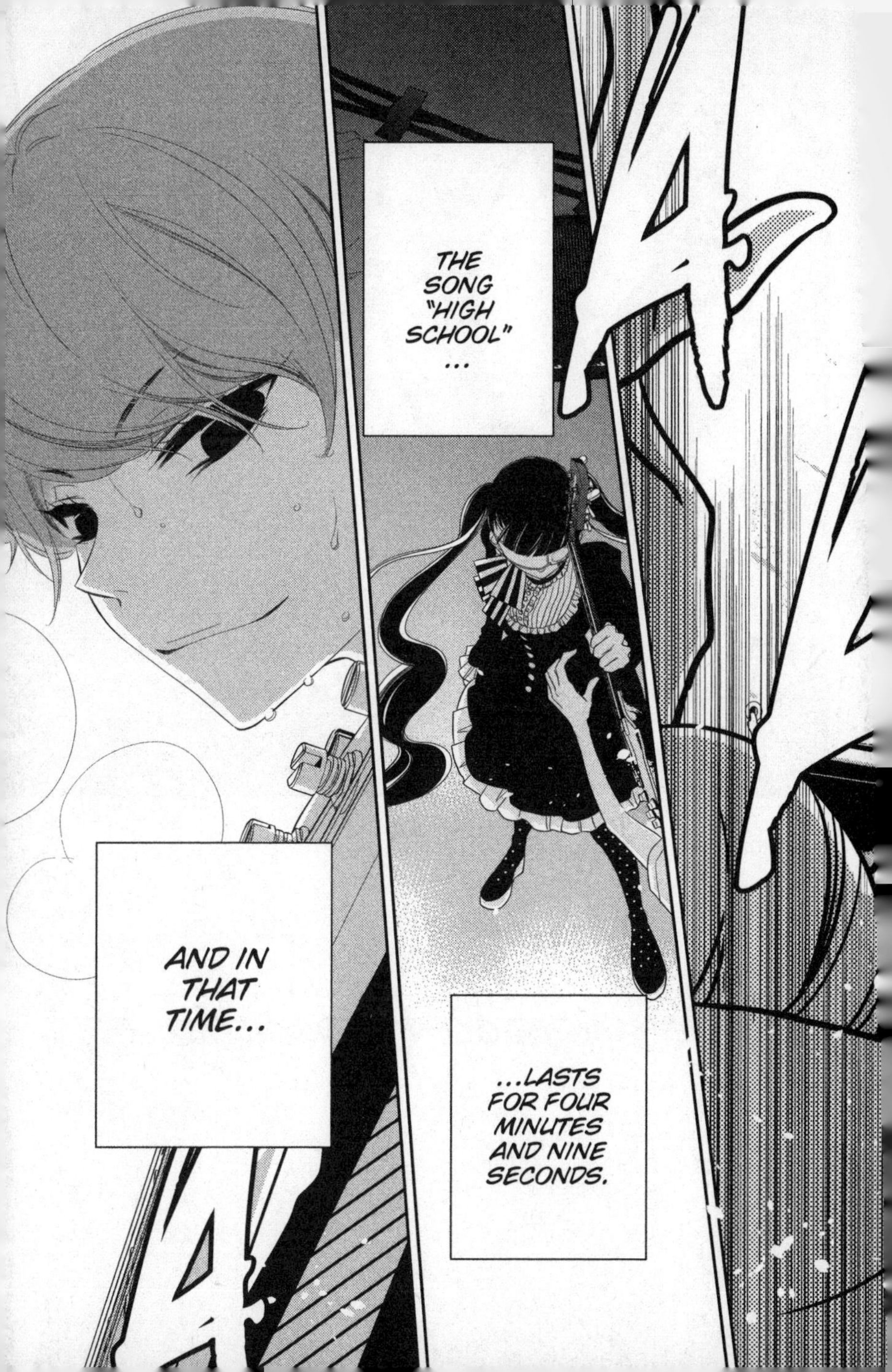
THE SONG "HIGH SCHOOL"...
...LASTS FOR FOUR MINUTES AND NINE SECONDS.
AND IN THAT TIME...

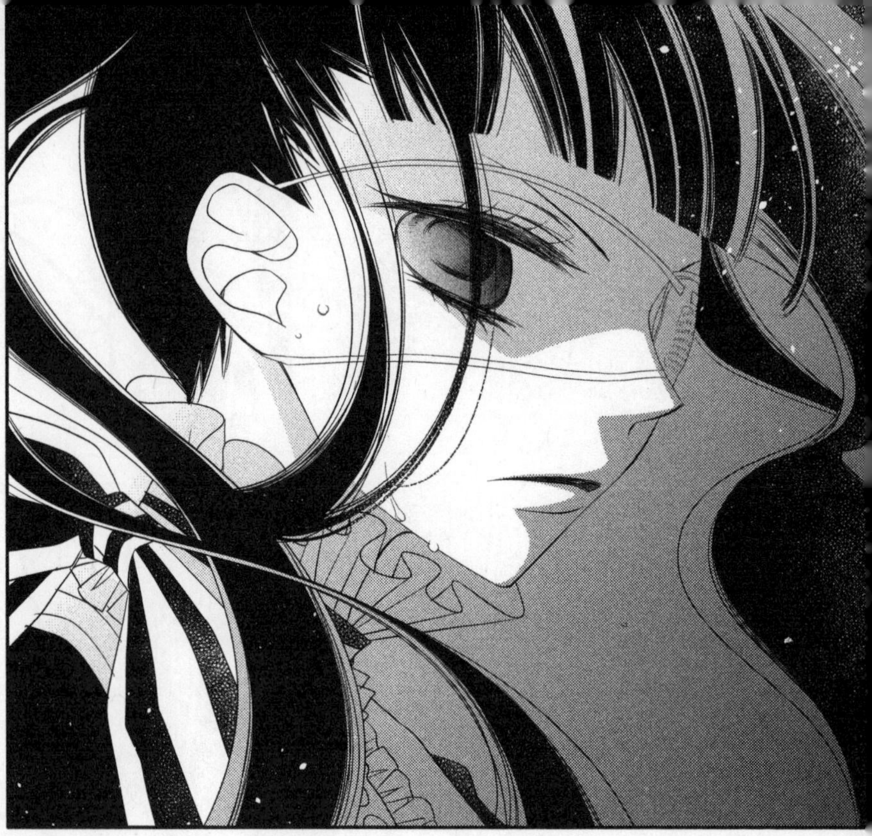

...THIS MAN IS GOING TO UNLOCK ME.

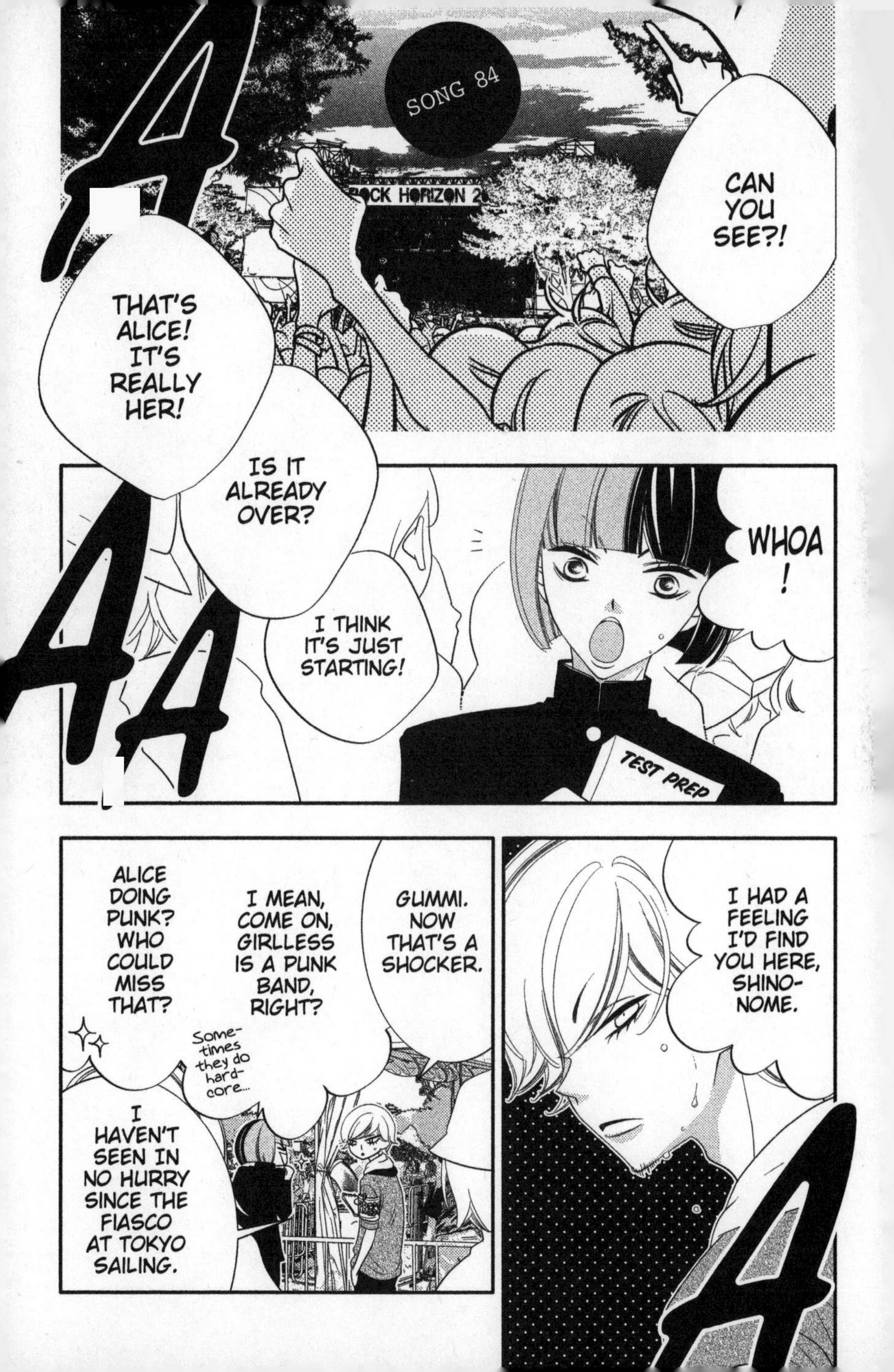
SONG 84
ROCK HORIZON 2
CAN YOU SEE?!
THAT'S ALICE! IT'S REALLY HER!
AAAA
WHOA!
IS IT ALREADY OVER?
I THINK IT'S JUST STARTING!
TEST PREP
I HAD A FEELING I'D FIND YOU HERE, SHINO-NOME.
GUMMI. NOW THAT'S A SHOCKER.
I MEAN, COME ON, GIRLLESS IS A PUNK BAND, RIGHT?
ALICE DOING PUNK? WHO COULD MISS THAT?
Some-times they do hard-core...
I HAVEN'T SEEN IN NO HURRY SINCE THE FIASCO AT TOKYO SAILING.

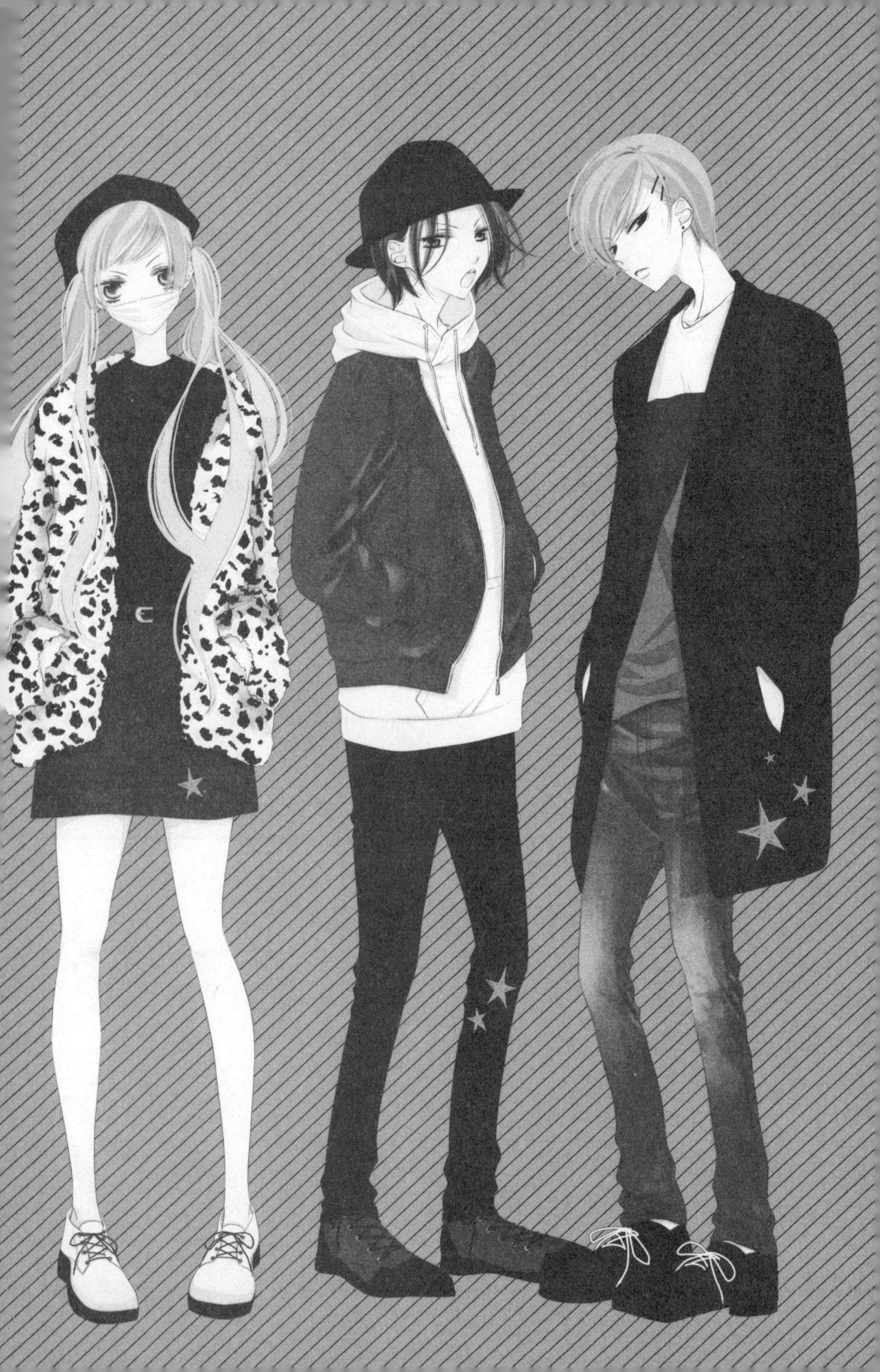

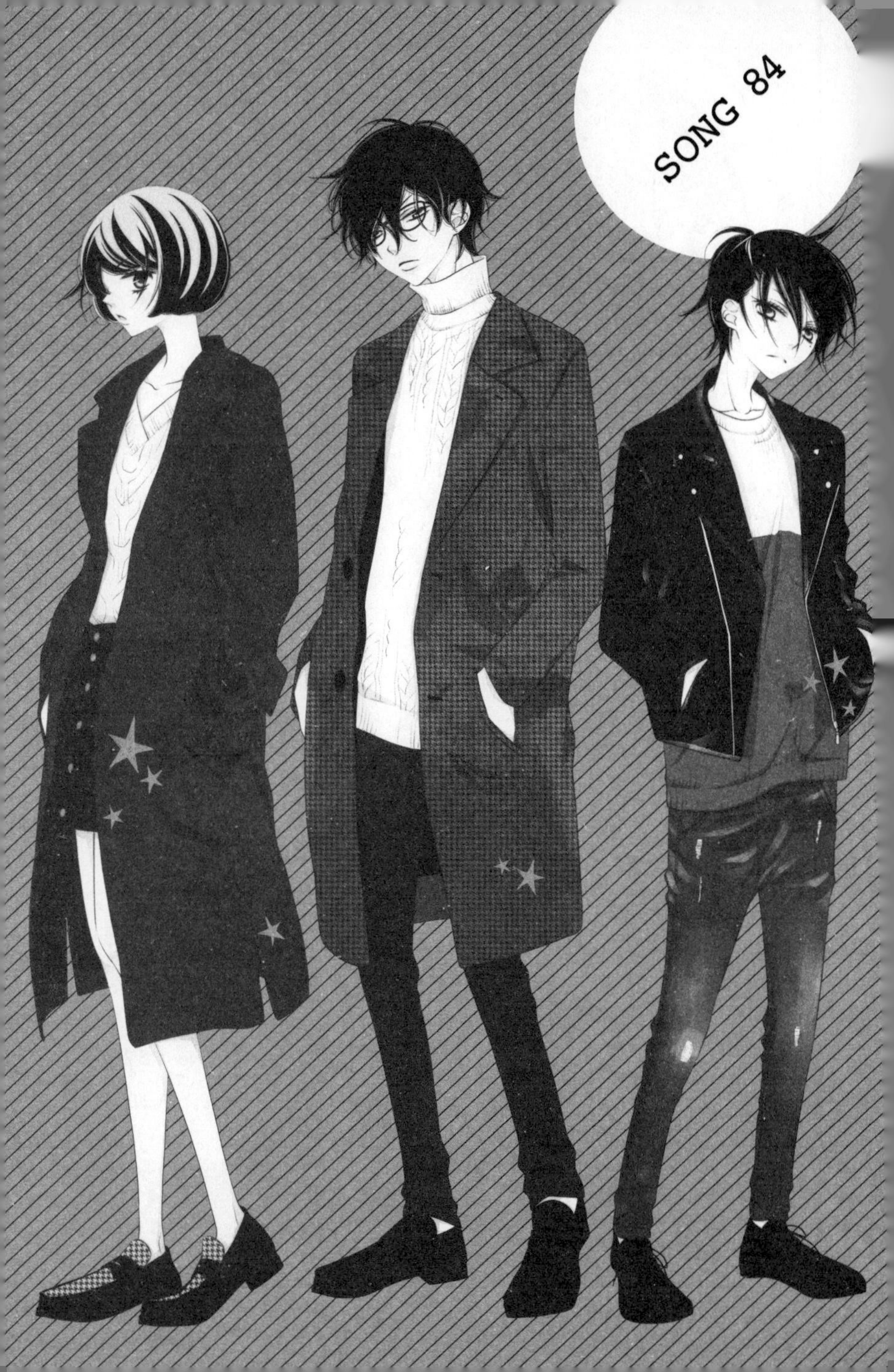
SONG 84

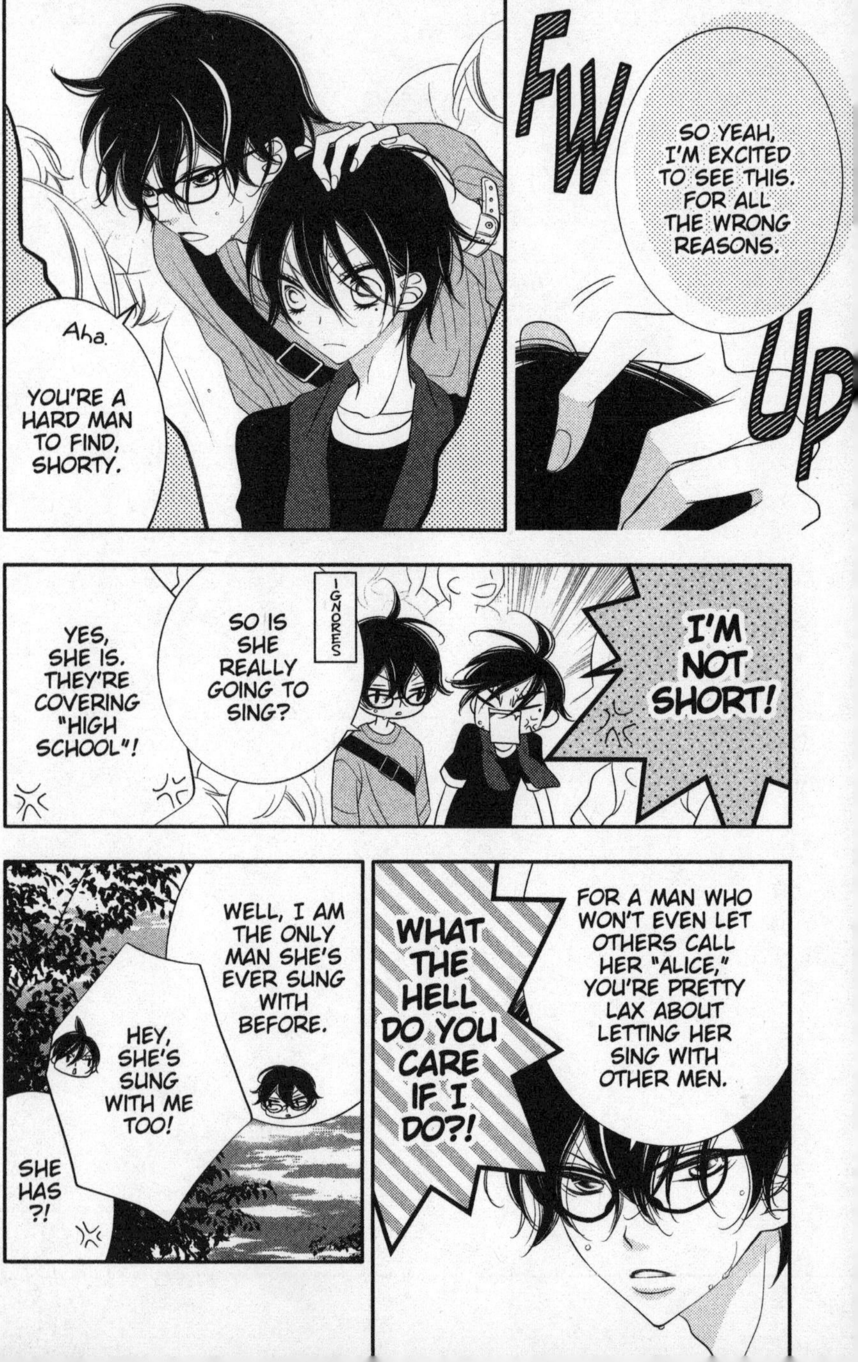
FWUP
SO YEAH, I'M EXCITED TO SEE THIS. FOR ALL THE WRONG REASONS.
Aha.
YOU'RE A HARD MAN TO FIND, SHORTY.
I'M NOT SHORT!
IGNORES
SO IS SHE REALLY GOING TO SING?
YES, SHE IS. THEY'RE COVERING "HIGH SCHOOL"!
FOR A MAN WHO WON'T EVEN LET OTHERS CALL HER "ALICE," YOU'RE PRETTY LAX ABOUT LETTING HER SING WITH OTHER MEN.
WHAT THE HELL DO YOU CARE IF I DO?!
WELL, I AM THE ONLY MAN SHE'S EVER SUNG WITH BEFORE.
HEY, SHE'S SUNG WITH ME TOO!
SHE HAS?!

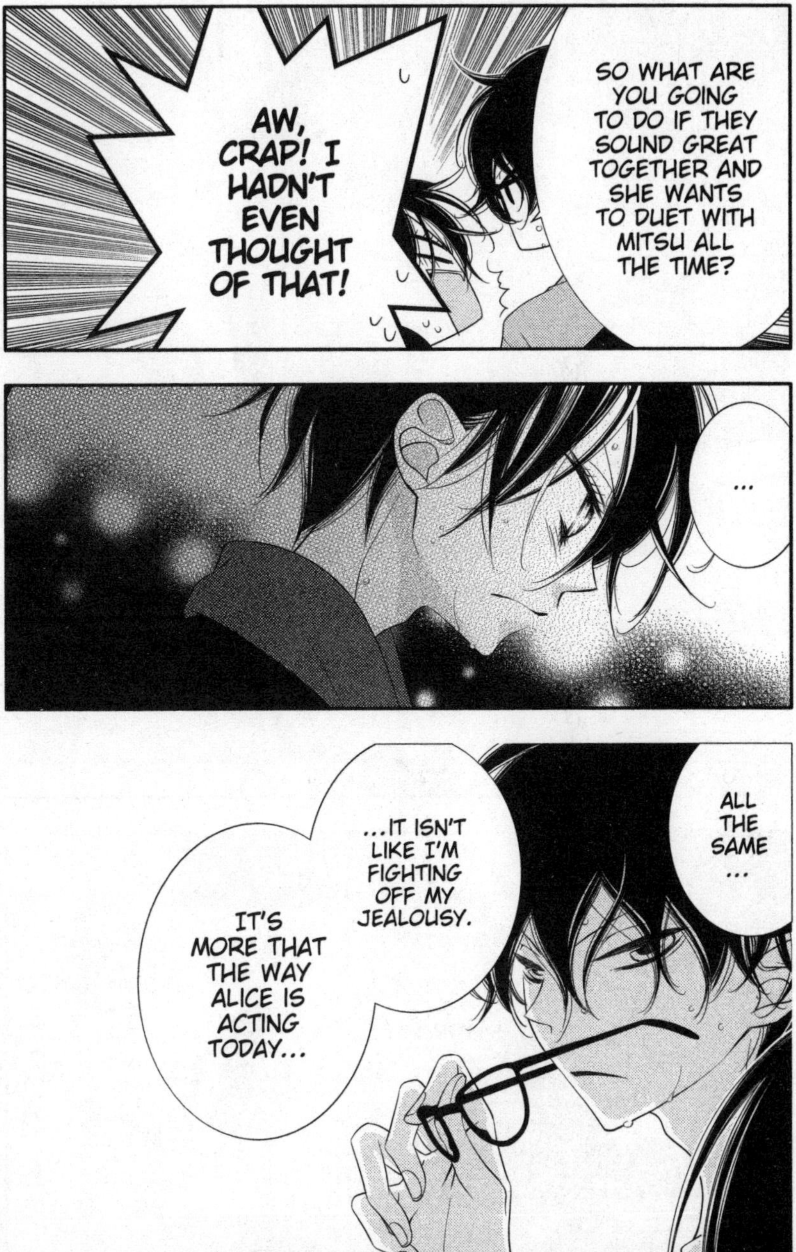
SO WHAT ARE YOU GOING TO DO IF THEY SOUND GREAT TOGETHER AND SHE WANTS TO DUET WITH MITSU ALL THE TIME?
AW, CRAP! I HADN'T EVEN THOUGHT OF THAT!
...
ALL THE SAME...
...IT ISN'T LIKE I'M FIGHTING OFF MY JEALOUSY.
IT'S MORE THAT THE WAY ALICE IS ACTING TODAY...

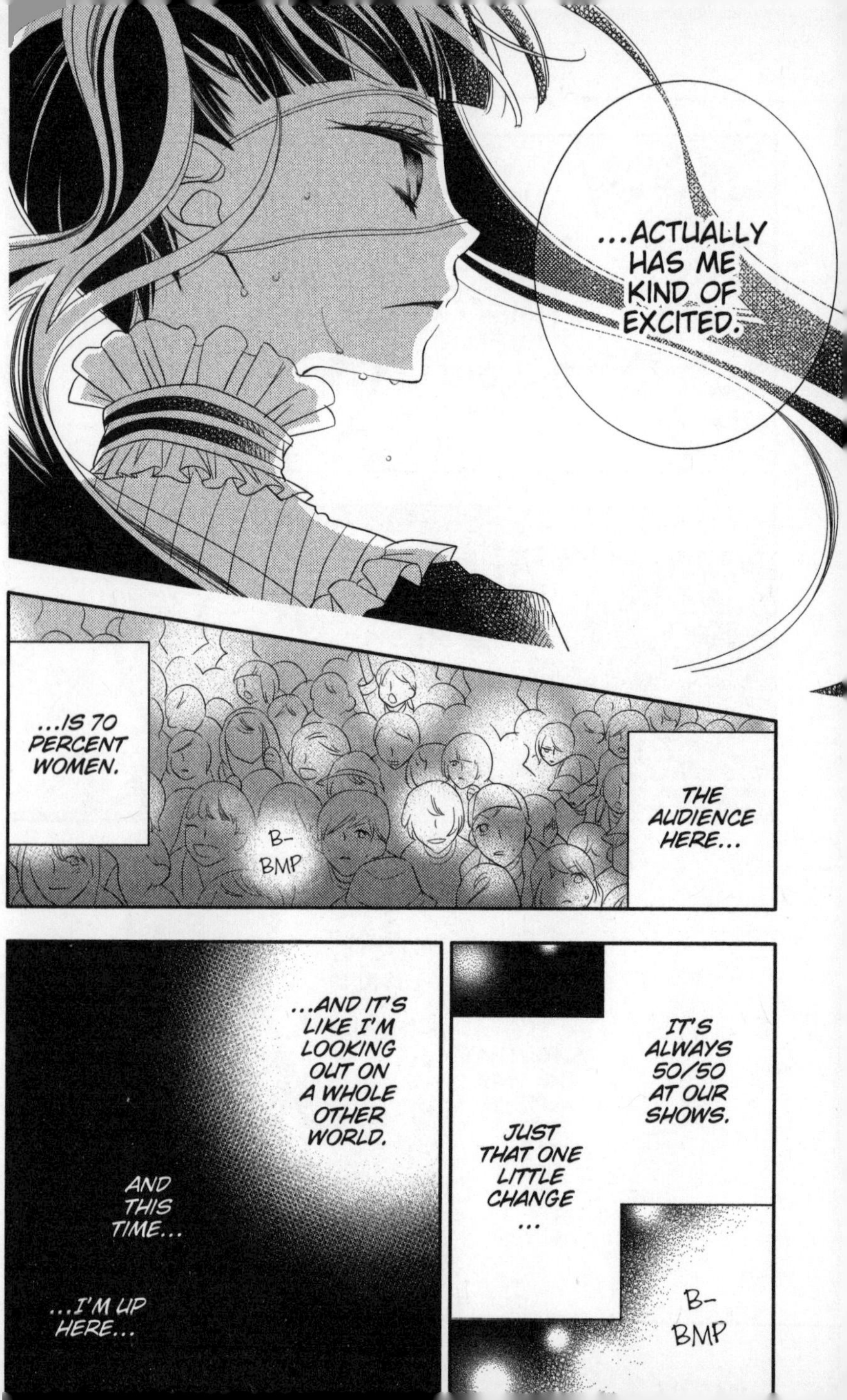
...ACTUALLY HAS ME KIND OF EXCITED.
THE AUDIENCE HERE...
B-BMP
...IS 70 PERCENT WOMEN.
IT'S ALWAYS 50/50 AT OUR SHOWS.
JUST THAT ONE LITTLE CHANGE...
B-BMP
...AND IT'S LIKE I'M LOOKING OUT ON A WHOLE OTHER WORLD.
AND THIS TIME...
...I'M UP HERE...

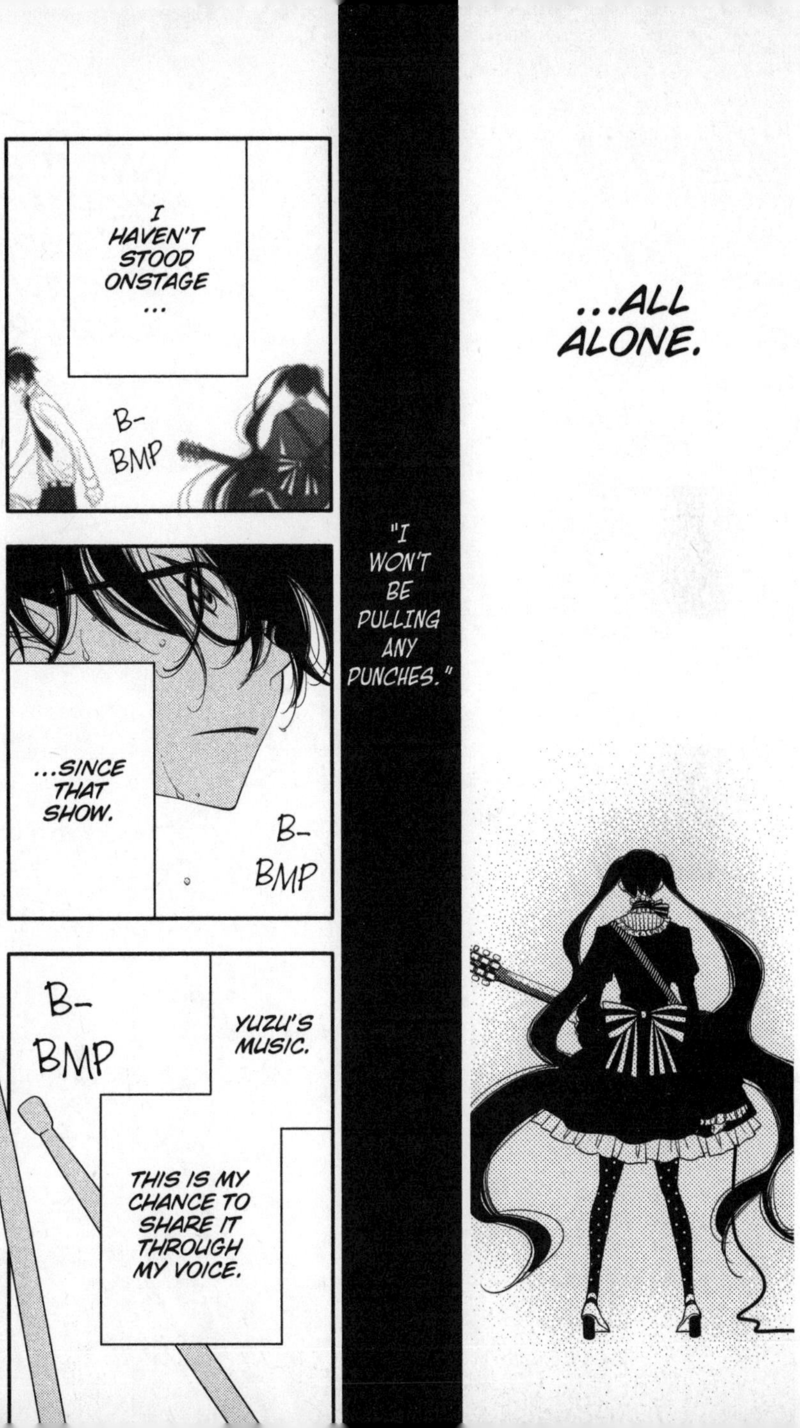
...ALL ALONE.
"I WON'T BE PULLING ANY PUNCHES."
I HAVEN'T STOOD ONSTAGE ...
B-BMP
...SINCE THAT SHOW.
B-BMP
YUZU'S MUSIC.
THIS IS MY CHANCE TO SHARE IT THROUGH MY VOICE.
B-BMP

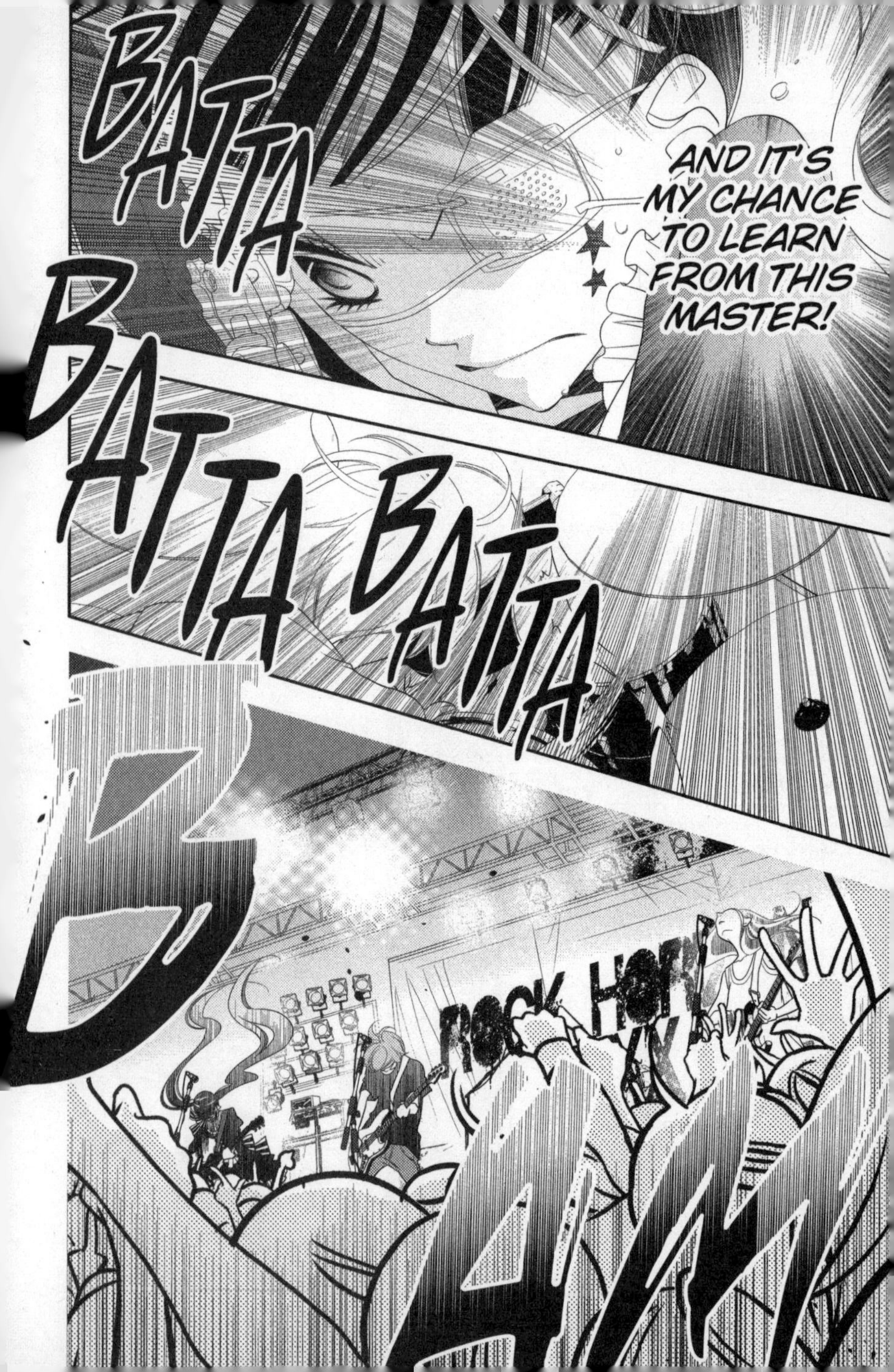
AND IT'S MY CHANCE TO LEARN FROM THIS MASTER!
BATTA
BATTA
BATTA
BATTA

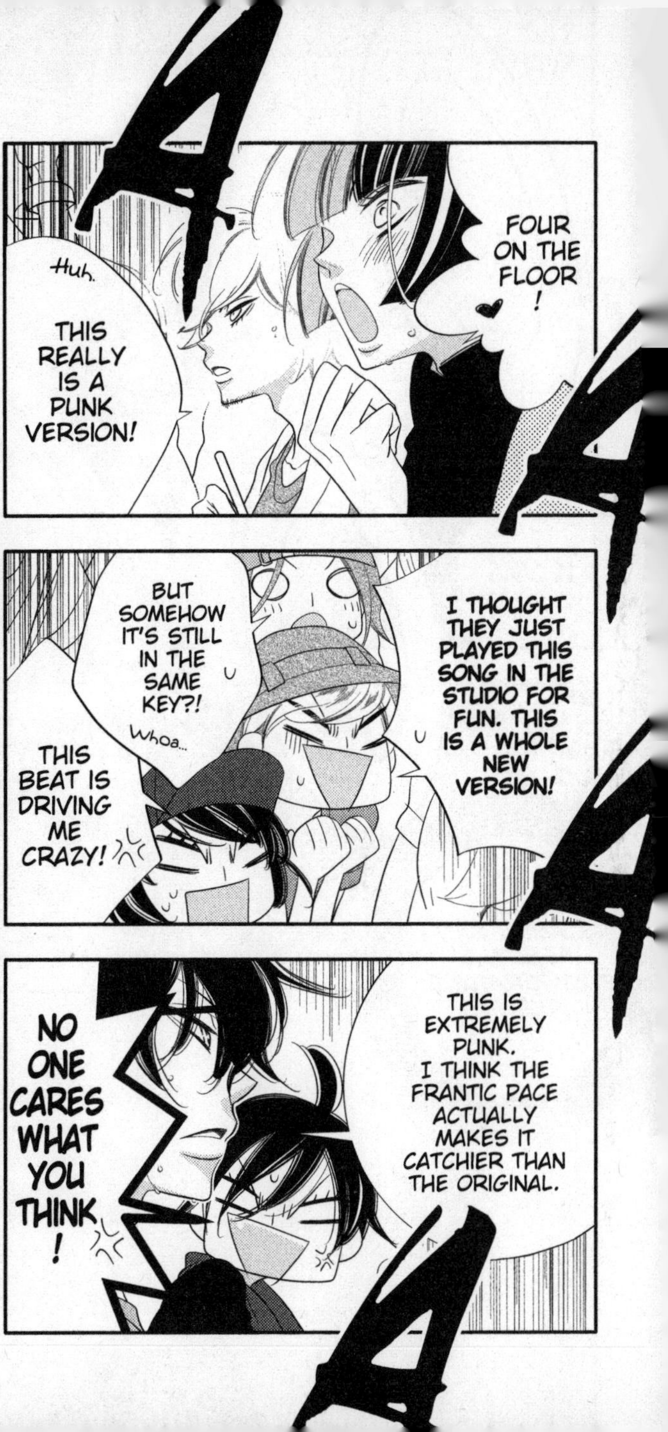
AAAAA
FOUR ON THE FLOOR ♥ !
Huh.
THIS REALLY IS A PUNK VERSION!
I THOUGHT THEY JUST PLAYED THIS SONG IN THE STUDIO FOR FUN. THIS IS A WHOLE NEW VERSION!
BUT SOMEHOW IT'S STILL IN THE SAME KEY?!
Whoa...
THIS BEAT IS DRIVING ME CRAZY!
THIS IS EXTREMELY PUNK. I THINK THE FRANTIC PACE ACTUALLY MAKES IT CATCHIER THAN THE ORIGINAL.
NO ONE CARES WHAT YOU THINK!

3

So what have I been doing on my vacation? Cleaning, photography, cleaning, drinking, cleaning, shopping, that sort of thing. But really, mostly just cleaning. I've lived in this apartment for ten years, and over that time a massive amount of stuff has piled up and I've been so busy that I've just pretended not to notice. But now I'm finally throwing it all out: my broken paper shredder, my busted vacuum, clothes I no longer wear, cans of long-since-expired cat food, etc. Every day as I clean, I can't help but wonder, "Where did all this stuff come from?"

AM I IN A FOURTH-DIMENSIONAL POCKET...?

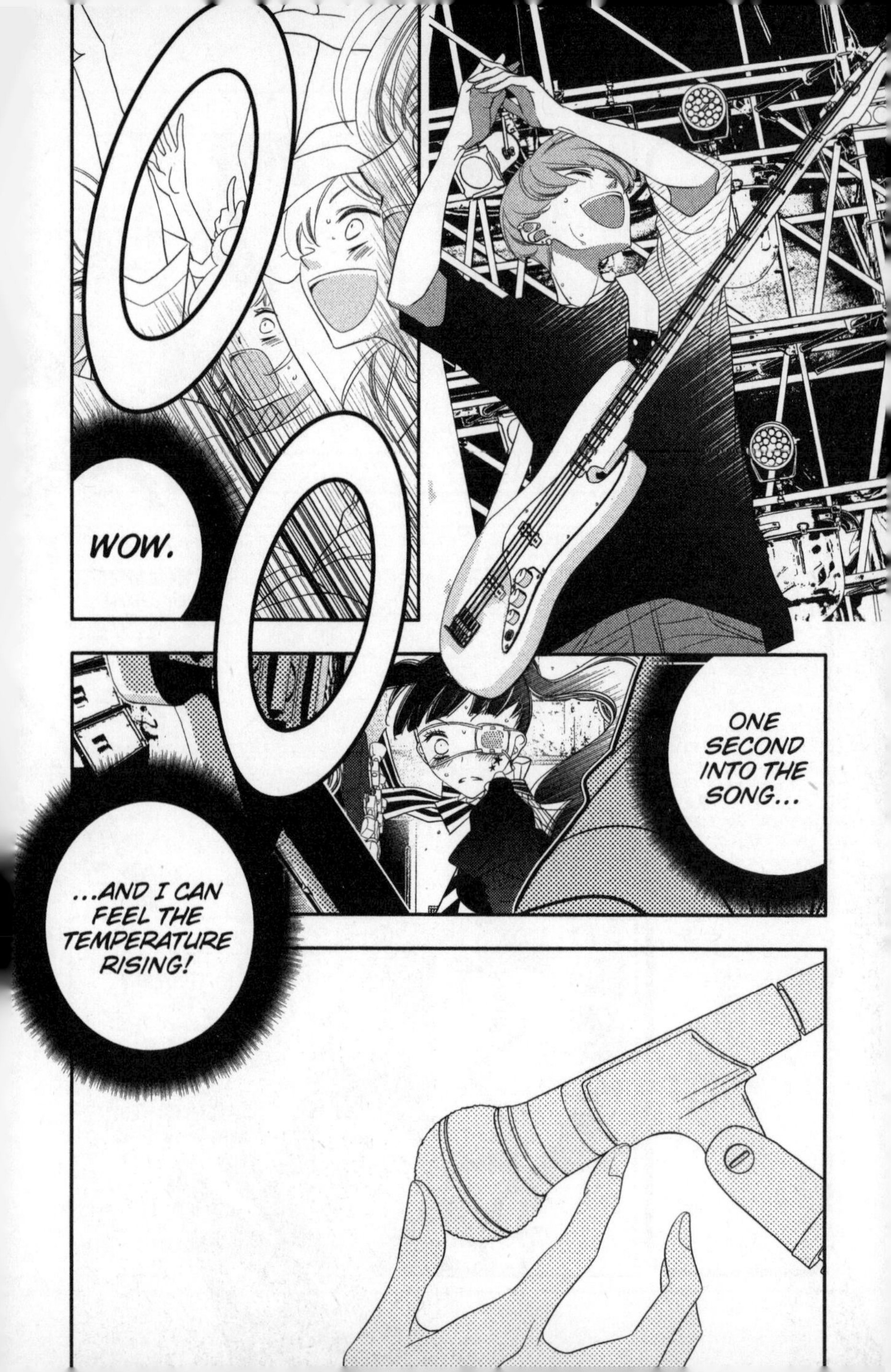
WOW.
ONE SECOND INTO THE SONG...
...AND I CAN FEEL THE TEMPERATURE RISING!

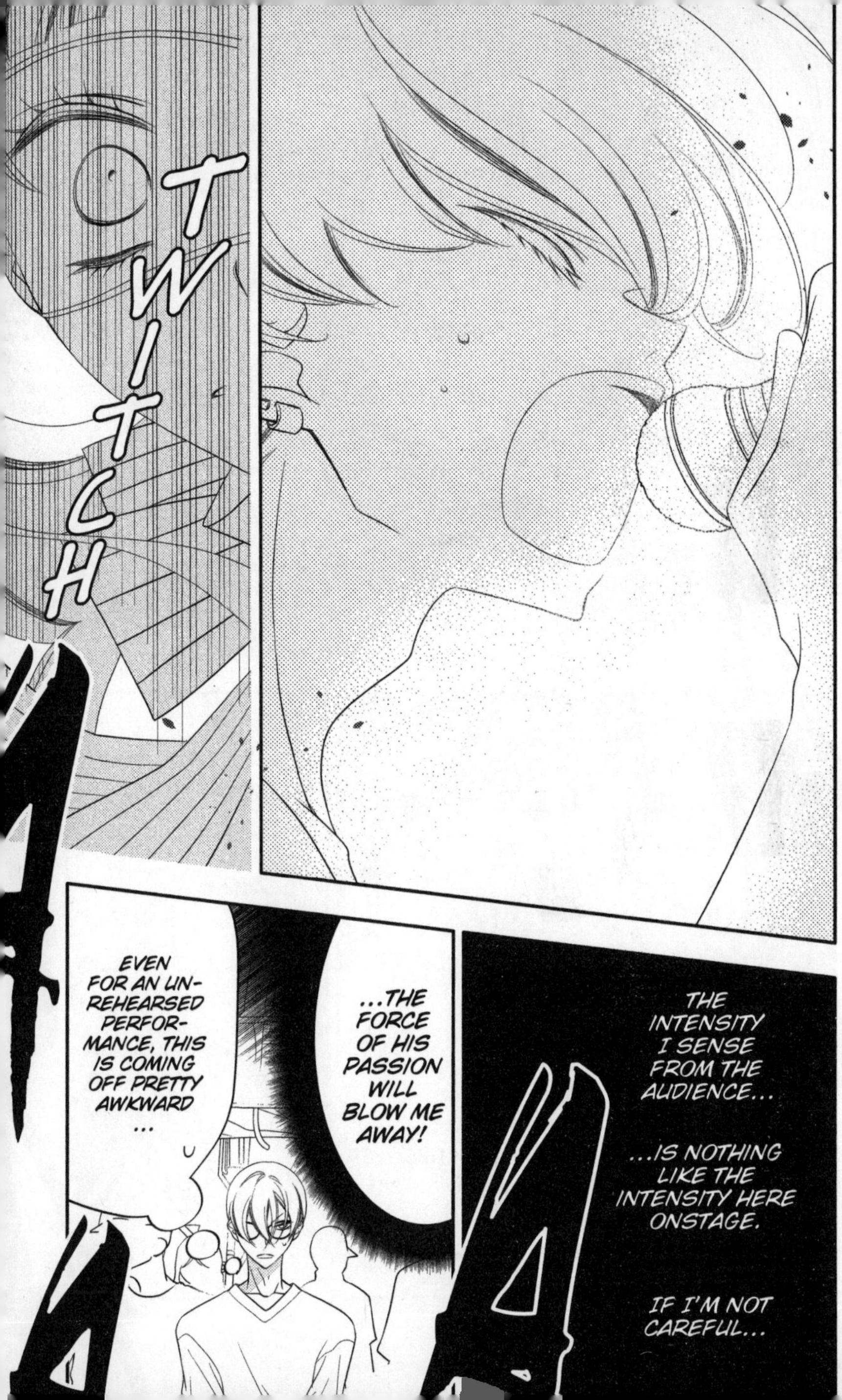
TWITCH
THE INTENSITY I SENSE FROM THE AUDIENCE...
...IS NOTHING LIKE THE INTENSITY HERE ONSTAGE.
IF I'M NOT CAREFUL...
...THE FORCE OF HIS PASSION WILL BLOW ME AWAY!
EVEN FOR AN UN-REHEARSED PERFOR-MANCE, THIS IS COMING OFF PRETTY AWKWARD ...

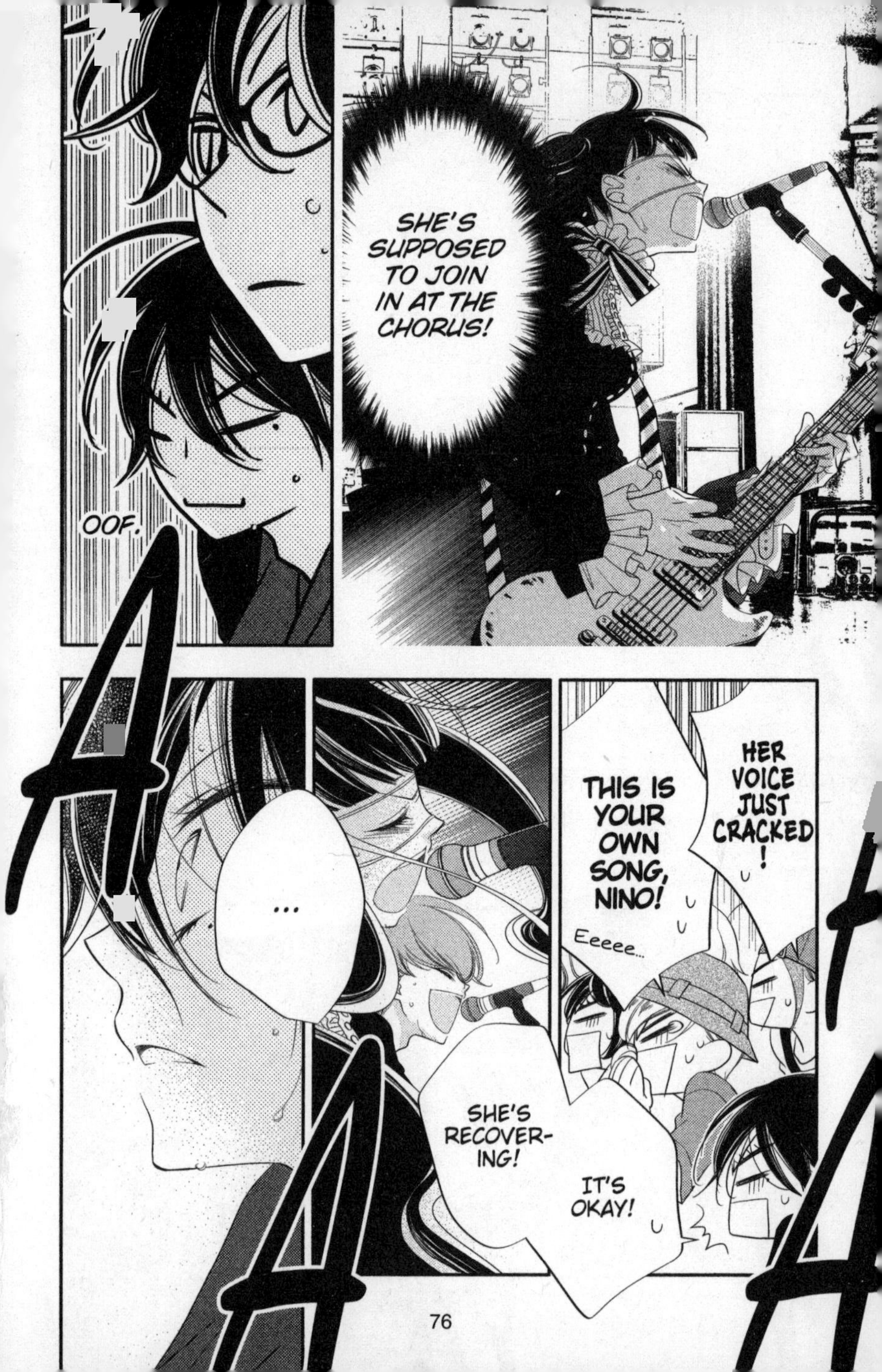
SHE'S SUPPOSED TO JOIN IN AT THE CHORUS!
OOF.
HER VOICE JUST CRACKED!
THIS IS YOUR OWN SONG, NINO!
Eeeee...
SHE'S RECOVER-ING!
IT'S OKAY!
...

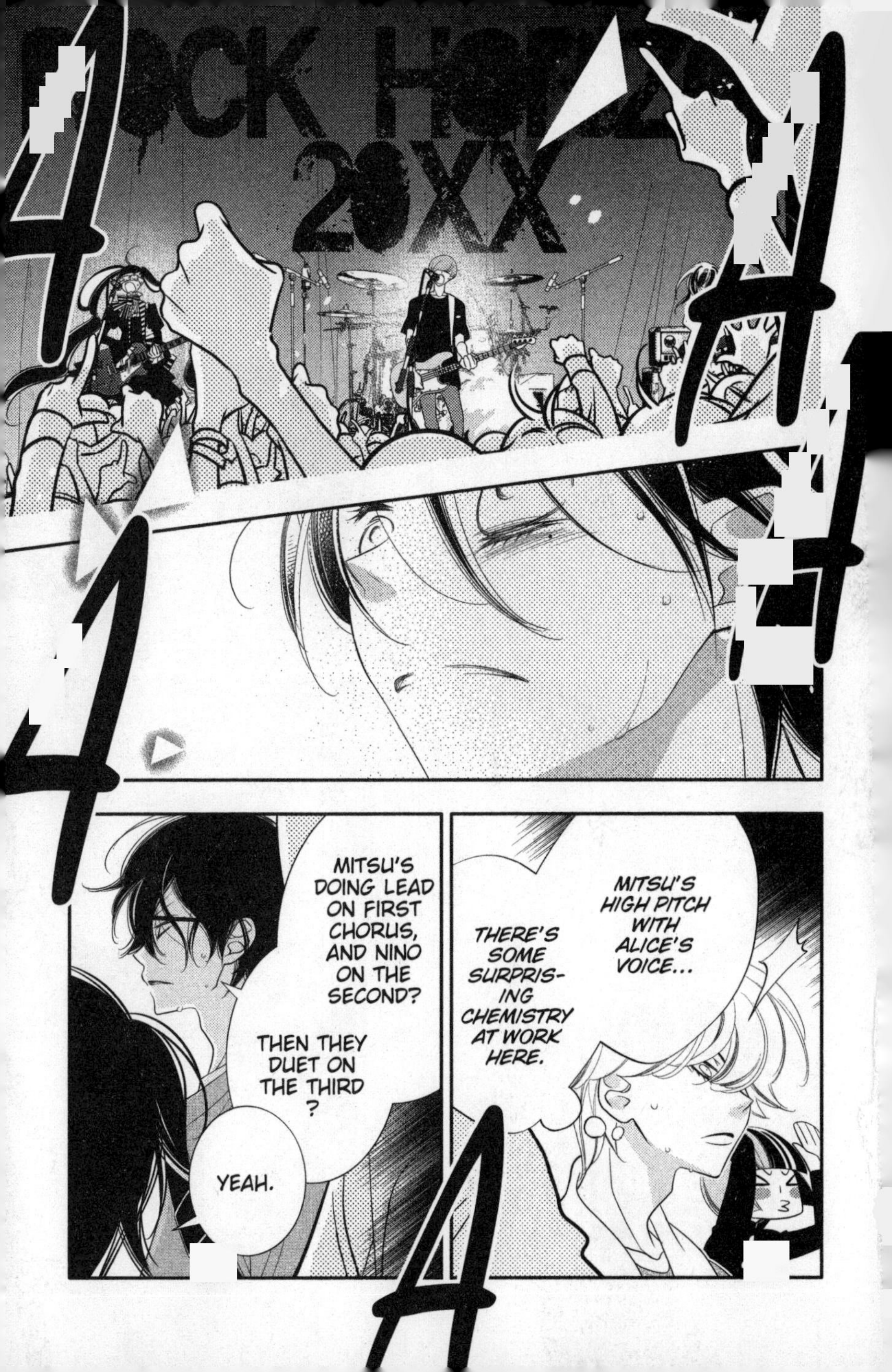
20XX
MITSU'S HIGH PITCH WITH ALICE'S VOICE...
THERE'S SOME SURPRIS-ING CHEMISTRY AT WORK HERE.
MITSU'S DOING LEAD ON FIRST CHORUS, AND NINO ON THE SECOND?
THEN THEY DUET ON THE THIRD?
YEAH.

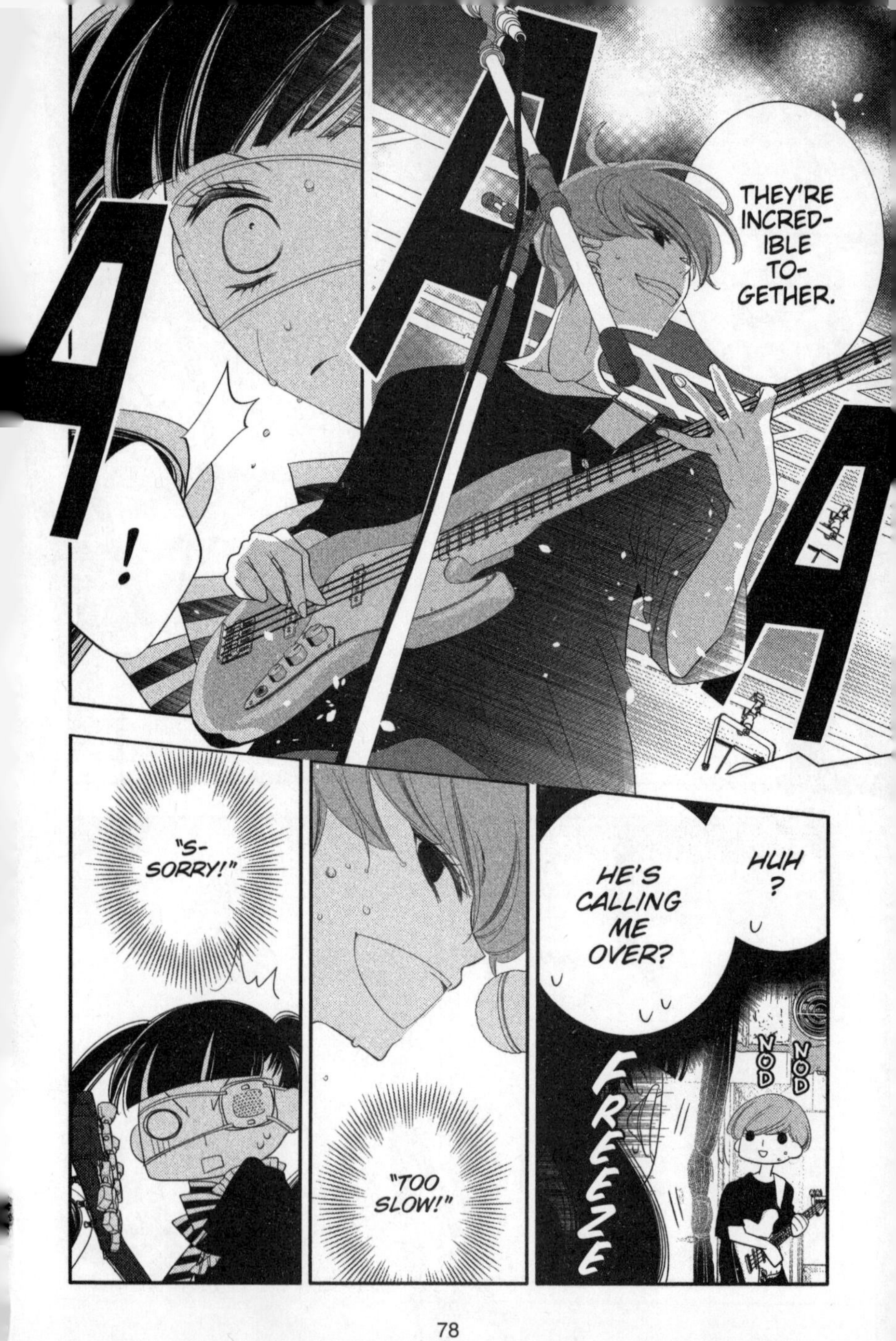

THEY'RE INCREDIBLE TOGETHER.
!
HUH?
HE'S CALLING ME OVER?
NOD NOD
FREEZE
"TOO SLOW!"
"S-SORRY!"

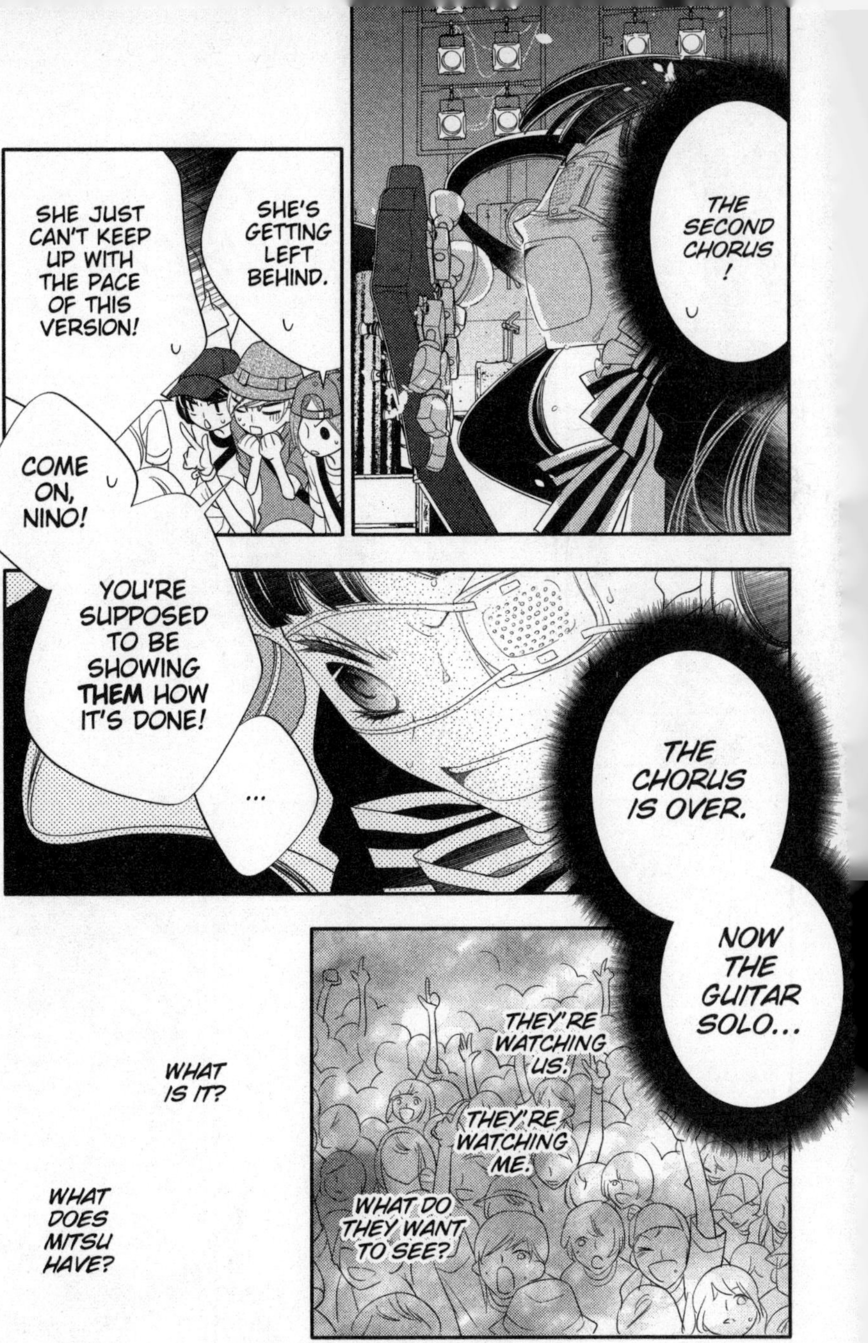
THE SECOND CHORUS!
SHE'S GETTING LEFT BEHIND.
SHE JUST CAN'T KEEP UP WITH THE PACE OF THIS VERSION!
COME ON, NINO!
YOU'RE SUPPOSED TO BE SHOWING **THEM** HOW IT'S DONE!
...
THE CHORUS IS OVER.
NOW THE GUITAR SOLO...
THEY'RE WATCHING US!
THEY'RE WATCHING ME.
WHAT DO THEY WANT TO SEE?
WHAT IS IT?
WHAT DOES MITSU HAVE?

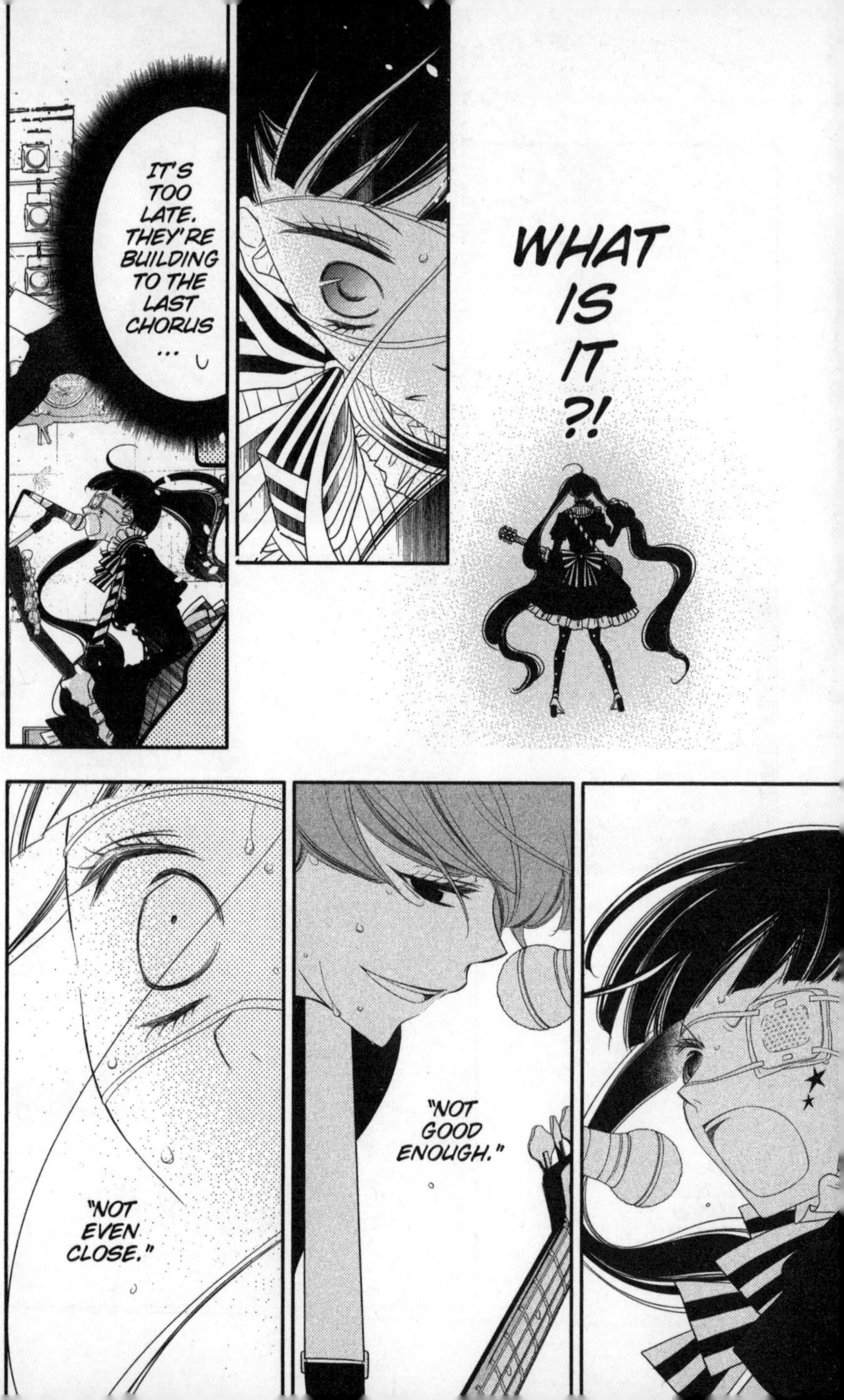
WHAT IS IT?!
IT'S TOO LATE. THEY'RE BUILDING TO THE LAST CHORUS...
"NOT GOOD ENOUGH."
"NOT EVEN CLOSE."

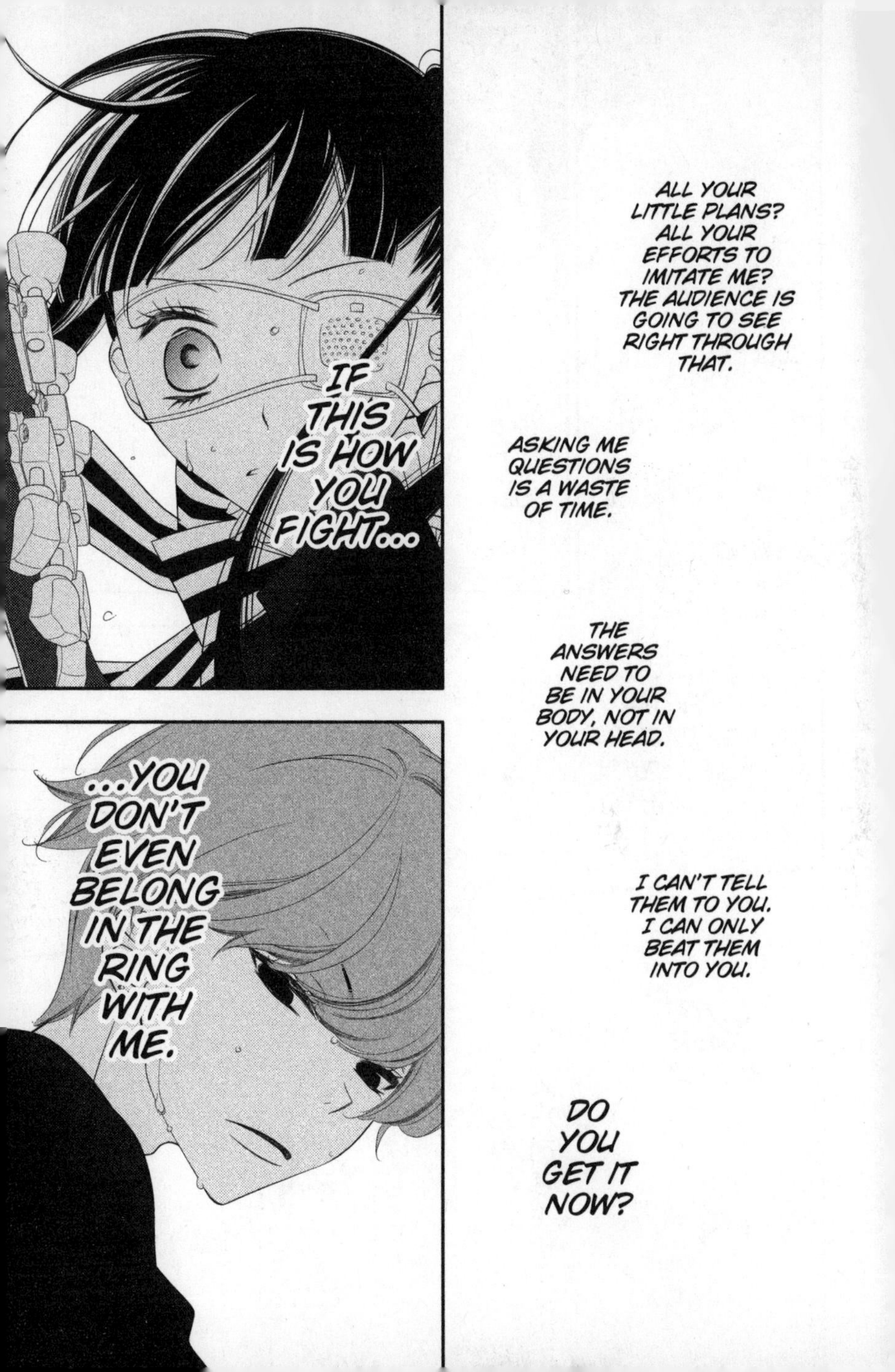
ALL YOUR LITTLE PLANS? ALL YOUR EFFORTS TO IMITATE ME? THE AUDIENCE IS GOING TO SEE RIGHT THROUGH THAT.
ASKING ME QUESTIONS IS A WASTE OF TIME.
THE ANSWERS NEED TO BE IN YOUR BODY, NOT IN YOUR HEAD.
I CAN'T TELL THEM TO YOU. I CAN ONLY BEAT THEM INTO YOU.
DO YOU GET IT NOW?
IF THIS IS HOW YOU FIGHT...
...YOU DON'T EVEN BELONG IN THE RING WITH ME.

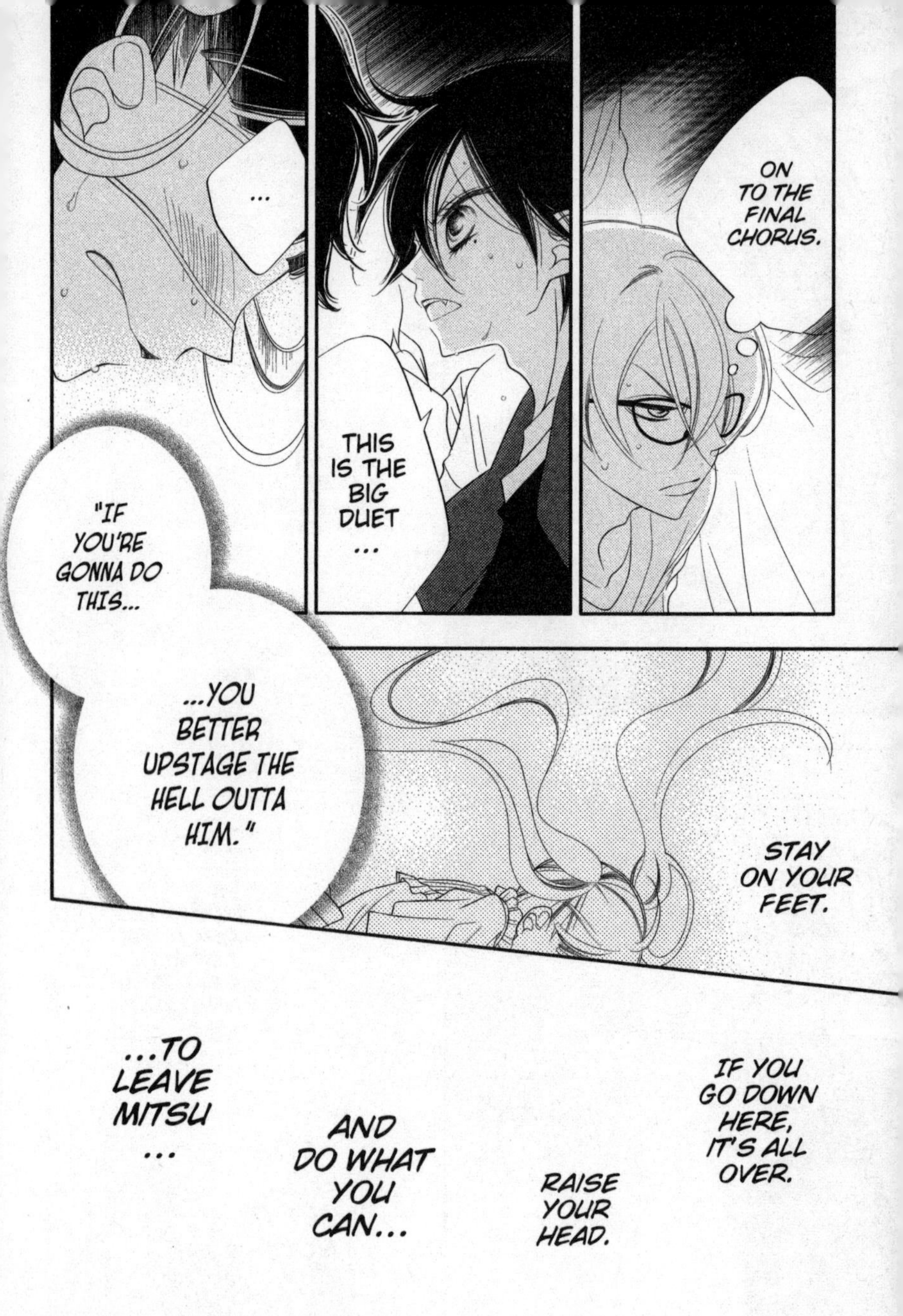
ON TO THE FINAL CHORUS.
THIS IS THE BIG DUET...
...
"IF YOU'RE GONNA DO THIS...
...YOU BETTER UPSTAGE THE HELL OUTTA HIM."
STAY ON YOUR FEET.
IF YOU GO DOWN HERE, IT'S ALL OVER.
RAISE YOUR HEAD.
AND DO WHAT YOU CAN...
...TO LEAVE MITSU...

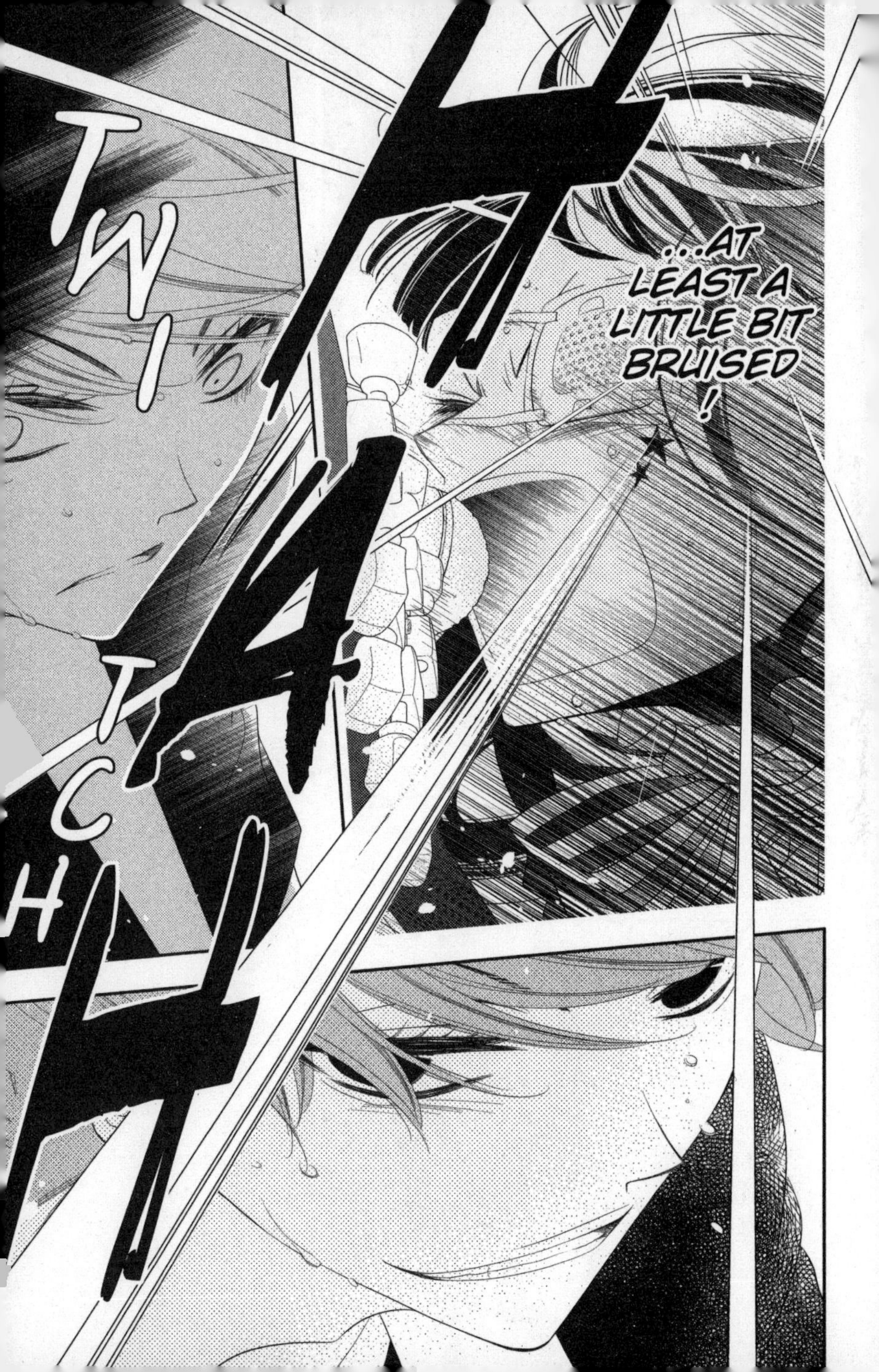
...AT LEAST A LITTLE BIT BRUISED!
TWITCH

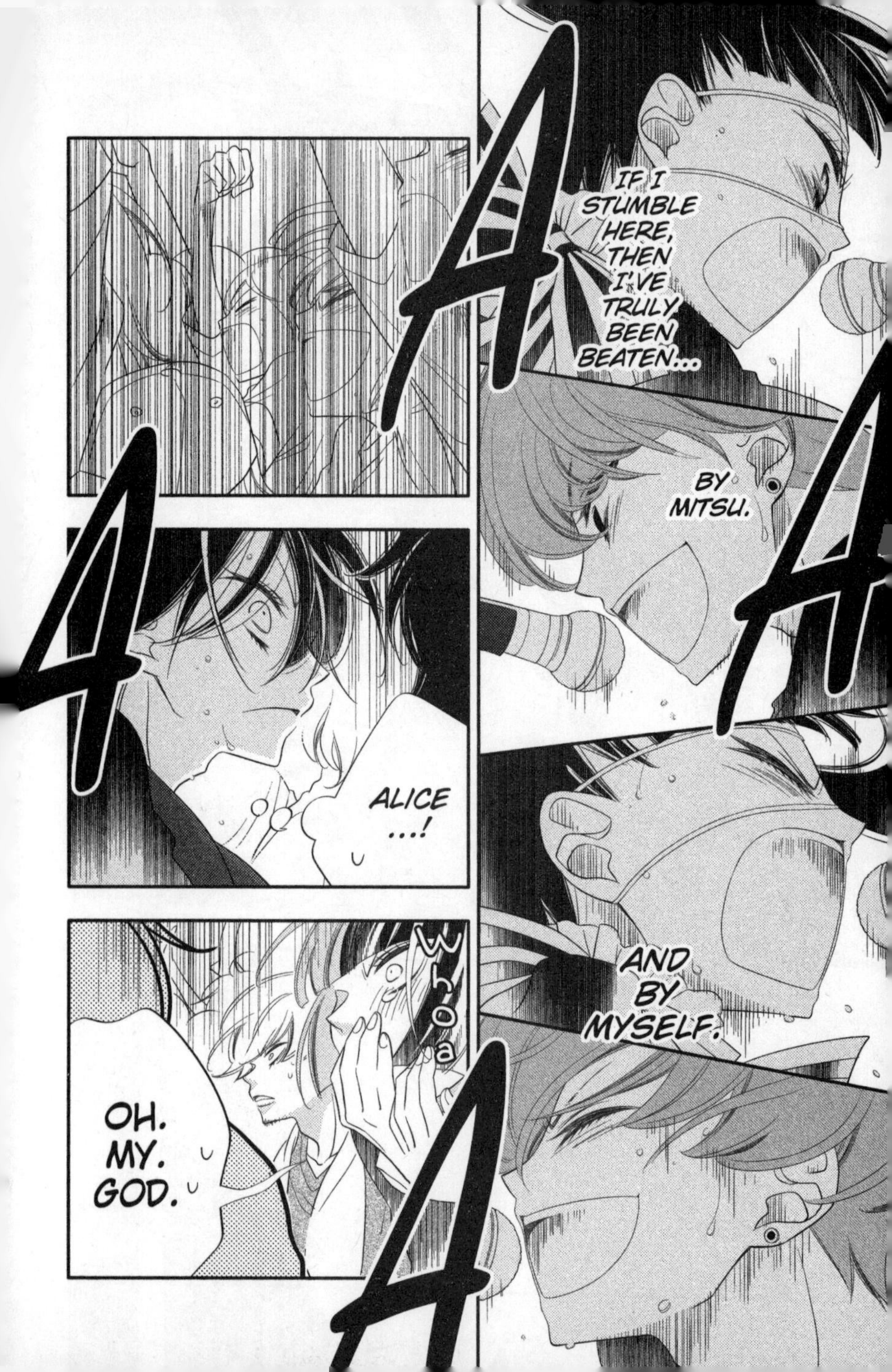
IF I STUMBLE HERE, THEN I'VE TRULY BEEN BEATEN...
BY MITSU.
AND BY MYSELF.
AAAAA
ALICE ...!
Whoa
OH. MY. GOD.

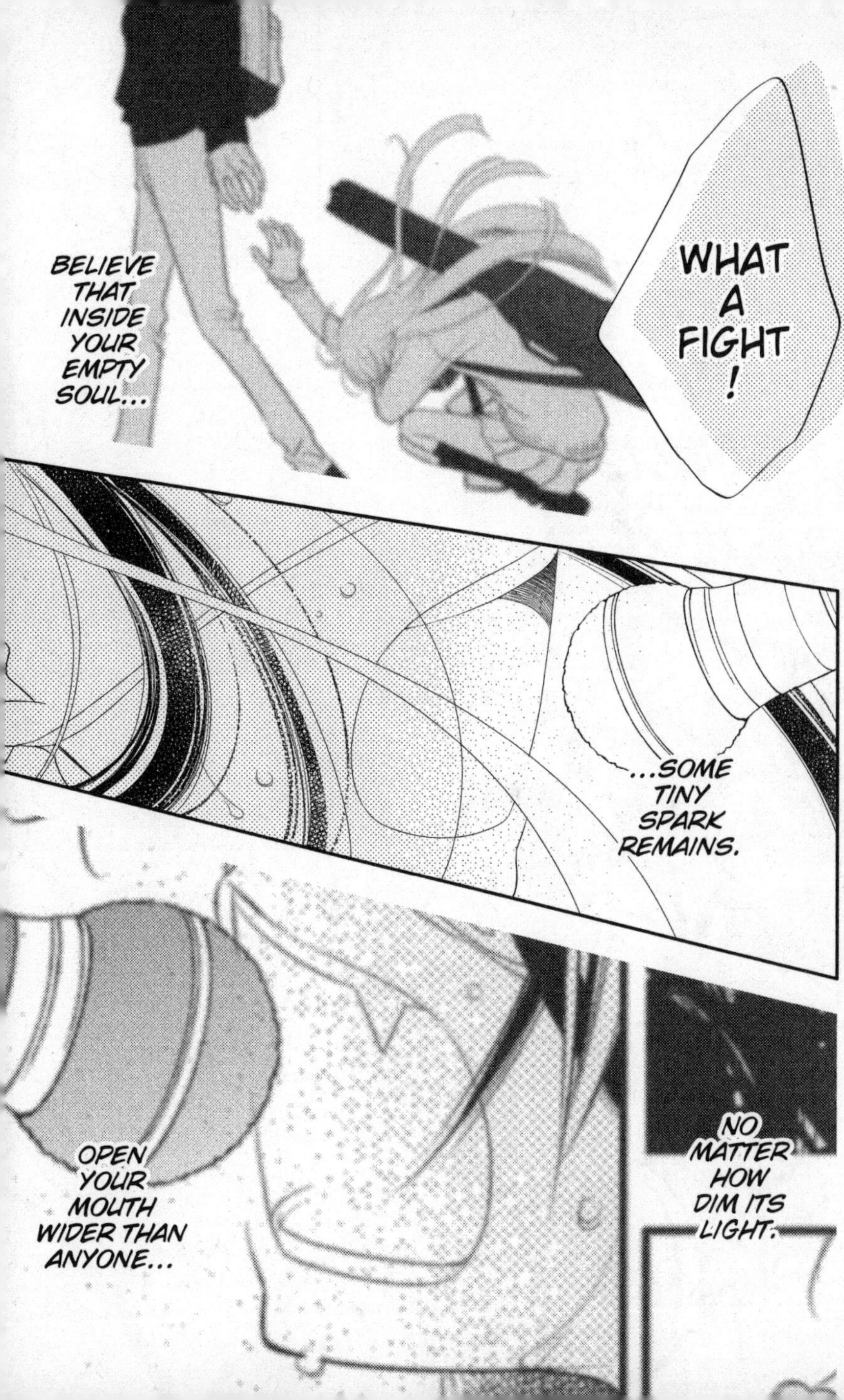
WHAT A FIGHT!
BELIEVE THAT INSIDE YOUR EMPTY SOUL...
...SOME TINY SPARK REMAINS.
NO MATTER HOW DIM ITS LIGHT.
OPEN YOUR MOUTH WIDER THAN ANYONE...

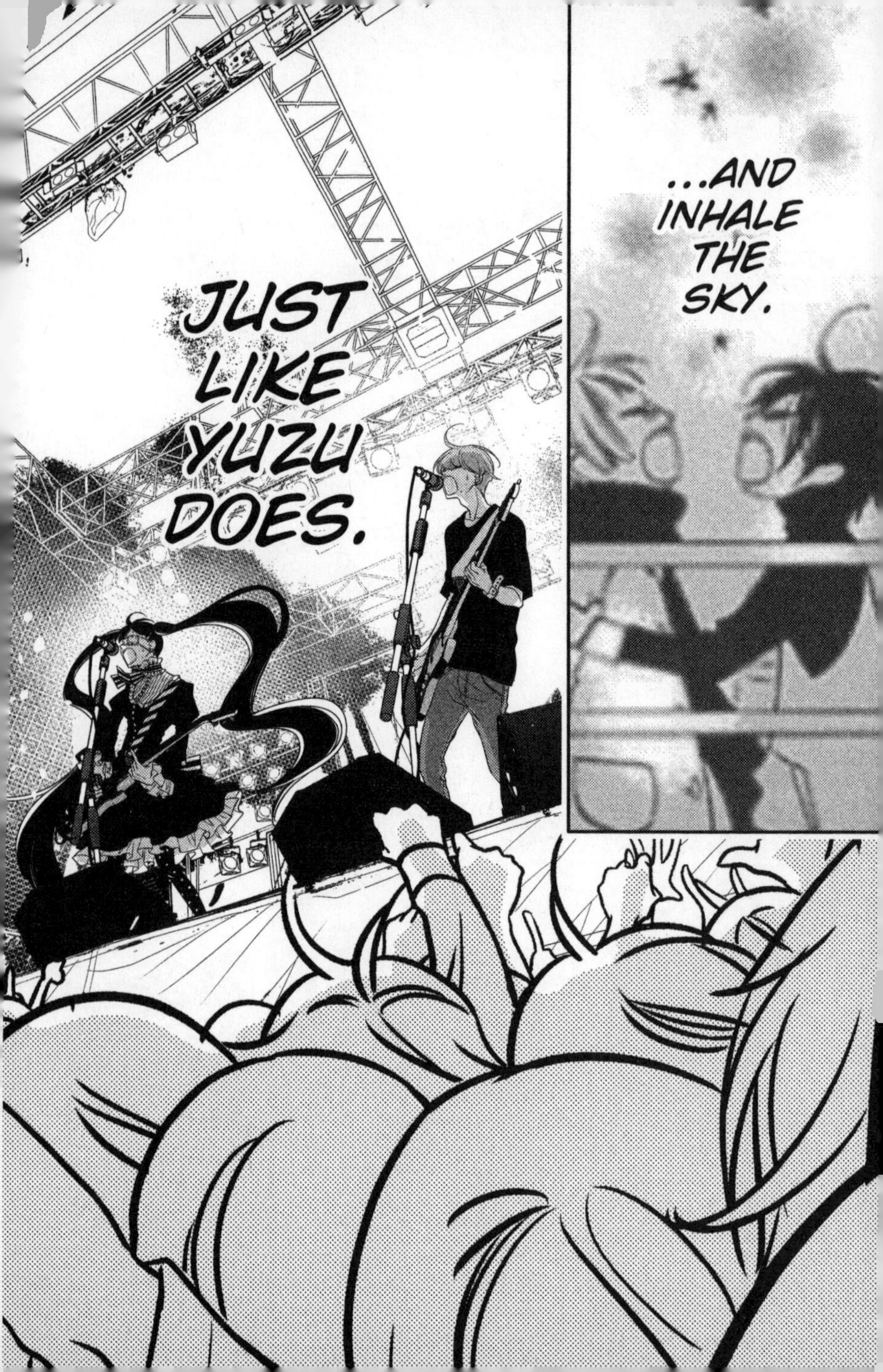
...AND INHALE THE SKY.
JUST LIKE YUZU DOES.

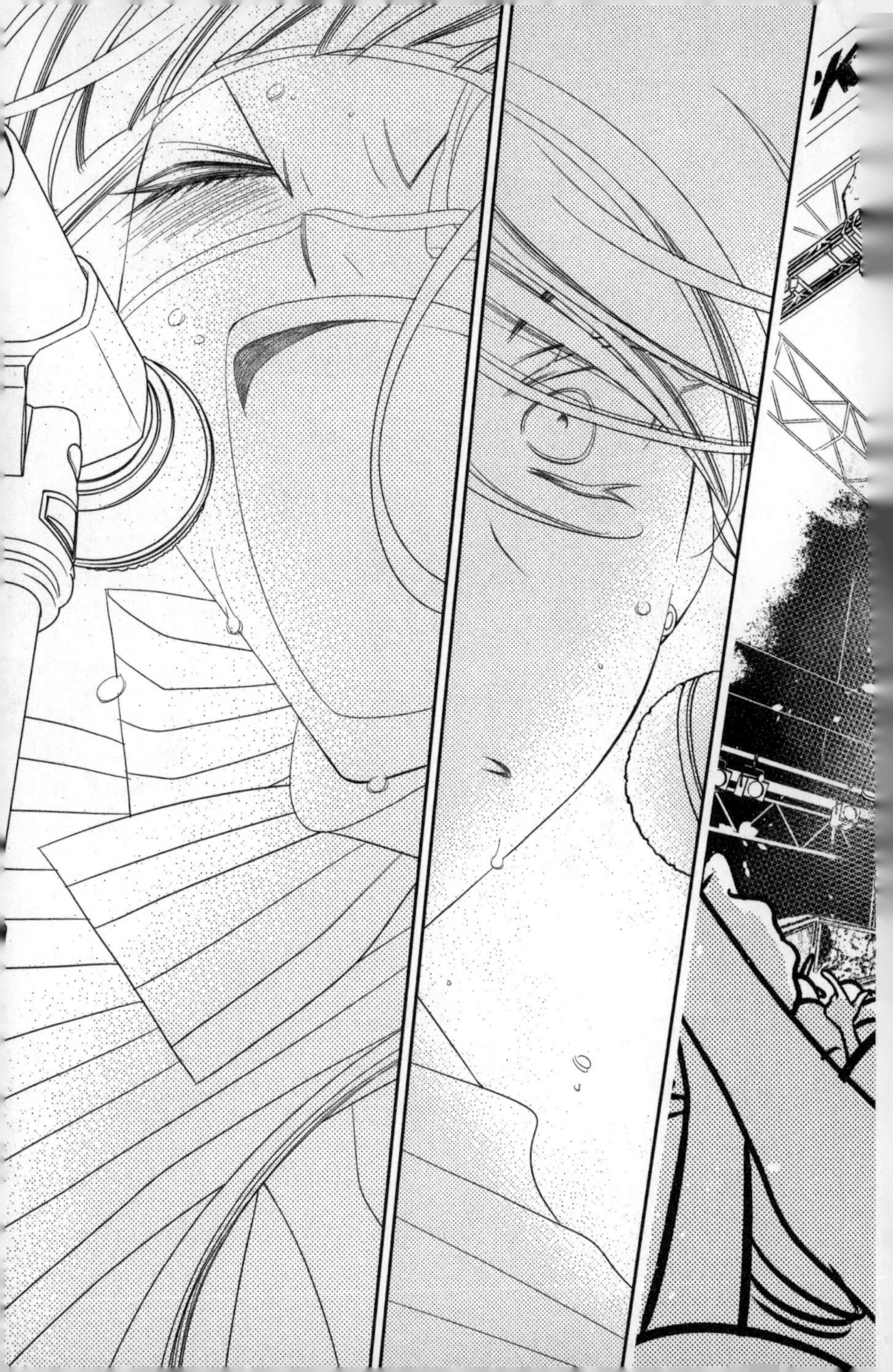

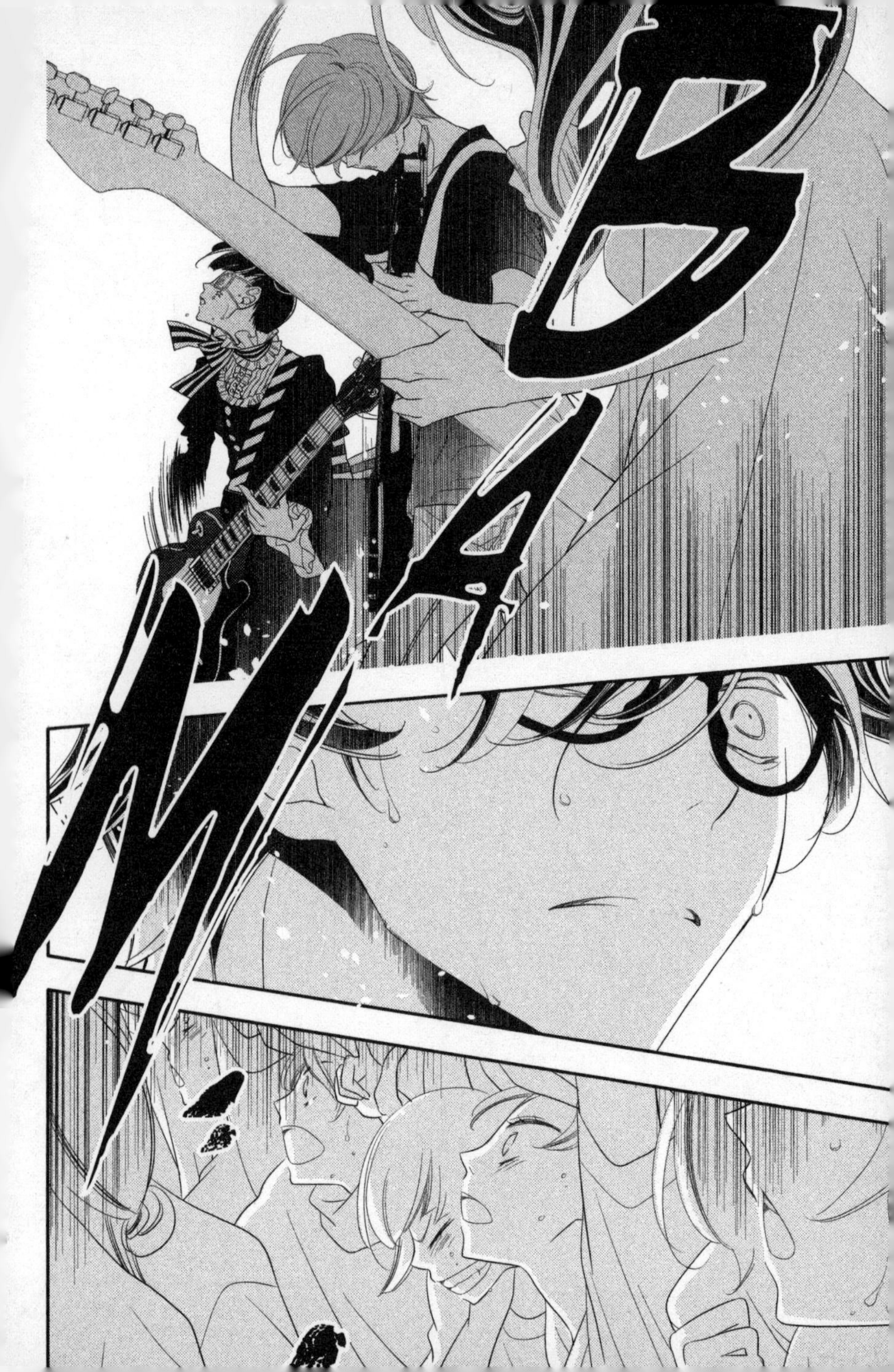

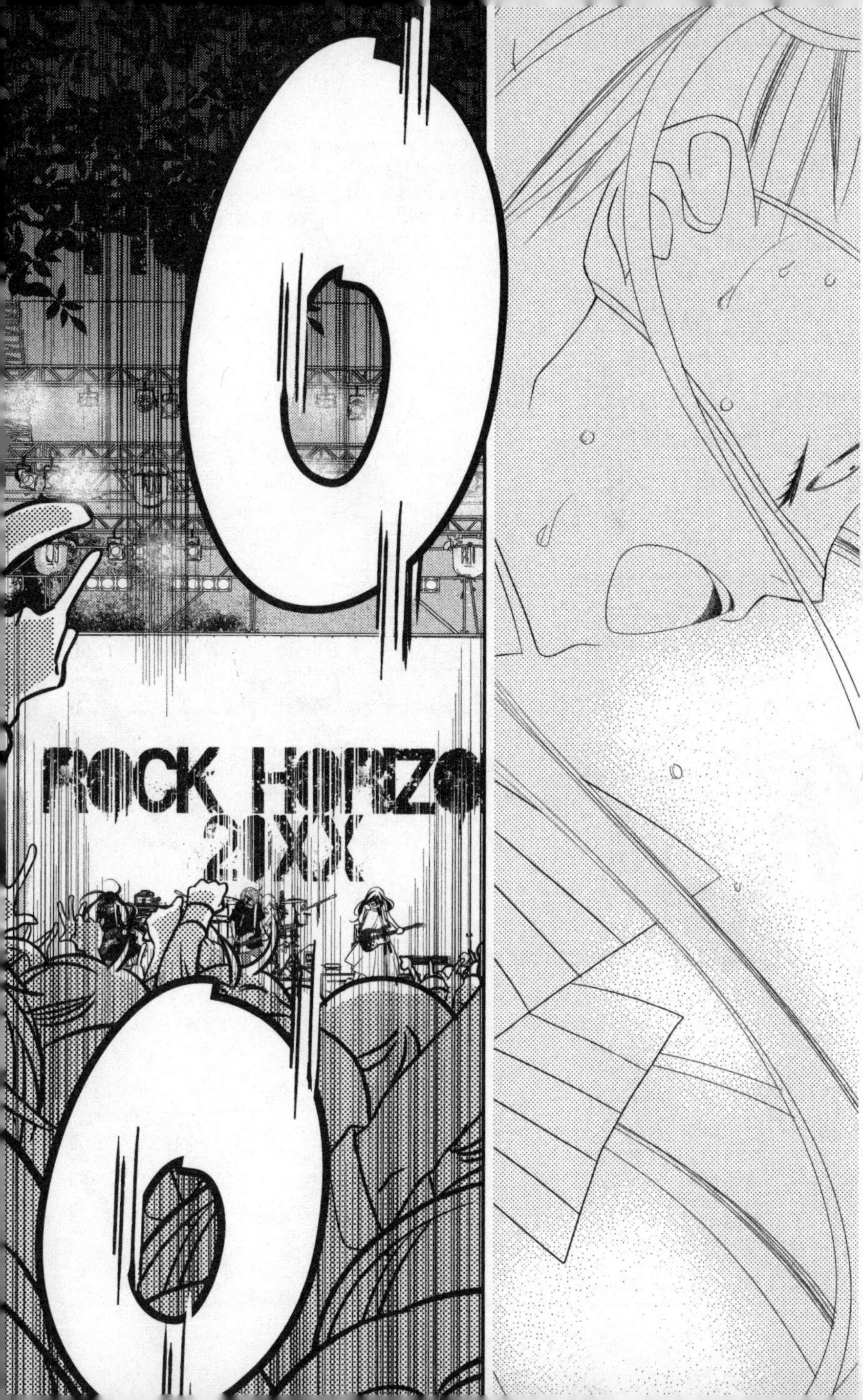
O
ROCK HORIZO
2XX
O

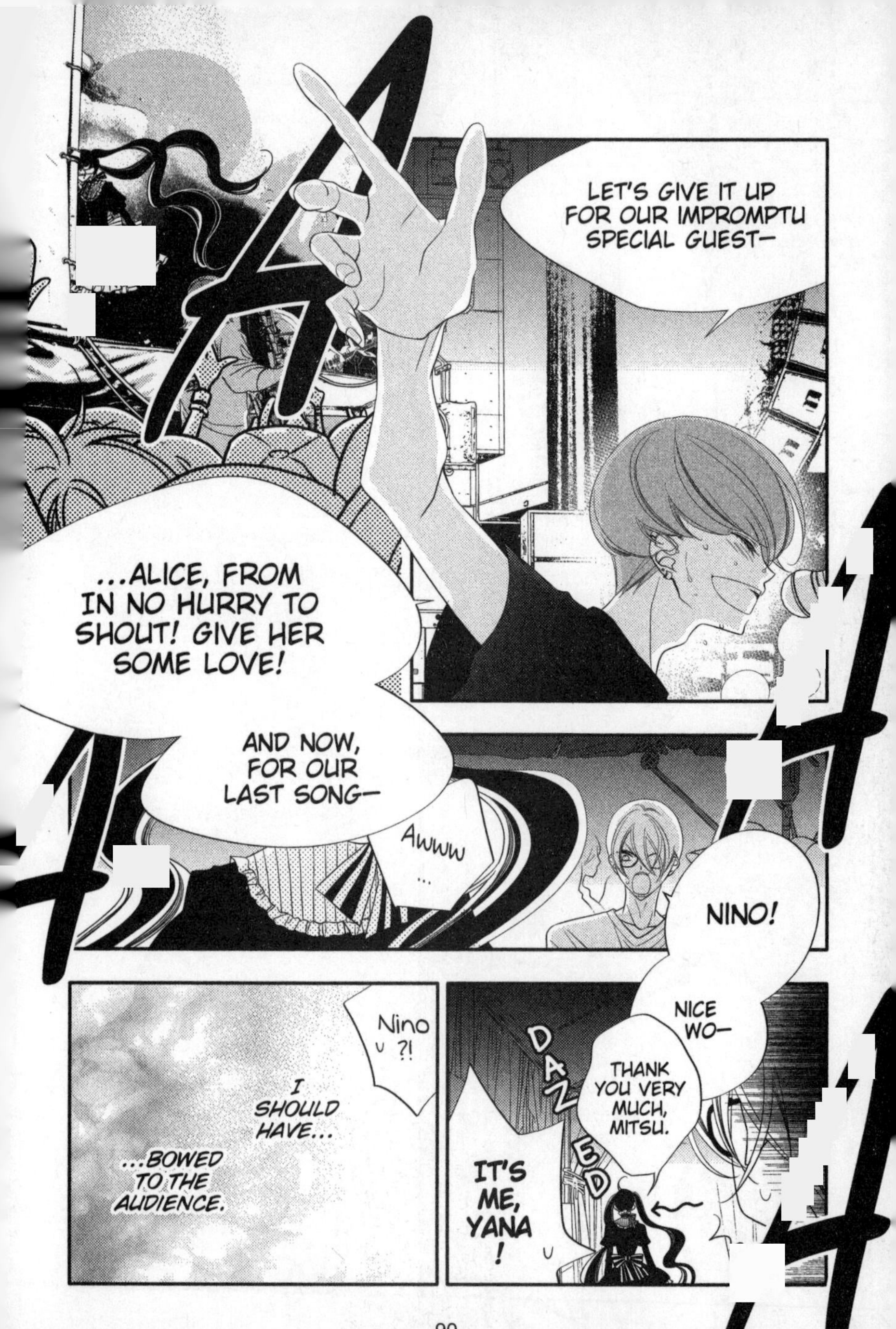
LET'S GIVE IT UP FOR OUR IMPROMPTU SPECIAL GUEST—
...ALICE, FROM IN NO HURRY TO SHOUT! GIVE HER SOME LOVE!
AND NOW, FOR OUR LAST SONG—
Awww...
NINO!
NICE WO—
THANK YOU VERY MUCH, MITSU.
DAZED
IT'S ME, YANA!
Nino ?!
I SHOULD HAVE...
...BOWED TO THE AUDIENCE.

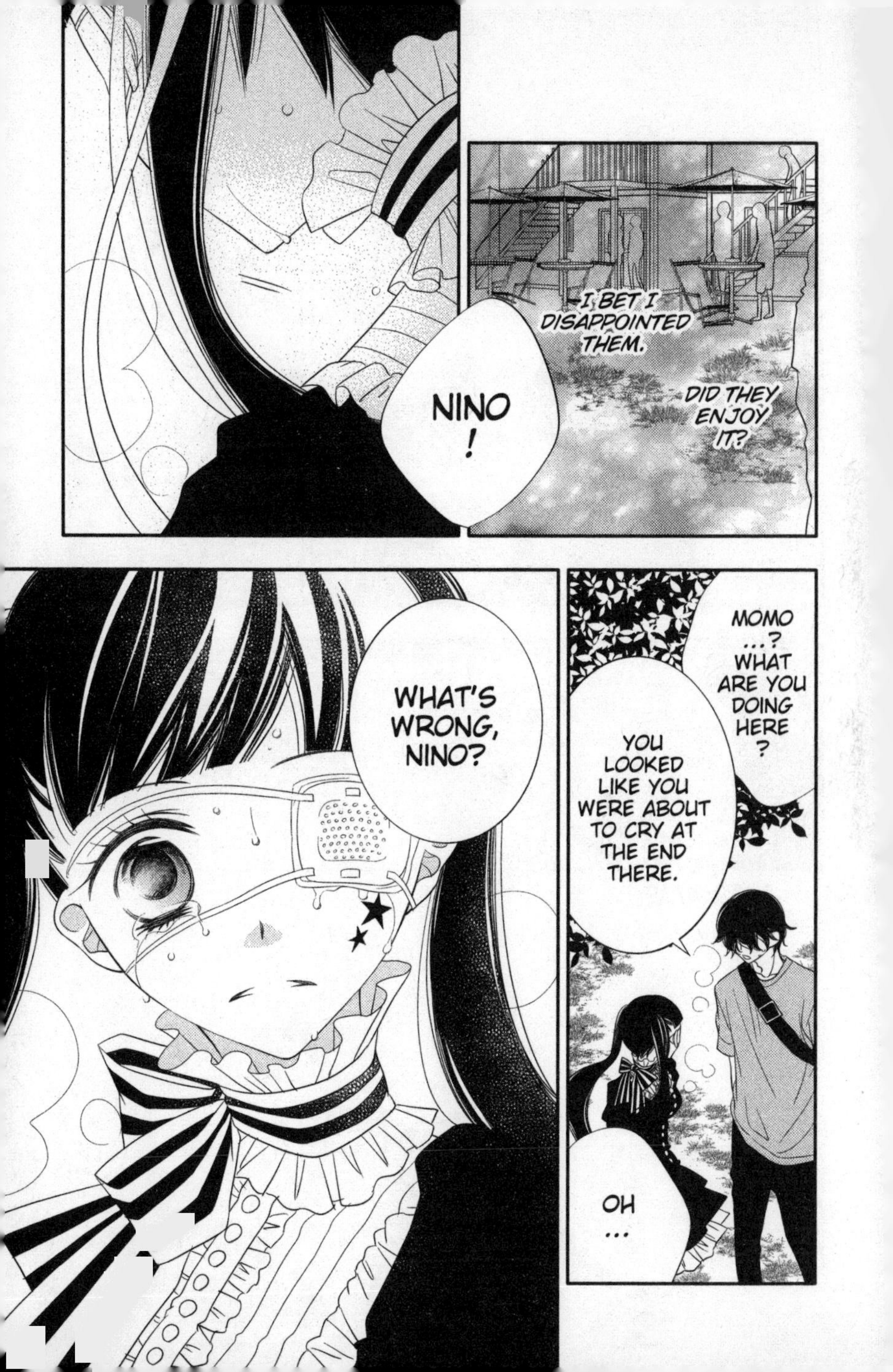
I BET I DISAPPOINTED THEM.
DID THEY ENJOY IT?
NINO!
MOMO...? WHAT ARE YOU DOING HERE?
YOU LOOKED LIKE YOU WERE ABOUT TO CRY AT THE END THERE.
OH...
WHAT'S WRONG, NINO?

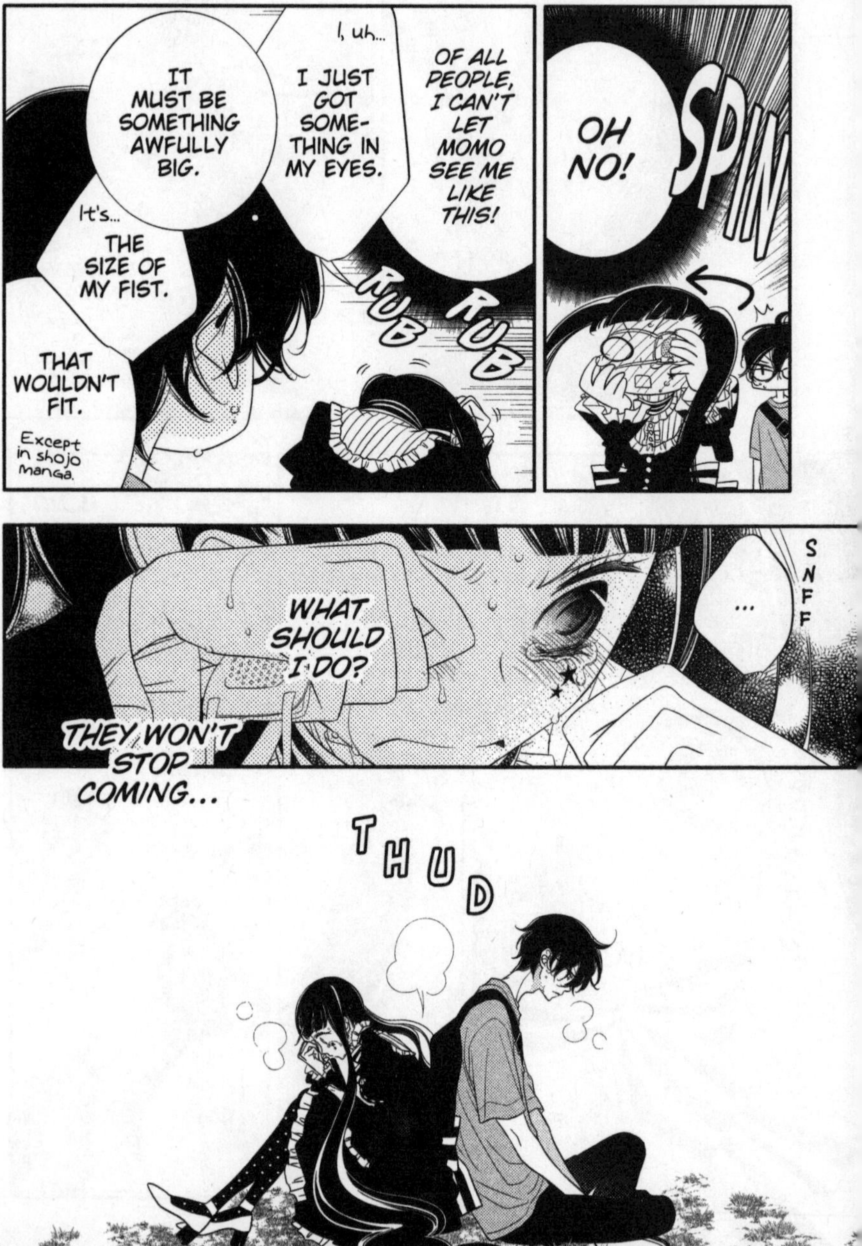
SPIN
OH NO!
OF ALL PEOPLE, I CAN'T LET MOMO SEE ME LIKE THIS!
I, uh...
I JUST GOT SOME-THING IN MY EYES.
IT MUST BE SOMETHING AWFULLY BIG.
RUB RUB
It's...
THE SIZE OF MY FIST.
THAT WOULDN'T FIT.
Except in shojo manga.
SNFF
...
WHAT SHOULD I DO?
THEY WON'T STOP COMING...
THUD

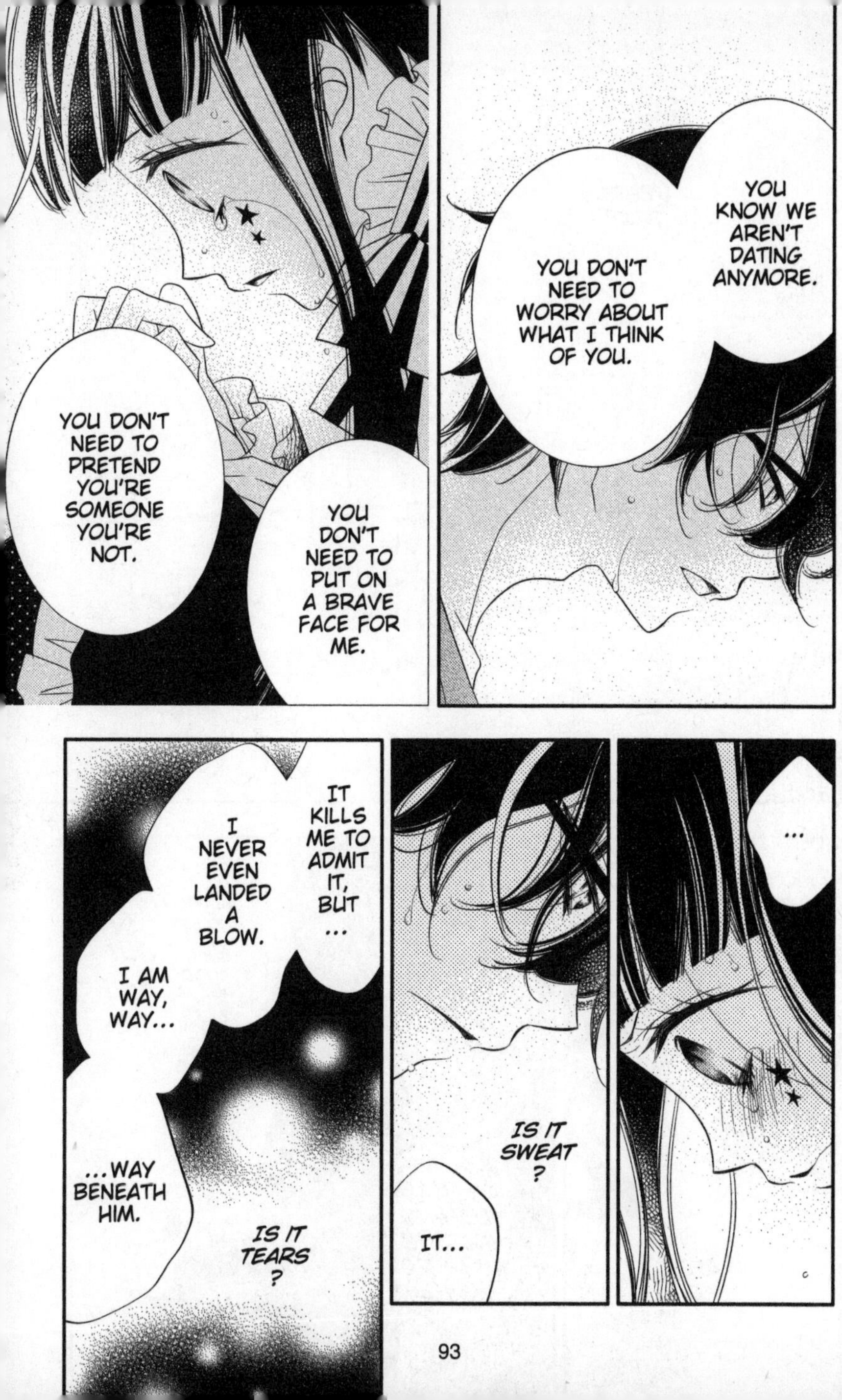
YOU KNOW WE AREN'T DATING ANYMORE.
YOU DON'T NEED TO WORRY ABOUT WHAT I THINK OF YOU.
YOU DON'T NEED TO PUT ON A BRAVE FACE FOR ME.
YOU DON'T NEED TO PRETEND YOU'RE SOMEONE YOU'RE NOT.
...
IS IT SWEAT?
IT...
IT KILLS ME TO ADMIT IT, BUT...
I NEVER EVEN LANDED A BLOW.
I AM WAY, WAY...
...WAY BENEATH HIM.
IS IT TEARS?

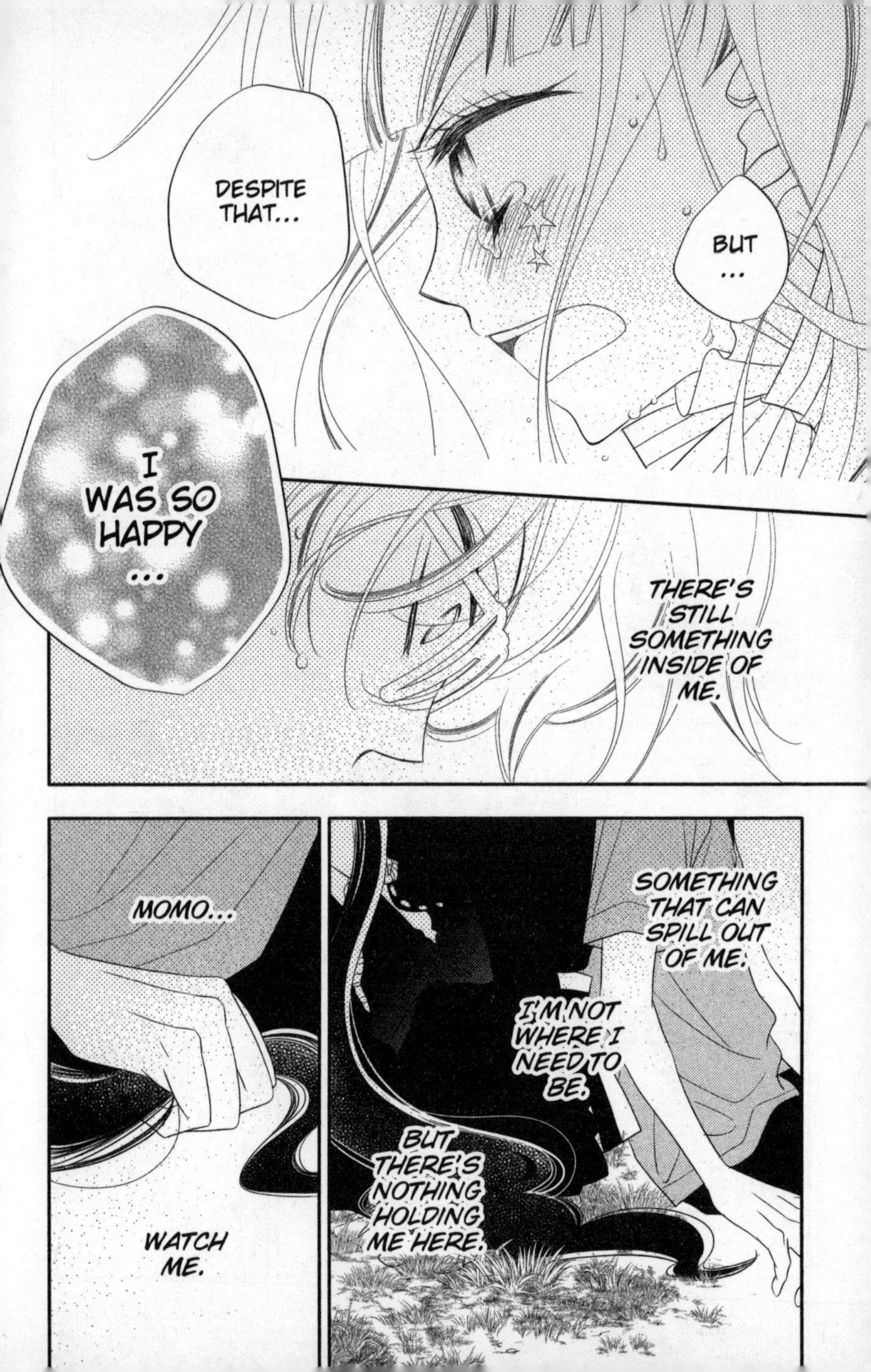
BUT ...
DESPITE THAT...
I WAS SO HAPPY ...
THERE'S STILL SOMETHING INSIDE OF ME.
SOMETHING THAT CAN SPILL OUT OF ME.
I'M NOT WHERE I NEED TO BE.
BUT THERE'S NOTHING HOLDING ME HERE.
MOMO...
WATCH ME.

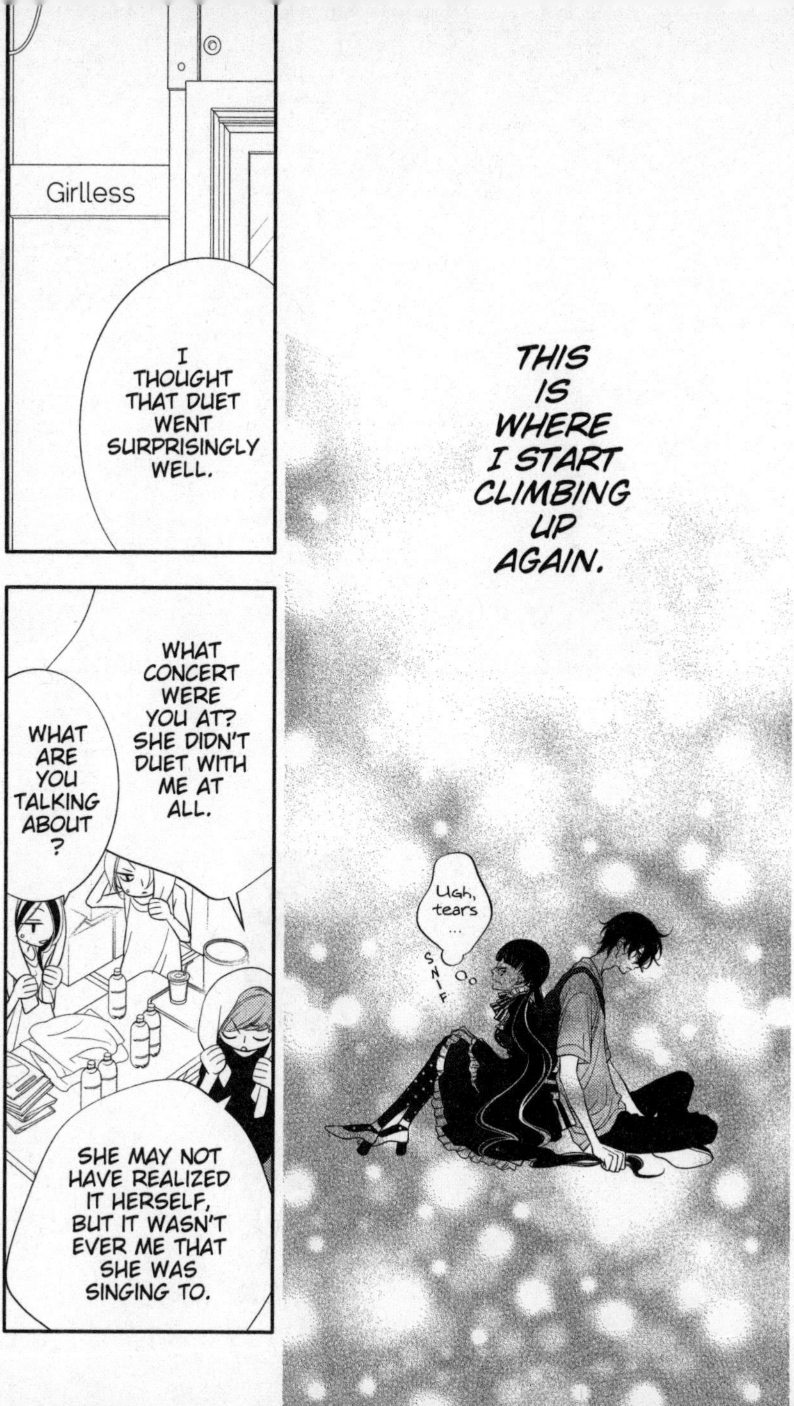
THIS IS WHERE I START CLIMBING UP AGAIN.
Ugh, tears ...
SNIF
Girlless
I THOUGHT THAT DUET WENT SURPRISINGLY WELL.
WHAT CONCERT WERE YOU AT? SHE DIDN'T DUET WITH ME AT ALL.
WHAT ARE YOU TALKING ABOUT?
SHE MAY NOT HAVE REALIZED IT HERSELF, BUT IT WASN'T EVER ME THAT SHE WAS SINGING TO.

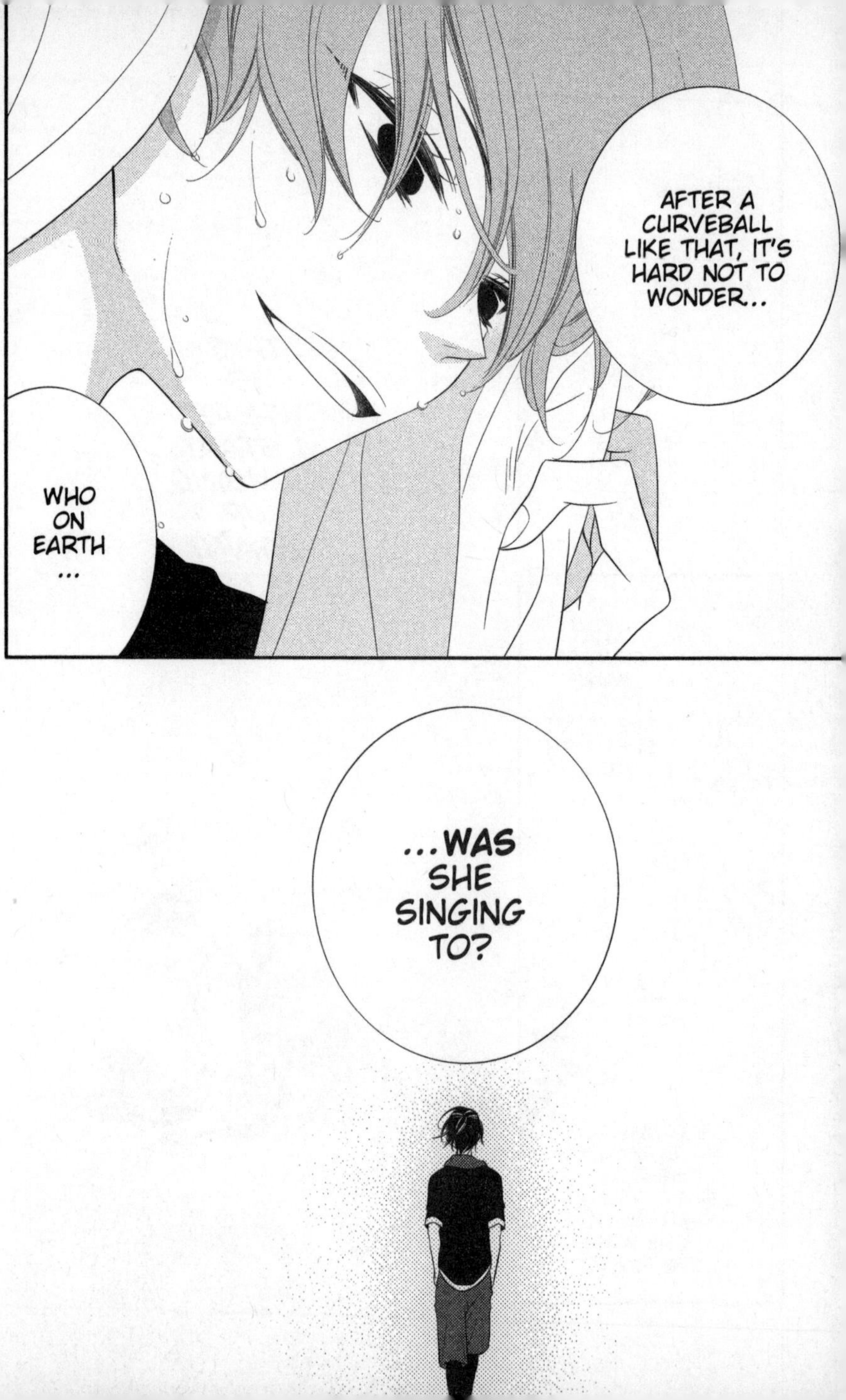
AFTER A CURVEBALL LIKE THAT, IT'S HARD NOT TO WONDER...
WHO ON EARTH ...
...WAS SHE SINGING TO?

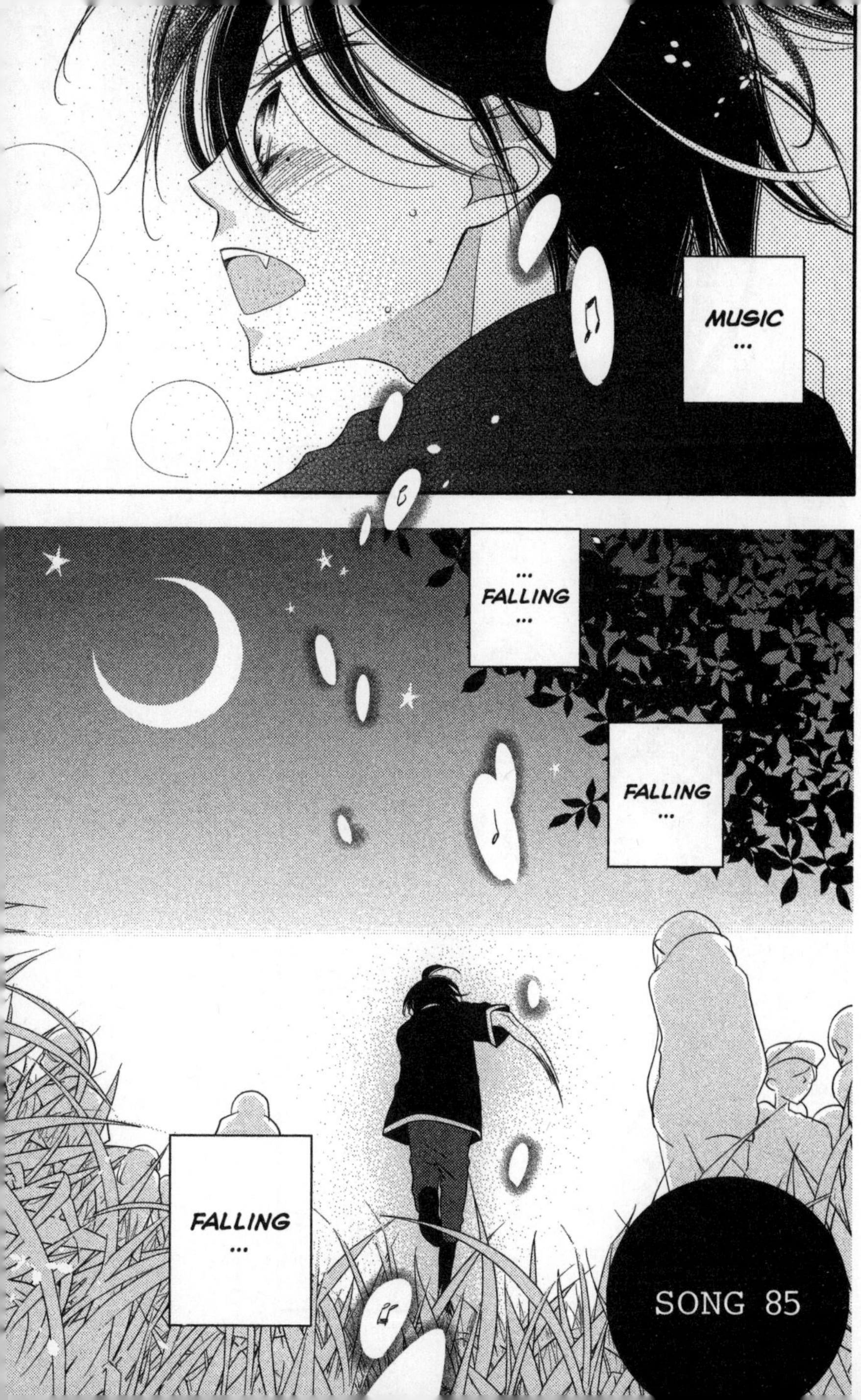
MUSIC ...
... FALLING ...
FALLING ...
FALLING ...
SONG 85

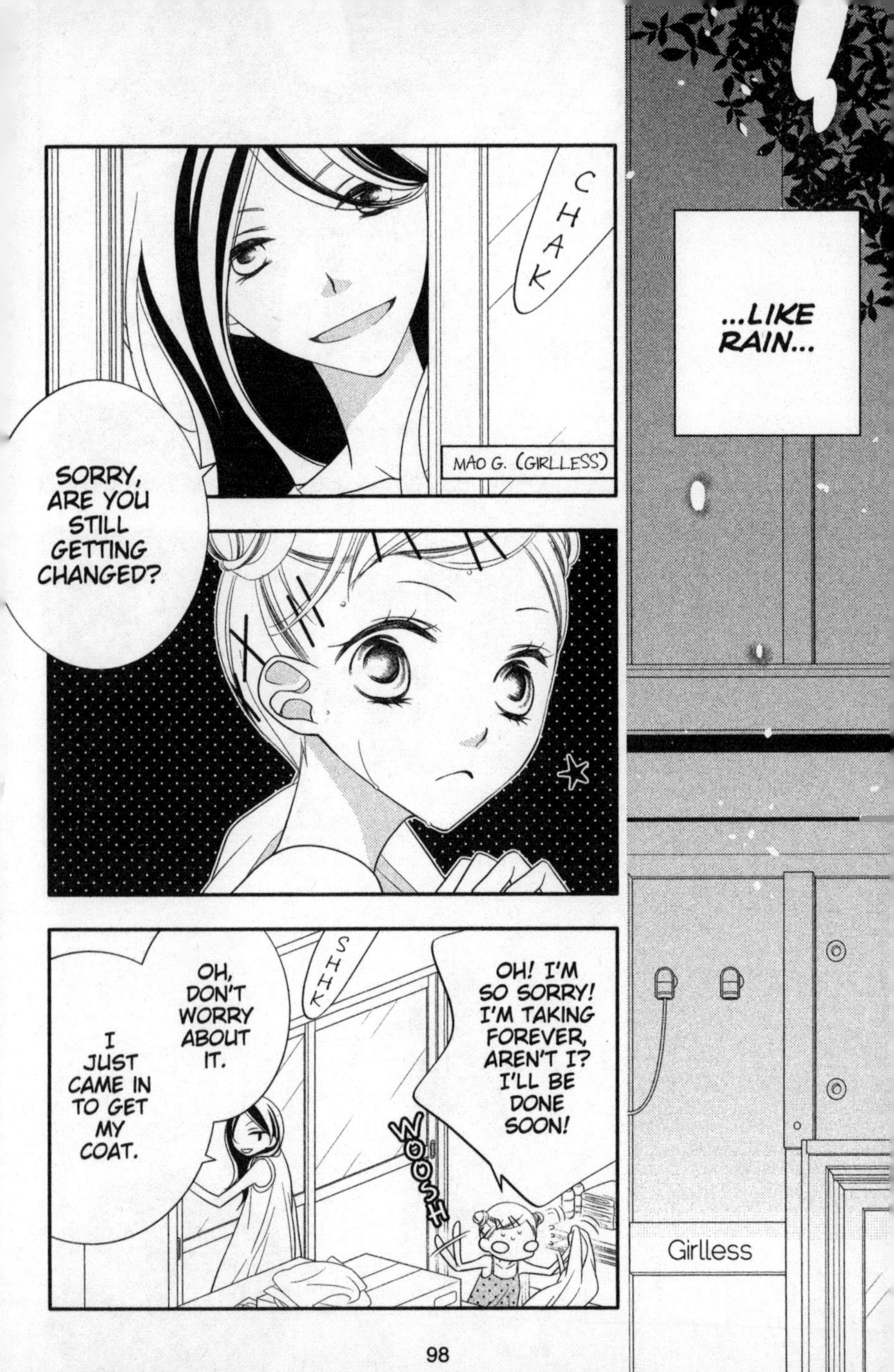
...LIKE RAIN...
Girlless
CHAK
MAO G. (GIRLLESS)
SORRY, ARE YOU STILL GETTING CHANGED?
OH! I'M SO SORRY! I'M TAKING FOREVER, AREN'T I? I'LL BE DONE SOON!
WOOSH
SHHK
OH, DON'T WORRY ABOUT IT.
I JUST CAME IN TO GET MY COAT.

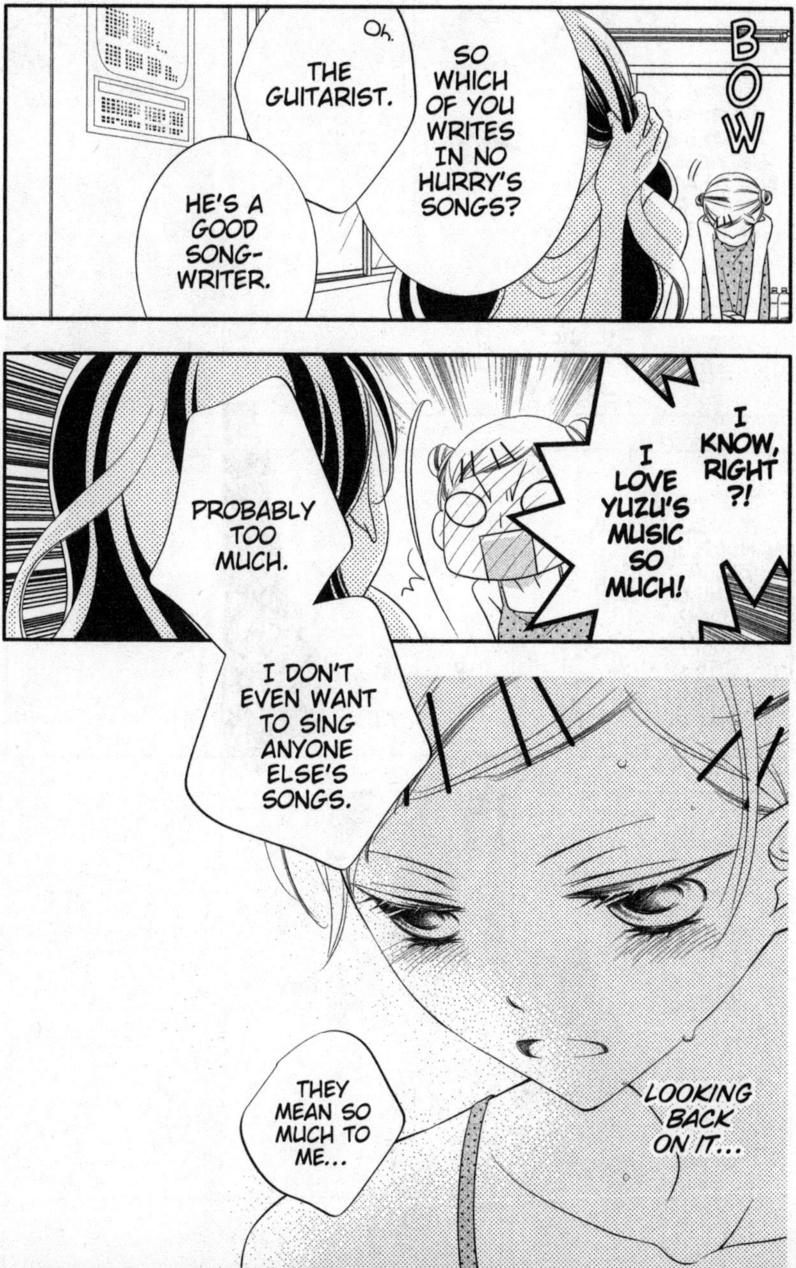
BOW
SO WHICH OF YOU WRITES IN NO HURRY'S SONGS?
Oh.
THE GUITARIST.
HE'S A GOOD SONG-WRITER.
I KNOW, RIGHT?!
I LOVE YUZU'S MUSIC SO MUCH!
PROBABLY TOO MUCH.
I DON'T EVEN WANT TO SING ANYONE ELSE'S SONGS.
LOOKING BACK ON IT...
THEY MEAN SO MUCH TO ME...

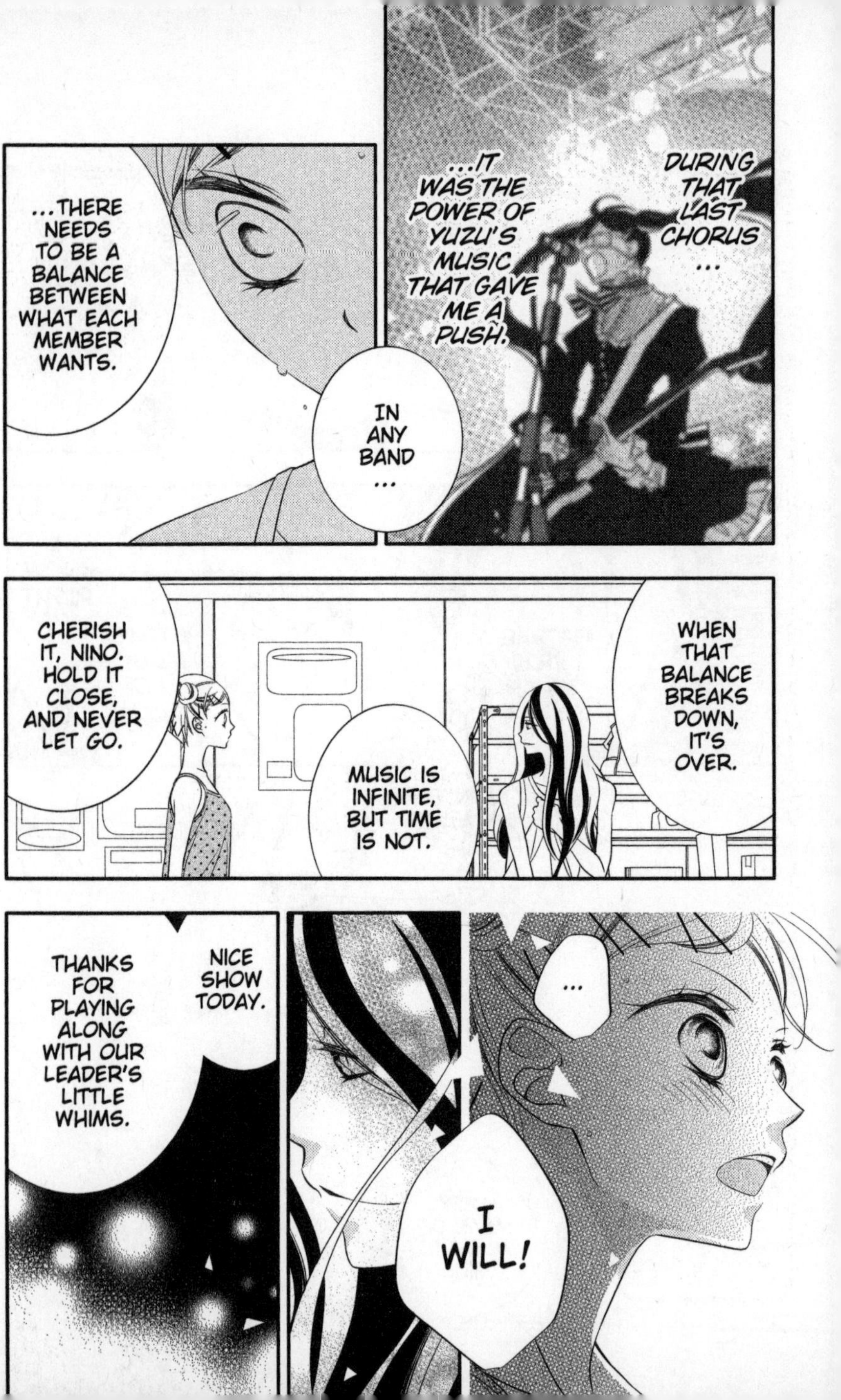
DURING THAT LAST CHORUS...
...IT WAS THE POWER OF YUZU'S MUSIC THAT GAVE ME A PUSH.
IN ANY BAND...
...THERE NEEDS TO BE A BALANCE BETWEEN WHAT EACH MEMBER WANTS.
WHEN THAT BALANCE BREAKS DOWN, IT'S OVER.
MUSIC IS INFINITE, BUT TIME IS NOT.
CHERISH IT, NINO. HOLD IT CLOSE, AND NEVER LET GO.
...
I WILL!
NICE SHOW TODAY.
THANKS FOR PLAYING ALONG WITH OUR LEADER'S LITTLE WHIMS.

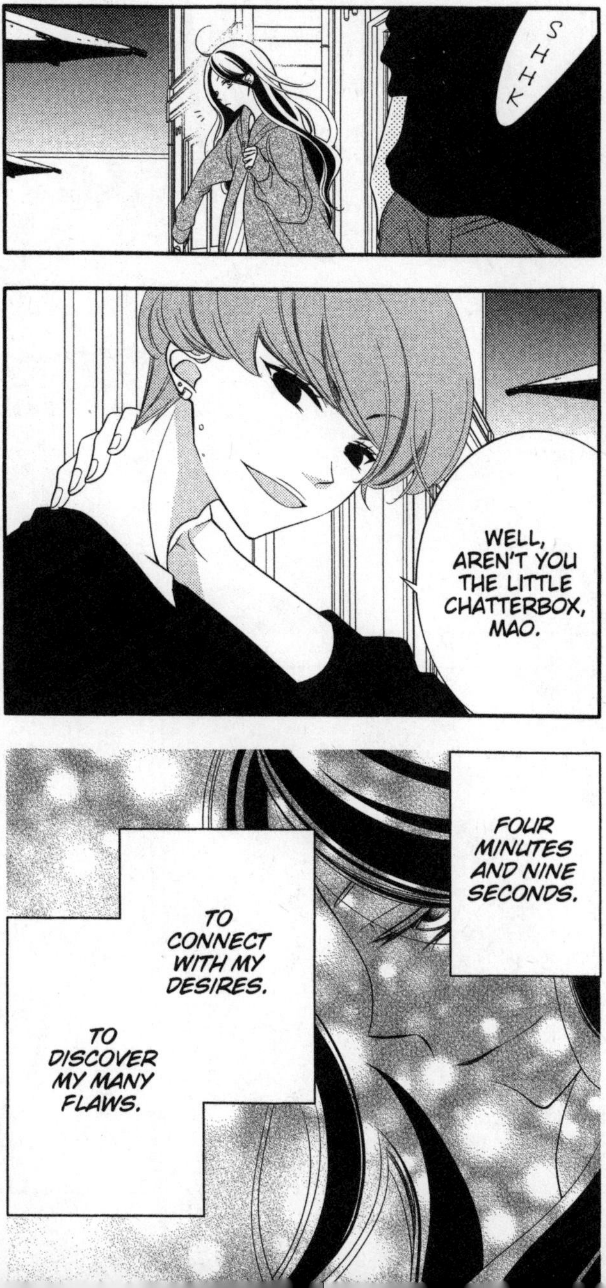
SHHK
WELL, AREN'T YOU THE LITTLE CHATTERBOX, MAO.
FOUR MINUTES AND NINE SECONDS.
TO CONNECT WITH MY DESIRES.
TO DISCOVER MY MANY FLAWS.

4

Despite being on vacation, I managed to drag myself down to all the In No Hurry song and drama CD recording sessions. (Although if I hadn't, I'm sure one of my assistants would have... Ha ha...) By now, I'm sure you've heard the new In No Hurry song "Signs" recorded for the limited edition of volume 15? I figured hearing that would be a big "Oh!" moment for fans who have been reading the manga from the start. I had such a clear image for what I wanted the song to be, and that's probably why I was able to write it in one sitting and get it approved on the first try! I really am so lucky to be able to work with such a great team and such wonderful musicians. I'm avoiding the past tense here because I have faith that we'll have a chance to work together again! WOW!

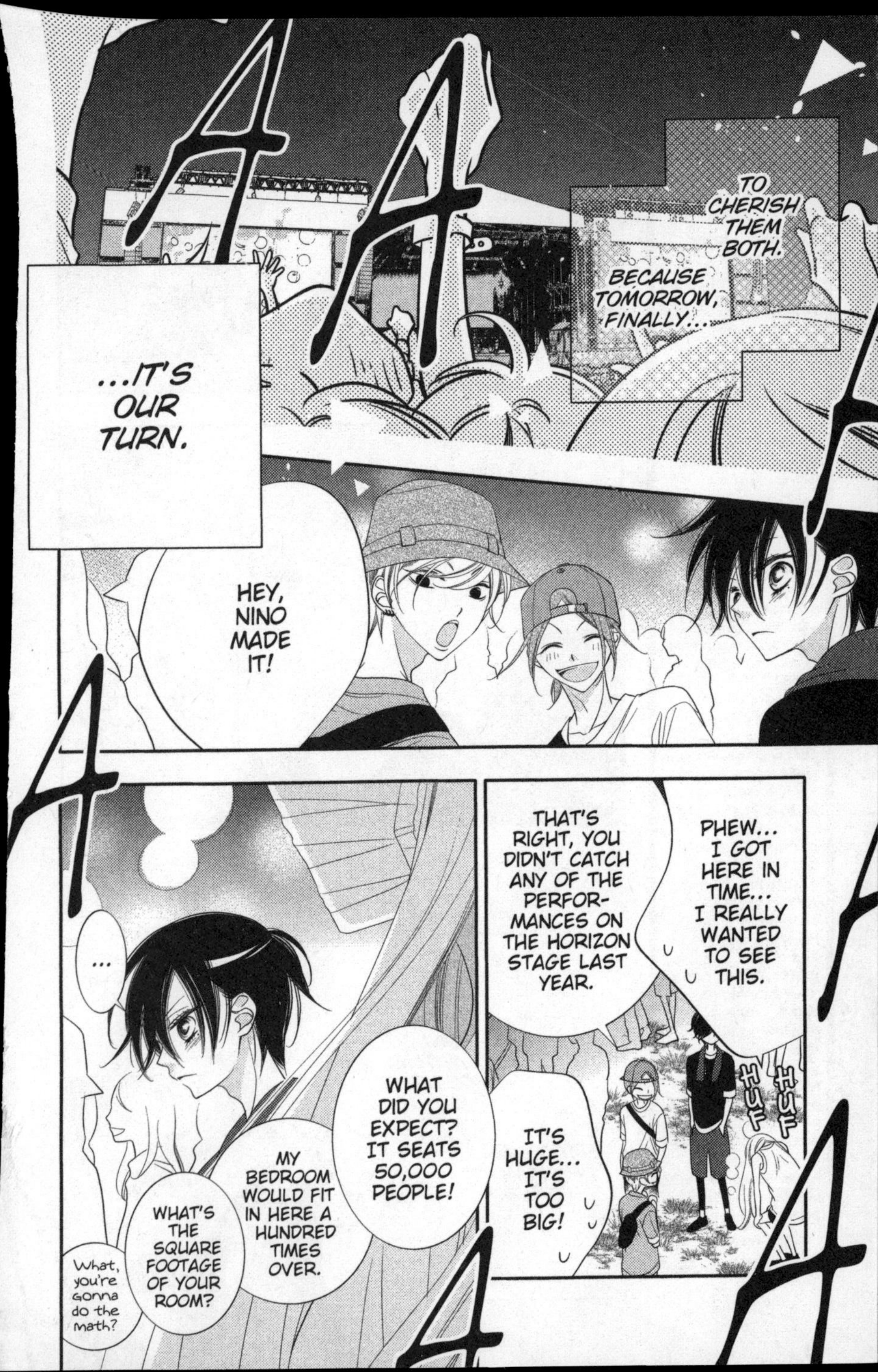
TO CHERISH THEM BOTH.
BECAUSE TOMORROW, FINALLY...
...IT'S OUR TURN.
HEY, NINO MADE IT!
PHEW... I GOT HERE IN TIME... I REALLY WANTED TO SEE THIS.
THAT'S RIGHT, YOU DIDN'T CATCH ANY OF THE PERFOR-MANCES ON THE HORIZON STAGE LAST YEAR.
HUF HUF
IT'S HUGE... IT'S TOO BIG!
...
WHAT DID YOU EXPECT? IT SEATS 50,000 PEOPLE!
MY BEDROOM WOULD FIT IN HERE A HUNDRED TIMES OVER.
WHAT'S THE SQUARE FOOTAGE OF YOUR ROOM?
What, you're gonna do the math?

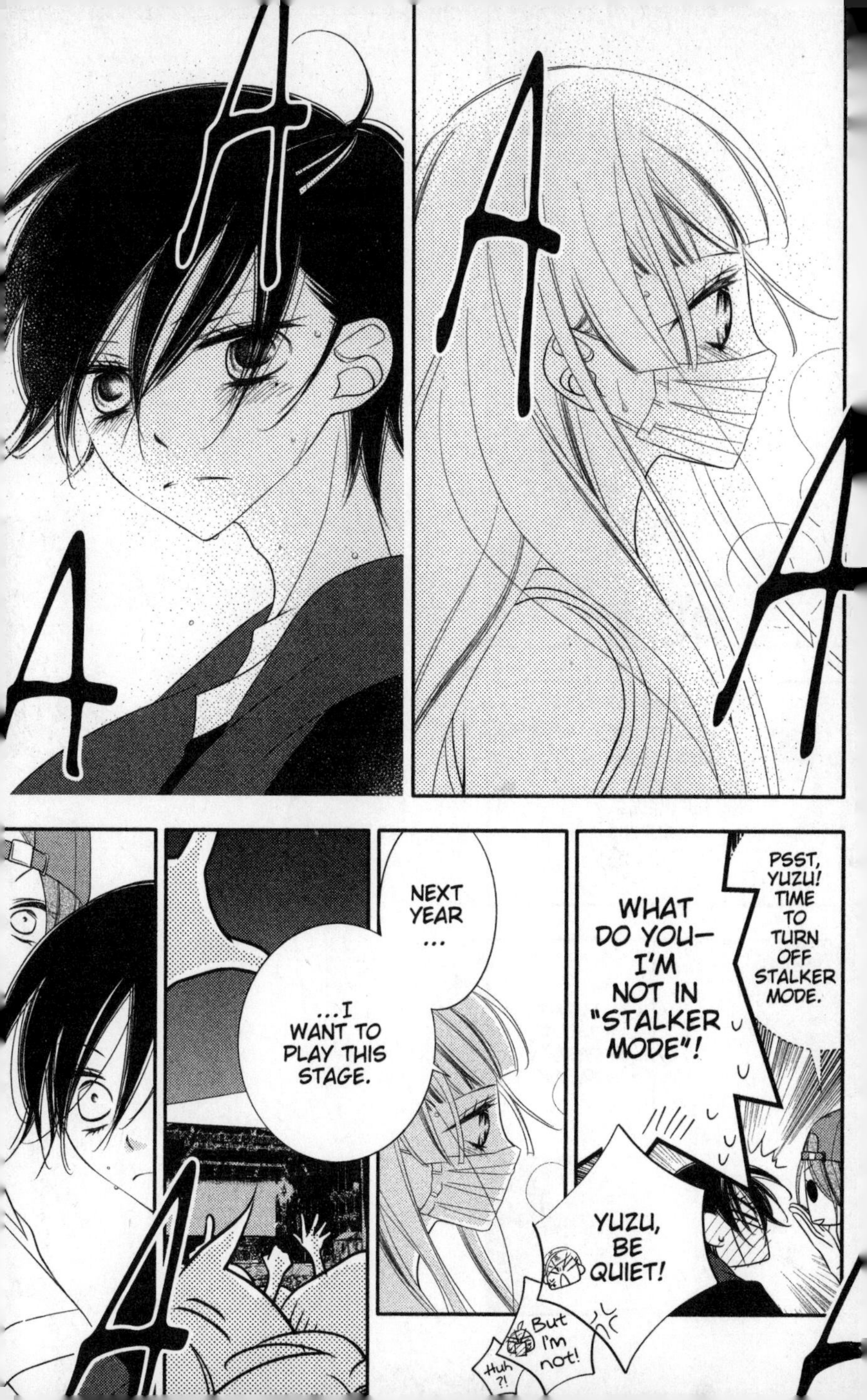

AAAA
PSST, YUZU! TIME TO TURN OFF STALKER MODE.
WHAT DO YOU— I'M NOT IN "STALKER MODE"!
YUZU, BE QUIET!
But I'm not!
Huh ?!
NEXT YEAR...
...I WANT TO PLAY THIS STAGE.

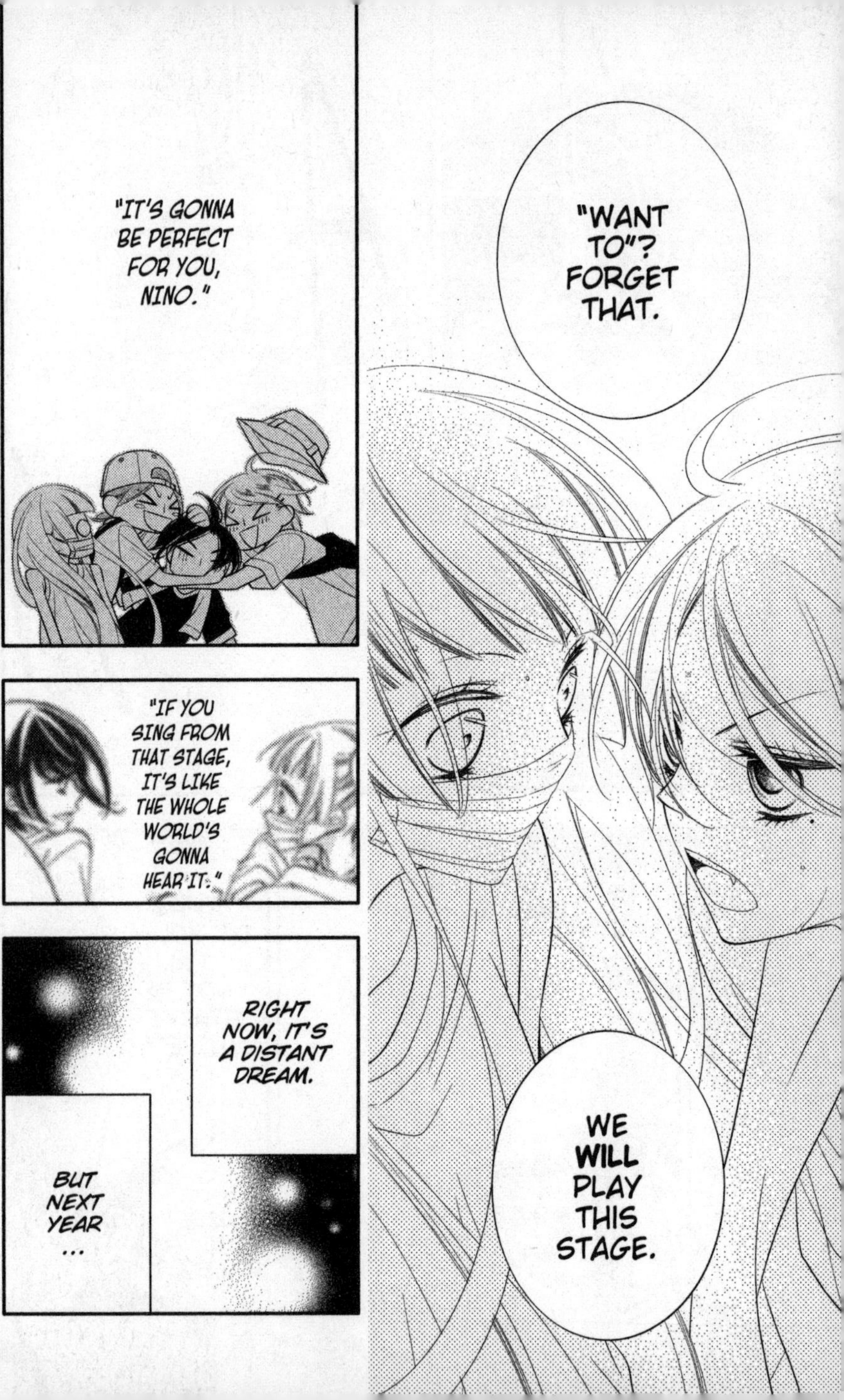
"WANT TO"? FORGET THAT.
WE WILL PLAY THIS STAGE.
"IT'S GONNA BE PERFECT FOR YOU, NINO."
"IF YOU SING FROM THAT STAGE, IT'S LIKE THE WHOLE WORLD'S GONNA HEAR IT."
RIGHT NOW, IT'S A DISTANT DREAM.
BUT NEXT YEAR ...

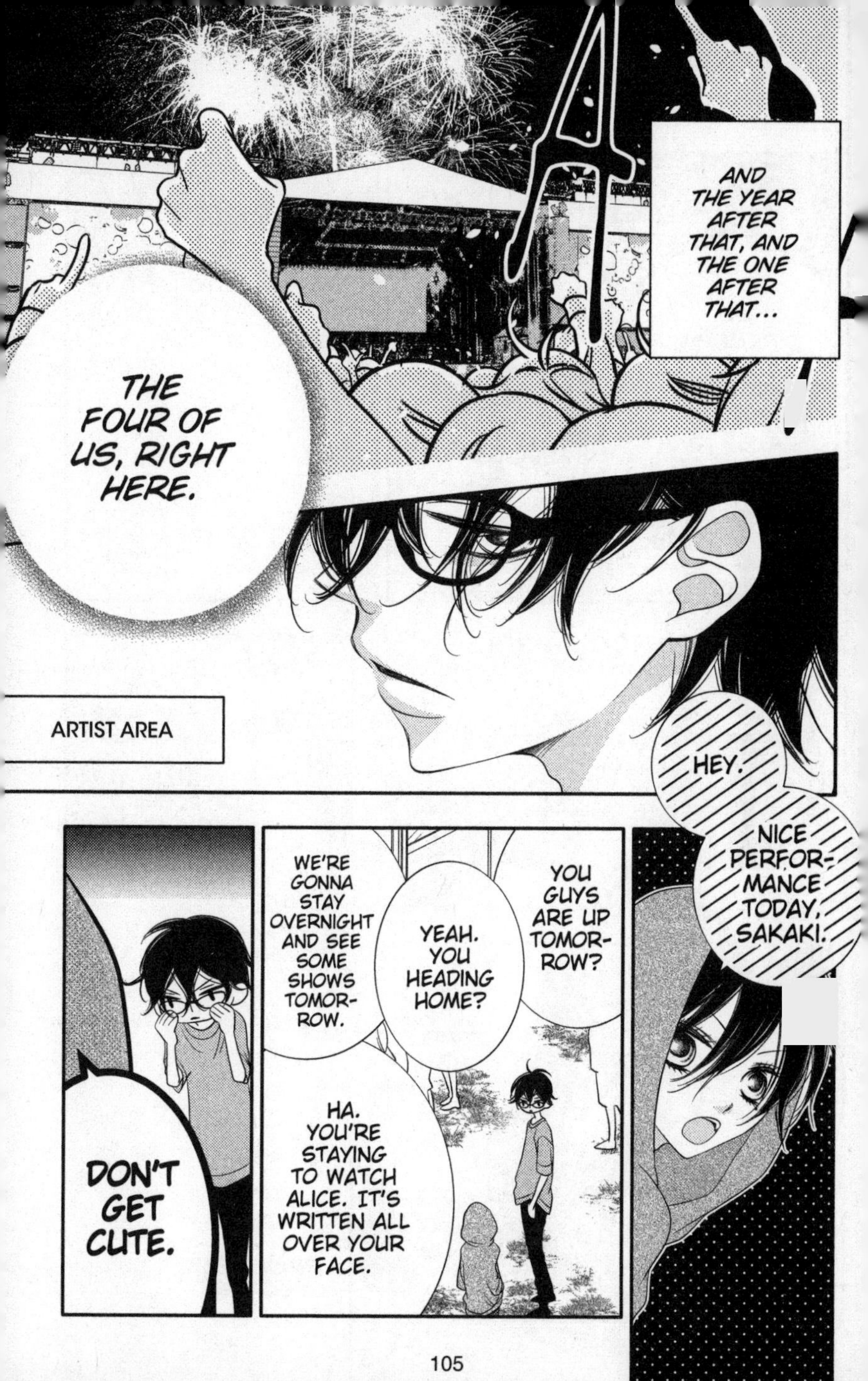
AND THE YEAR AFTER THAT, AND THE ONE AFTER THAT...
THE FOUR OF US, RIGHT HERE.
ARTIST AREA
HEY.
NICE PERFORMANCE TODAY, SAKAKI.
YOU GUYS ARE UP TOMORROW?
YEAH. YOU HEADING HOME?
WE'RE GONNA STAY OVERNIGHT AND SEE SOME SHOWS TOMORROW.
HA. YOU'RE STAYING TO WATCH ALICE. IT'S WRITTEN ALL OVER YOUR FACE.
DON'T GET CUTE.

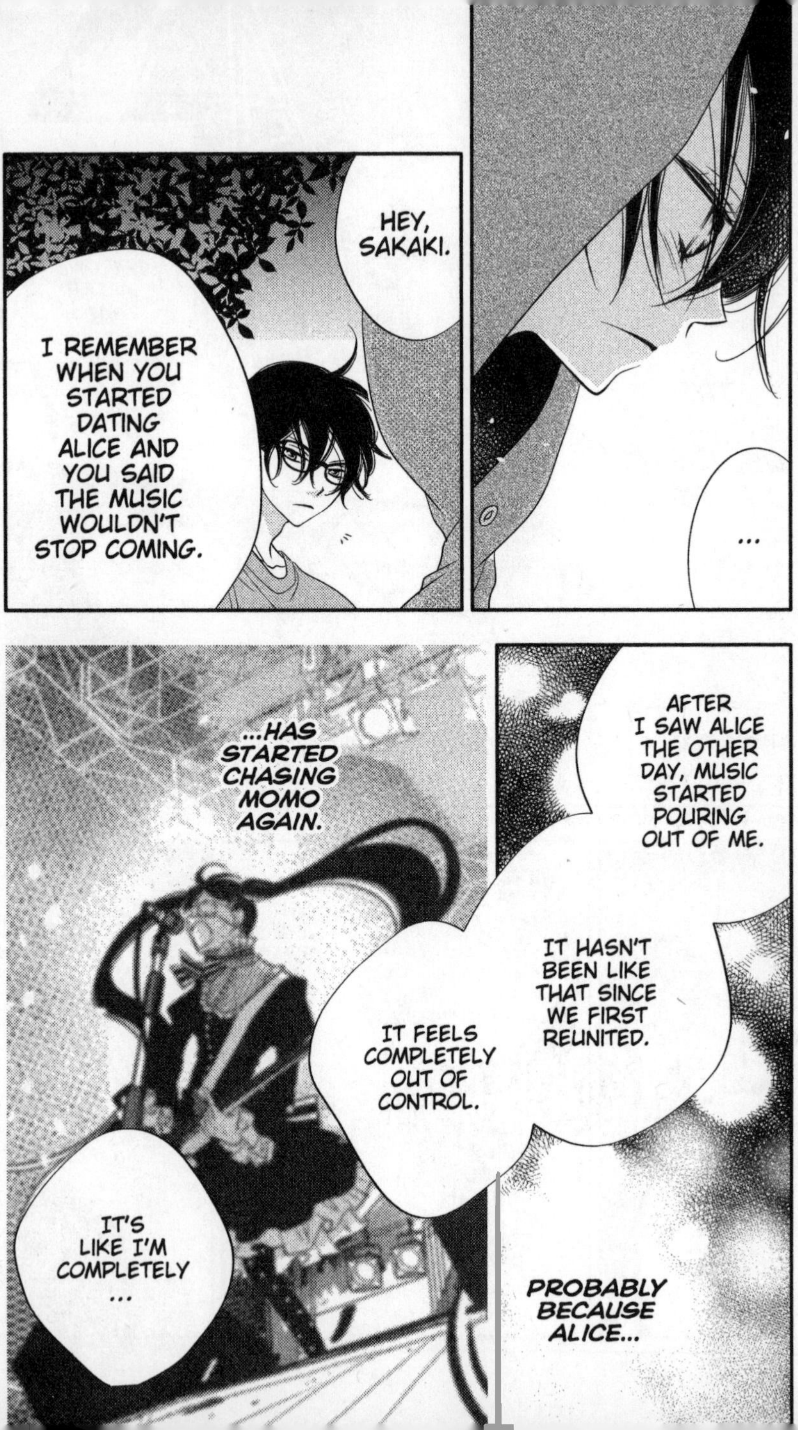
...
HEY, SAKAKI.
I REMEMBER WHEN YOU STARTED DATING ALICE AND YOU SAID THE MUSIC WOULDN'T STOP COMING.
AFTER I SAW ALICE THE OTHER DAY, MUSIC STARTED POURING OUT OF ME.
IT HASN'T BEEN LIKE THAT SINCE WE FIRST REUNITED.
IT FEELS COMPLETELY OUT OF CONTROL.
PROBABLY BECAUSE ALICE...
...HAS STARTED CHASING MOMO AGAIN.
IT'S LIKE I'M COMPLETELY ...

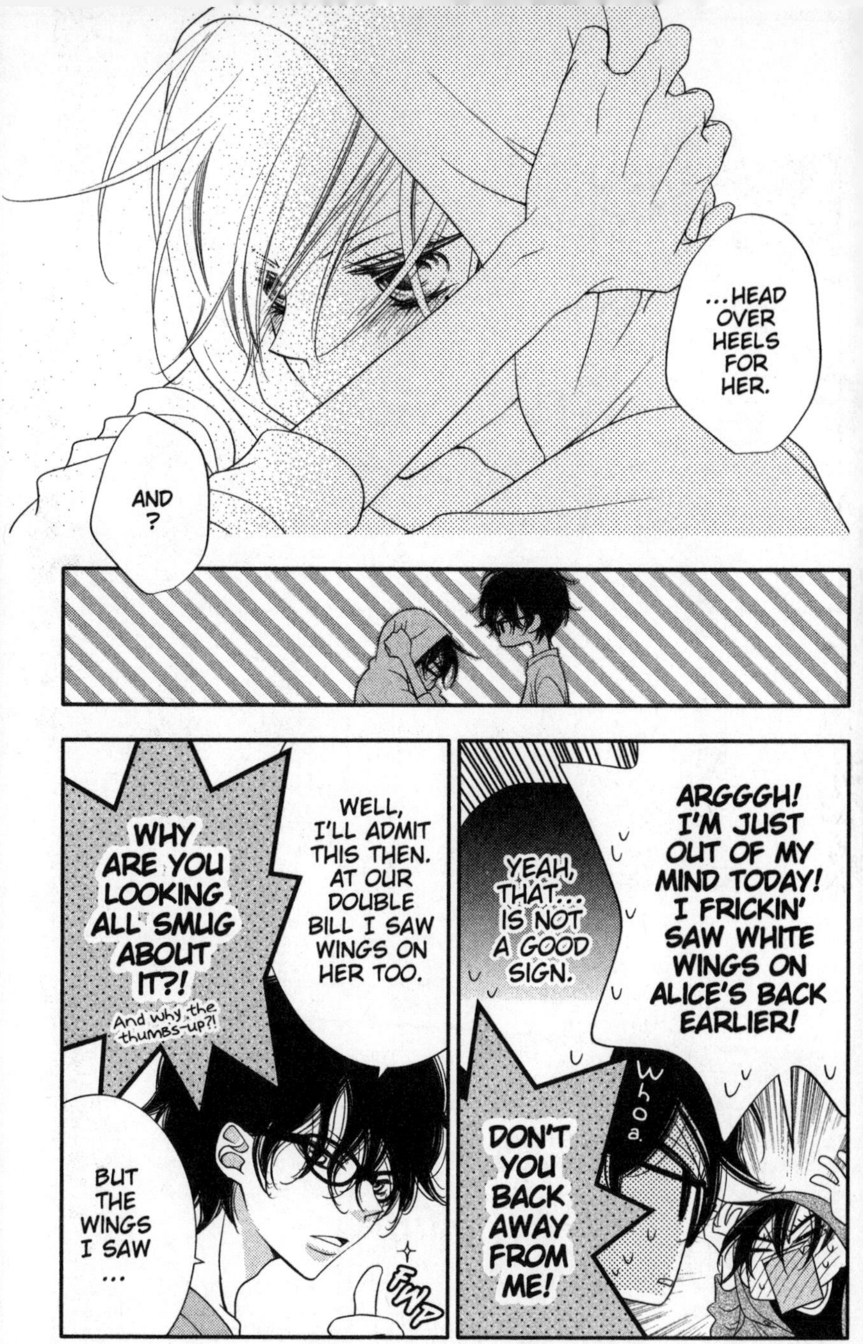
...HEAD OVER HEELS FOR HER.
AND ?
ARGGGH! I'M JUST OUT OF MY MIND TODAY! I FRICKIN' SAW WHITE WINGS ON ALICE'S BACK EARLIER!
YEAH, THAT... IS NOT A GOOD SIGN.
Whoa.
DON'T YOU BACK AWAY FROM ME!
WELL, I'LL ADMIT THIS THEN. AT OUR DOUBLE BILL I SAW WINGS ON HER TOO.
WHY ARE YOU LOOKING ALL SMUG ABOUT IT?!
And why the thumbs-up?!
FWP
BUT THE WINGS I SAW ...

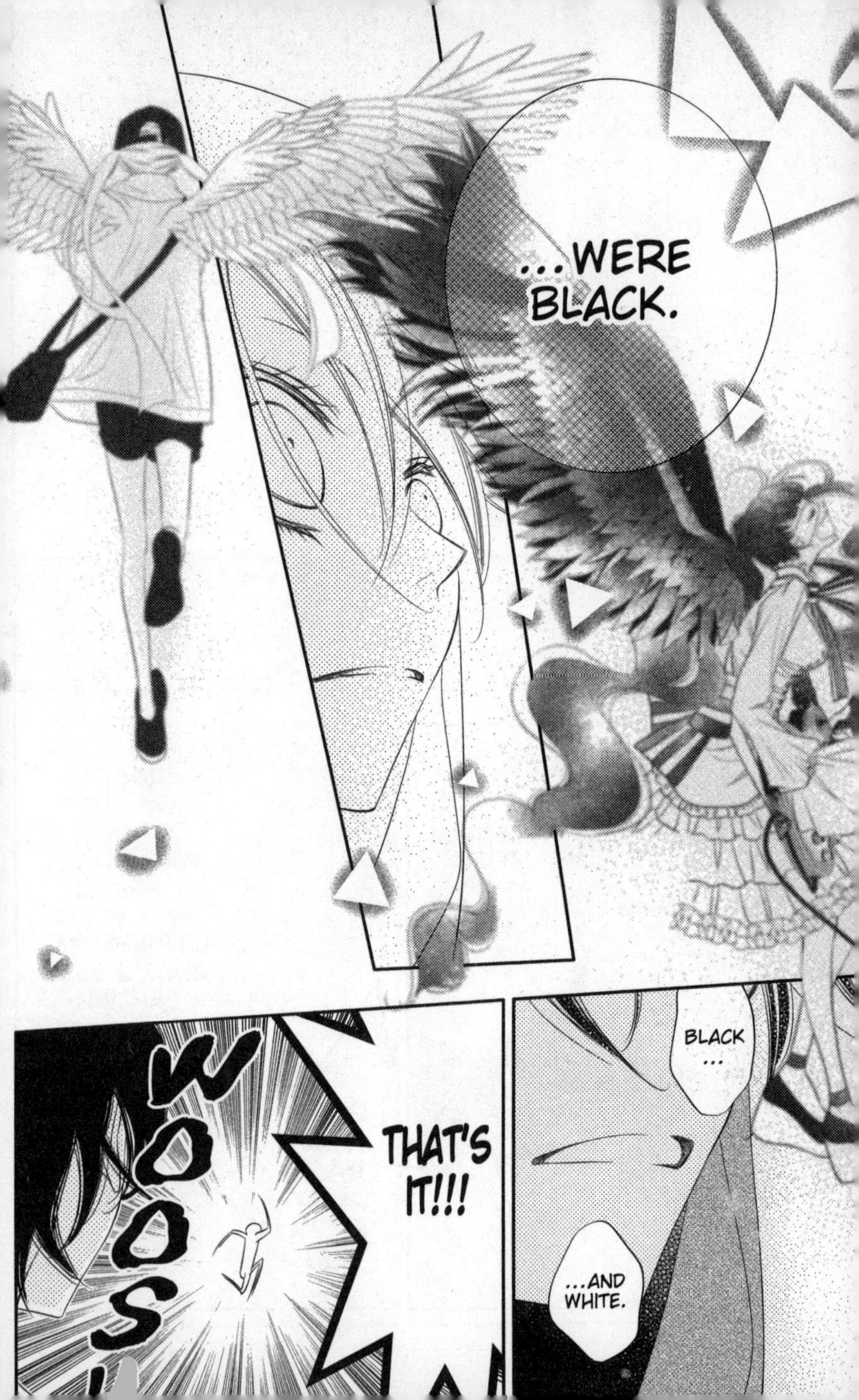
...WERE BLACK.
BLACK...
...AND WHITE.
THAT'S IT!!!
WOOOS

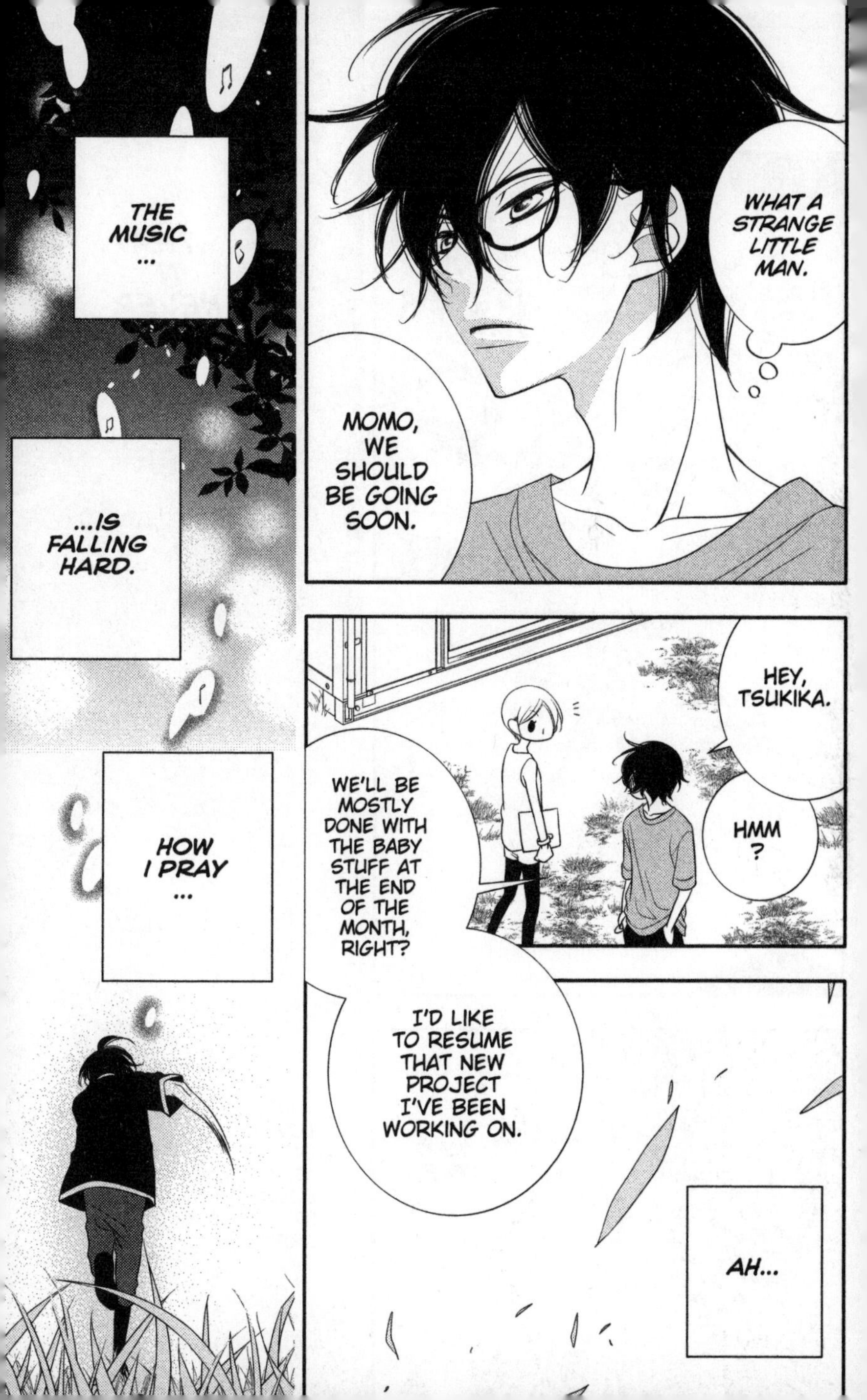
WHAT A STRANGE LITTLE MAN.
MOMO, WE SHOULD BE GOING SOON.
HEY, TSUKIKA.
HMM?
WE'LL BE MOSTLY DONE WITH THE BABY STUFF AT THE END OF THE MONTH, RIGHT?
I'D LIKE TO RESUME THAT NEW PROJECT I'VE BEEN WORKING ON.
AH...
THE MUSIC...
...IS FALLING HARD.
HOW I PRAY...

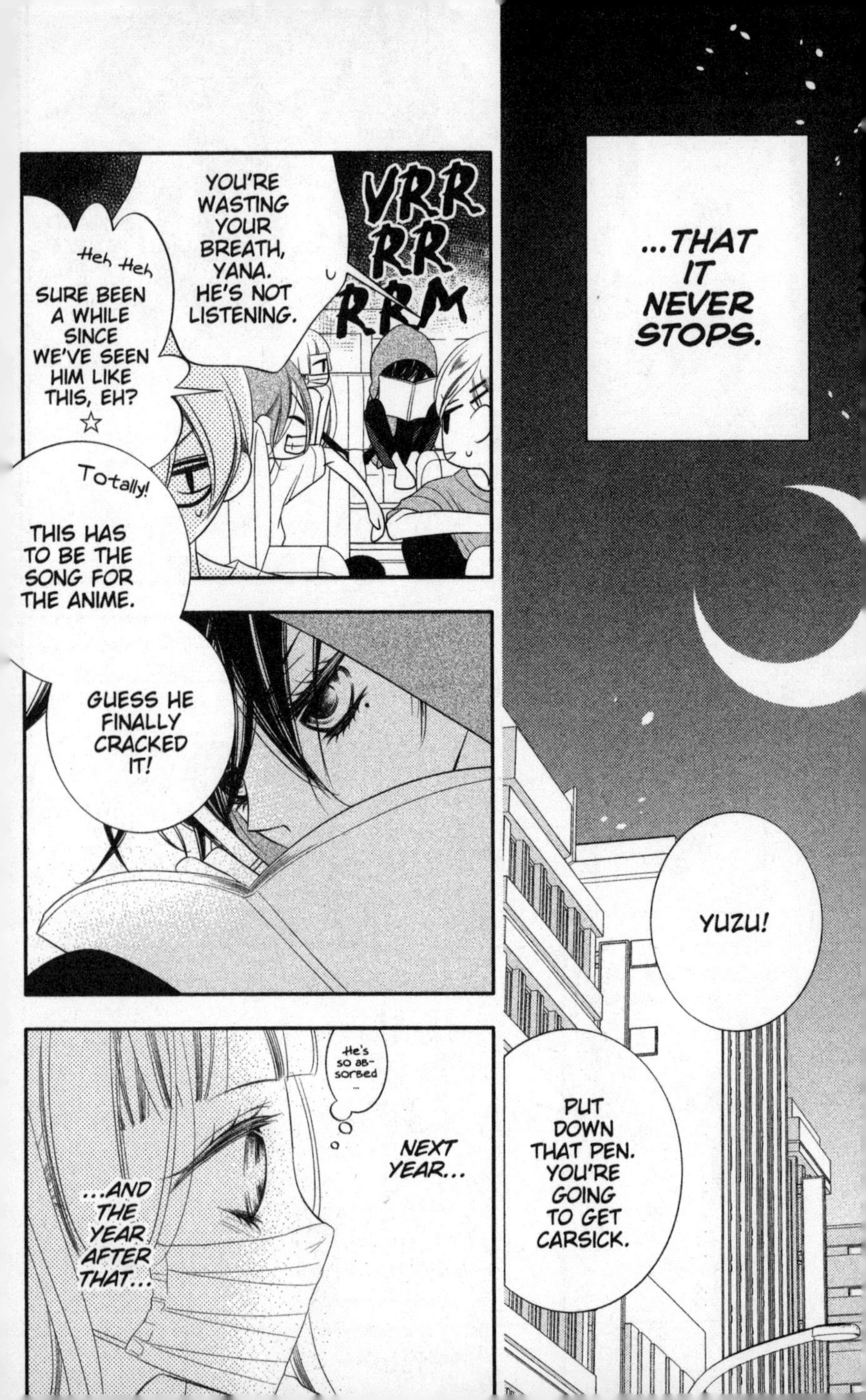
...THAT IT NEVER STOPS.
YUZU!
PUT DOWN THAT PEN. YOU'RE GOING TO GET CARSICK.
VRRRRRRRM
YOU'RE WASTING YOUR BREATH, YANA. HE'S NOT LISTENING.
Heh Heh SURE BEEN A WHILE SINCE WE'VE SEEN HIM LIKE THIS, EH? ☆
Totally! THIS HAS TO BE THE SONG FOR THE ANIME.
GUESS HE FINALLY CRACKED IT!
He's so absorbed...
NEXT YEAR...
...AND THE YEAR AFTER THAT...

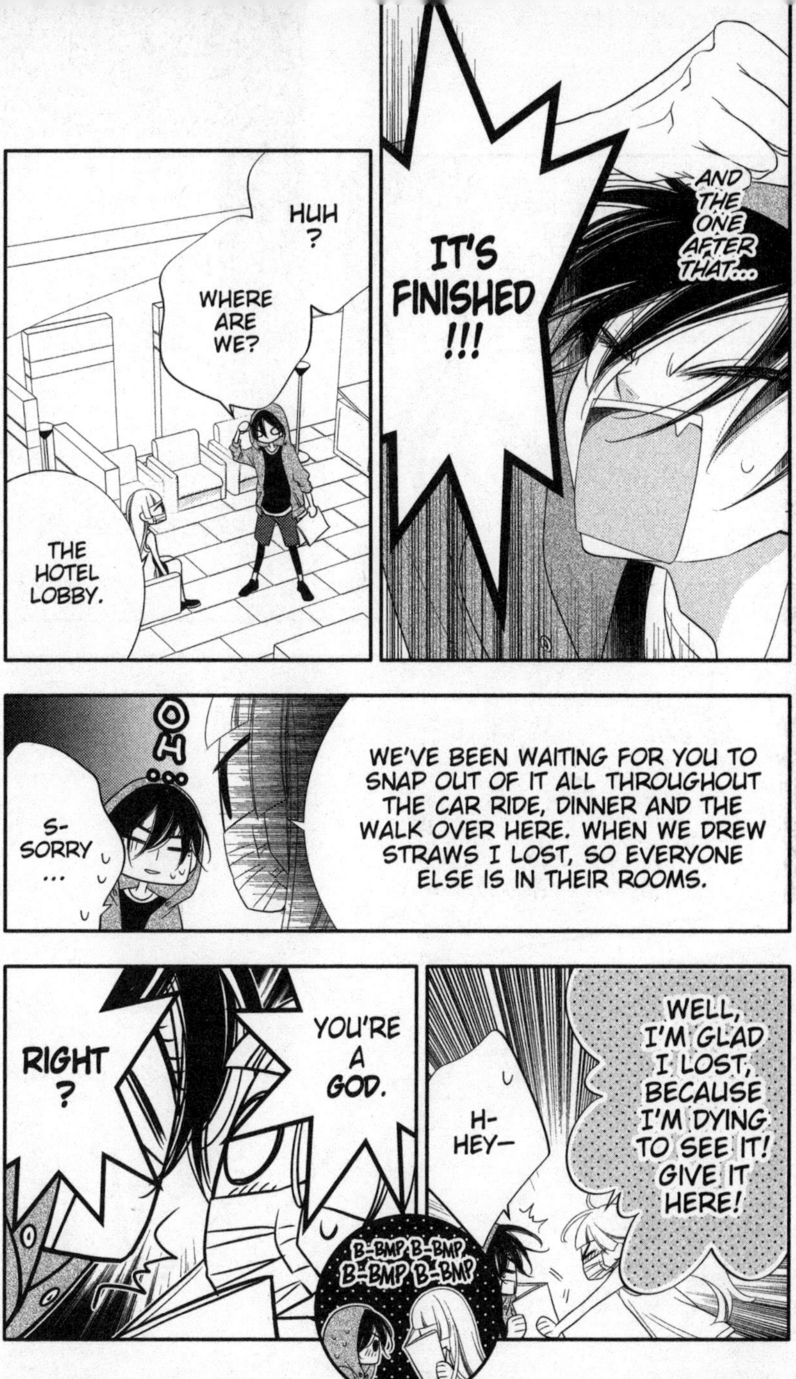
AND THE ONE AFTER THAT...
IT'S FINISHED!!!
HUH?
WHERE ARE WE?
THE HOTEL LOBBY.
WE'VE BEEN WAITING FOR YOU TO SNAP OUT OF IT ALL THROUGHOUT THE CAR RIDE, DINNER AND THE WALK OVER HERE. WHEN WE DREW STRAWS I LOST, SO EVERYONE ELSE IS IN THEIR ROOMS.
OH...
S-SORRY...
WELL, I'M GLAD I LOST, BECAUSE I'M DYING TO SEE IT! GIVE IT HERE!
H-HEY—
B-BMP B-BMP B-BMP B-BMP
YOU'RE A GOD.
RIGHT?

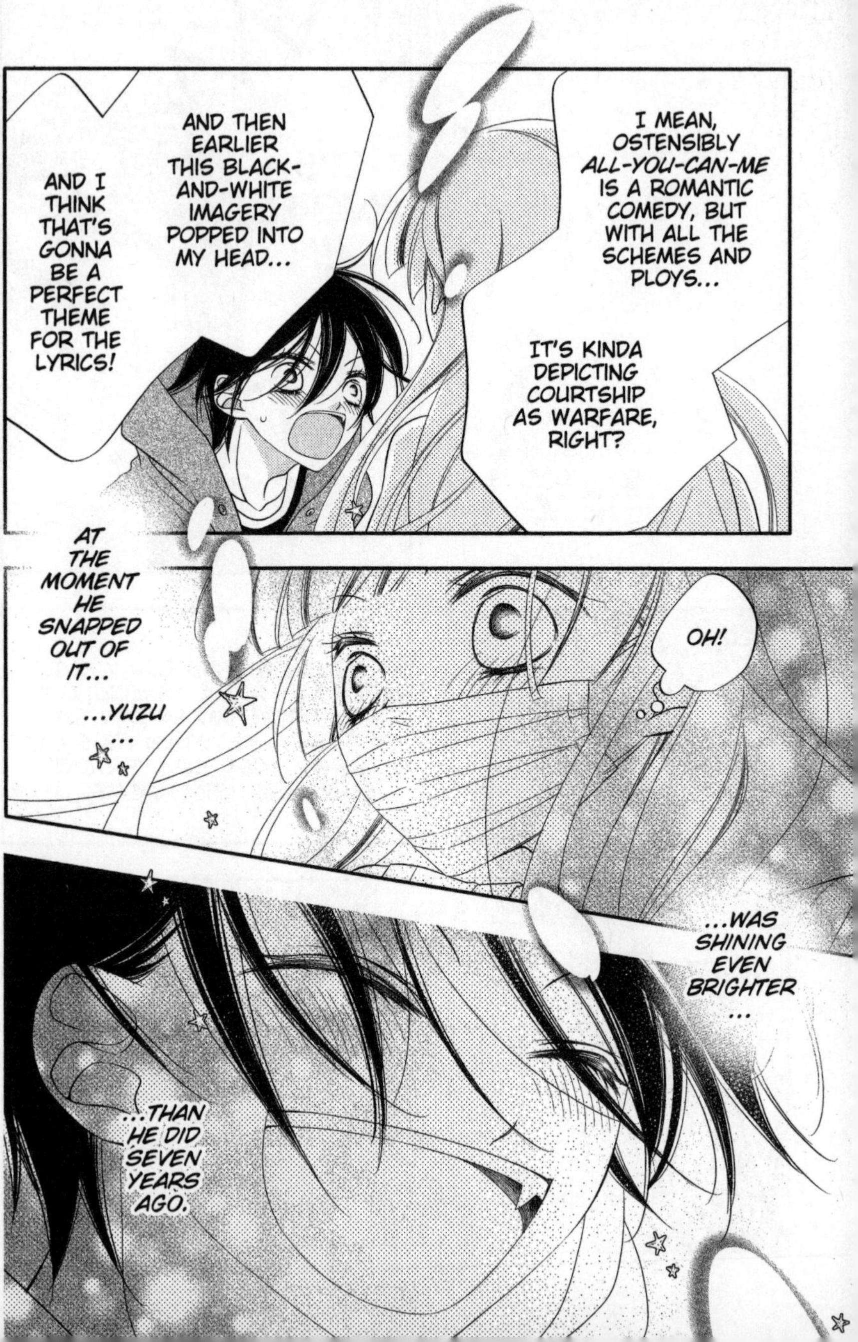

I MEAN, OSTENSIBLY ALL-YOU-CAN-ME IS A ROMANTIC COMEDY, BUT WITH ALL THE SCHEMES AND PLOYS...
IT'S KINDA DEPICTING COURTSHIP AS WARFARE, RIGHT?
AND THEN EARLIER THIS BLACK-AND-WHITE IMAGERY POPPED INTO MY HEAD...
AND I THINK THAT'S GONNA BE A PERFECT THEME FOR THE LYRICS!
OH!
AT THE MOMENT HE SNAPPED OUT OF IT...
...YUZU...
...WAS SHINING EVEN BRIGHTER...
...THAN HE DID SEVEN YEARS AGO.

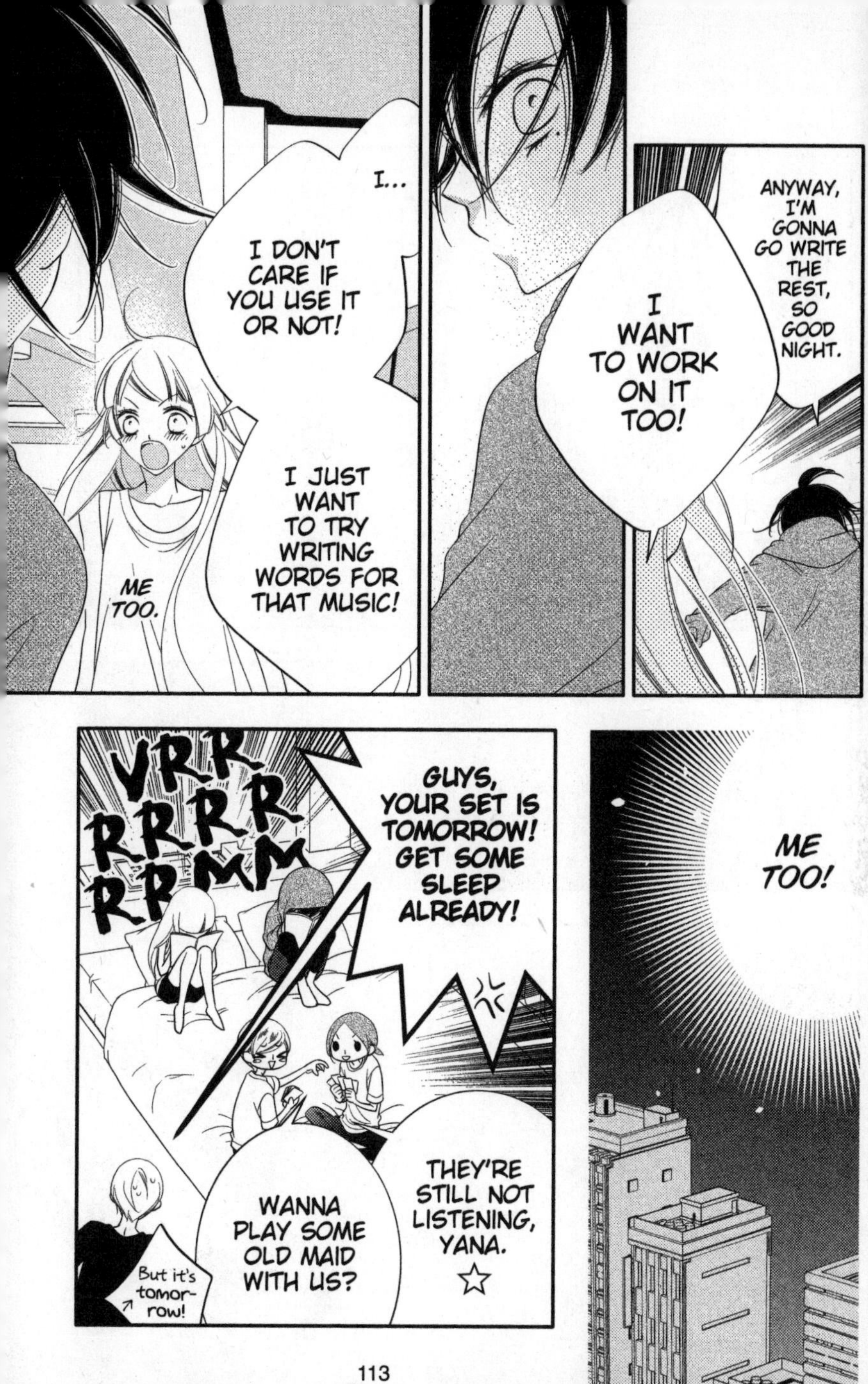
ANYWAY, I'M GONNA GO WRITE THE REST, SO GOOD NIGHT.
I WANT TO WORK ON IT TOO!
I...
I DON'T CARE IF YOU USE IT OR NOT!
I JUST WANT TO TRY WRITING WORDS FOR THAT MUSIC!
ME TOO.
ME TOO!
VRRRRRRRRMM
GUYS, YOUR SET IS TOMORROW! GET SOME SLEEP ALREADY!
THEY'RE STILL NOT LISTENING, YANA. ☆
WANNA PLAY SOME OLD MAID WITH US?
But it's tomorrow!

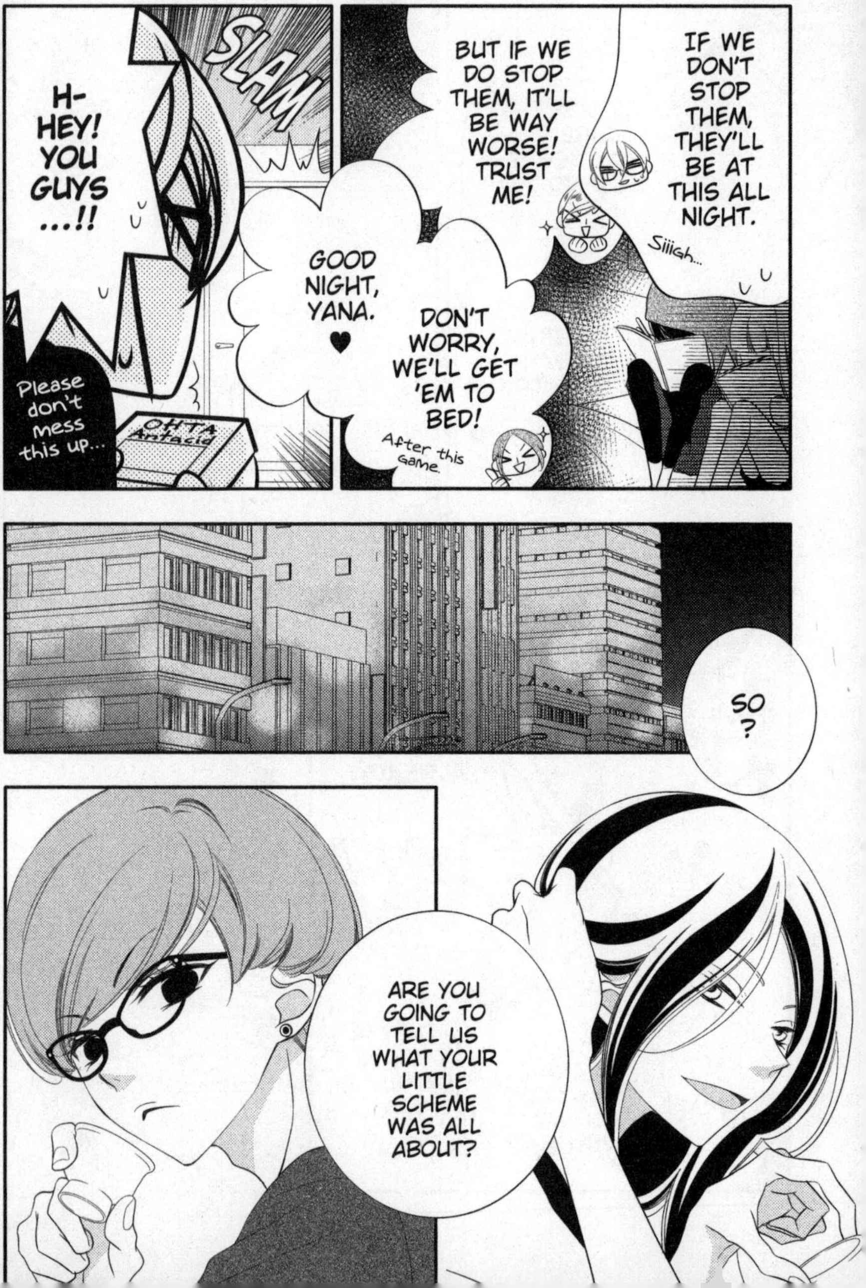
IF WE DON'T STOP THEM, THEY'LL BE AT THIS ALL NIGHT.
Siiigh...
BUT IF WE DO STOP THEM, IT'LL BE WAY WORSE! TRUST ME!
DON'T WORRY, WE'LL GET 'EM TO BED!
After this game.
GOOD NIGHT, YANA. ♥
SLAM
H-HEY! YOU GUYS ...!!
Please don't mess this up...
OHTA Antacid
SO?
ARE YOU GOING TO TELL US WHAT YOUR LITTLE SCHEME WAS ALL ABOUT?

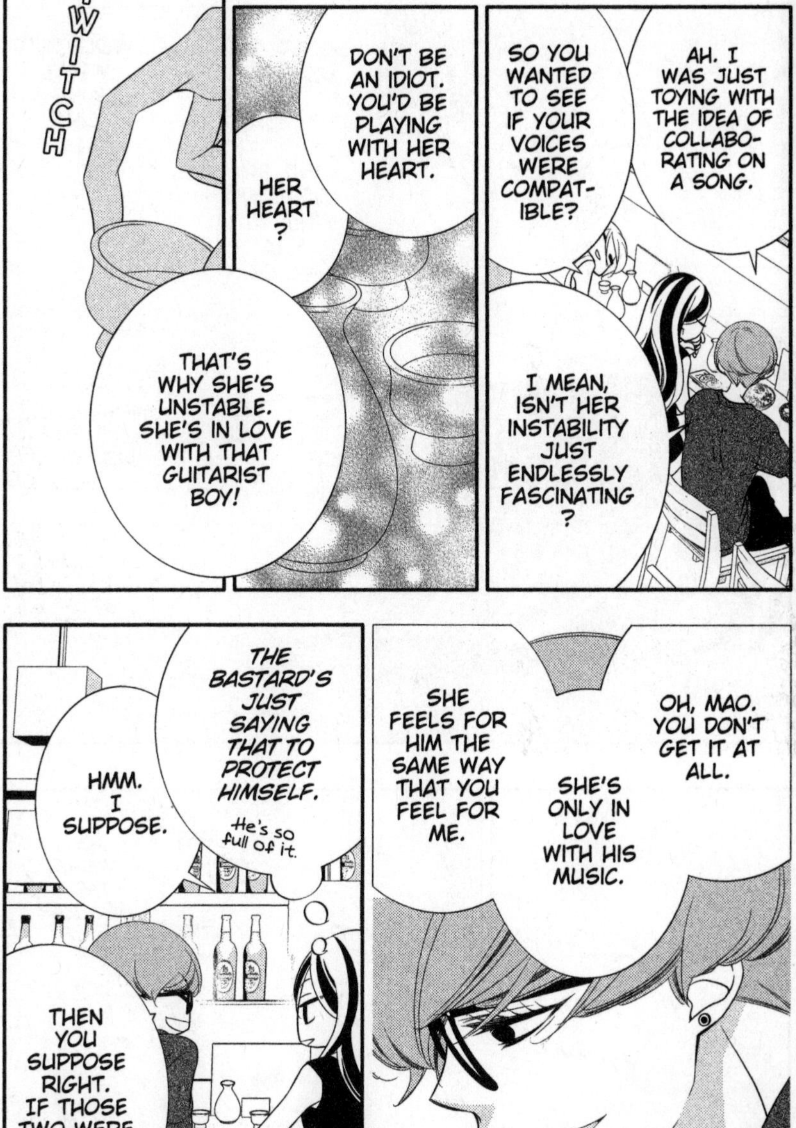
AH. I WAS JUST TOYING WITH THE IDEA OF COLLABO-RATING ON A SONG.
SO YOU WANTED TO SEE IF YOUR VOICES WERE COMPAT-IBLE?
I MEAN, ISN'T HER INSTABILITY JUST ENDLESSLY FASCINATING?
DON'T BE AN IDIOT. YOU'D BE PLAYING WITH HER HEART.
HER HEART?
TWITCH
THAT'S WHY SHE'S UNSTABLE. SHE'S IN LOVE WITH THAT GUITARIST BOY!
OH, MAO. YOU DON'T GET IT AT ALL.
SHE'S ONLY IN LOVE WITH HIS MUSIC.
SHE FEELS FOR HIM THE SAME WAY THAT YOU FEEL FOR ME.
THE BASTARD'S JUST SAYING THAT TO PROTECT HIMSELF.
He's so full of it.
HMM. I SUPPOSE.
THEN YOU SUPPOSE RIGHT. IF THOSE TWO WERE IN LOVE...

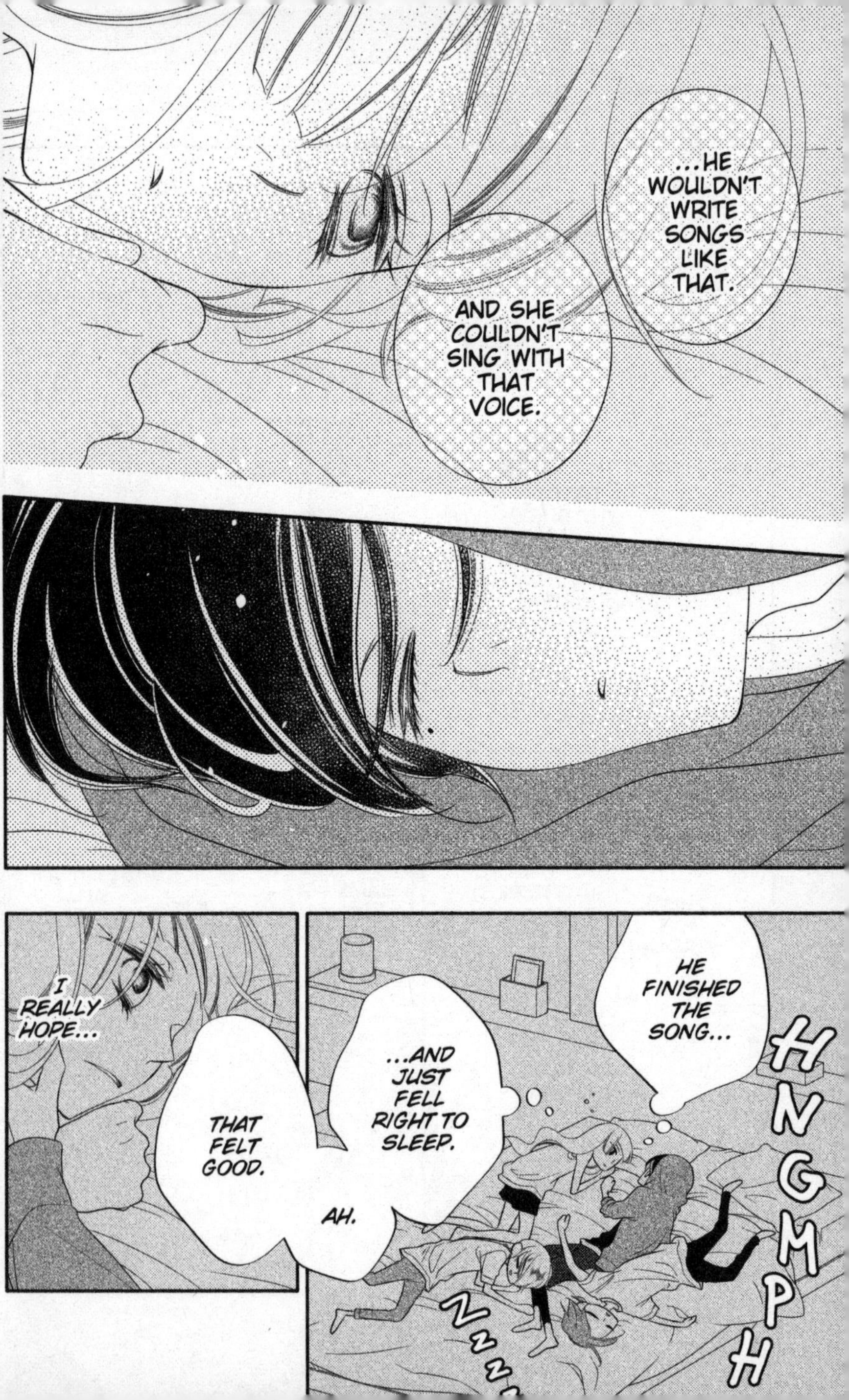
...HE WOULDN'T WRITE SONGS LIKE THAT.
AND SHE COULDN'T SING WITH THAT VOICE.
HE FINISHED THE SONG...
HNGMPH
...AND JUST FELL RIGHT TO SLEEP.
ZZZ
AH.
THAT FELT GOOD.
I REALLY HOPE...

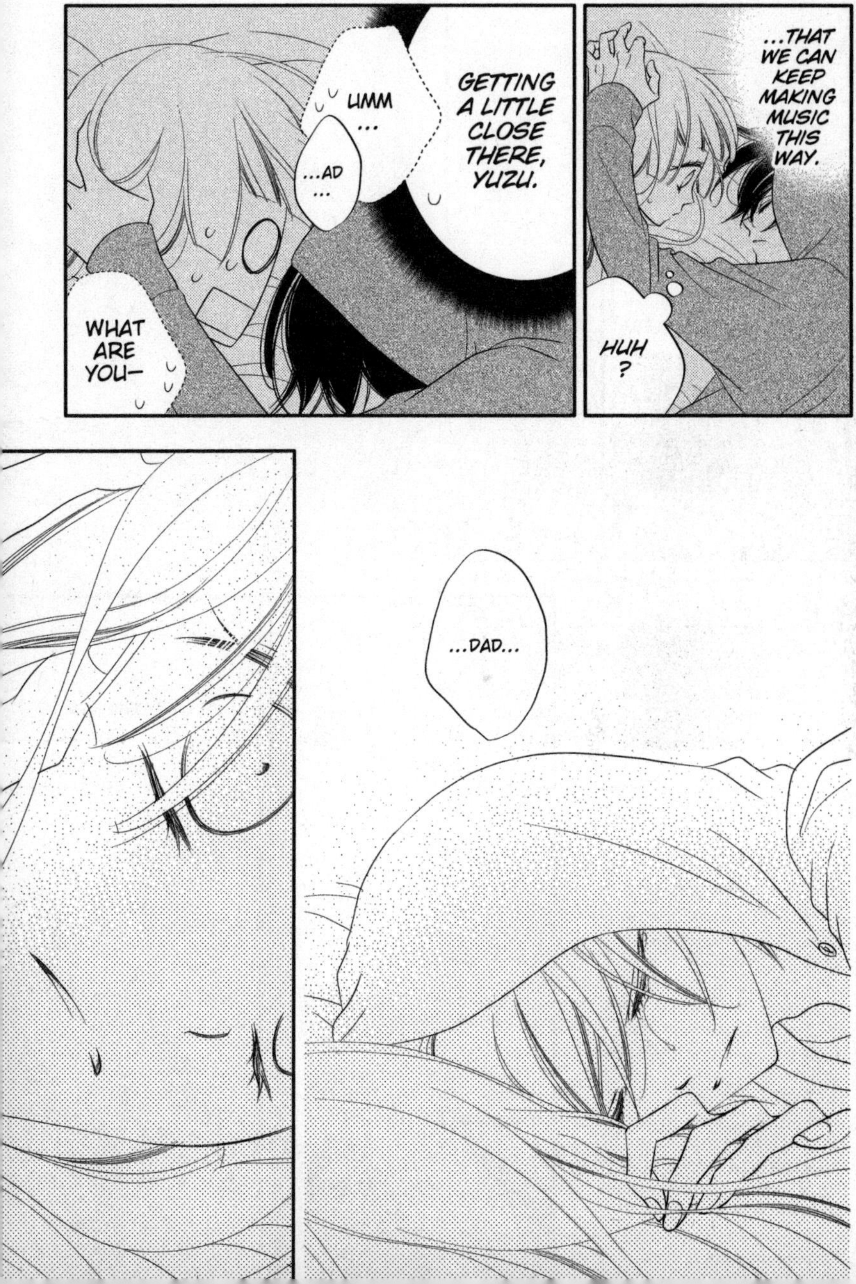
...THAT WE CAN KEEP MAKING MUSIC THIS WAY.
HUH?
GETTING A LITTLE CLOSE THERE, YUZU.
UMM ...
...AD ...
WHAT ARE YOU—
...DAD...

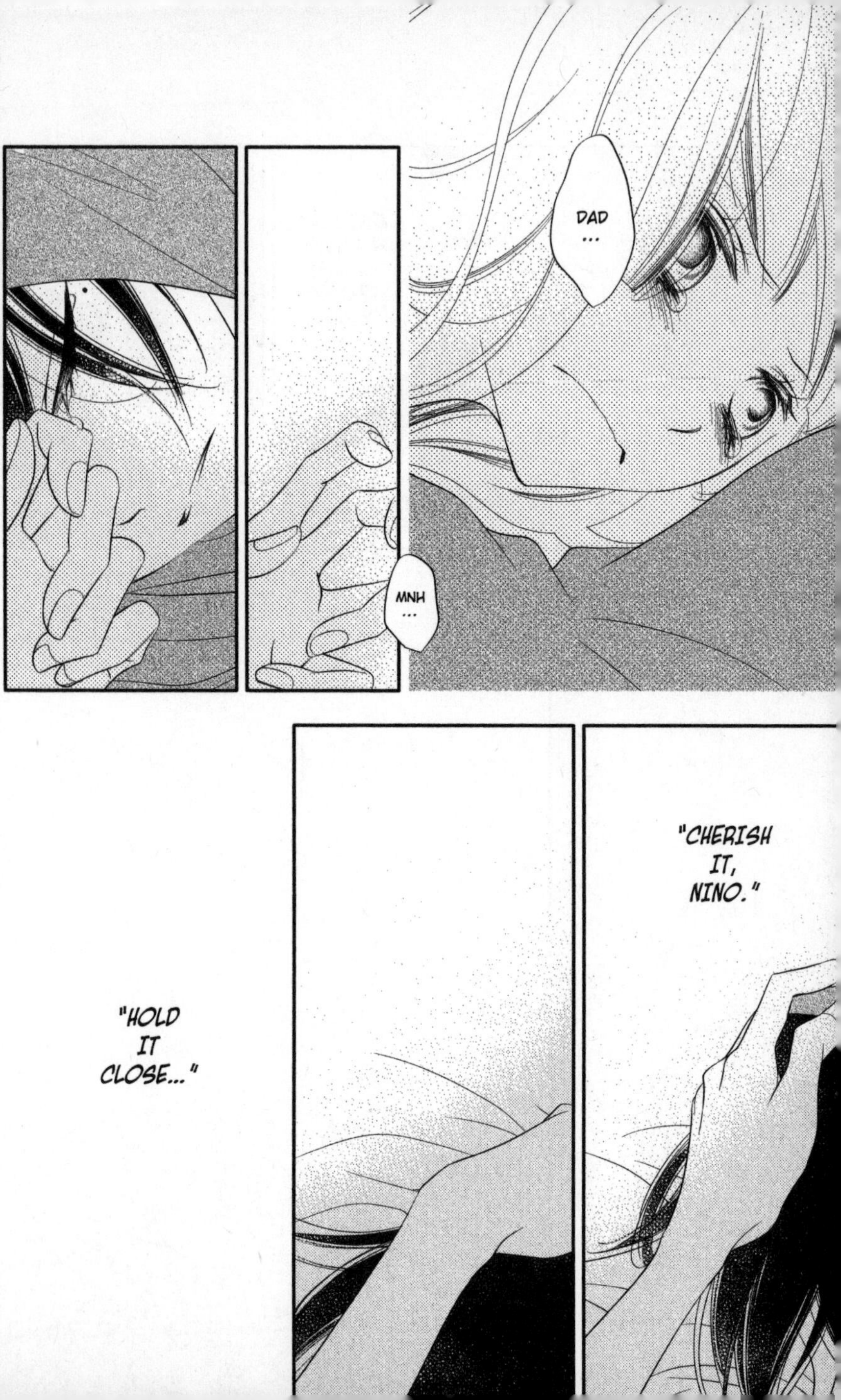
DAD...
MNH...
"CHERISH IT, NINO."
"HOLD IT CLOSE..."

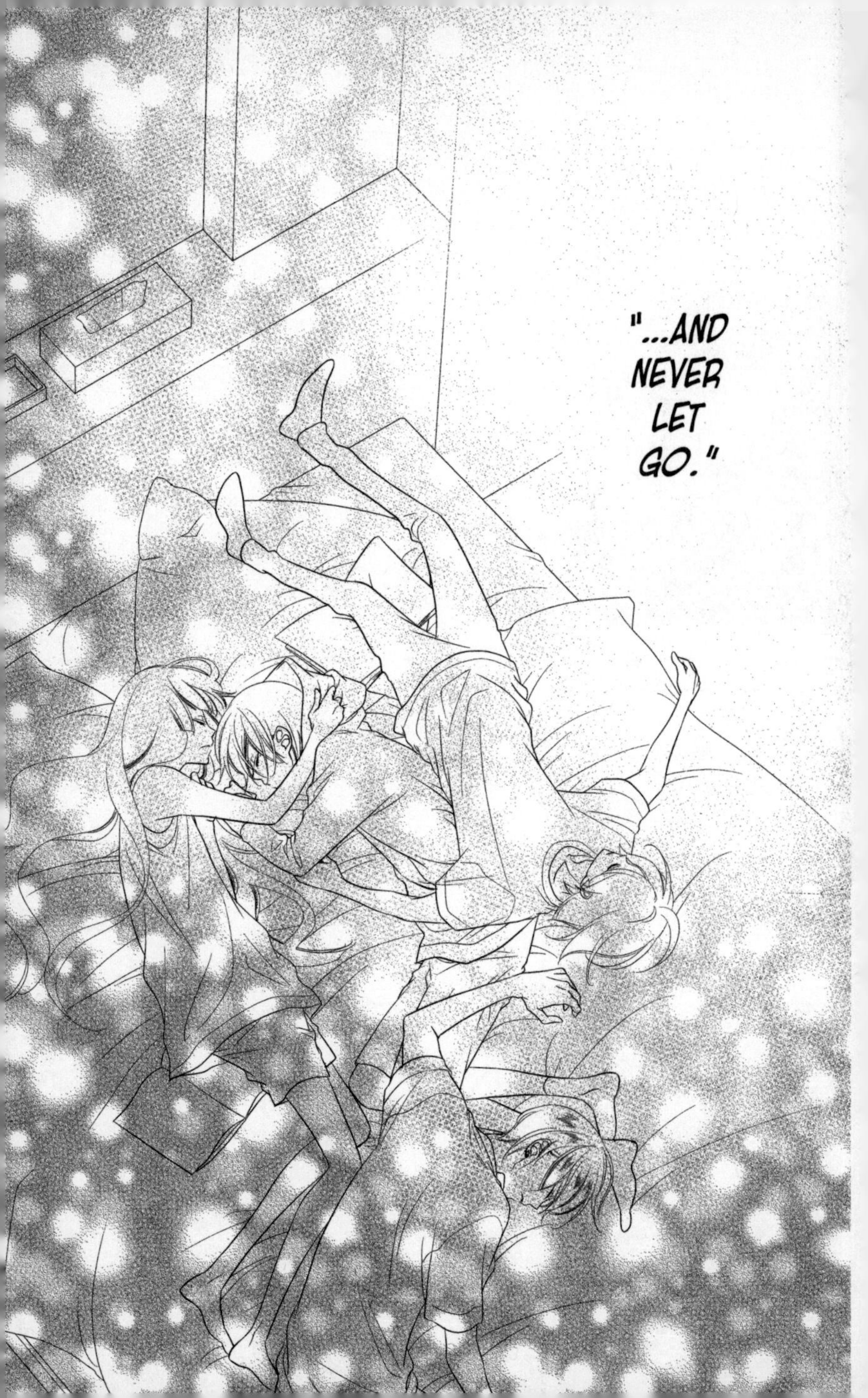
"...AND NEVER LET GO."

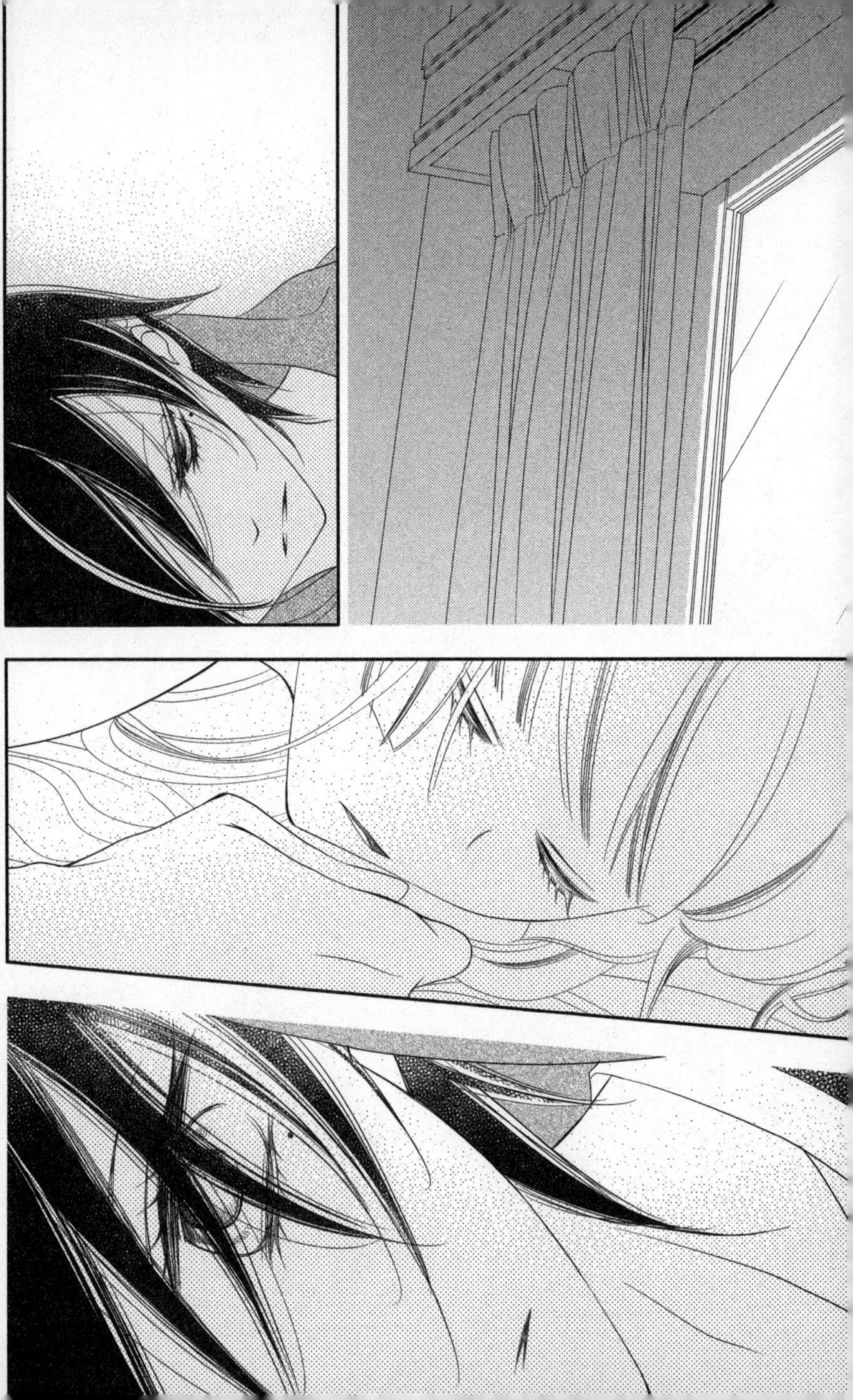

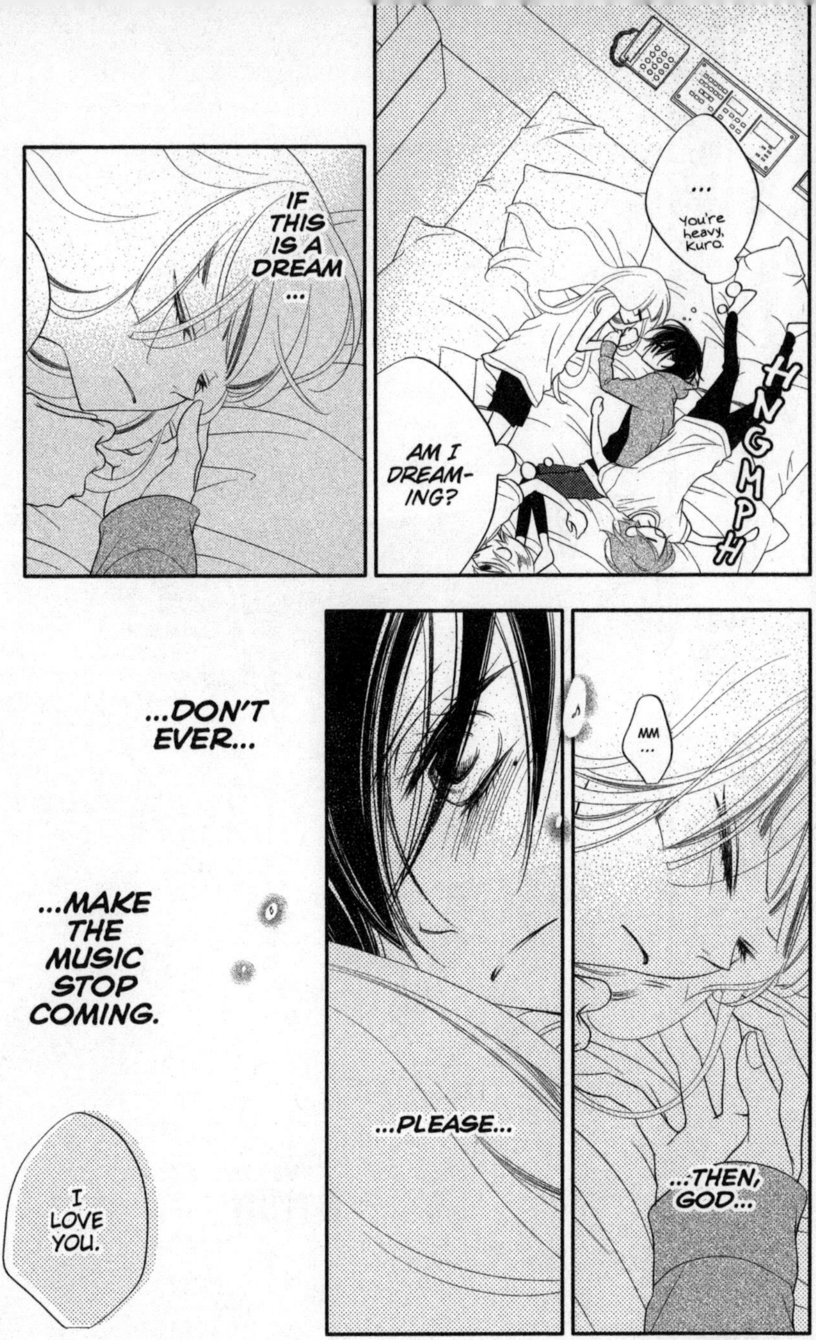
...
You're heavy, Kuro.
HNGMPH
AM I DREAMING?
IF THIS IS A DREAM...
MM...
...THEN, GOD...
...PLEASE...
...DON'T EVER...
...MAKE THE MUSIC STOP COMING.
I LOVE YOU.

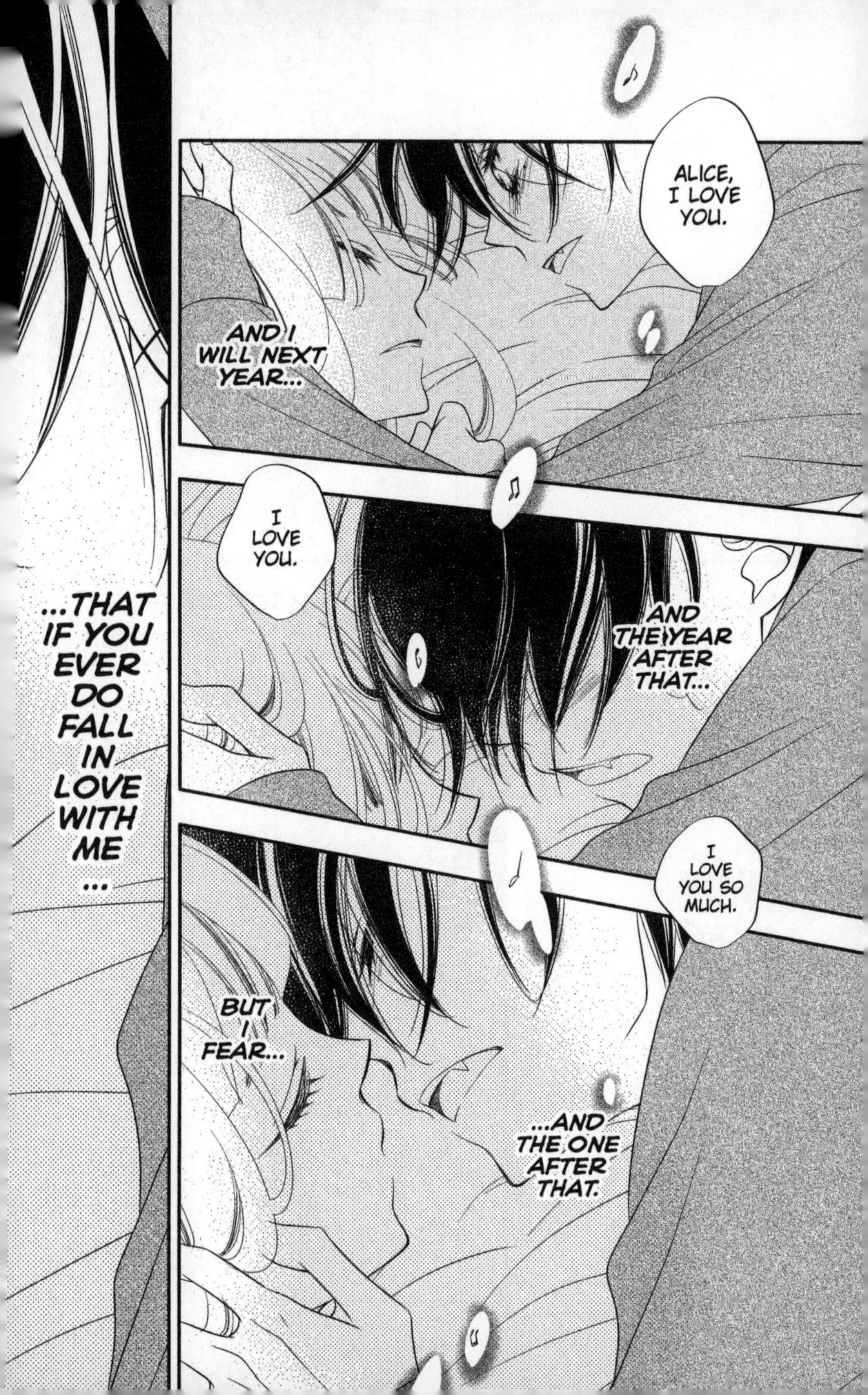
ALICE, I LOVE YOU.
AND I WILL NEXT YEAR...
I LOVE YOU.
AND THE YEAR AFTER THAT...
I LOVE YOU SO MUCH.
...AND THE ONE AFTER THAT.
BUT I FEAR...
...THAT IF YOU EVER DO FALL IN LOVE WITH ME...

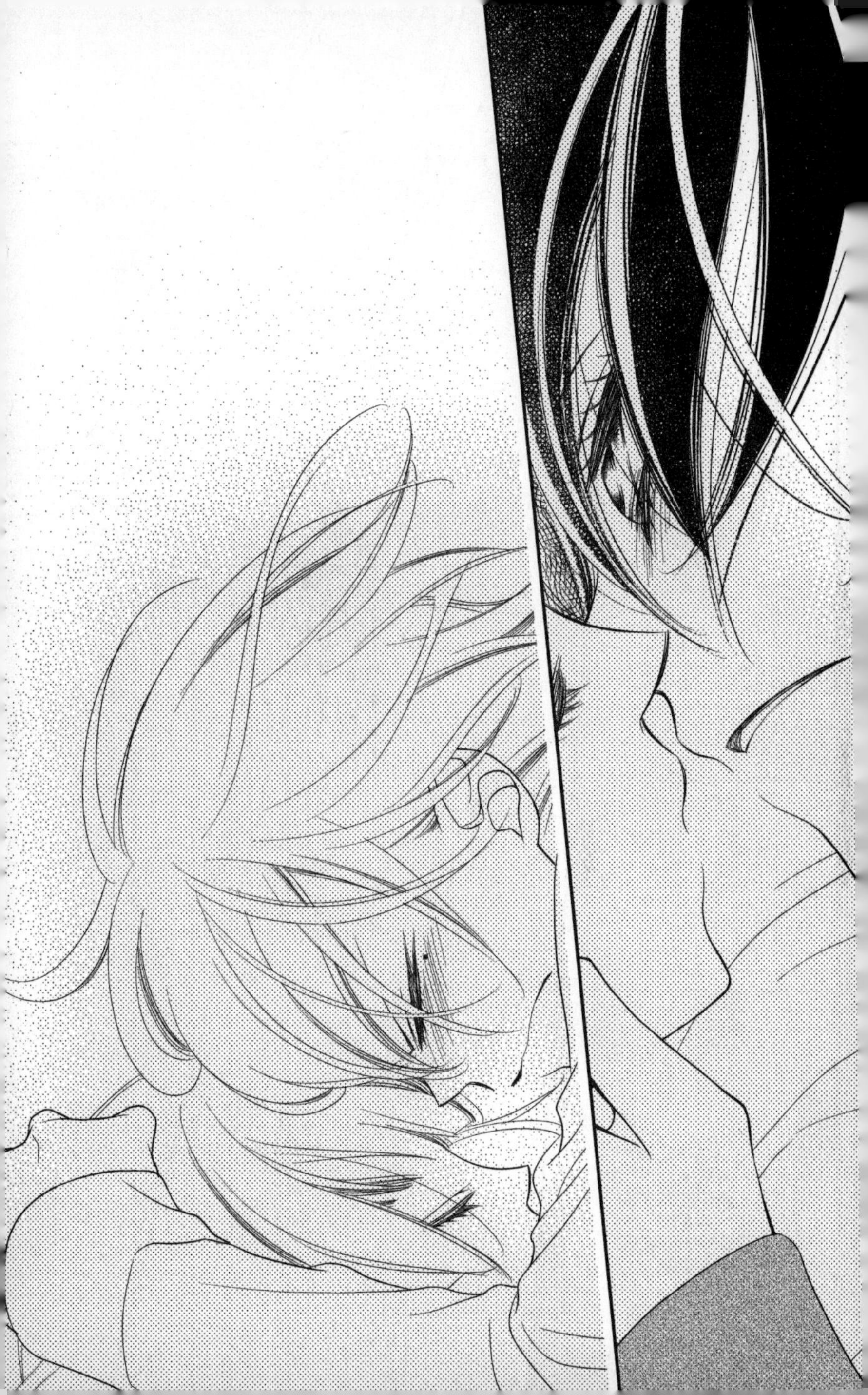

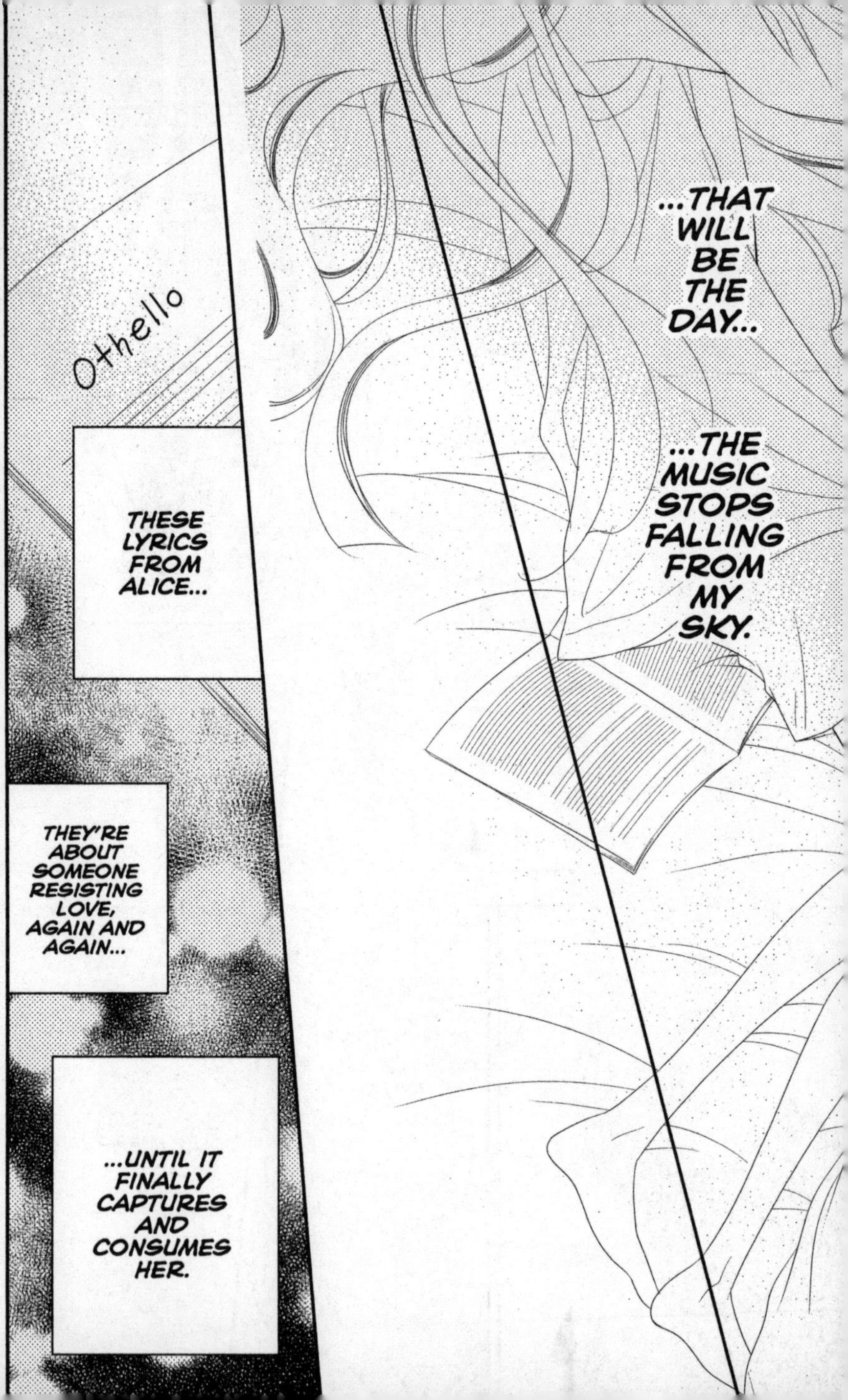
...THAT WILL BE THE DAY...
...THE MUSIC STOPS FALLING FROM MY SKY.
Othello
THESE LYRICS FROM ALICE...
THEY'RE ABOUT SOMEONE RESISTING LOVE, AGAIN AND AGAIN...
...UNTIL IT FINALLY CAPTURES AND CONSUMES HER.

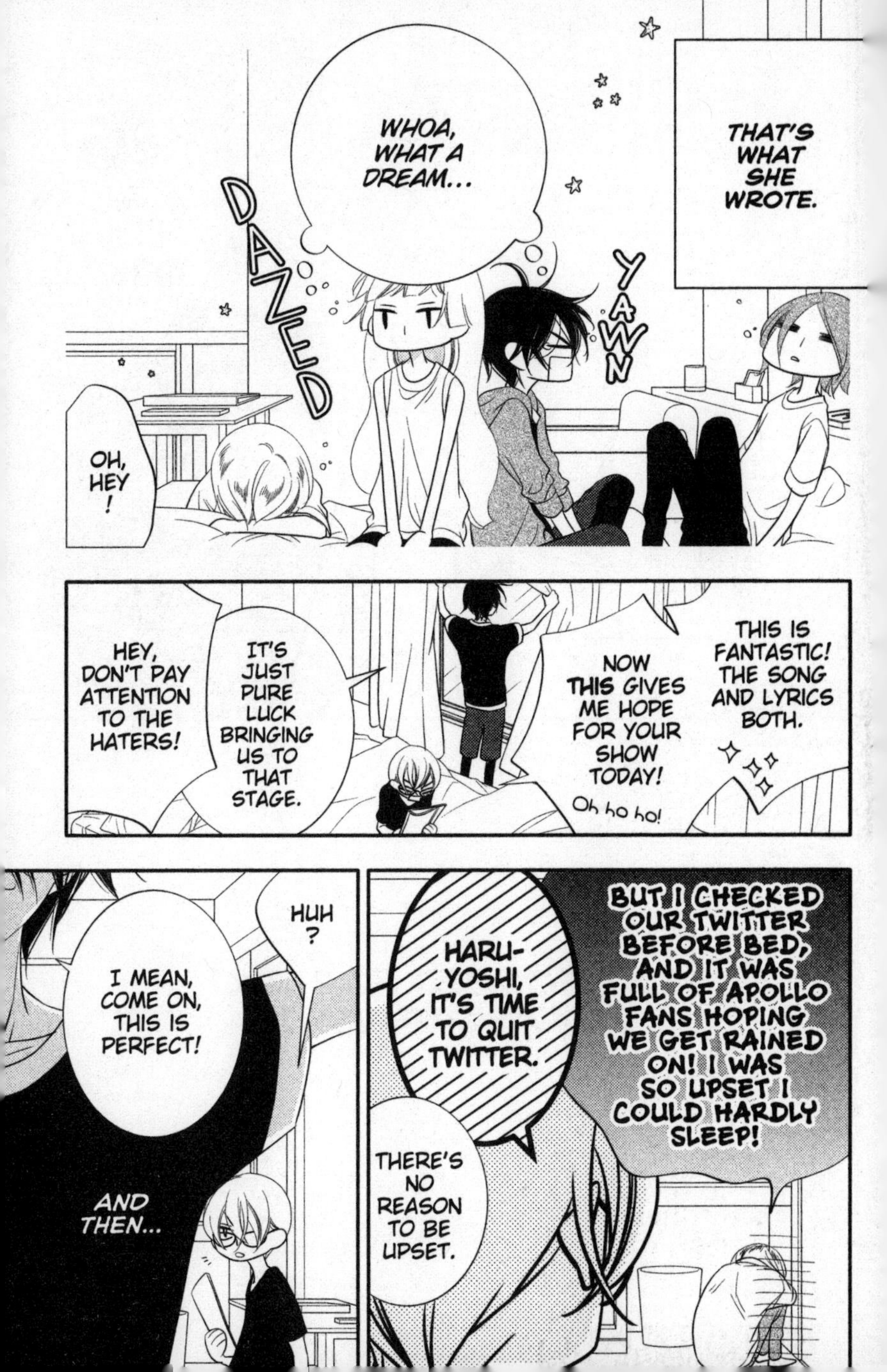
THAT'S WHAT SHE WROTE.
YAWN
WHOA, WHAT A DREAM...
DAZED
OH, HEY!
THIS IS FANTASTIC! THE SONG AND LYRICS BOTH.
NOW THIS GIVES ME HOPE FOR YOUR SHOW TODAY!
Oh ho ho!
IT'S JUST PURE LUCK BRINGING US TO THAT STAGE.
HEY, DON'T PAY ATTENTION TO THE HATERS!
BUT I CHECKED OUR TWITTER BEFORE BED, AND IT WAS FULL OF APOLLO FANS HOPING WE GET RAINED ON! I WAS SO UPSET I COULD HARDLY SLEEP!
HARU-YOSHI, IT'S TIME TO QUIT TWITTER.
THERE'S NO REASON TO BE UPSET.
HUH?
I MEAN, COME ON, THIS IS PERFECT!
AND THEN...

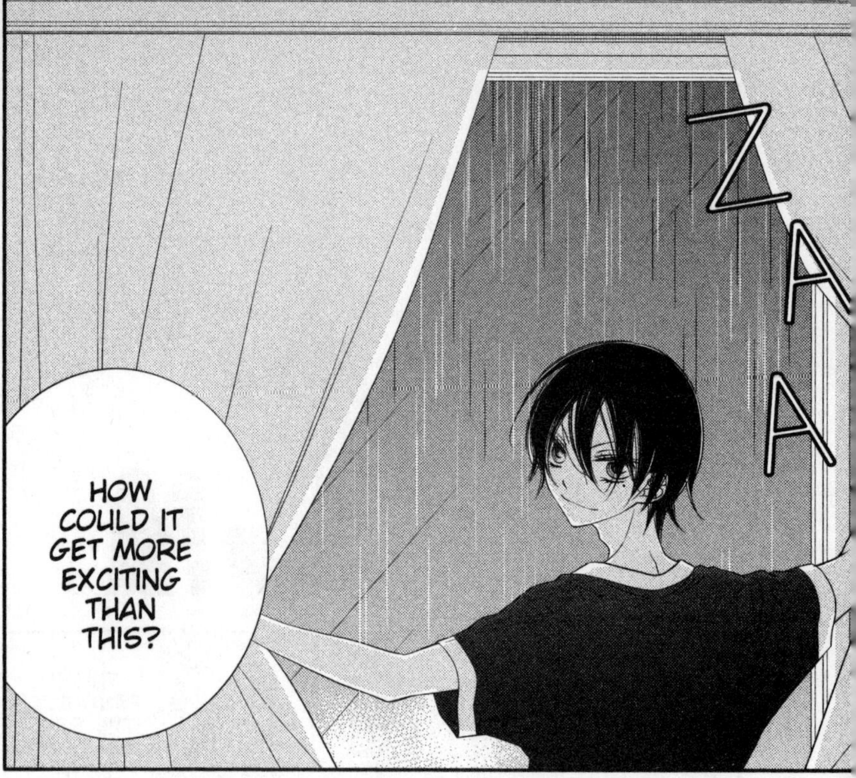
ZAA
HOW COULD IT GET MORE EXCITING THAN THIS?

...IT POURED FOR TWO DAYS STRAIGHT.

SONG 86

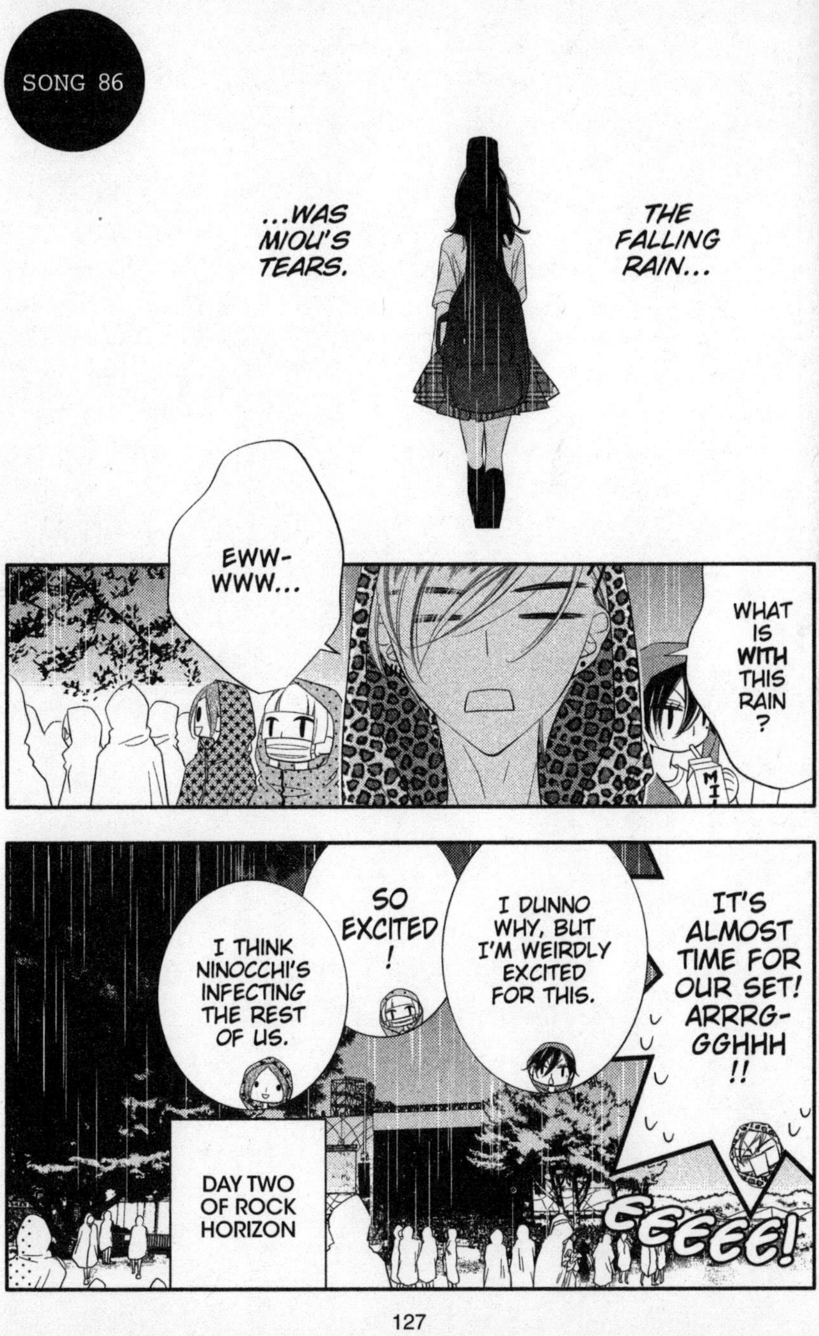
THE FALLING RAIN...
...WAS MIOU'S TEARS.
WHAT IS WITH THIS RAIN?
EWWWWW...
IT'S ALMOST TIME FOR OUR SET! ARRRGGHHH!!
EEEEE!
I DUNNO WHY, BUT I'M WEIRDLY EXCITED FOR THIS.
SO EXCITED!
I THINK NINOCCHI'S INFECTING THE REST OF US.
DAY TWO OF ROCK HORIZON

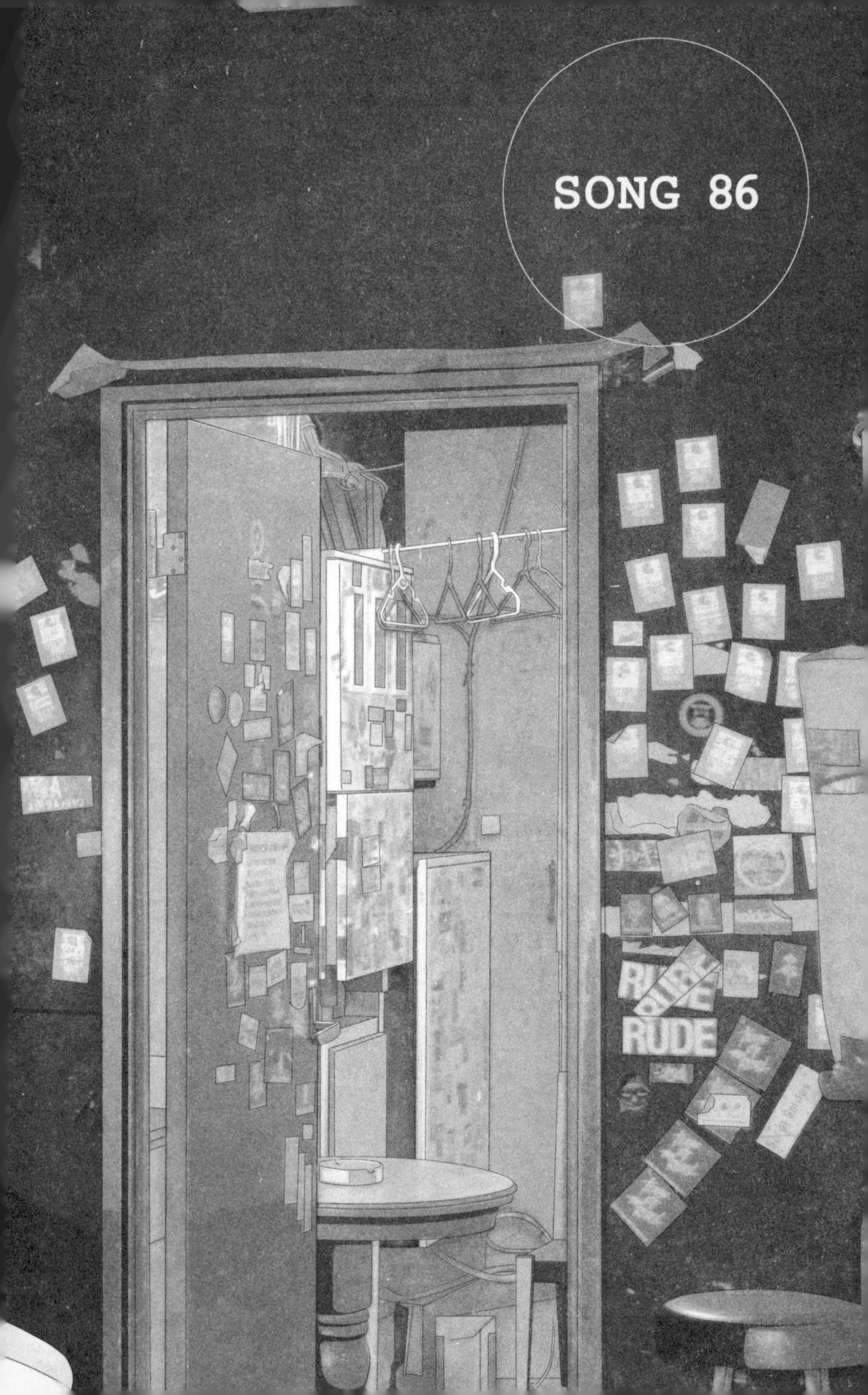
SONG 86
RUDE
RUDE
RUDE

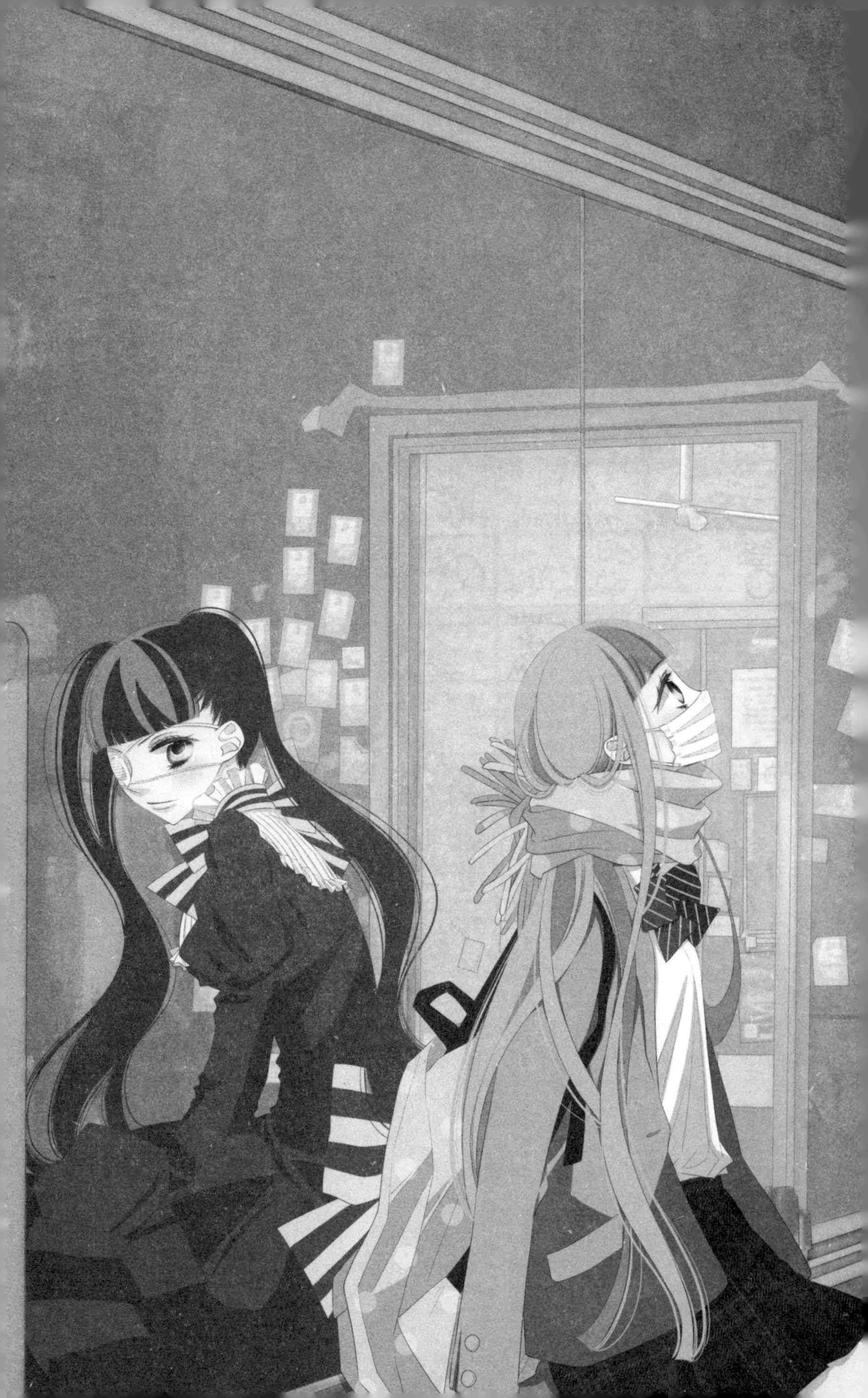

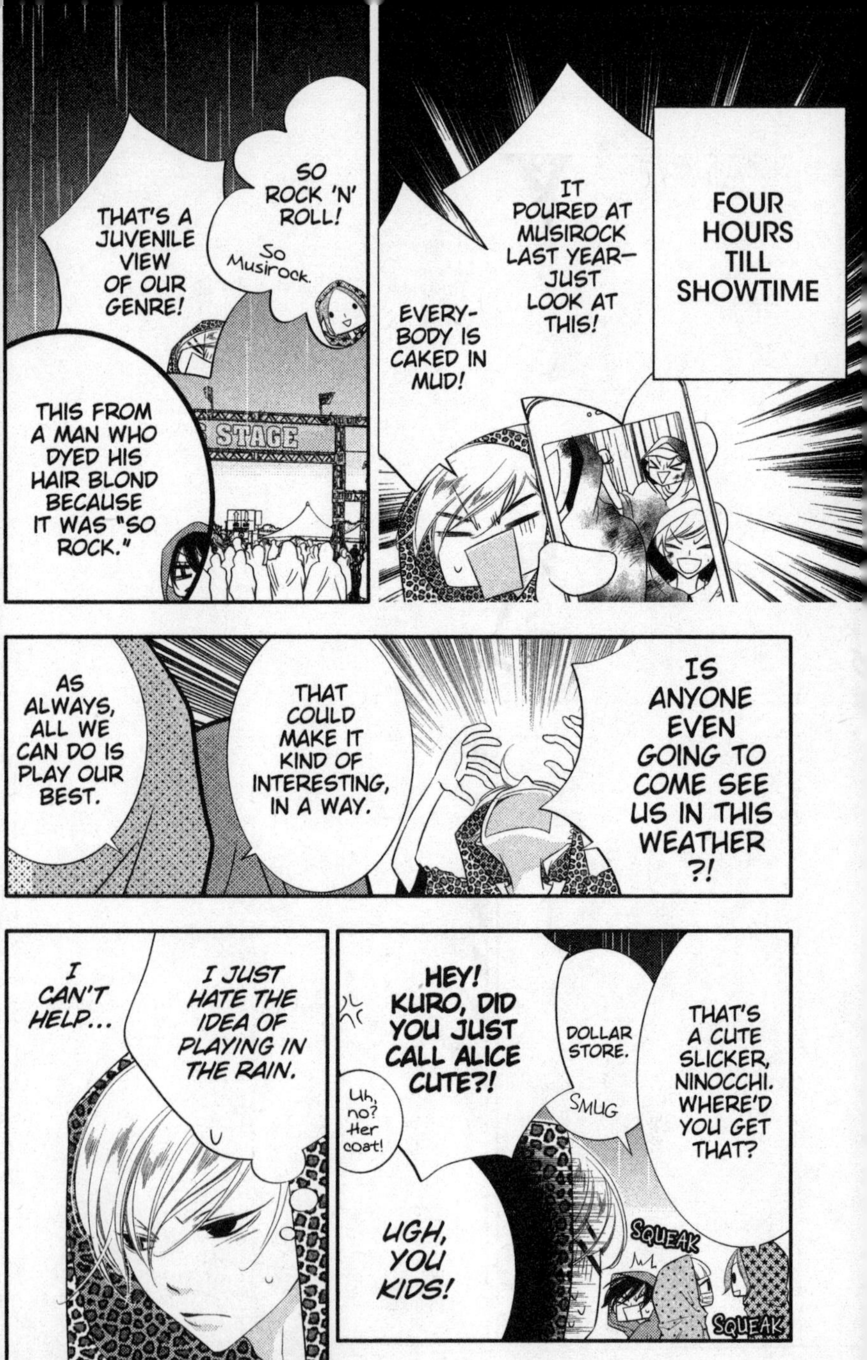
FOUR HOURS TILL SHOWTIME
IT POURED AT MUSIROCK LAST YEAR—JUST LOOK AT THIS!
EVERYBODY IS CAKED IN MUD!
SO ROCK 'N' ROLL!
So Musirock.
THAT'S A JUVENILE VIEW OF OUR GENRE!
STAGE
THIS FROM A MAN WHO DYED HIS HAIR BLOND BECAUSE IT WAS "SO ROCK."
IS ANYONE EVEN GOING TO COME SEE US IN THIS WEATHER?!
THAT COULD MAKE IT KIND OF INTERESTING, IN A WAY.
AS ALWAYS, ALL WE CAN DO IS PLAY OUR BEST.
THAT'S A CUTE SLICKER, NINOCCHI. WHERE'D YOU GET THAT?
DOLLAR STORE.
SMUG
HEY! KURO, DID YOU JUST CALL ALICE CUTE?!
Uh, no? Her coat!
UGH, YOU KIDS!
SQUEAK
SQUEAK
I JUST HATE THE IDEA OF PLAYING IN THE RAIN.
I CAN'T HELP...

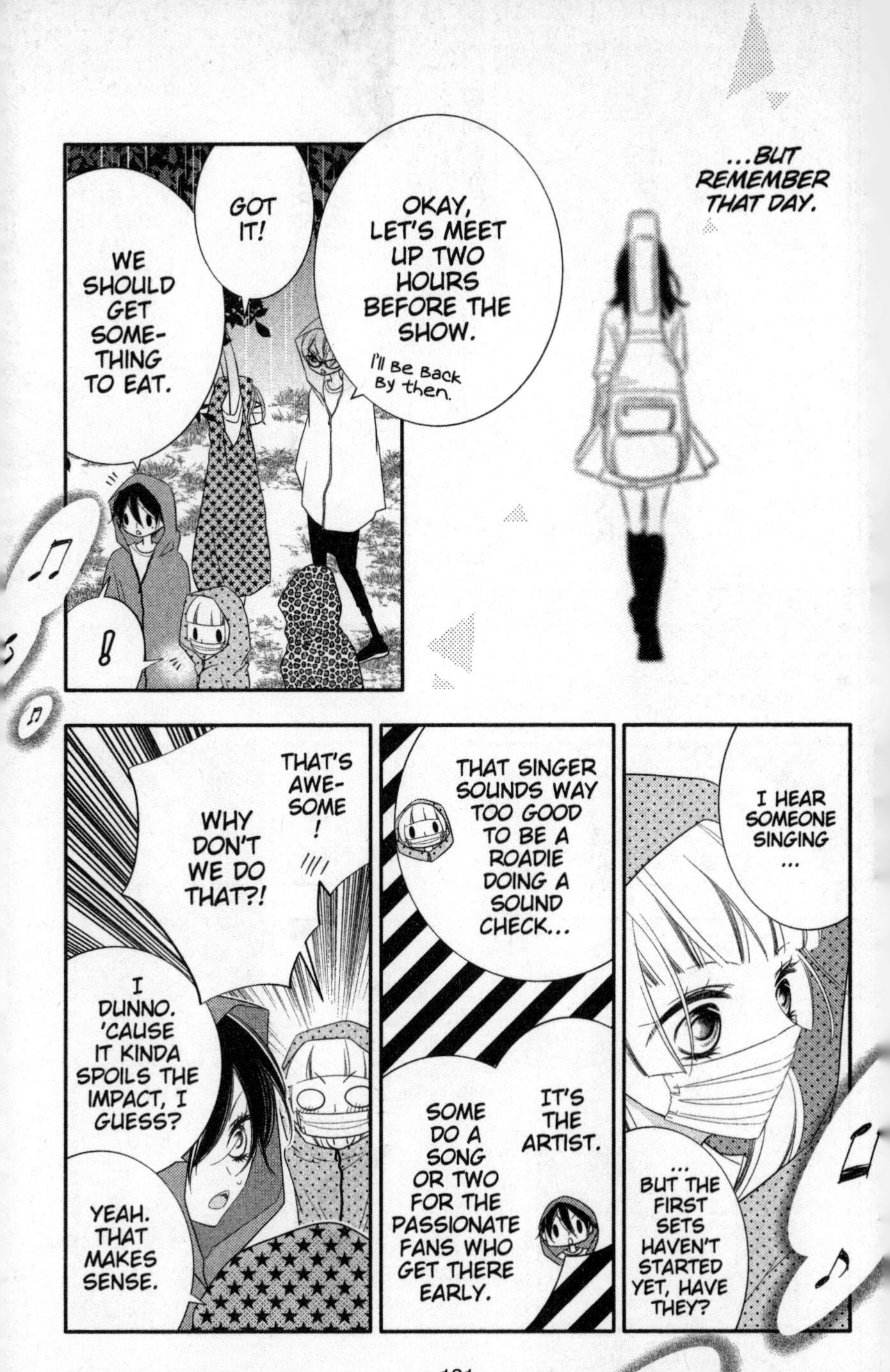
...BUT REMEMBER THAT DAY.
OKAY, LET'S MEET UP TWO HOURS BEFORE THE SHOW.
I'll be back by then.
GOT IT!
WE SHOULD GET SOME-THING TO EAT.
!
I HEAR SOMEONE SINGING...
...BUT THE FIRST SETS HAVEN'T STARTED YET, HAVE THEY?
THAT SINGER SOUNDS WAY TOO GOOD TO BE A ROADIE DOING A SOUND CHECK...
IT'S THE ARTIST.
SOME DO A SONG OR TWO FOR THE PASSIONATE FANS WHO GET THERE EARLY.
THAT'S AWE-SOME!
WHY DON'T WE DO THAT?!
I DUNNO. 'CAUSE IT KINDA SPOILS THE IMPACT, I GUESS?
YEAH. THAT MAKES SENSE.

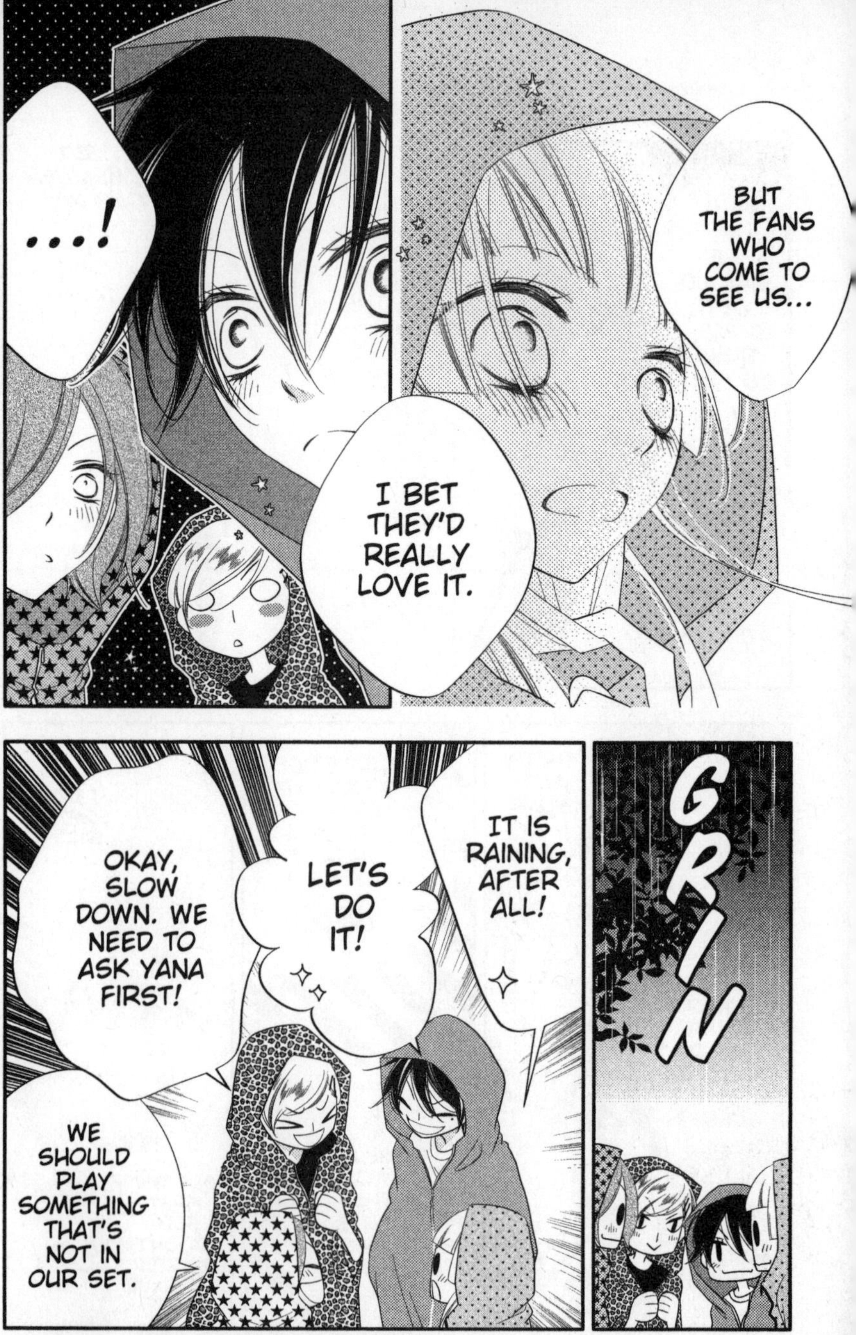
BUT THE FANS WHO COME TO SEE US...
I BET THEY'D REALLY LOVE IT.
...!
GRIN
IT IS RAINING, AFTER ALL!
LET'S DO IT!
OKAY, SLOW DOWN. WE NEED TO ASK YANA FIRST!
WE SHOULD PLAY SOMETHING THAT'S NOT IN OUR SET.

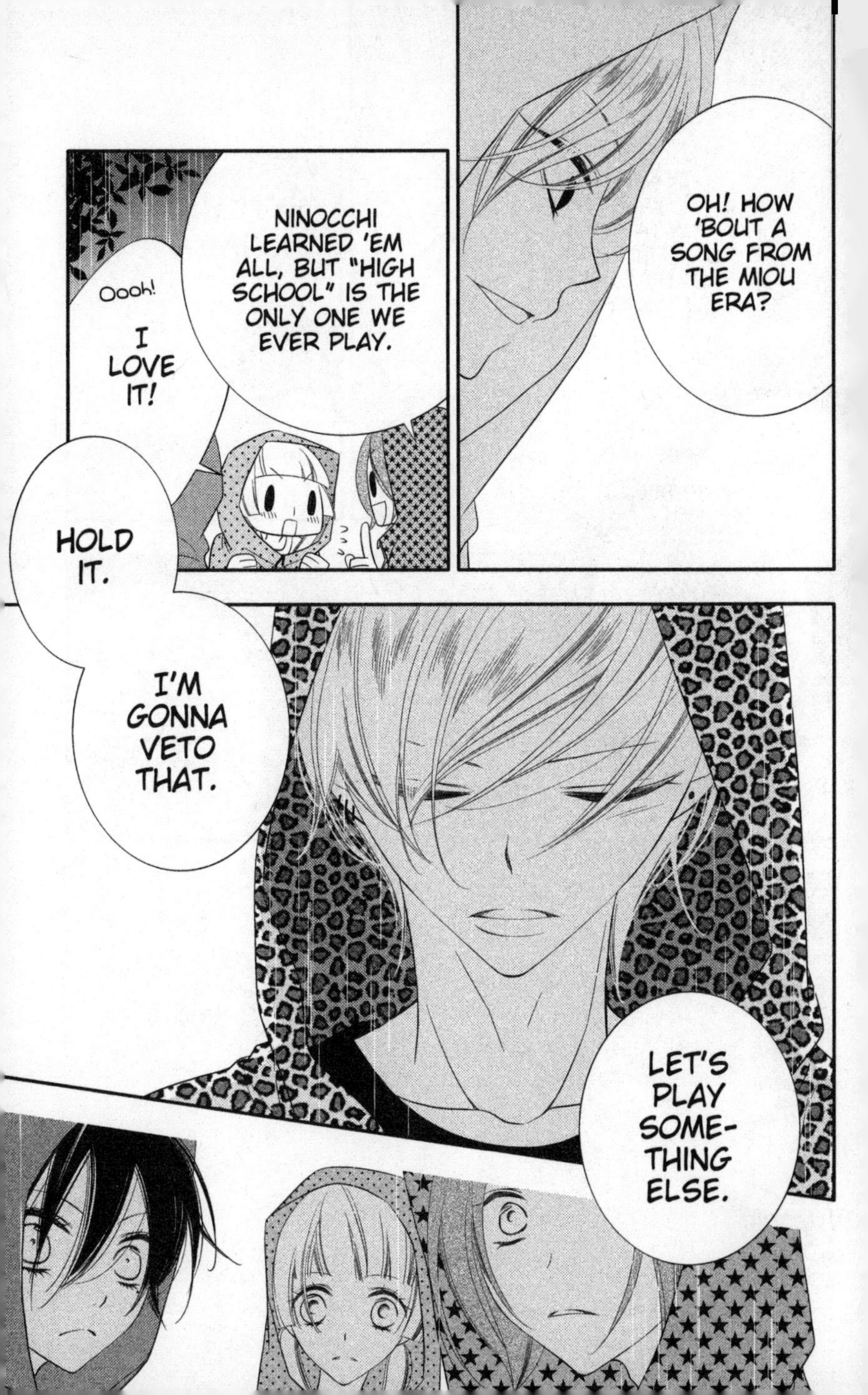
OH! HOW 'BOUT A SONG FROM THE MIOU ERA?
NINOCCHI LEARNED 'EM ALL, BUT "HIGH SCHOOL" IS THE ONLY ONE WE EVER PLAY.
Oooh!
I LOVE IT!
HOLD IT.
I'M GONNA VETO THAT.
LET'S PLAY SOME-THING ELSE.

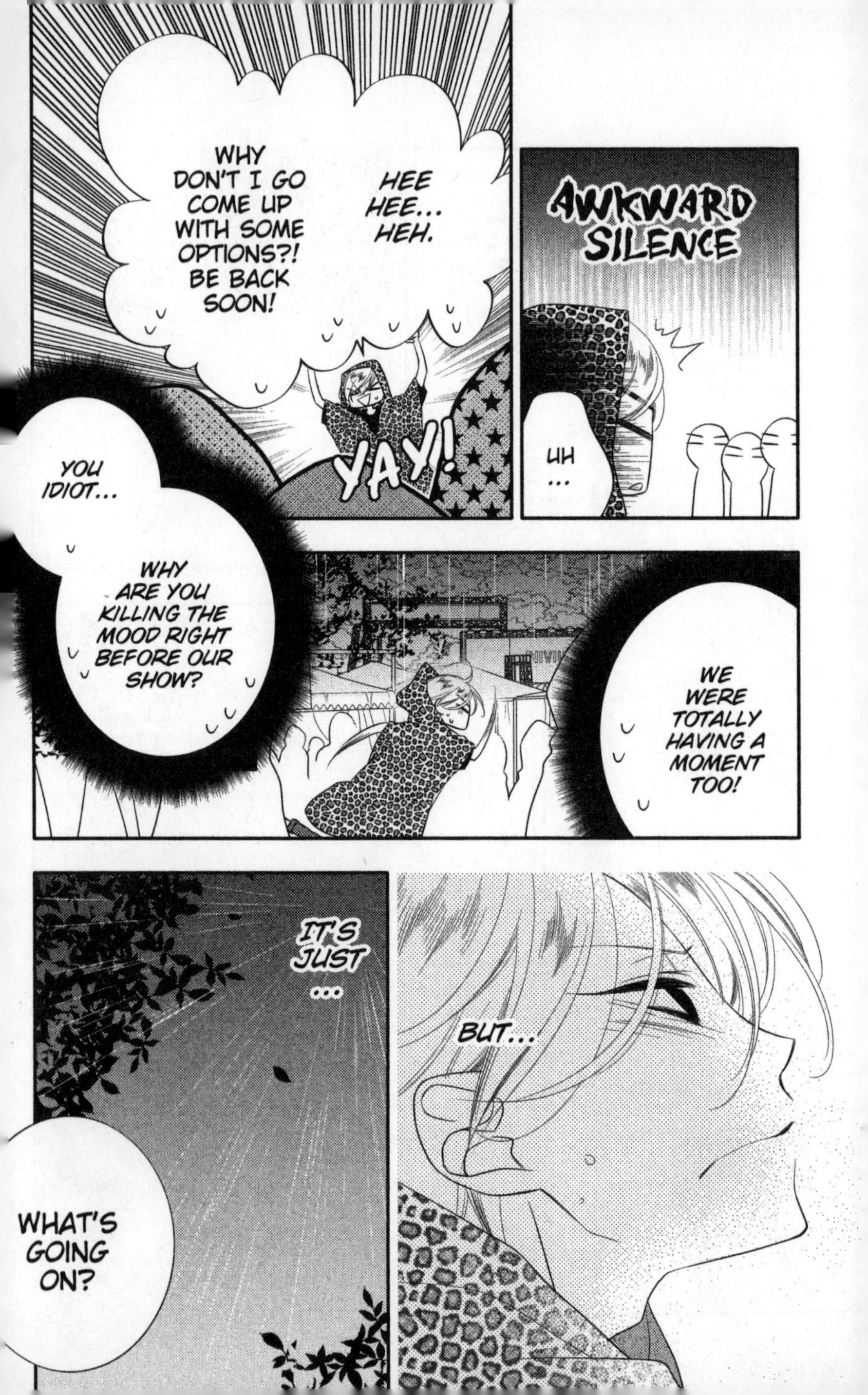
AWKWARD SILENCE
UH ...
HEE HEE... HEH.
WHY DON'T I GO COME UP WITH SOME OPTIONS?! BE BACK SOON!
YAY!
WE WERE TOTALLY HAVING A MOMENT TOO!
YOU IDIOT...
WHY ARE YOU KILLING THE MOOD RIGHT BEFORE OUR SHOW?
BUT...
IT'S JUST ...
WHAT'S GOING ON?

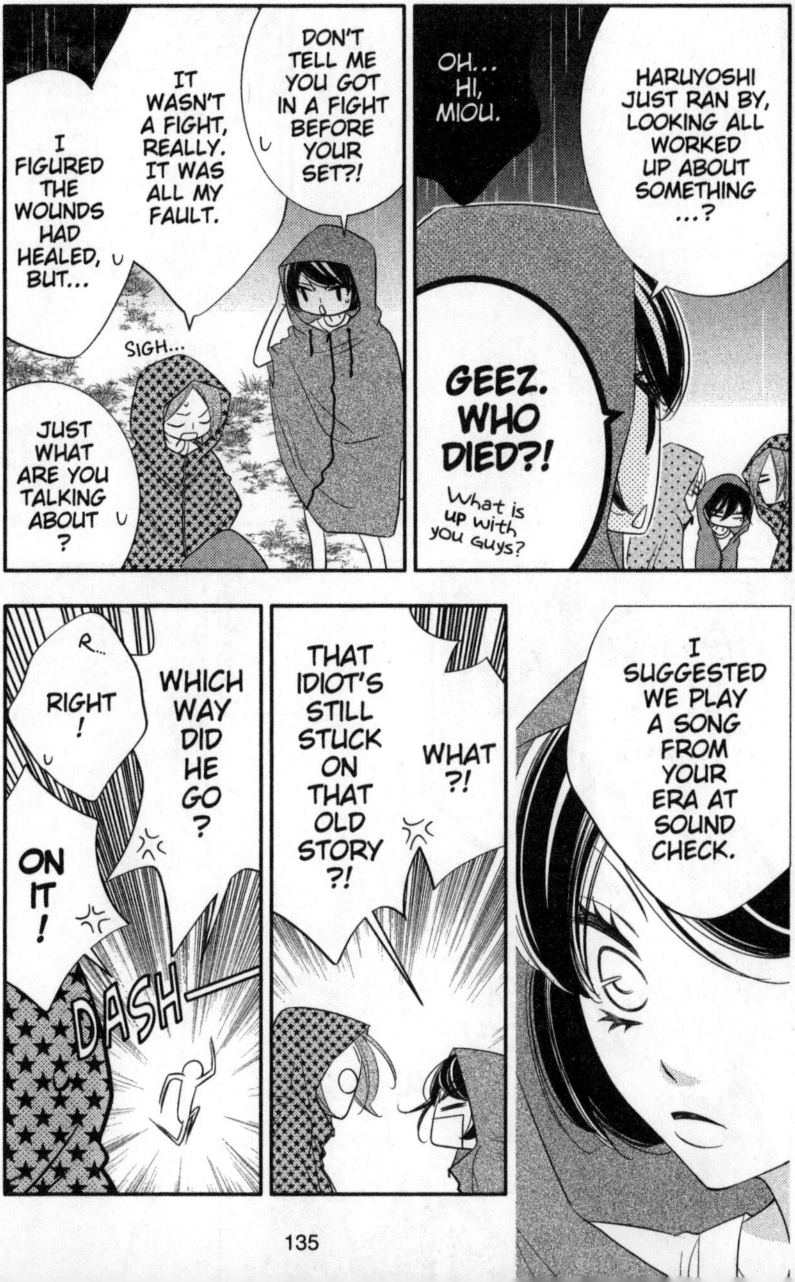
HARUYOSHI JUST RAN BY, LOOKING ALL WORKED UP ABOUT SOMETHING ...?
OH... HI, MIOU.
GEEZ. WHO DIED?!
What is up with you guys?
DON'T TELL ME YOU GOT IN A FIGHT BEFORE YOUR SET?!
IT WASN'T A FIGHT, REALLY. IT WAS ALL MY FAULT.
I FIGURED THE WOUNDS HAD HEALED, BUT...
SIGH...
JUST WHAT ARE YOU TALKING ABOUT?
I SUGGESTED WE PLAY A SONG FROM YOUR ERA AT SOUND CHECK.
WHAT?!
THAT IDIOT'S STILL STUCK ON THAT OLD STORY?!
WHICH WAY DID HE GO?
R... RIGHT!
ON IT!
DASH

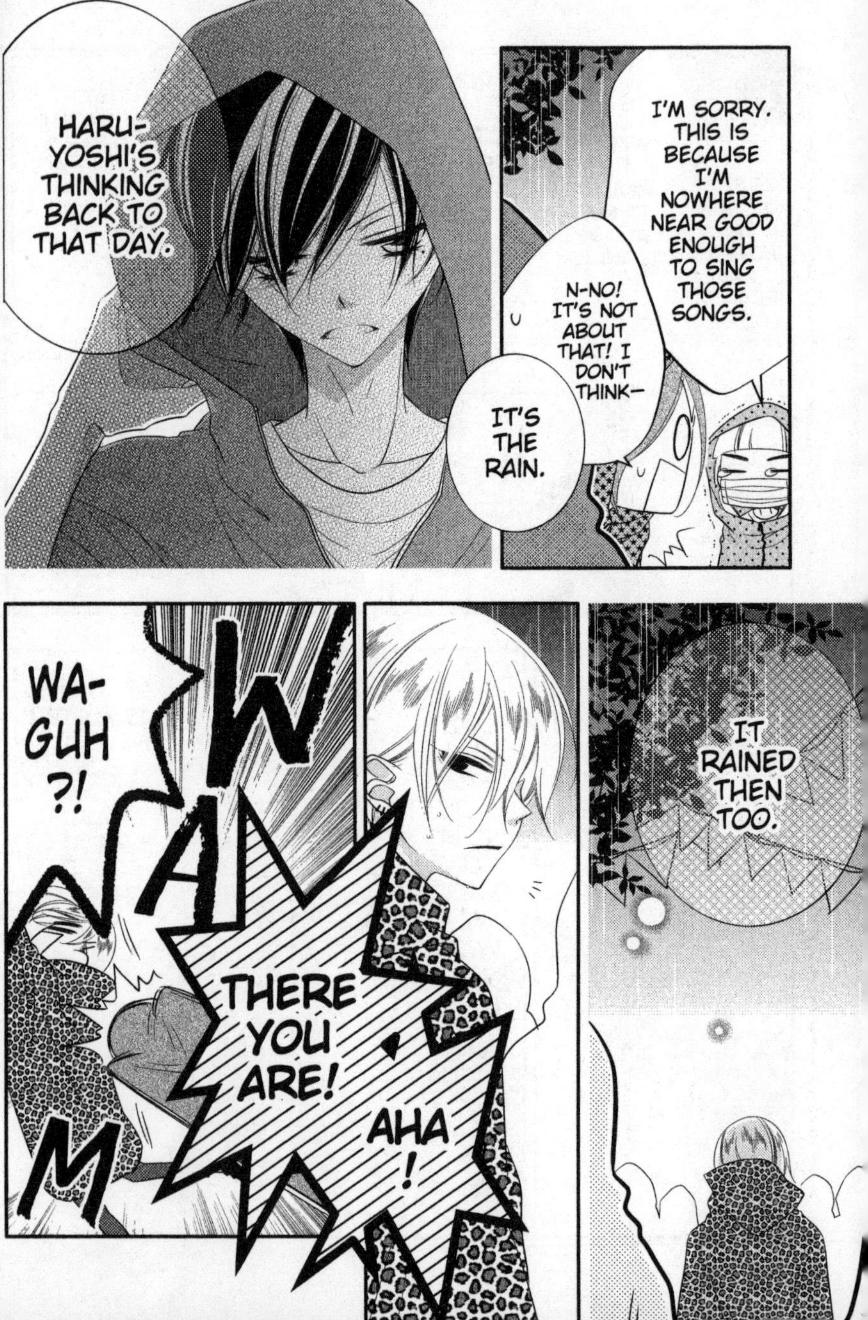
I'M SORRY. THIS IS BECAUSE I'M NOWHERE NEAR GOOD ENOUGH TO SING THOSE SONGS.
N-NO! IT'S NOT ABOUT THAT! I DON'T THINK—
IT'S THE RAIN.
HARU-YOSHI'S THINKING BACK TO THAT DAY.
IT RAINED THEN TOO.
WHAM
THERE YOU ARE!
AHA!
WA-GUH?!

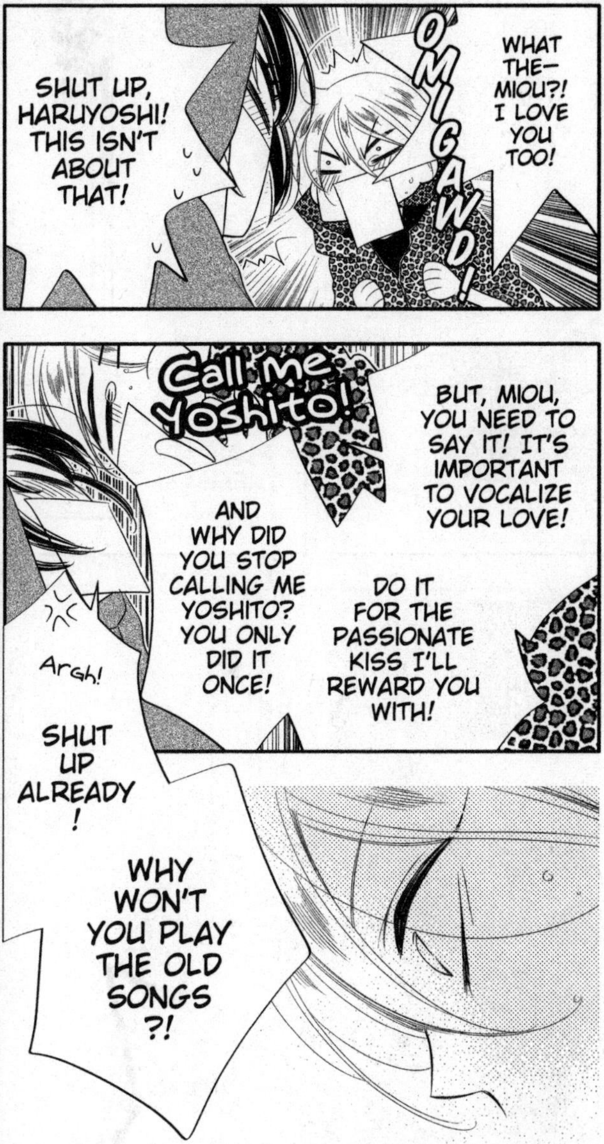
WHAT THE— MIOU?! I LOVE YOU TOO!
OMIGAWD!
SHUT UP, HARUYOSHI! THIS ISN'T ABOUT THAT!
BUT, MIOU, YOU NEED TO SAY IT! IT'S IMPORTANT TO VOCALIZE YOUR LOVE!
Call me Yoshito!
DO IT FOR THE PASSIONATE KISS I'LL REWARD YOU WITH!
AND WHY DID YOU STOP CALLING ME YOSHITO? YOU ONLY DID IT ONCE!
Argh!
SHUT UP ALREADY!
WHY WON'T YOU PLAY THE OLD SONGS?!

5

Incidentally, the entire song came rushing into my head when I heard Saori Hayami (Nino's voice actress) sing at a recording session. I was positively frantic trying to scribble it all down on my notepad! It was the first time I'd ever been inspired like that from hearing someone's voice.

The drama CD is a skit that was inspired by something that happened at an anime event. It's a sort of parallel story to the events of volumes 13 and 14 of the manga. The deadlines for the drama CD scripts are always a nightmare, but this time I was able to relax and enjoy writing it. I can't tell you how much I love the cast—make sure to listen all the way until the cast roundtable at the end!

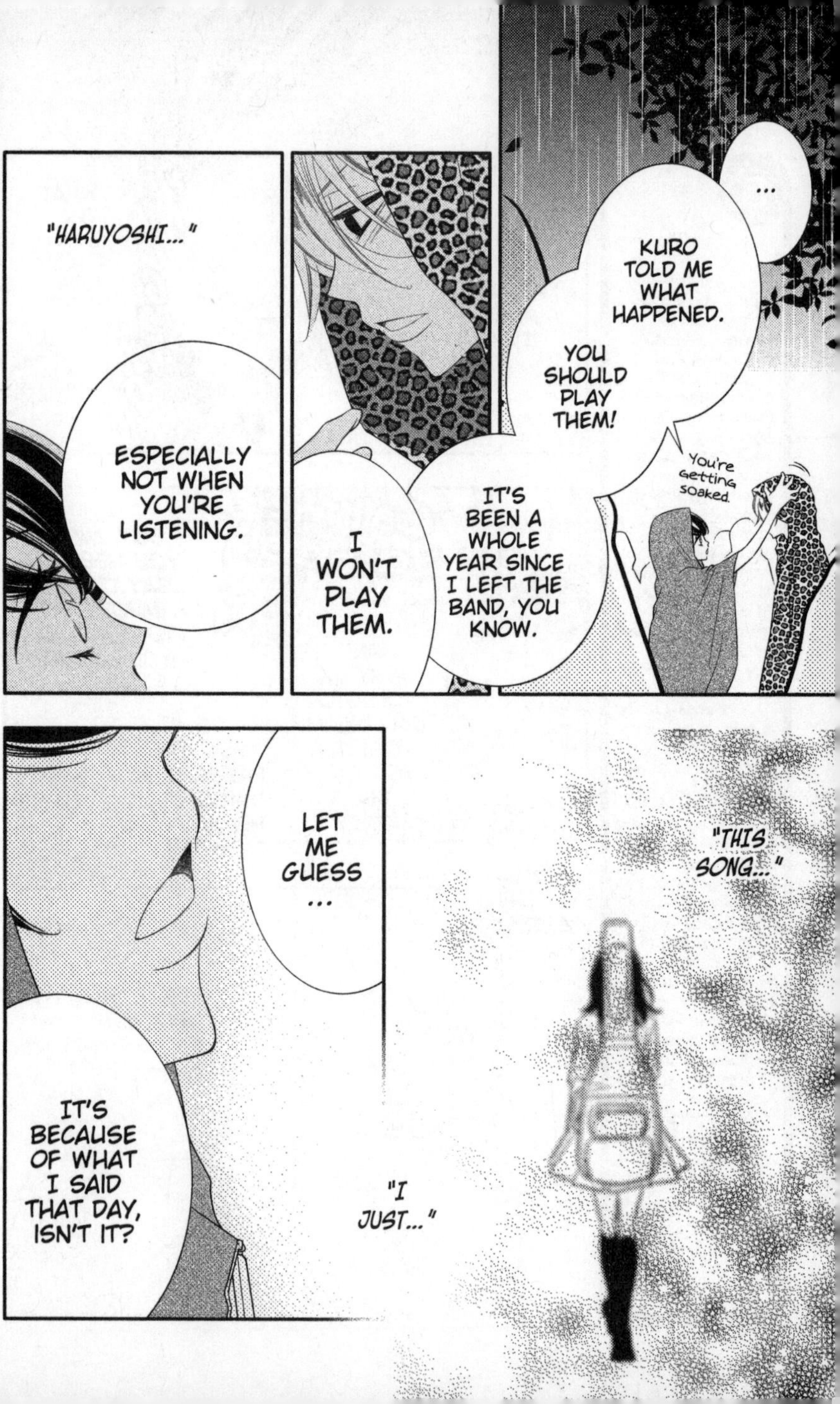
...
KURO TOLD ME WHAT HAPPENED.
YOU SHOULD PLAY THEM!
You're Getting soaked.
IT'S BEEN A WHOLE YEAR SINCE I LEFT THE BAND, YOU KNOW.
I WON'T PLAY THEM.
"HARUYOSHI..."
ESPECIALLY NOT WHEN YOU'RE LISTENING.
"THIS SONG..."
"I JUST..."
LET ME GUESS...
IT'S BECAUSE OF WHAT I SAID THAT DAY, ISN'T IT?

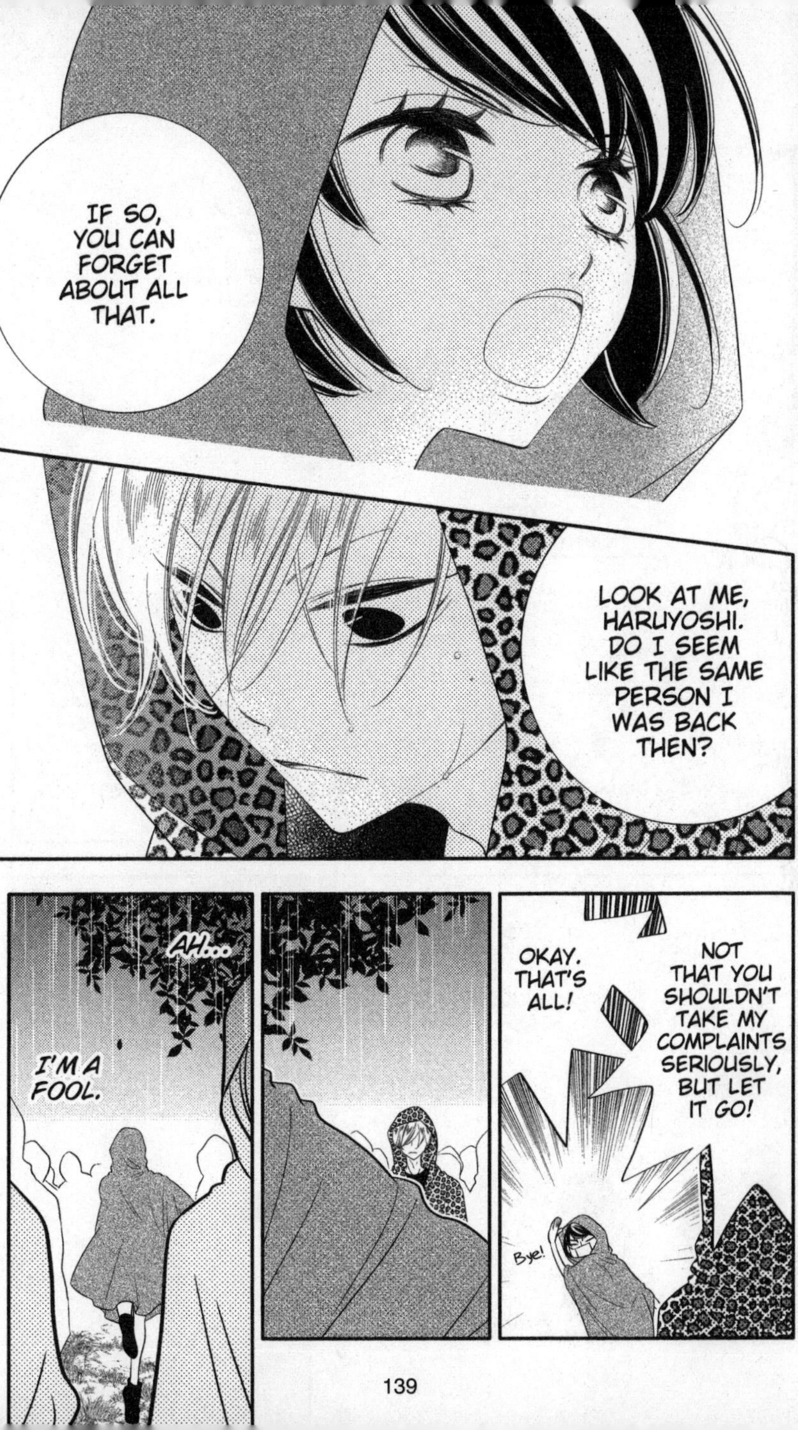
IF SO, YOU CAN FORGET ABOUT ALL THAT.
LOOK AT ME, HARUYOSHI. DO I SEEM LIKE THE SAME PERSON I WAS BACK THEN?
NOT THAT YOU SHOULDN'T TAKE MY COMPLAINTS SERIOUSLY, BUT LET IT GO!
OKAY. THAT'S ALL!
Bye!
AH...
I'M A FOOL.

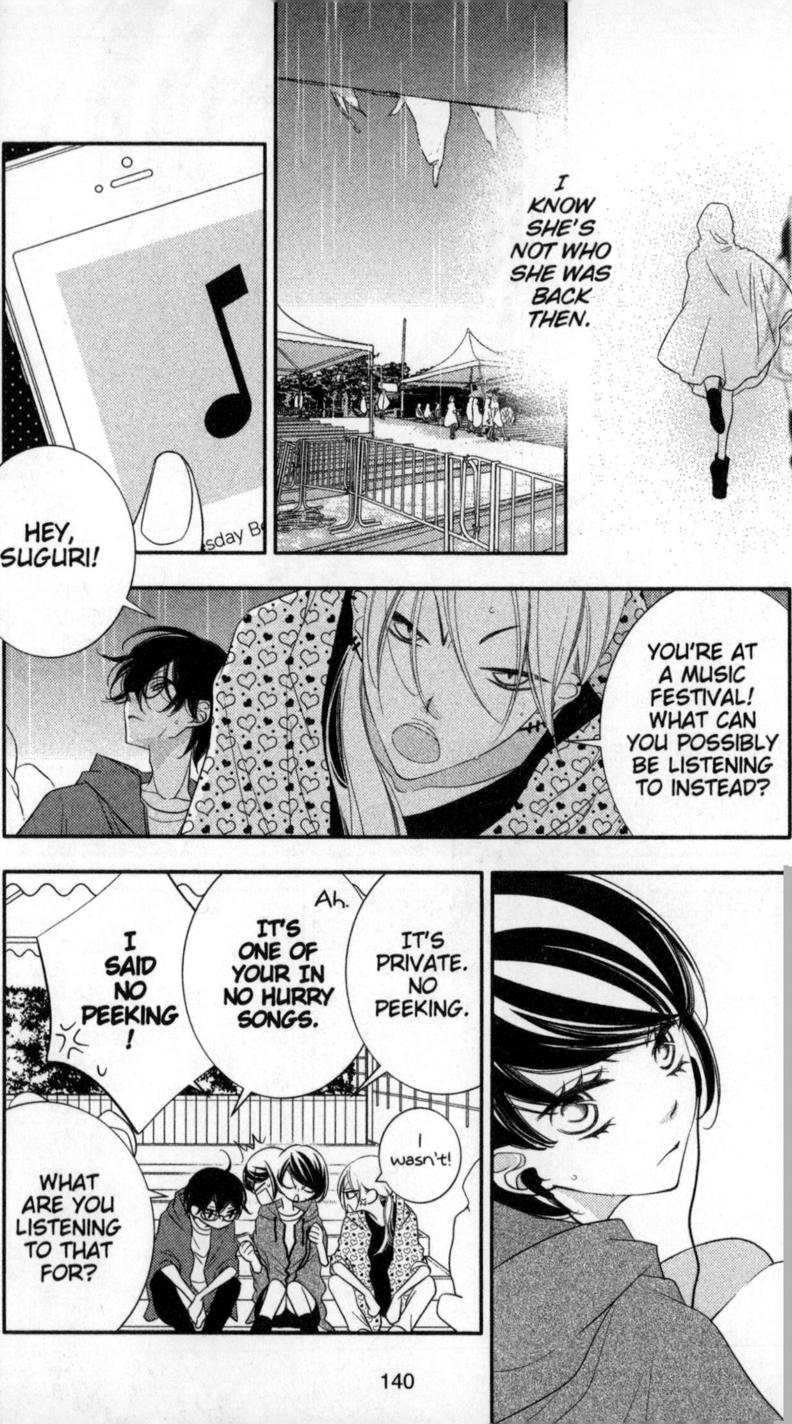
I KNOW SHE'S NOT WHO SHE WAS BACK THEN.
HEY, SUGURI!
YOU'RE AT A MUSIC FESTIVAL! WHAT CAN YOU POSSIBLY BE LISTENING TO INSTEAD?
IT'S PRIVATE. NO PEEKING.
Ah.
IT'S ONE OF YOUR IN NO HURRY SONGS.
I SAID NO PEEKING!
I wasn't!
WHAT ARE YOU LISTENING TO THAT FOR?

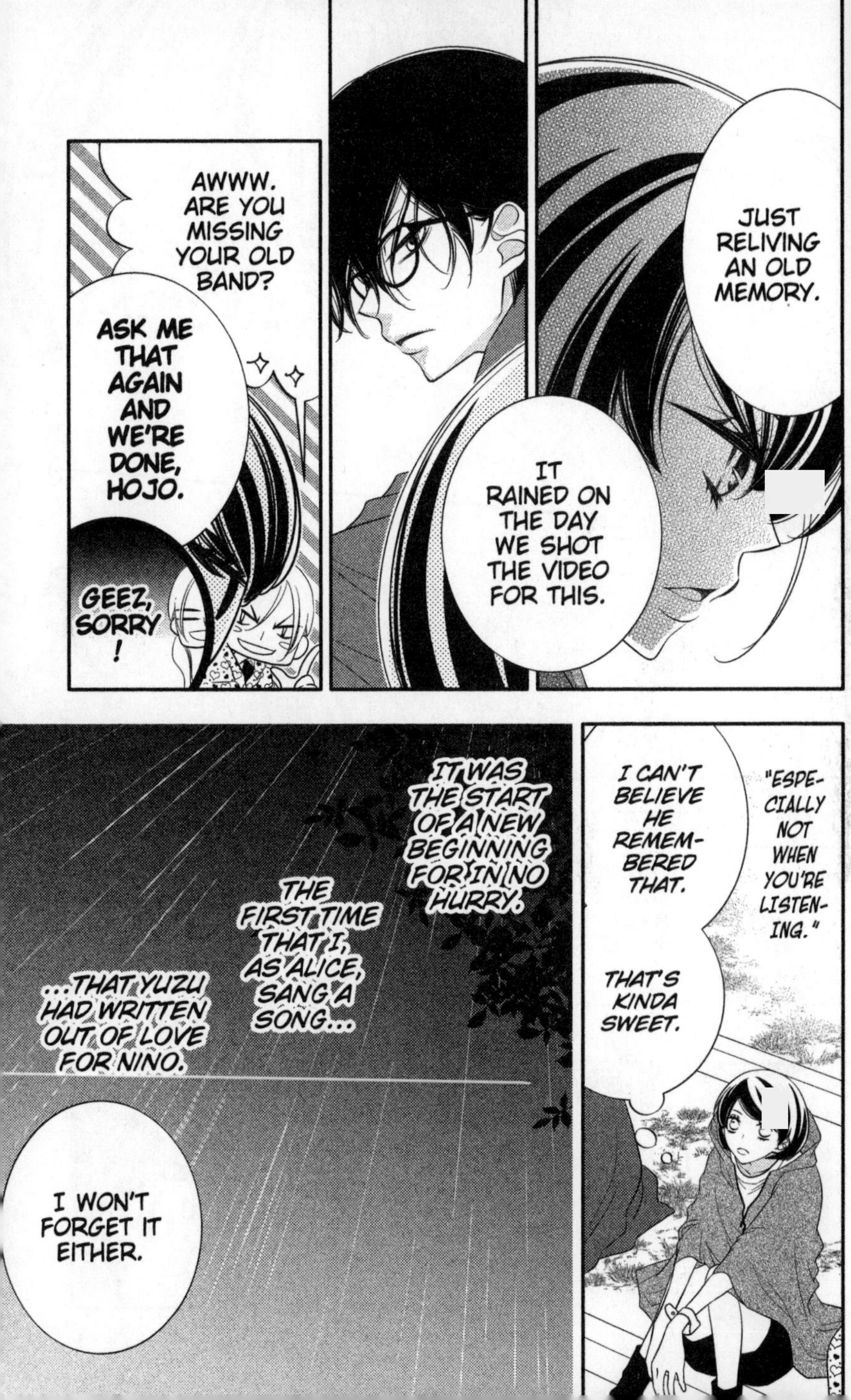
JUST RELIVING AN OLD MEMORY.
IT RAINED ON THE DAY WE SHOT THE VIDEO FOR THIS.
AWWW. ARE YOU MISSING YOUR OLD BAND?
ASK ME THAT AGAIN AND WE'RE DONE, HOJO.
GEEZ, SORRY!
"ESPECIALLY NOT WHEN YOU'RE LISTENING."
I CAN'T BELIEVE HE REMEMBERED THAT.
THAT'S KINDA SWEET.
IT WAS THE START OF A NEW BEGINNING FOR IN NO HURRY.
THE FIRST TIME THAT I, AS ALICE, SANG A SONG...
...THAT YUZU HAD WRITTEN OUT OF LOVE FOR NINO.
I WON'T FORGET IT EITHER.

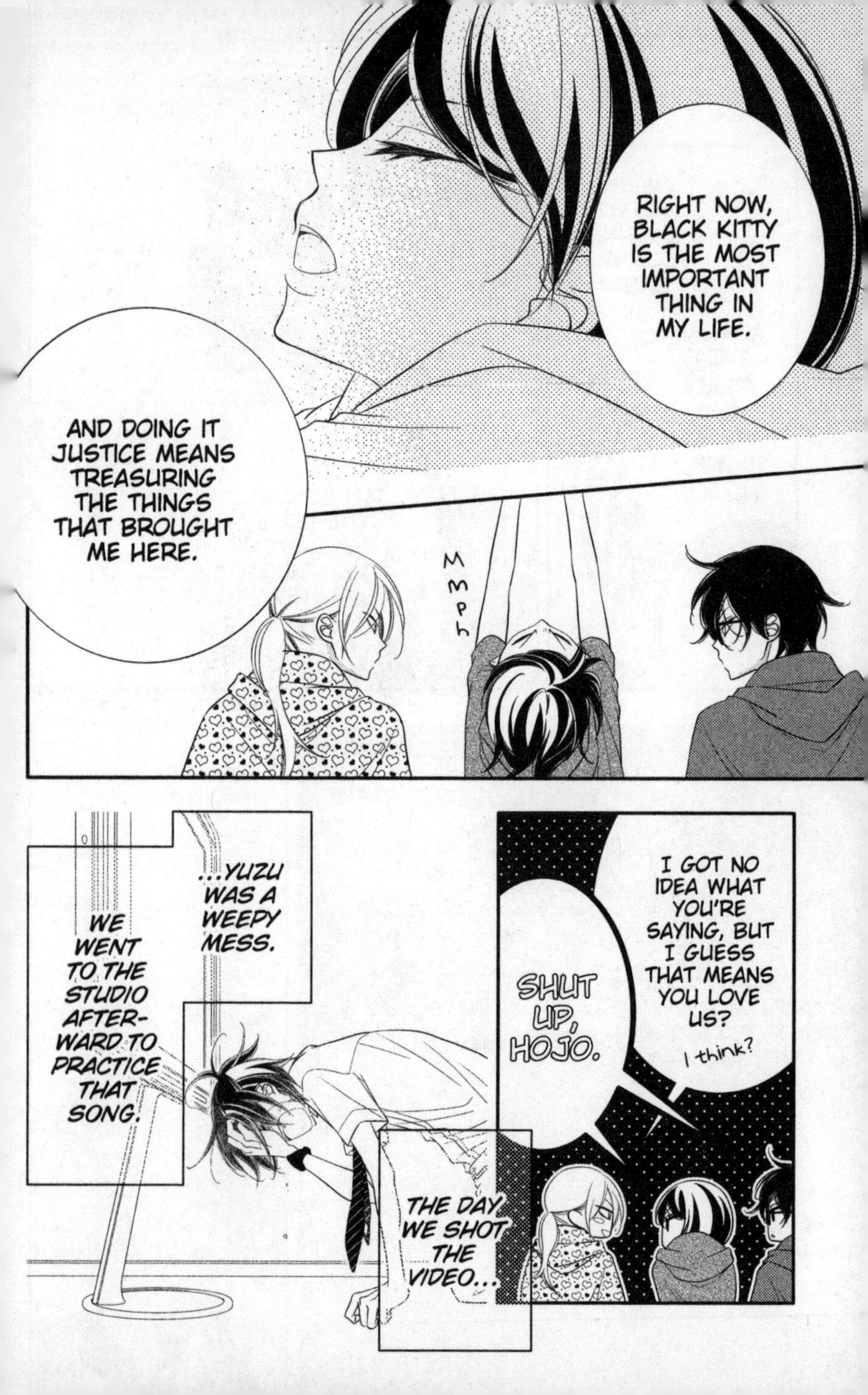
RIGHT NOW, BLACK KITTY IS THE MOST IMPORTANT THING IN MY LIFE.
AND DOING IT JUSTICE MEANS TREASURING THE THINGS THAT BROUGHT ME HERE.
Mmph
I GOT NO IDEA WHAT YOU'RE SAYING, BUT I GUESS THAT MEANS YOU LOVE US?
I think?
SHUT UP, HOJO.
THE DAY WE SHOT THE VIDEO...
...YUZU WAS A WEEPY MESS.
WE WENT TO THE STUDIO AFTERWARD TO PRACTICE THAT SONG.

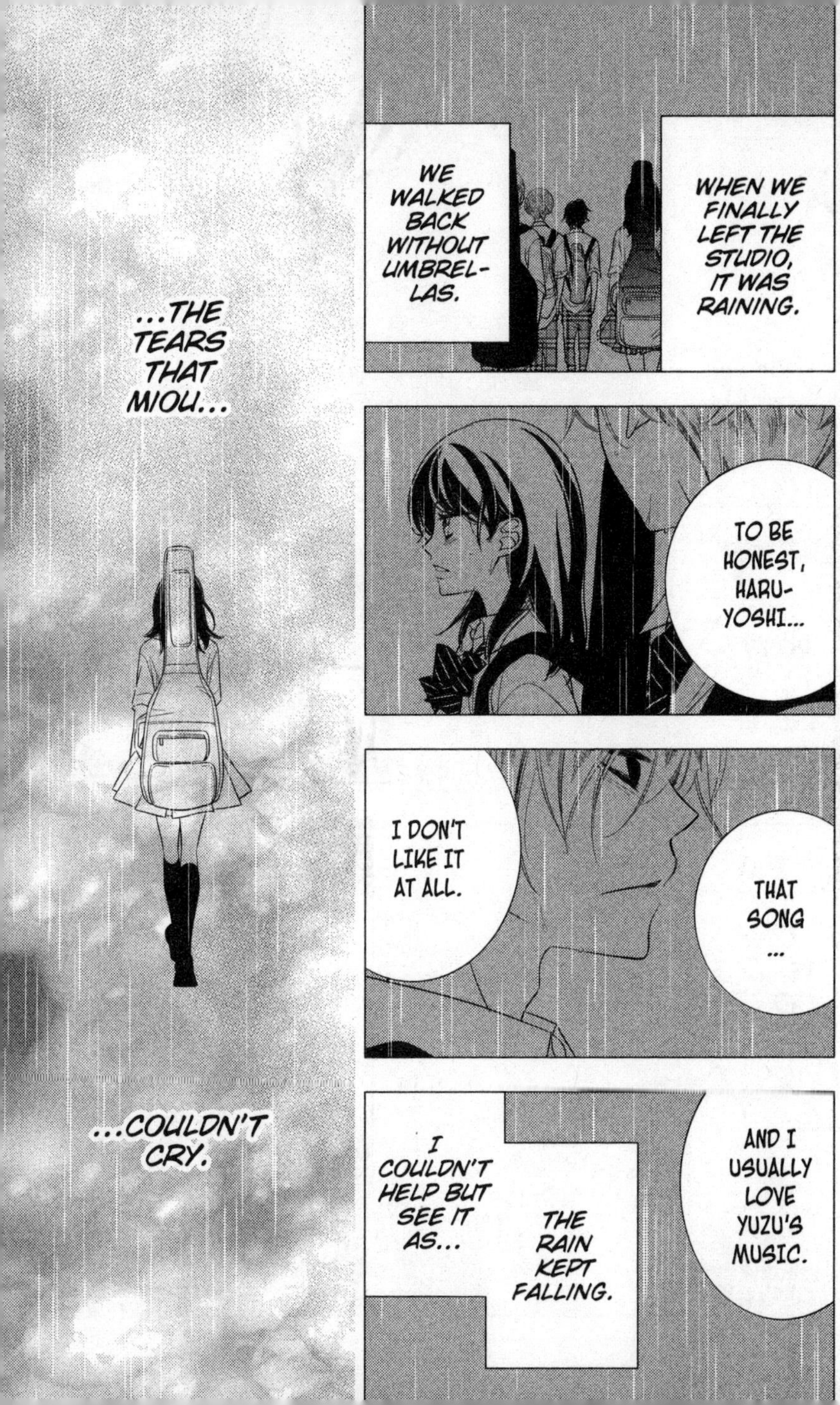
WHEN WE FINALLY LEFT THE STUDIO, IT WAS RAINING.
WE WALKED BACK WITHOUT UMBRELLAS.
TO BE HONEST, HARUYOSHI...
THAT SONG ...
I DON'T LIKE IT AT ALL.
AND I USUALLY LOVE YUZU'S MUSIC.
THE RAIN KEPT FALLING.
I COULDN'T HELP BUT SEE IT AS...
...THE TEARS THAT MIOU...
...COULDN'T CRY.

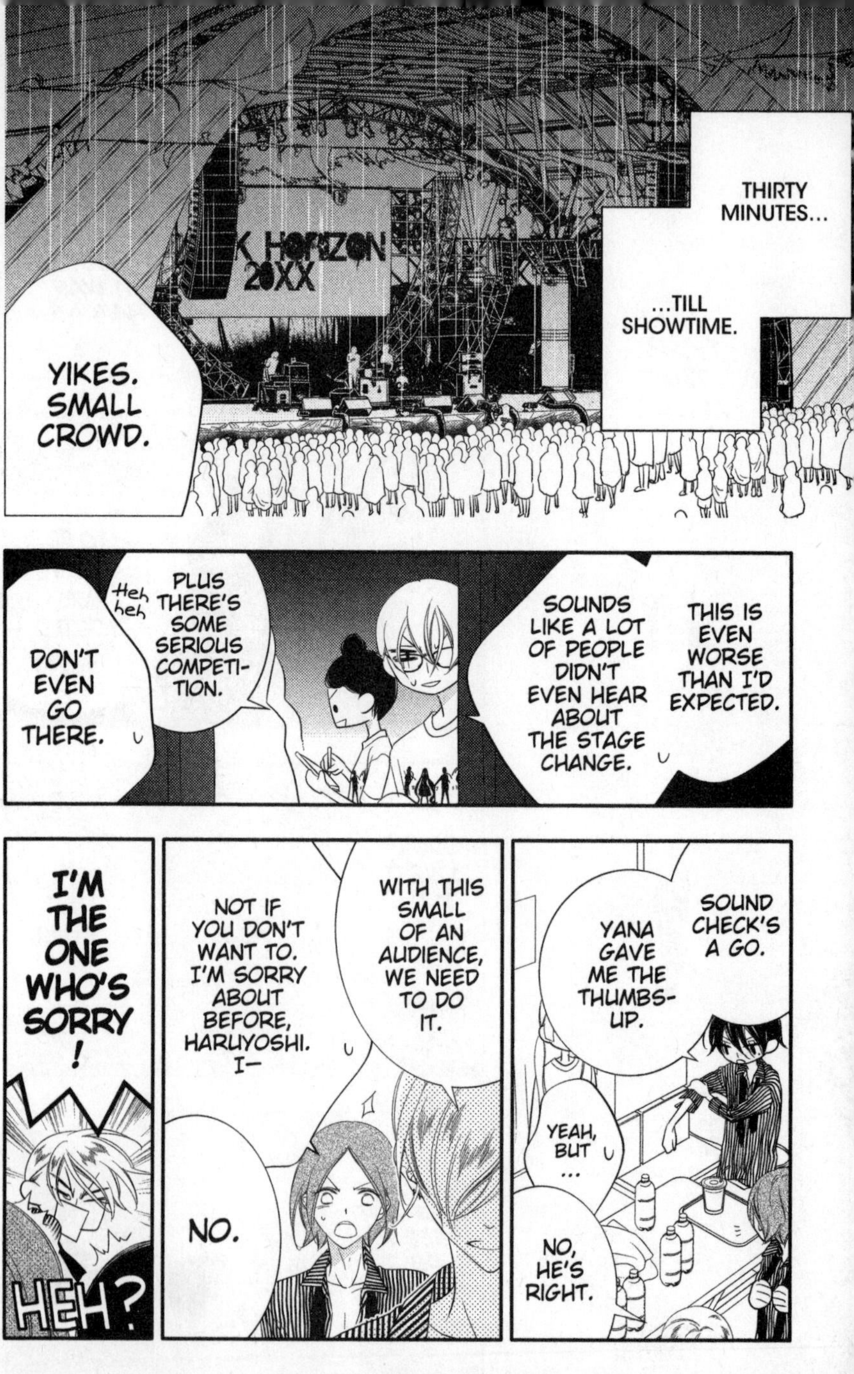
THIRTY MINUTES...
...TILL SHOWTIME.
K HORIZON 20XX
YIKES. SMALL CROWD.
THIS IS EVEN WORSE THAN I'D EXPECTED.
SOUNDS LIKE A LOT OF PEOPLE DIDN'T EVEN HEAR ABOUT THE STAGE CHANGE.
PLUS THERE'S SOME SERIOUS COMPETITION.
Heh heh
DON'T EVEN GO THERE.
SOUND CHECK'S A GO.
YANA GAVE ME THE THUMBS-UP.
YEAH, BUT...
NO, HE'S RIGHT.
WITH THIS SMALL OF AN AUDIENCE, WE NEED TO DO IT.
NOT IF YOU DON'T WANT TO. I'M SORRY ABOUT BEFORE, HARUYOSHI. I—
NO.
I'M THE ONE WHO'S SORRY!
HEH?

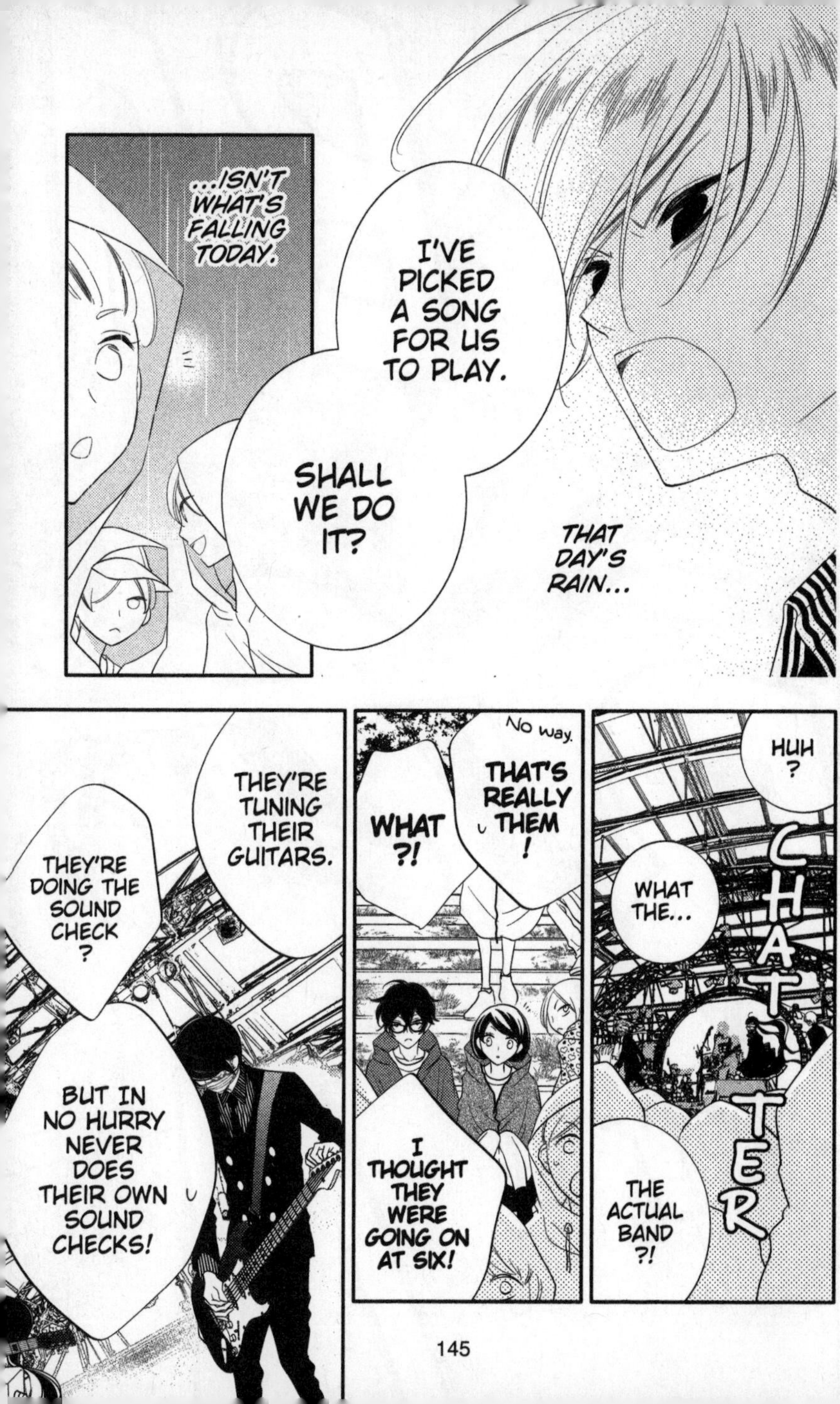
I'VE PICKED A SONG FOR US TO PLAY.
SHALL WE DO IT?
THAT DAY'S RAIN...
...ISN'T WHAT'S FALLING TODAY.
HUH?
WHAT THE...
CHATTER
THE ACTUAL BAND?!
No way.
THAT'S REALLY THEM!
WHAT?!
I THOUGHT THEY WERE GOING ON AT SIX!
THEY'RE TUNING THEIR GUITARS.
THEY'RE DOING THE SOUND CHECK?
BUT IN NO HURRY NEVER DOES THEIR OWN SOUND CHECKS!

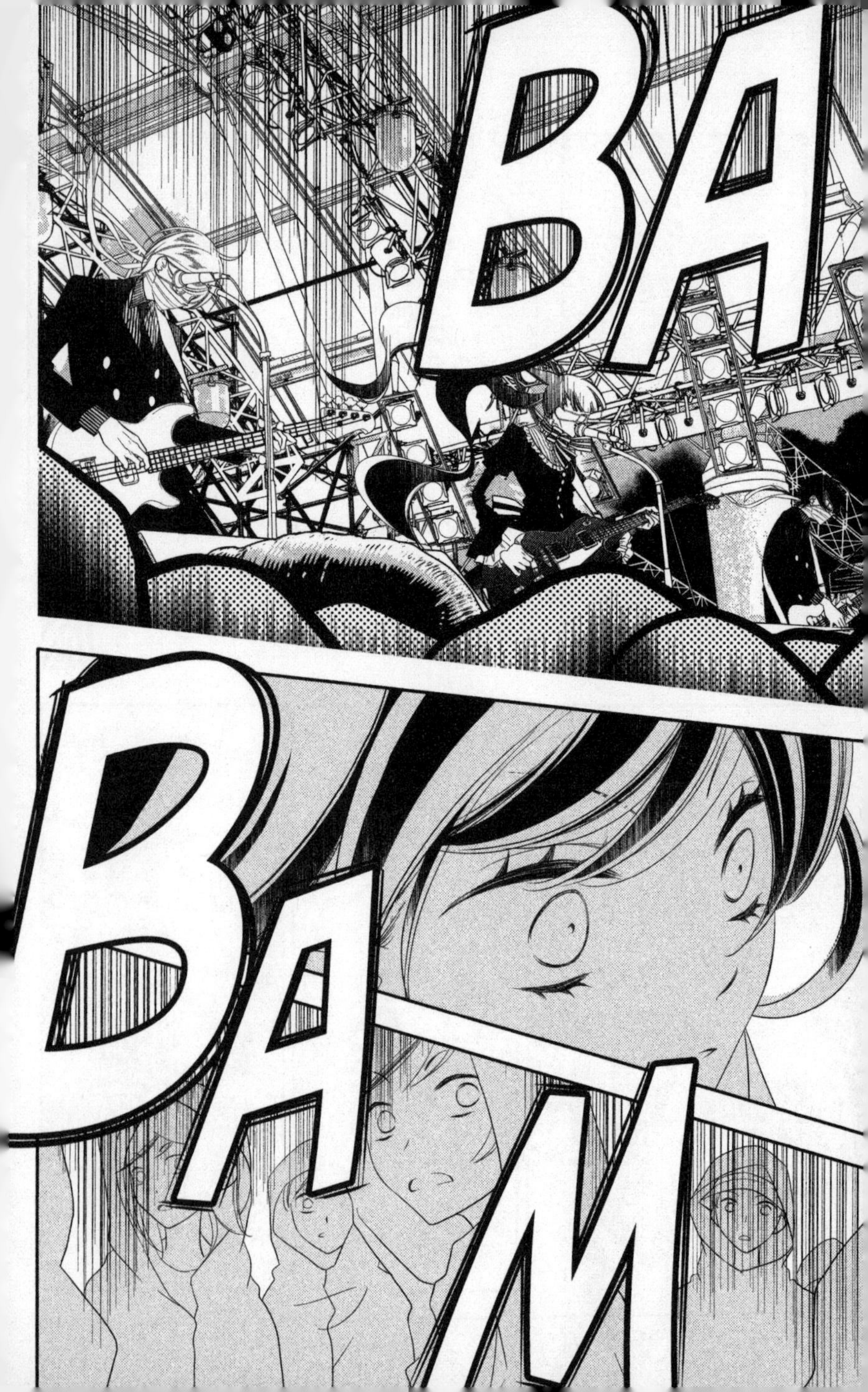
BA
BAM

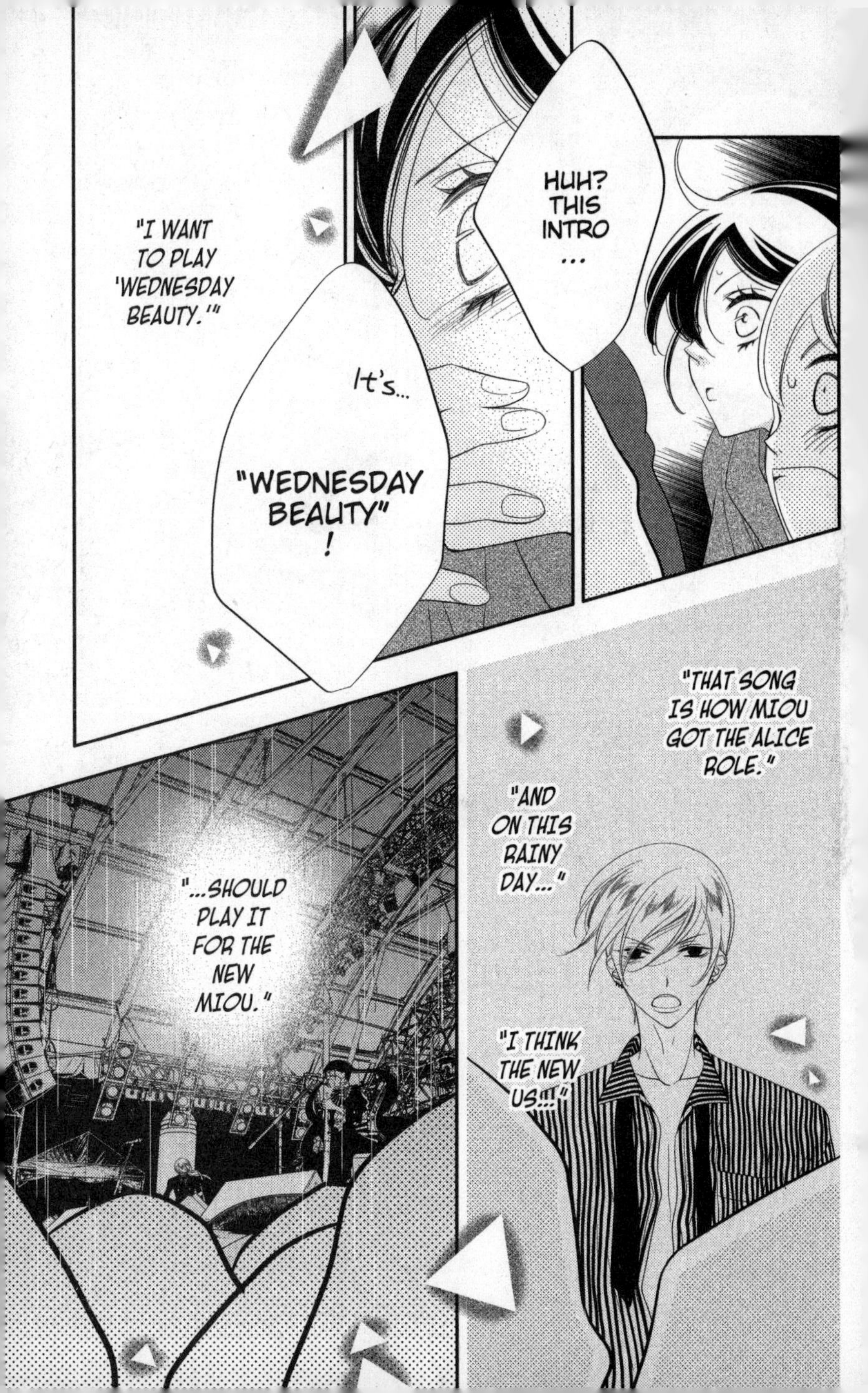
HUH? THIS INTRO ...
"I WANT TO PLAY 'WEDNESDAY BEAUTY.'"
It's...
"WEDNESDAY BEAUTY" !
"THAT SONG IS HOW MIOU GOT THE ALICE ROLE."
"AND ON THIS RAINY DAY..."
"I THINK THE NEW US!!"
"...SHOULD PLAY IT FOR THE NEW MIOU."

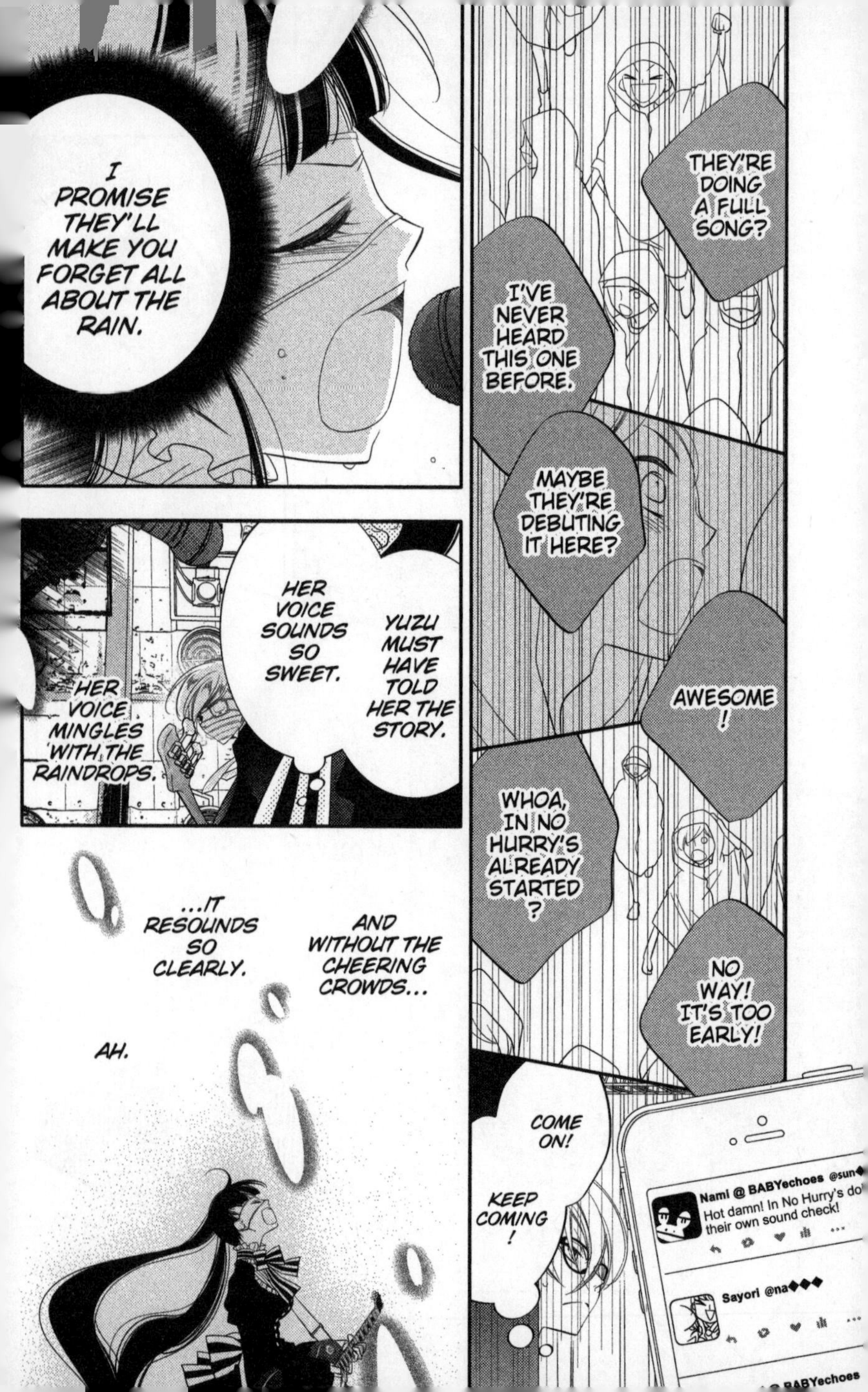
THEY'RE DOING A FULL SONG?
I'VE NEVER HEARD THIS ONE BEFORE.
MAYBE THEY'RE DEBUTING IT HERE?
AWESOME!
WHOA, IN NO HURRY'S ALREADY STARTED?
NO WAY! IT'S TOO EARLY!
COME ON!
KEEP COMING!
Nami @ BABYechoes
Hot damn! In No Hurry's do
their own sound check!
Sayori
I PROMISE THEY'LL MAKE YOU FORGET ALL ABOUT THE RAIN.
YUZU MUST HAVE TOLD HER THE STORY.
HER VOICE SOUNDS SO SWEET.
HER VOICE MINGLES WITH THE RAINDROPS.
AND WITHOUT THE CHEERING CROWDS...
...IT RESOUNDS SO CLEARLY.
AH.

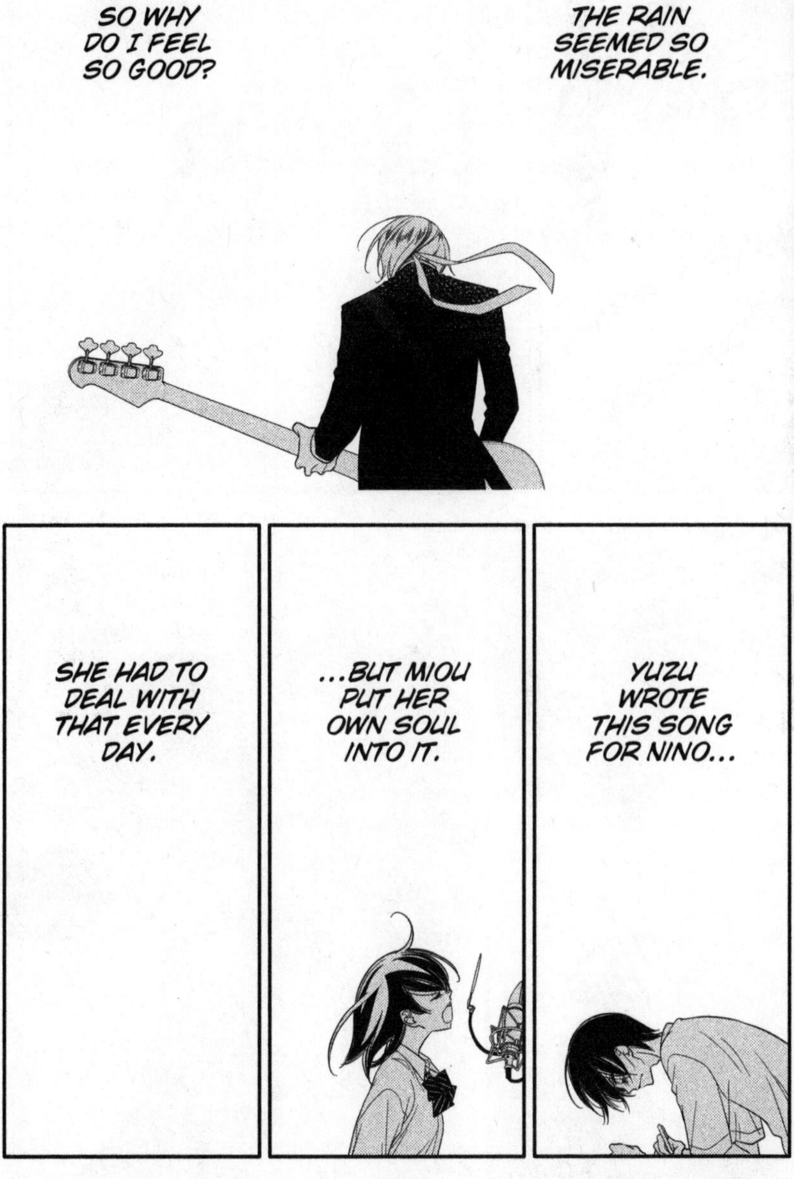
THE RAIN SEEMED SO MISERABLE.
SO WHY DO I FEEL SO GOOD?
YUZU WROTE THIS SONG FOR NINO...
...BUT MIOU PUT HER OWN SOUL INTO IT.
SHE HAD TO DEAL WITH THAT EVERY DAY.

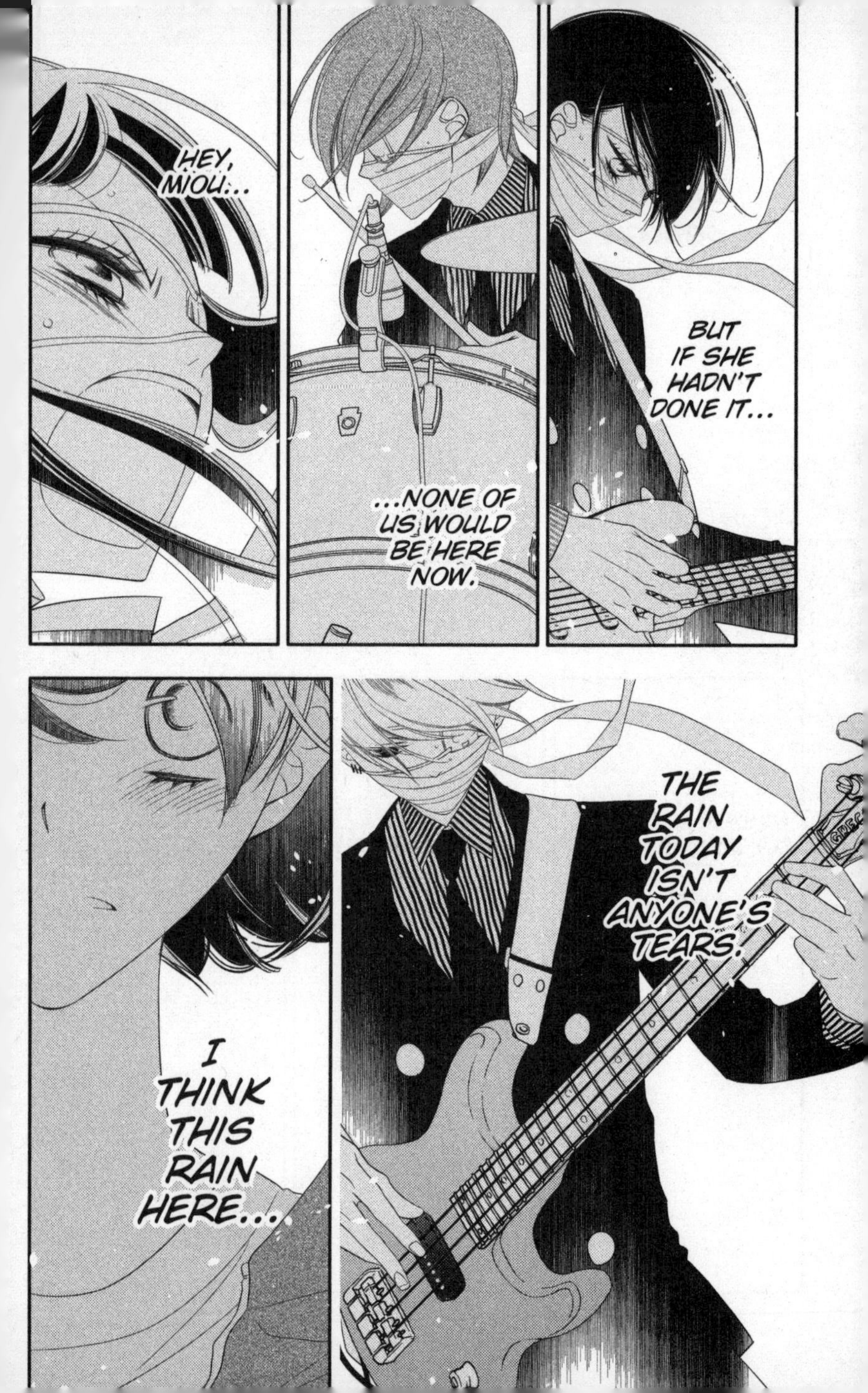
BUT IF SHE HADN'T DONE IT...
...NONE OF US WOULD BE HERE NOW.
HEY, MIOU...
THE RAIN TODAY ISN'T ANYONE'S TEARS.
I THINK THIS RAIN HERE...

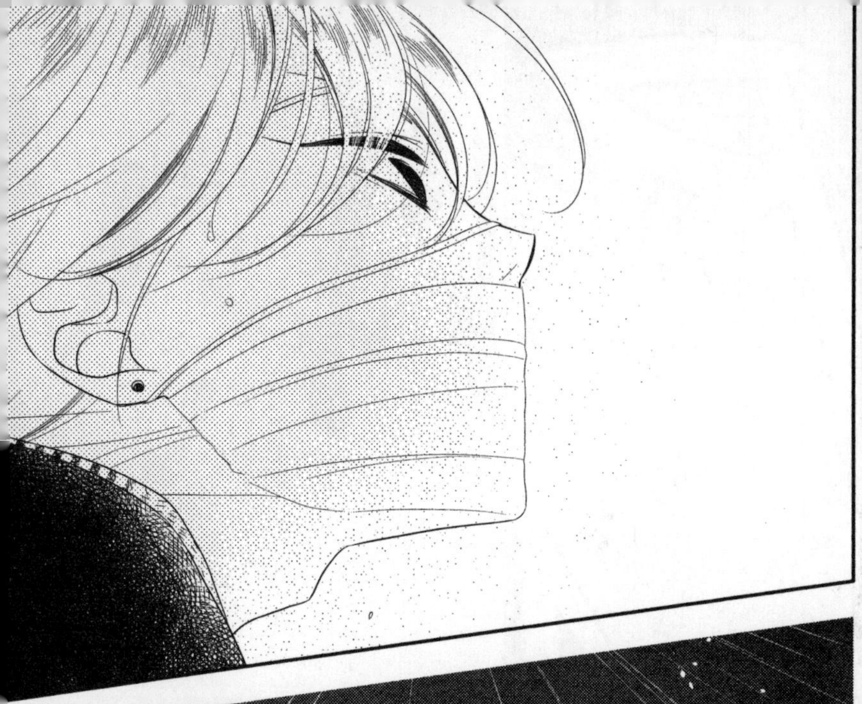
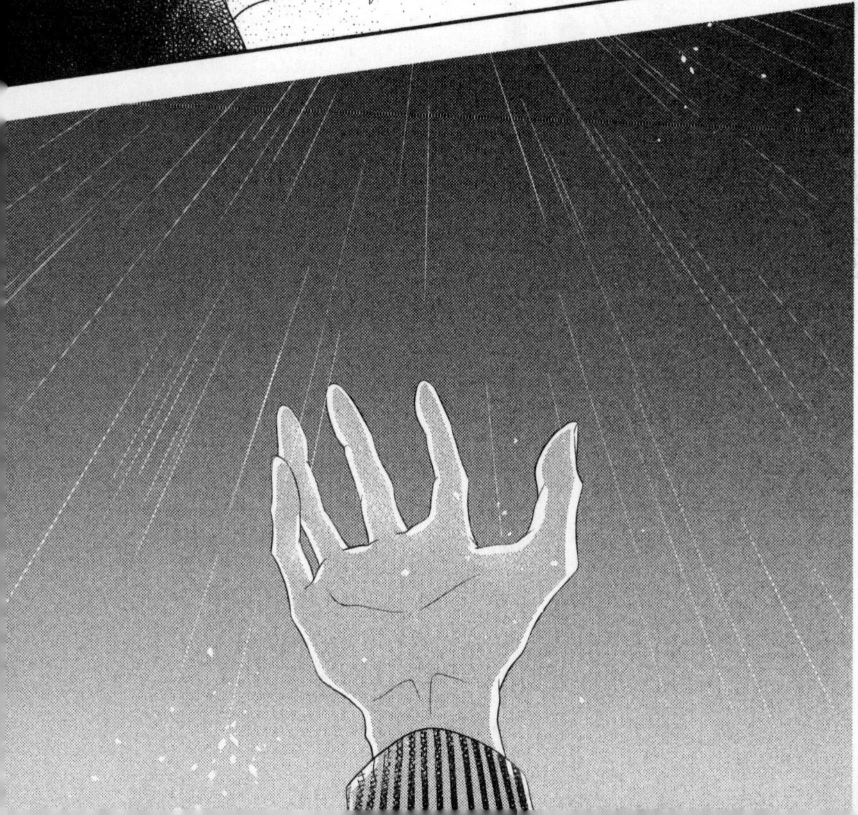

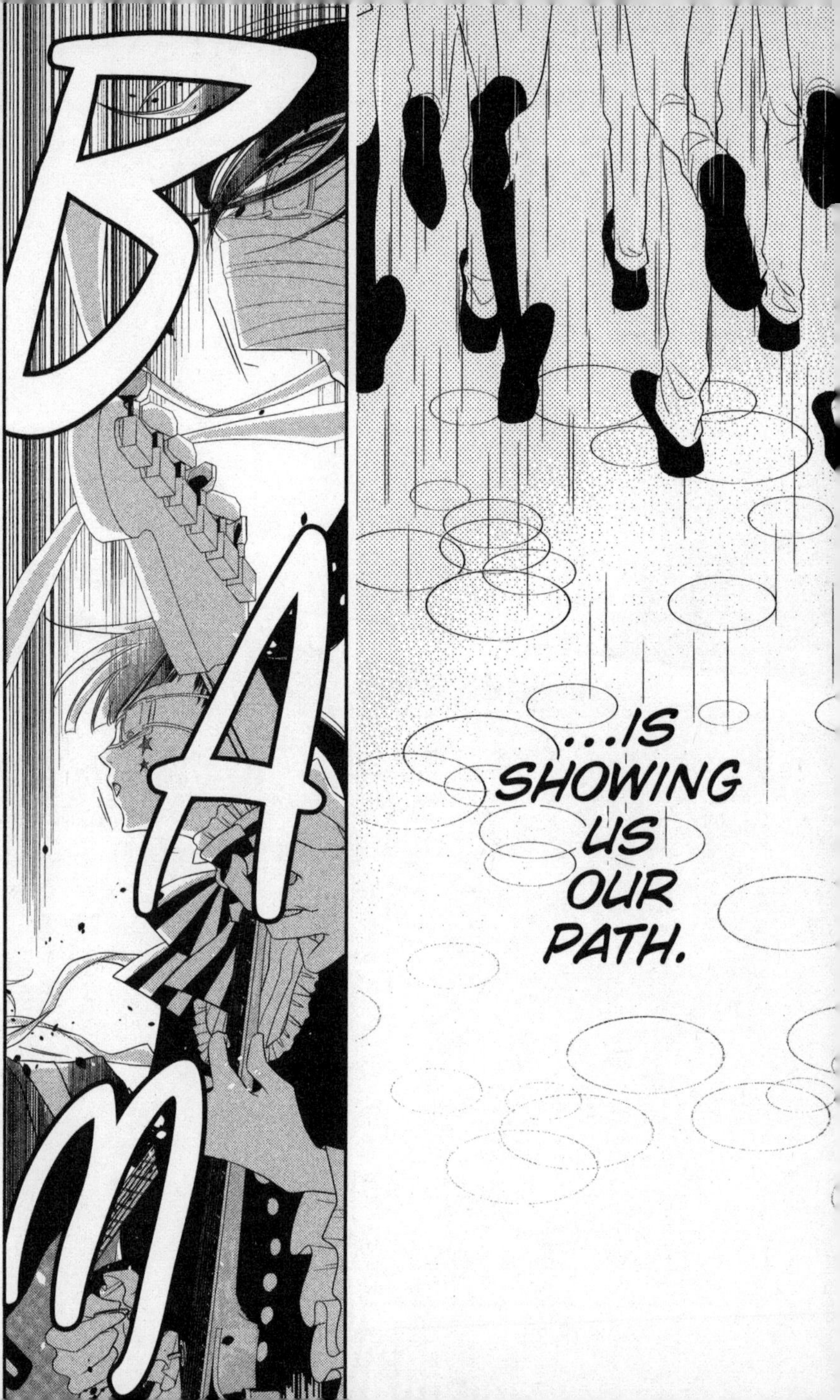
...IS SHOWING US OUR PATH.
BAM

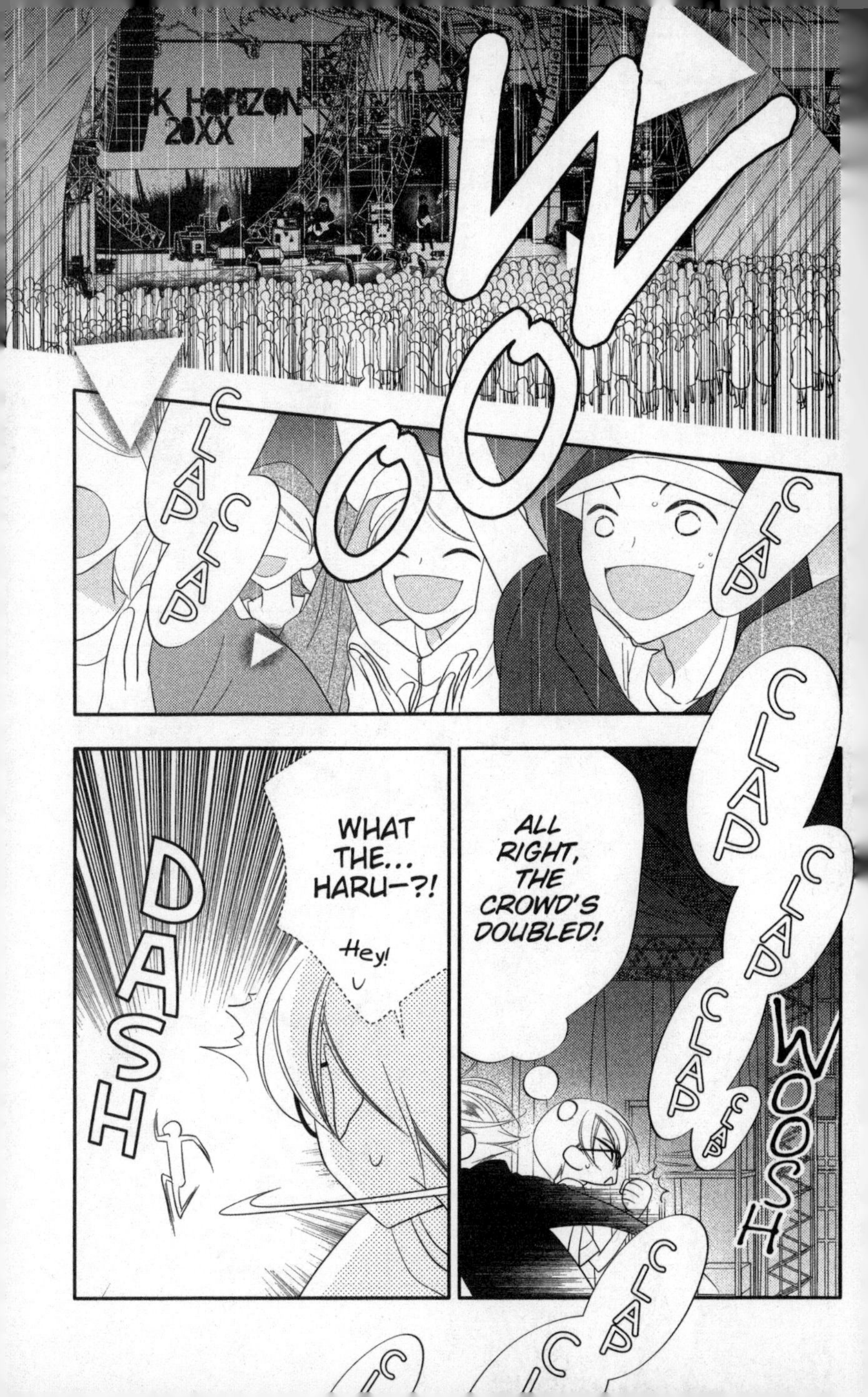
K HORIZON
20XX
WOOO
CLAP CLAP
CLAP CLAP
CLAP CLAP
ALL RIGHT, THE CROWD'S DOUBLED!
CLAP CLAP
WOOSH
CLAP
WHAT THE... HARU-?!
Hey!
DASH

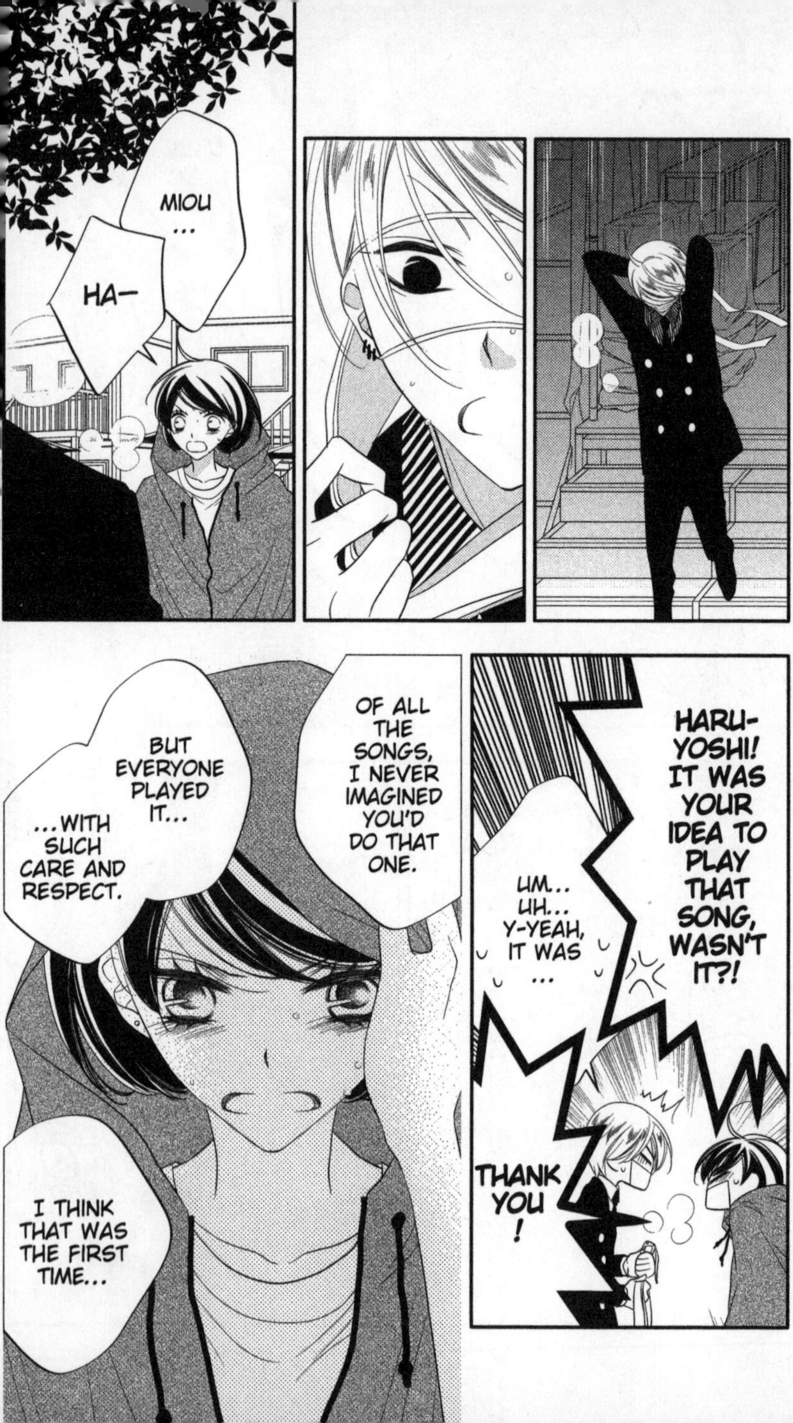
MIOU ...
HA—
HARU-YOSHI! IT WAS YOUR IDEA TO PLAY THAT SONG, WASN'T IT?!
UM... UH... Y-YEAH, IT WAS ...
THANK YOU!
OF ALL THE SONGS, I NEVER IMAGINED YOU'D DO THAT ONE.
BUT EVERYONE PLAYED IT...
...WITH SUCH CARE AND RESPECT.
I THINK THAT WAS THE FIRST TIME...

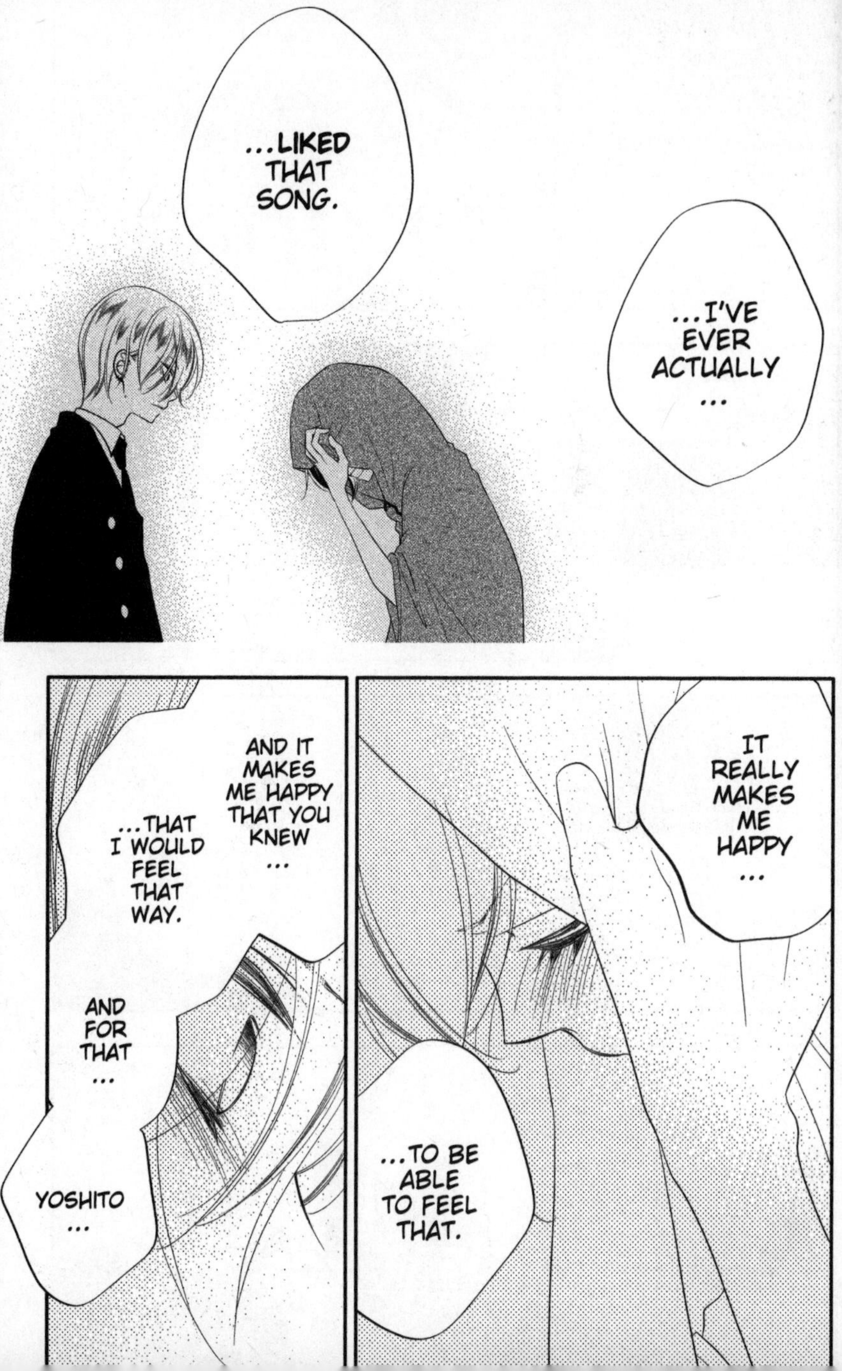
...I'VE EVER ACTUALLY ...
...LIKED THAT SONG.
IT REALLY MAKES ME HAPPY ...
...TO BE ABLE TO FEEL THAT.
AND IT MAKES ME HAPPY THAT YOU KNEW ...
...THAT I WOULD FEEL THAT WAY.
AND FOR THAT ...
YOSHITO ...

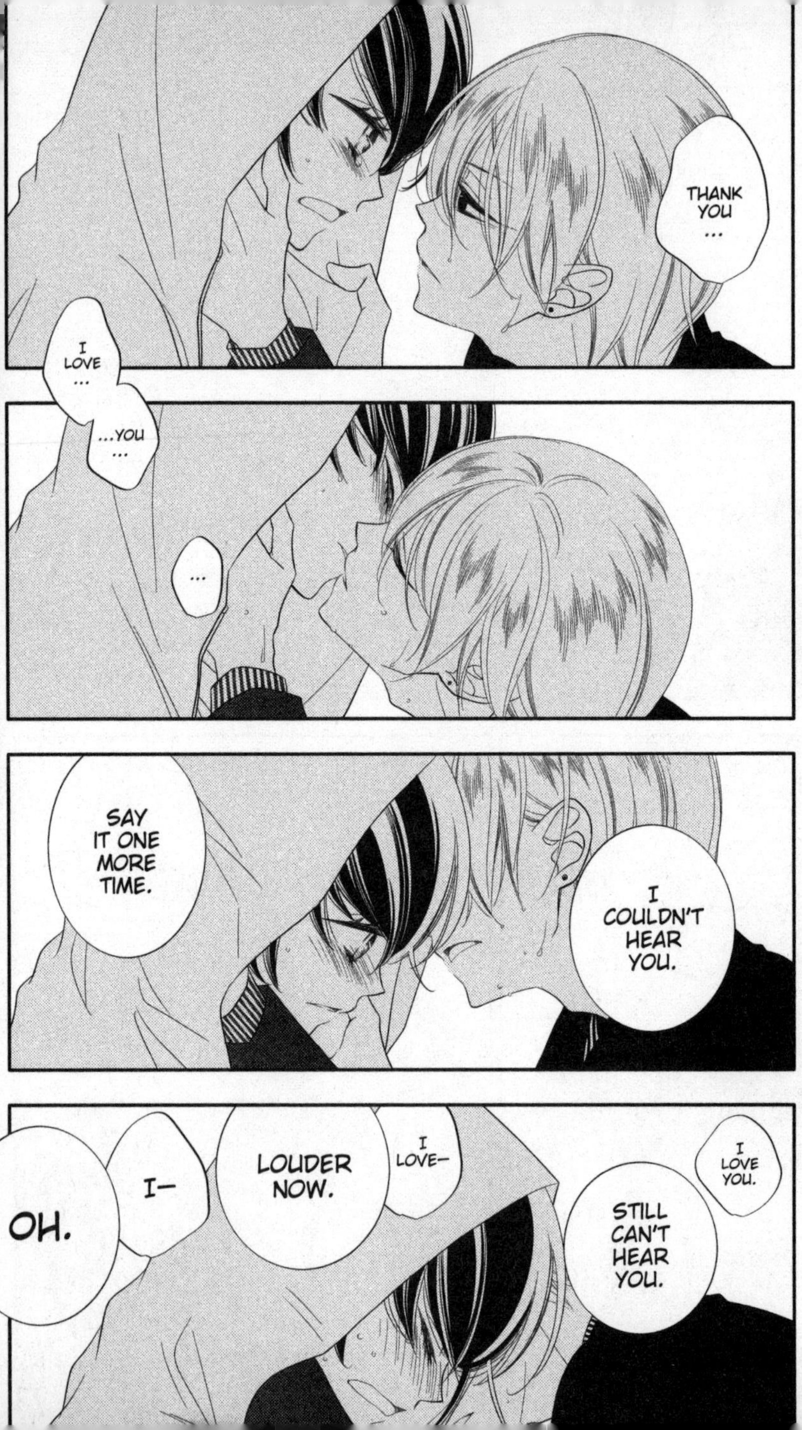
THANK YOU...
I LOVE...
...YOU...
...
I COULDN'T HEAR YOU.
SAY IT ONE MORE TIME.
I LOVE YOU.
STILL CAN'T HEAR YOU.
I LOVE—
LOUDER NOW.
I—
OH.

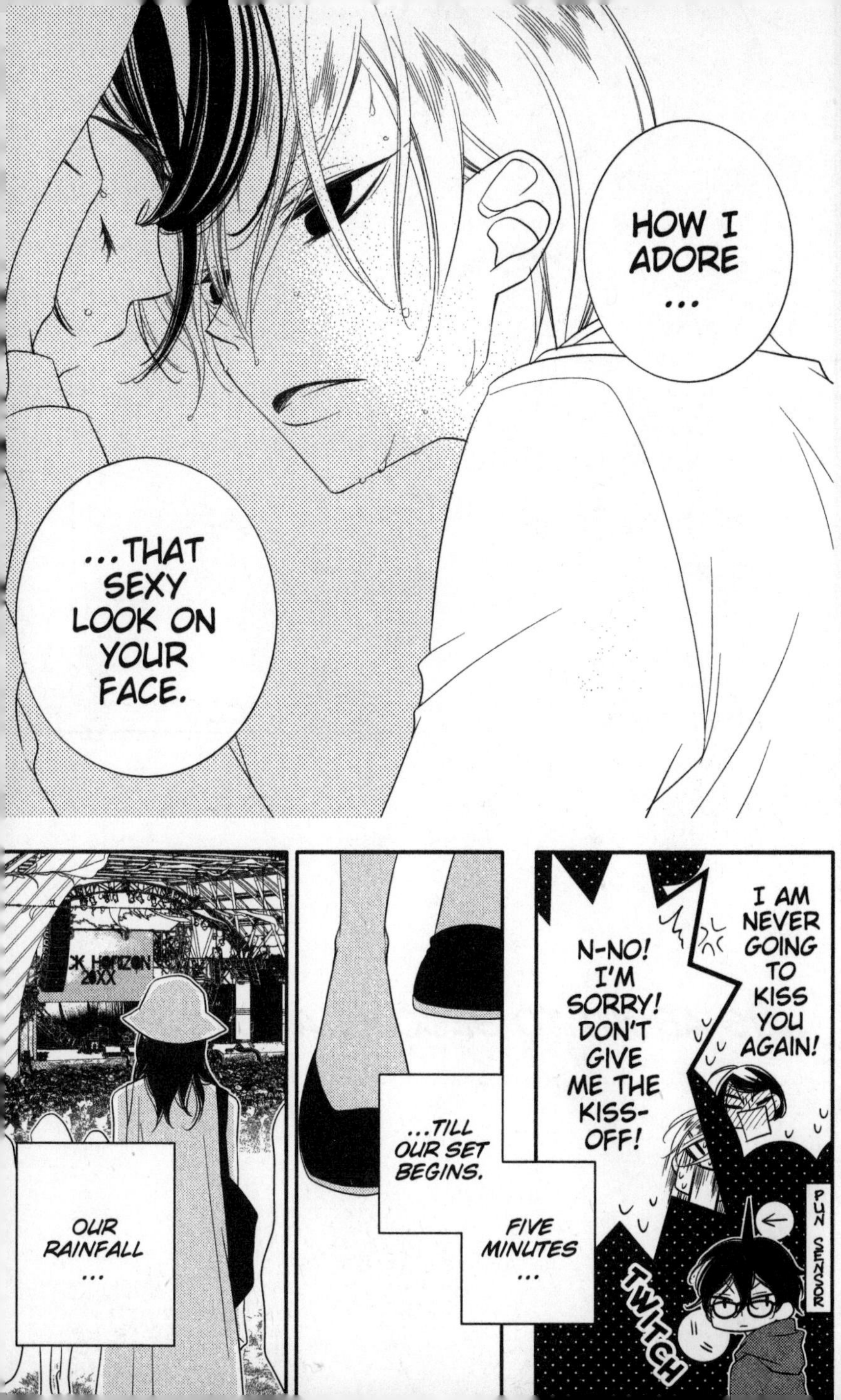
HOW I ADORE ...
...THAT SEXY LOOK ON YOUR FACE.
I AM NEVER GOING TO KISS YOU AGAIN!
N-NO! I'M SORRY! DON'T GIVE ME THE KISS-OFF!
PUN SENSOR
TWITCH
FIVE MINUTES ...
...TILL OUR SET BEGINS.
HORIZON 20XX
OUR RAINFALL ...

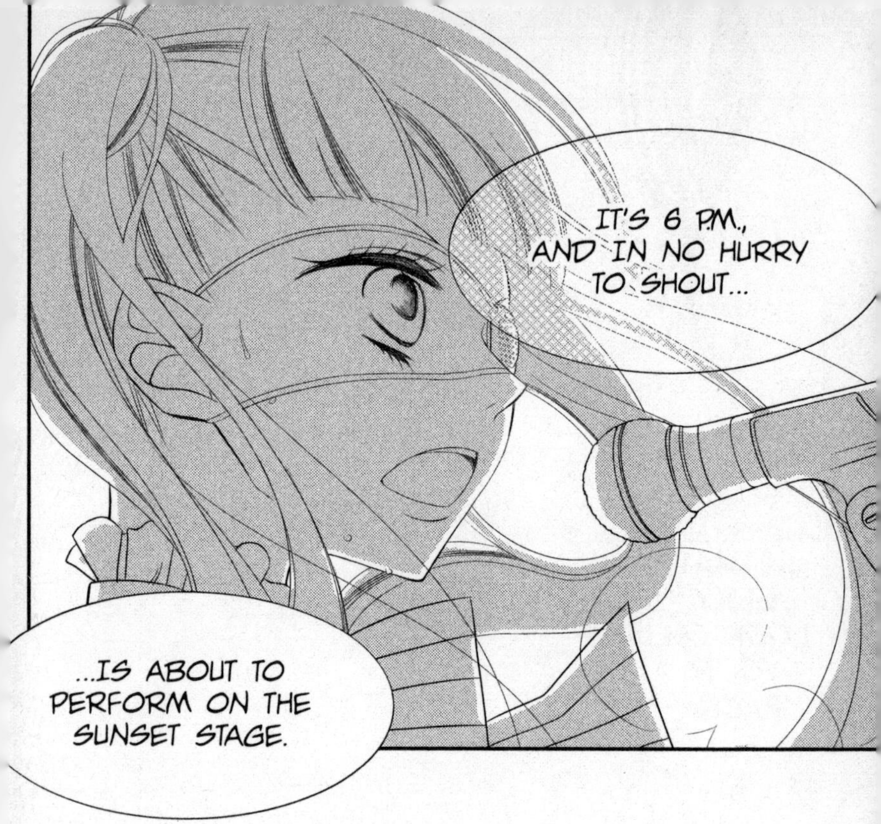
IT'S 6 P.M., AND IN NO HURRY TO SHOUT...
...IS ABOUT TO PERFORM ON THE SUNSET STAGE.

...IS ABOUT TO BECOME A DOWNPOUR.

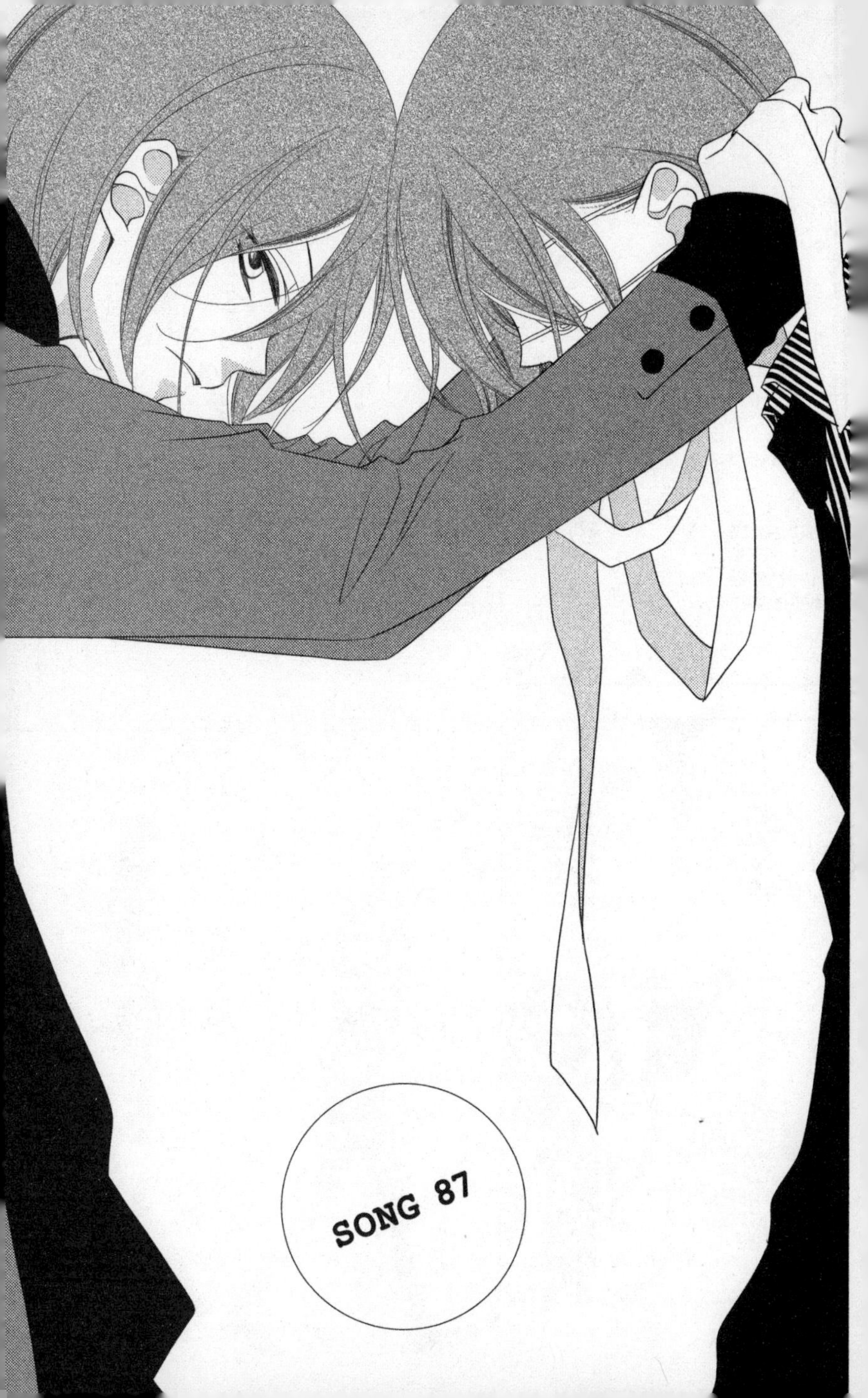
SONG 87

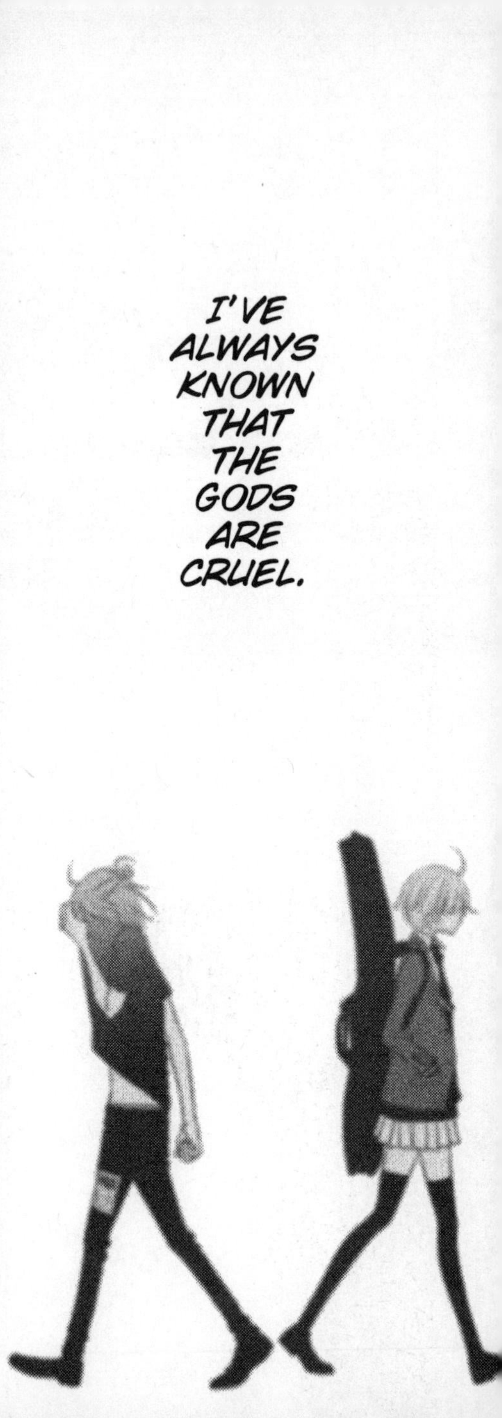
I'VE ALWAYS KNOWN THAT THE GODS ARE CRUEL.

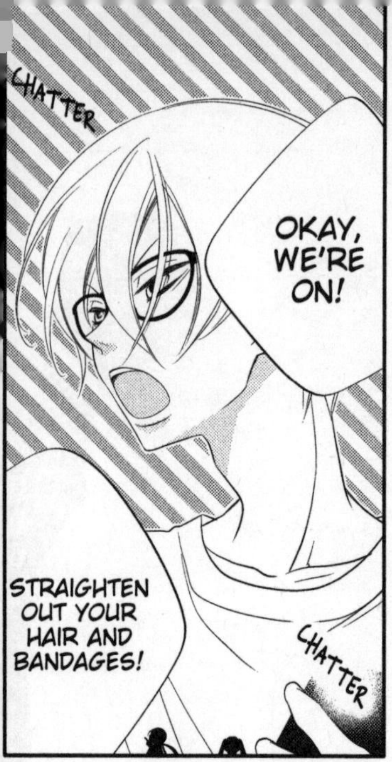
OKAY, WE'RE ON!
CHATTER
STRAIGHTEN OUT YOUR HAIR AND BANDAGES!
CHATTER

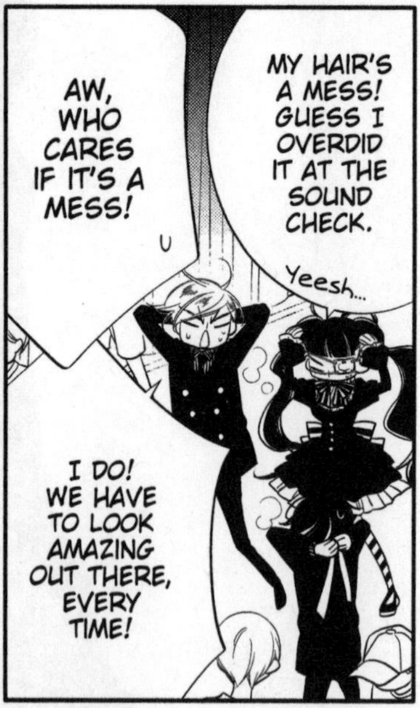
MY HAIR'S A MESS! GUESS I OVERDID IT AT THE SOUND CHECK.
AW, WHO CARES IF IT'S A MESS!
Yeesh...
I DO! WE HAVE TO LOOK AMAZING OUT THERE, EVERY TIME!

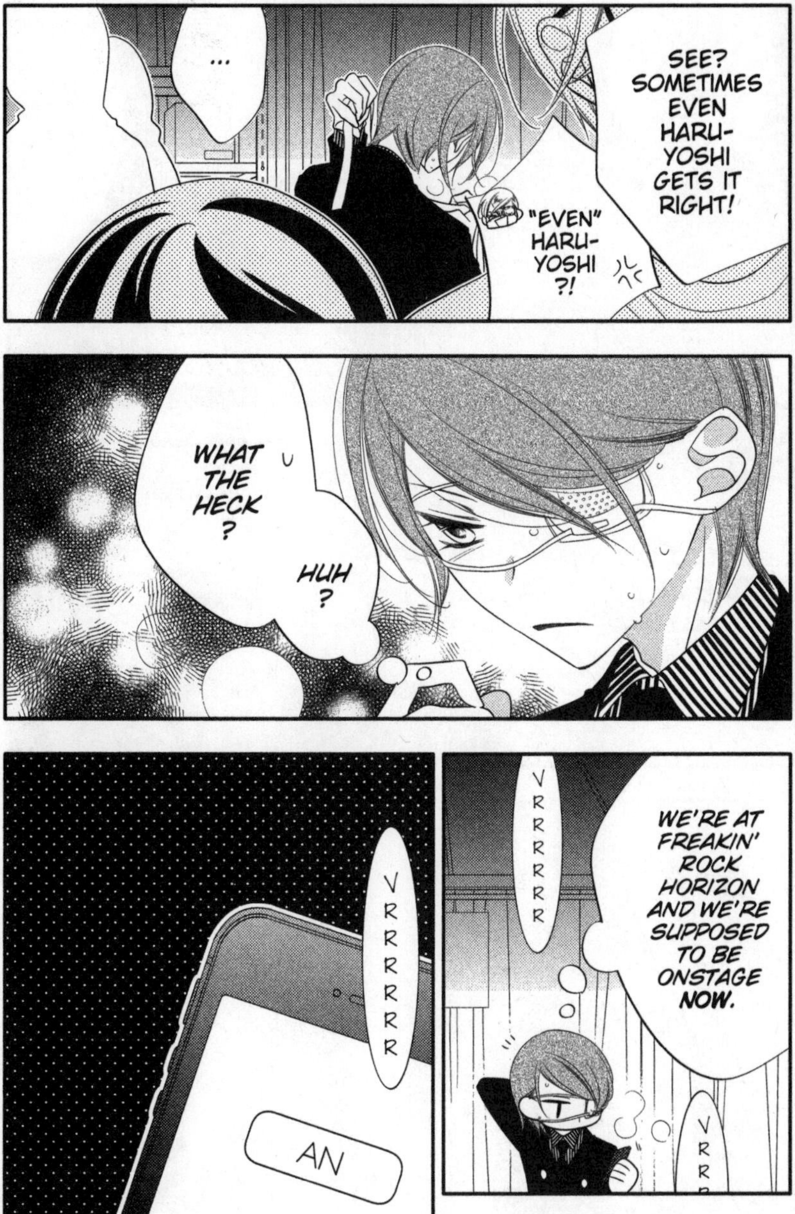
SEE? SOMETIMES EVEN HARU-YOSHI GETS IT RIGHT!
"EVEN" HARU-YOSHI ?!
...
WHAT THE HECK ?
HUH ?
WE'RE AT FREAKIN' ROCK HORIZON AND WE'RE SUPPOSED TO BE ONSTAGE NOW.
VRRRRRR
VRR
VRRRRRR
AN

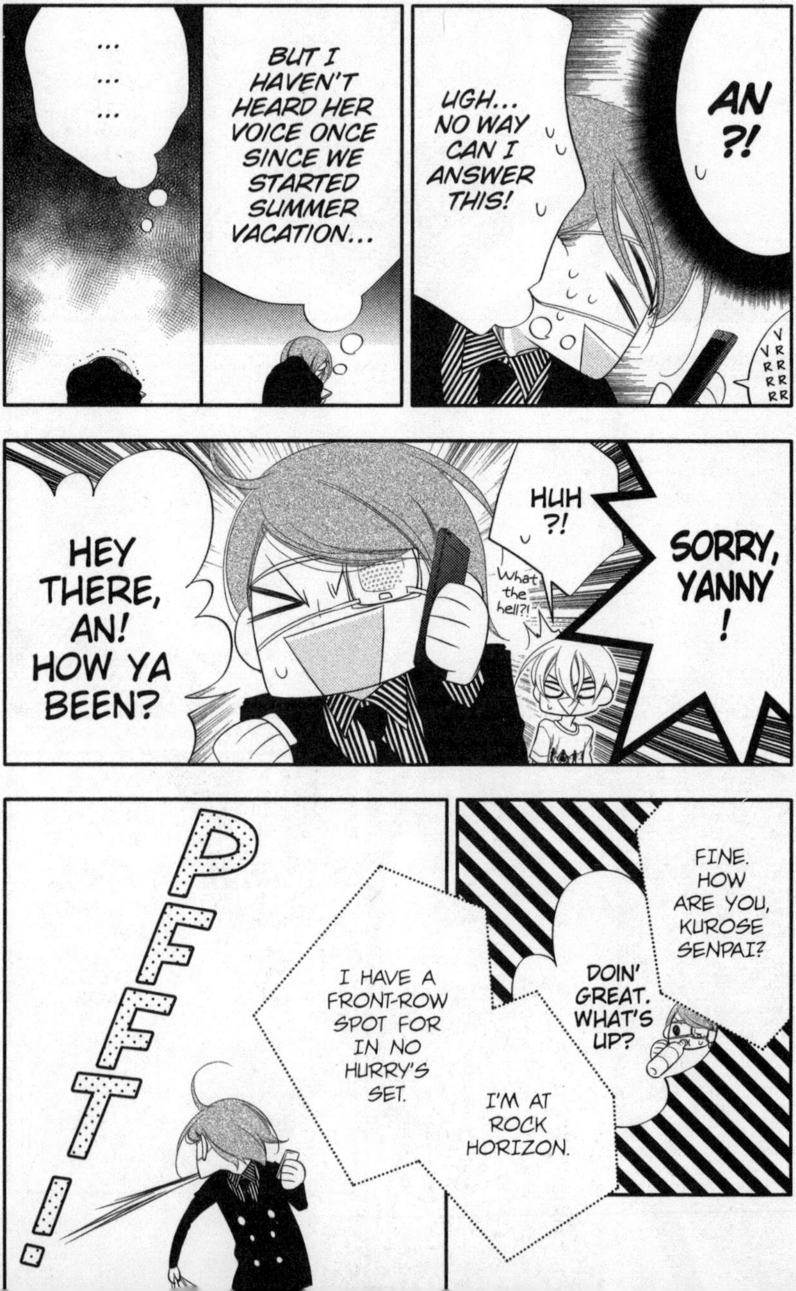
AN ?!
VRRR VRRRR
UGH... NO WAY CAN I ANSWER THIS!
BUT I HAVEN'T HEARD HER VOICE ONCE SINCE WE STARTED SUMMER VACATION...
... ...
SORRY, YANNY!
HUH ?!
What the hell?!
HEY THERE, AN! HOW YA BEEN?
FINE. HOW ARE YOU, KUROSE SENPAI?
DOIN' GREAT. WHAT'S UP?
I'M AT ROCK HORIZON.
I HAVE A FRONT-ROW SPOT FOR IN NO HURRY'S SET.
PFFFT!!

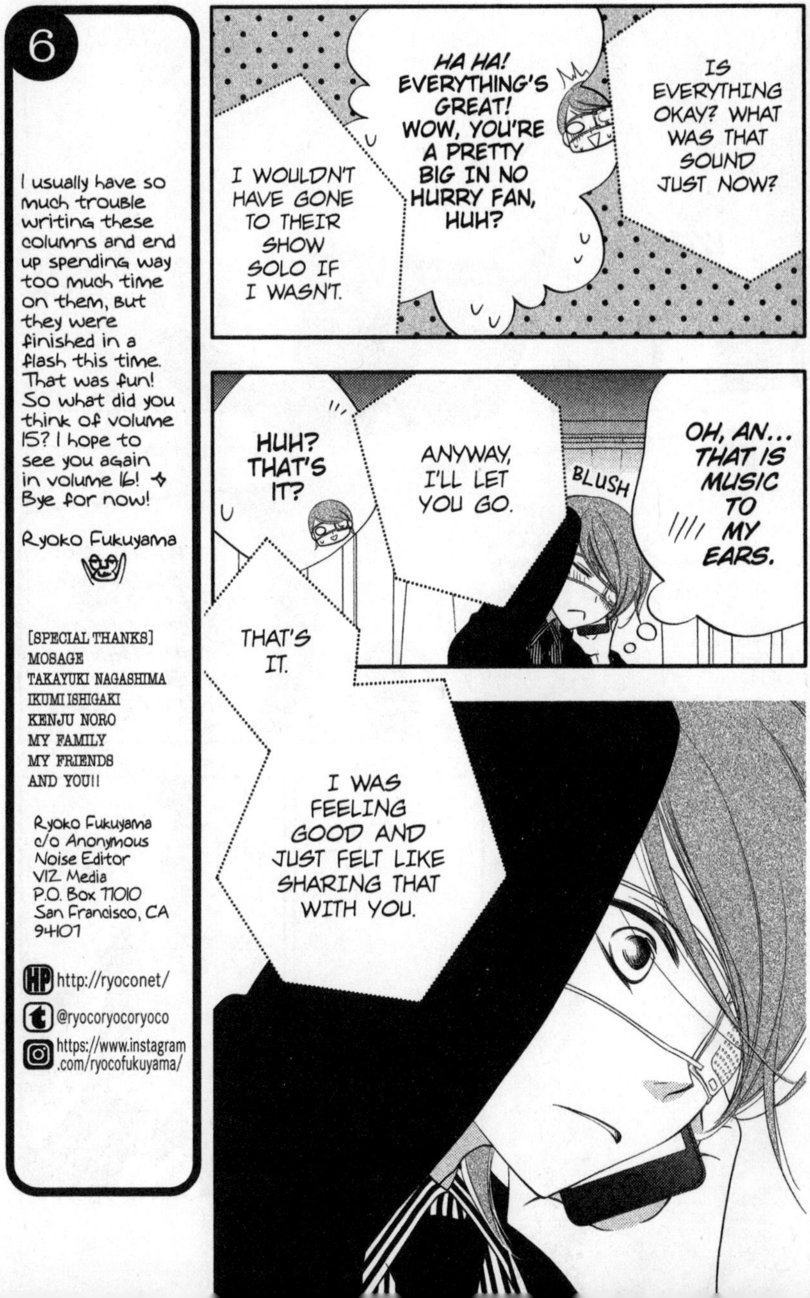
IS EVERYTHING OKAY? WHAT WAS THAT SOUND JUST NOW?
HA HA! EVERYTHING'S GREAT! WOW, YOU'RE A PRETTY BIG IN NO HURRY FAN, HUH?
I WOULDN'T HAVE GONE TO THEIR SHOW SOLO IF I WASN'T.
OH, AN... THAT IS MUSIC TO MY EARS.
BLUSH
ANYWAY, I'LL LET YOU GO.
HUH? THAT'S IT?
THAT'S IT.
I WAS FEELING GOOD AND JUST FELT LIKE SHARING THAT WITH YOU.

6

I usually have so much trouble writing these columns and end up spending way too much time on them, but they were finished in a flash this time. That was fun! So what did you think of volume 15? I hope to see you again in volume 16! ✧ Bye for now!

Ryoko Fukuyama

[SPECIAL THANKS]
MOSAGE
TAKAYUKI NAGASHIMA
IKUMI ISHIGAKI
KENJU NORO
MY FAMILY
MY FRIENDS
AND YOU!!

Ryoko Fukuyama
c/o Anonymous Noise Editor
VIZ Media
P.O. Box 77010
San Francisco, CA 94107

HP http://ryoconet/
@ryocoryocoryoco
https://www.instagram.com/ryocofukuyama/

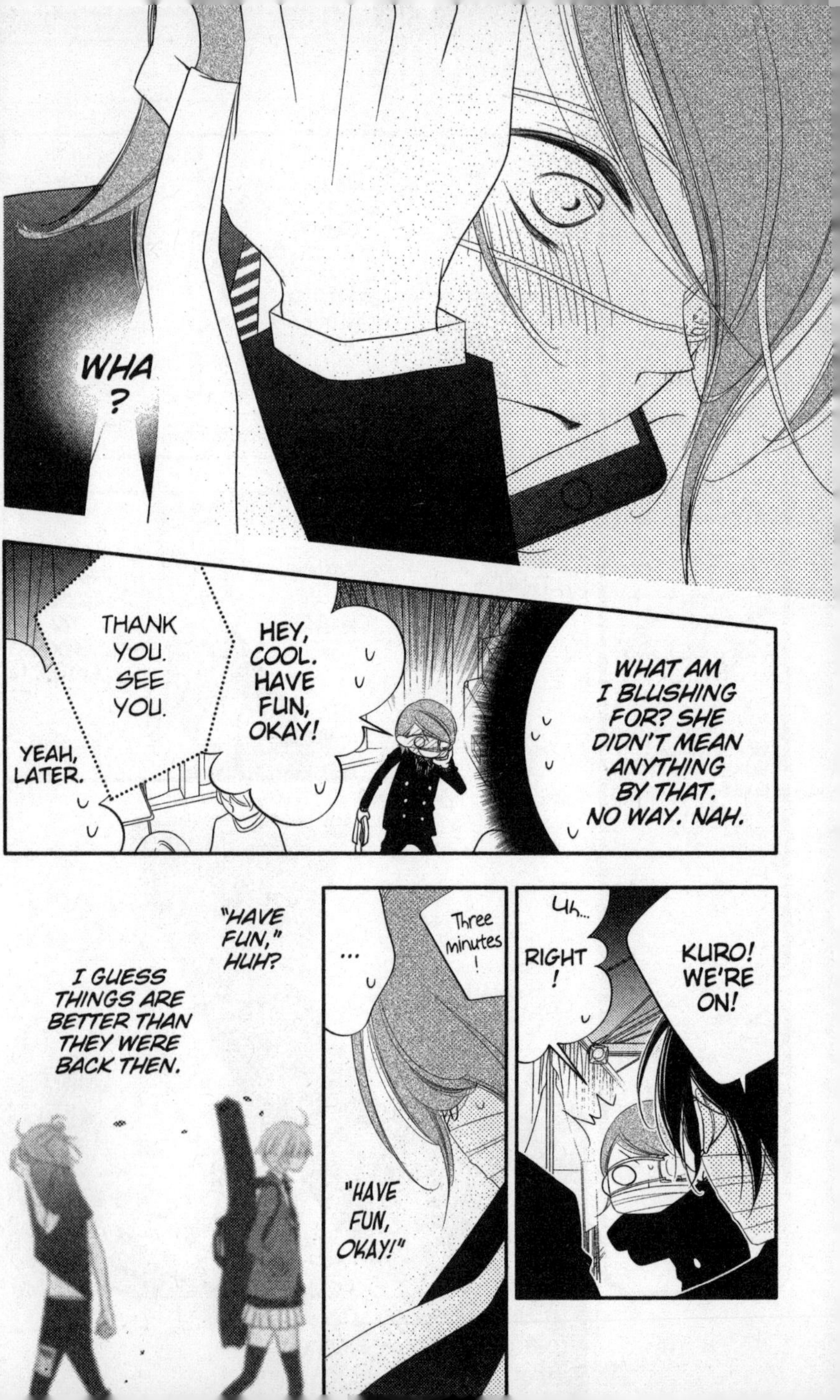
WHA ?
WHAT AM I BLUSHING FOR? SHE DIDN'T MEAN ANYTHING BY THAT. NO WAY. NAH.
HEY, COOL. HAVE FUN, OKAY!
THANK YOU. SEE YOU.
YEAH, LATER.
KURO! WE'RE ON!
Uh...
RIGHT!
Three minutes!
...
"HAVE FUN, OKAY!"
"HAVE FUN," HUH?
I GUESS THINGS ARE BETTER THAN THEY WERE BACK THEN.

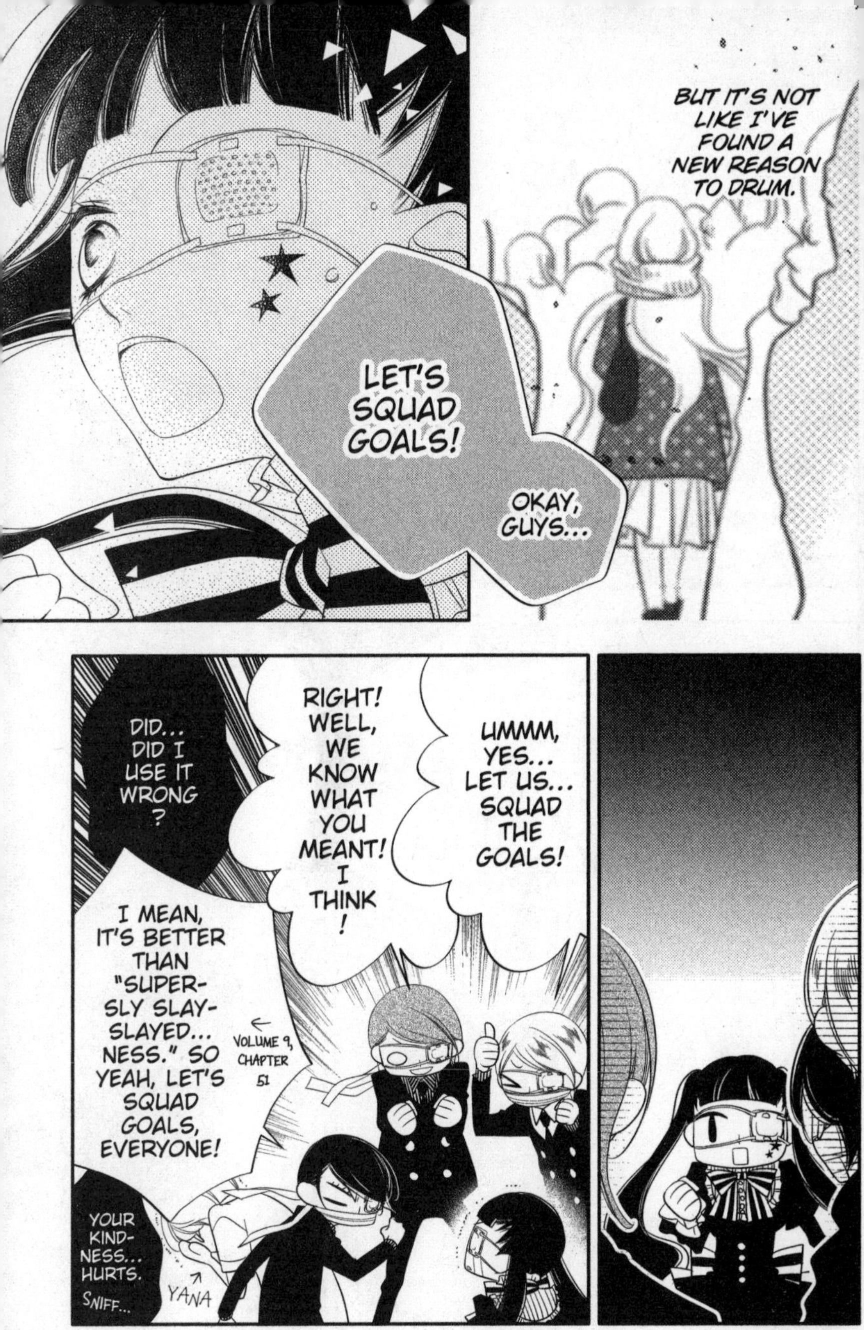
BUT IT'S NOT LIKE I'VE FOUND A NEW REASON TO DRUM.
OKAY, GUYS...
LET'S SQUAD GOALS!
UMMM, YES... LET US... SQUAD THE GOALS!
RIGHT! WELL, WE KNOW WHAT YOU MEANT! I THINK!
DID... DID I USE IT WRONG?
I MEAN, IT'S BETTER THAN "SUPER-SLY SLAY-SLAYED... NESS." SO YEAH, LET'S SQUAD GOALS, EVERYONE!
VOLUME 9, CHAPTER 51
YOUR KINDNESS... HURTS.
SNIFF...
YANA

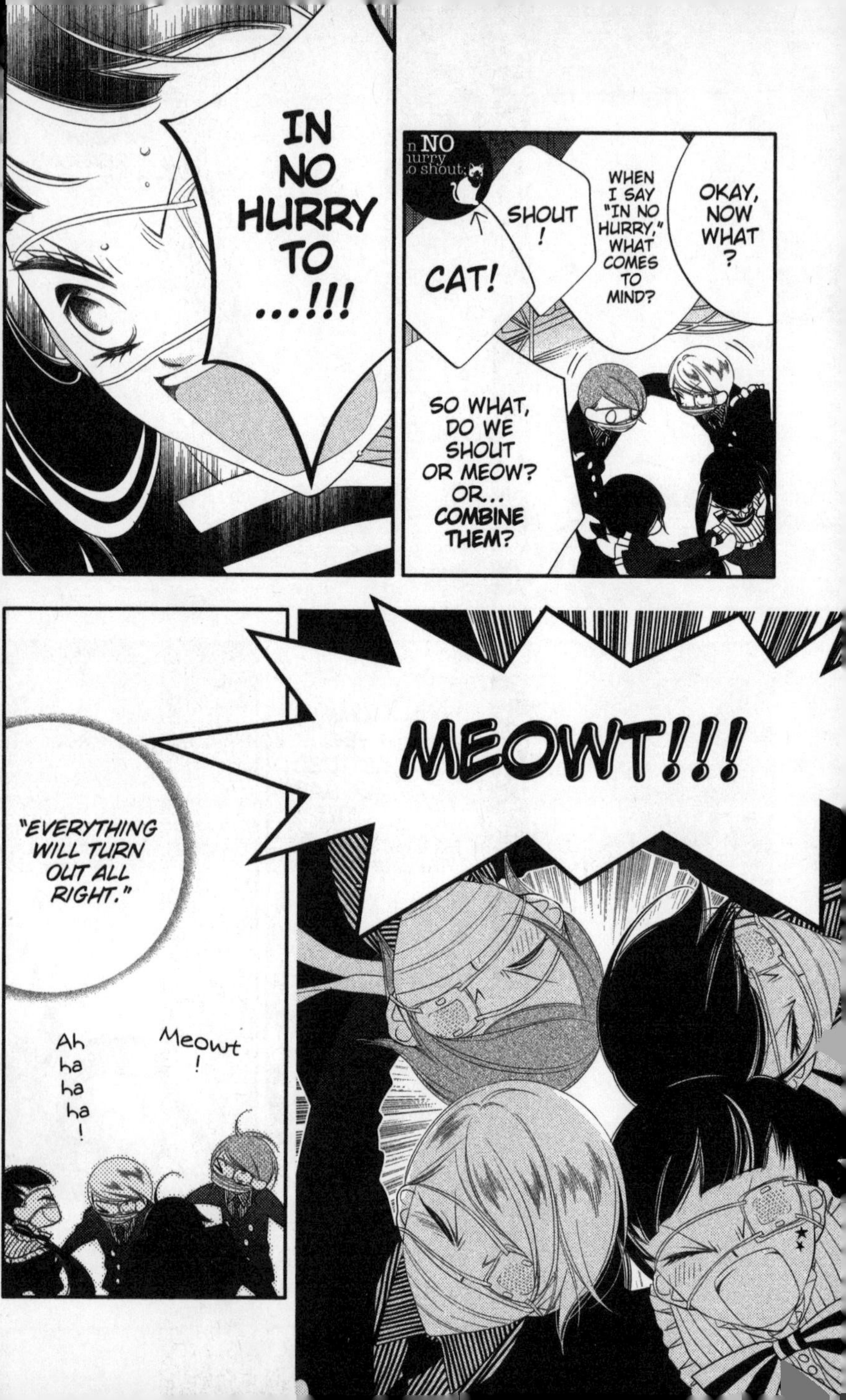
OKAY, NOW WHAT?
WHEN I SAY "IN NO HURRY," WHAT COMES TO MIND?
SHOUT!
CAT!
SO WHAT, DO WE SHOUT OR MEOW? OR.. COMBINE THEM?
IN NO HURRY TO ...!!!
MEOWT!!!
"EVERYTHING WILL TURN OUT ALL RIGHT."
Meowt!
Ah ha ha ha!

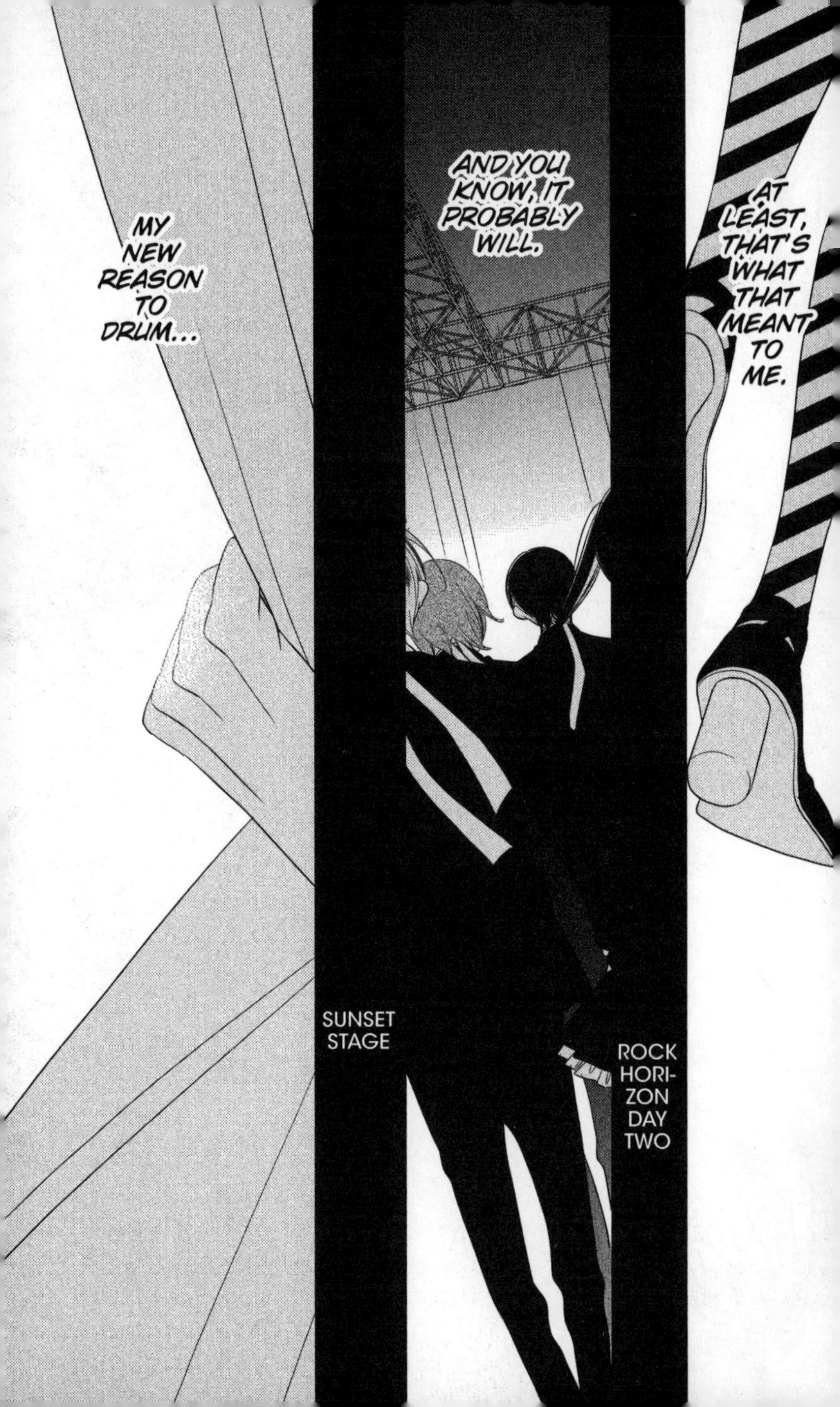
AT LEAST, THAT'S WHAT THAT MEANT TO ME.
ROCK HORIZON DAY TWO
AND YOU KNOW, IT PROBABLY WILL.
SUNSET STAGE
MY NEW REASON TO DRUM...

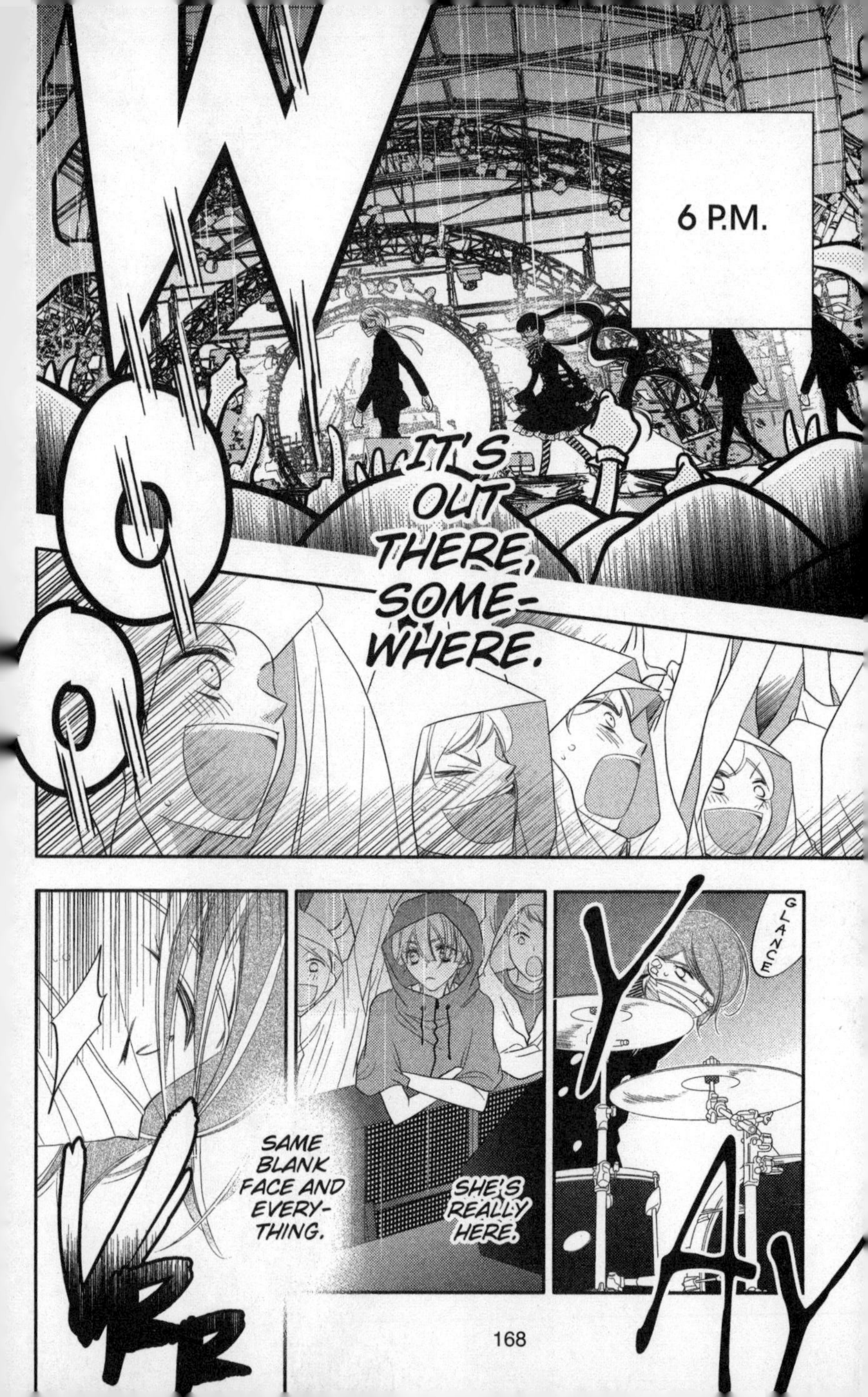
6 P.M.
WOO
IT'S OUT THERE, SOME-WHERE.
GLANCE
YAY
SHE'S REALLY HERE.
SAME BLANK FACE AND EVERY-THING.

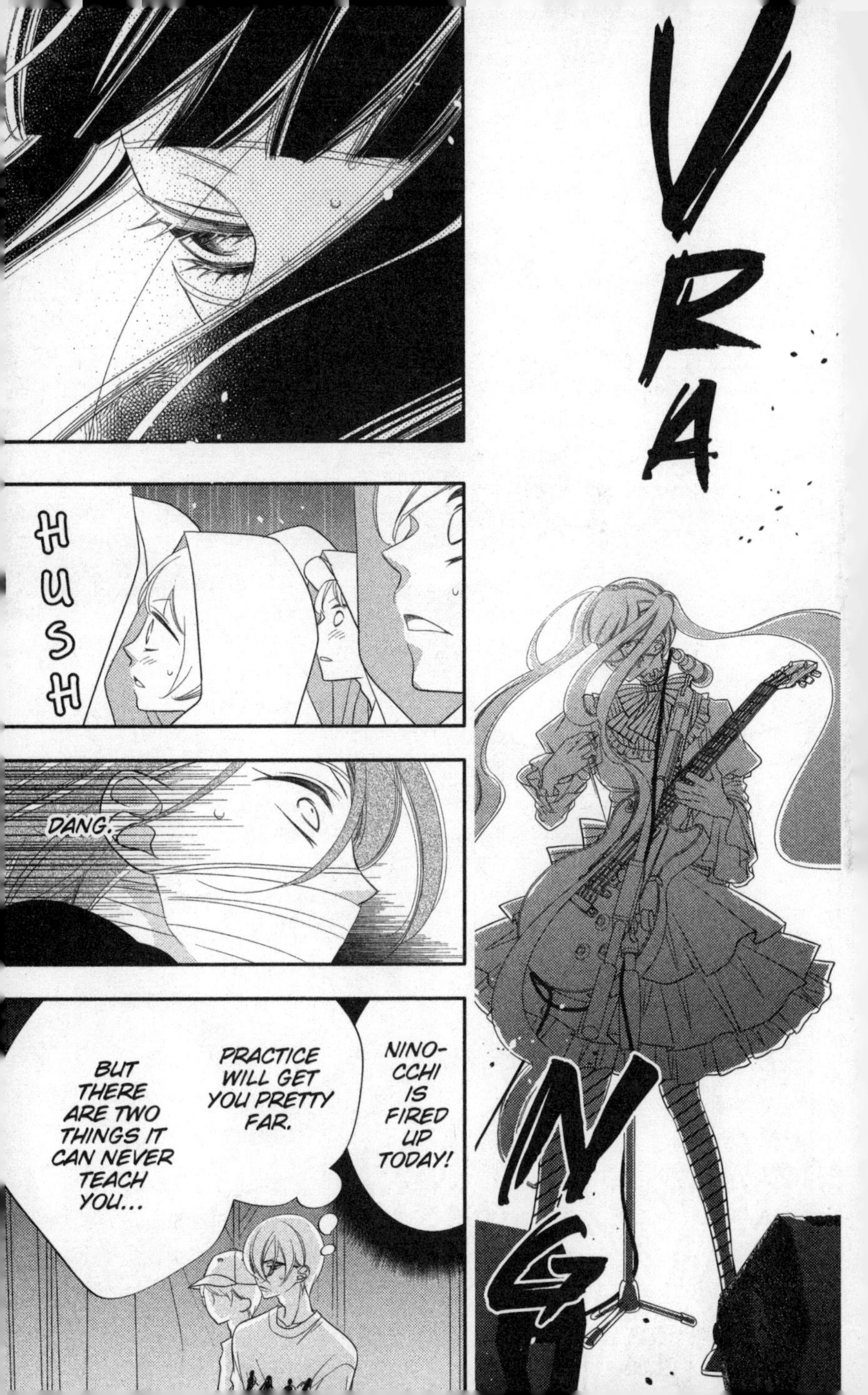
VRA
MNG
HUSH
DANG.
NINO-CCHI IS FIRED UP TODAY!
PRACTICE WILL GET YOU PRETTY FAR.
BUT THERE ARE TWO THINGS IT CAN NEVER TEACH YOU...

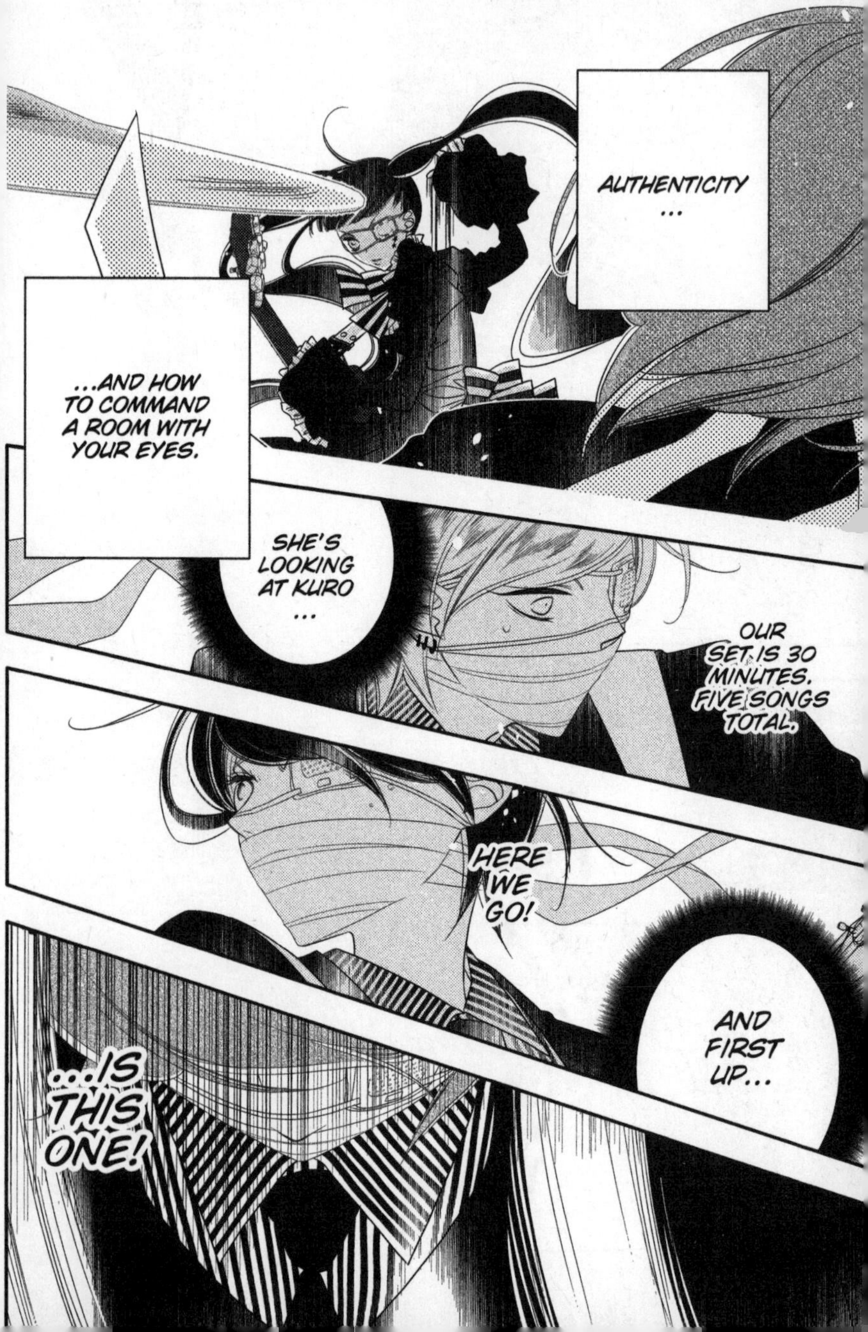
AUTHENTICITY...
...AND HOW TO COMMAND A ROOM WITH YOUR EYES.
SHE'S LOOKING AT KURO...
OUR SET IS 30 MINUTES. FIVE SONGS TOTAL.
HERE WE GO!
AND FIRST UP...
...IS THIS ONE!

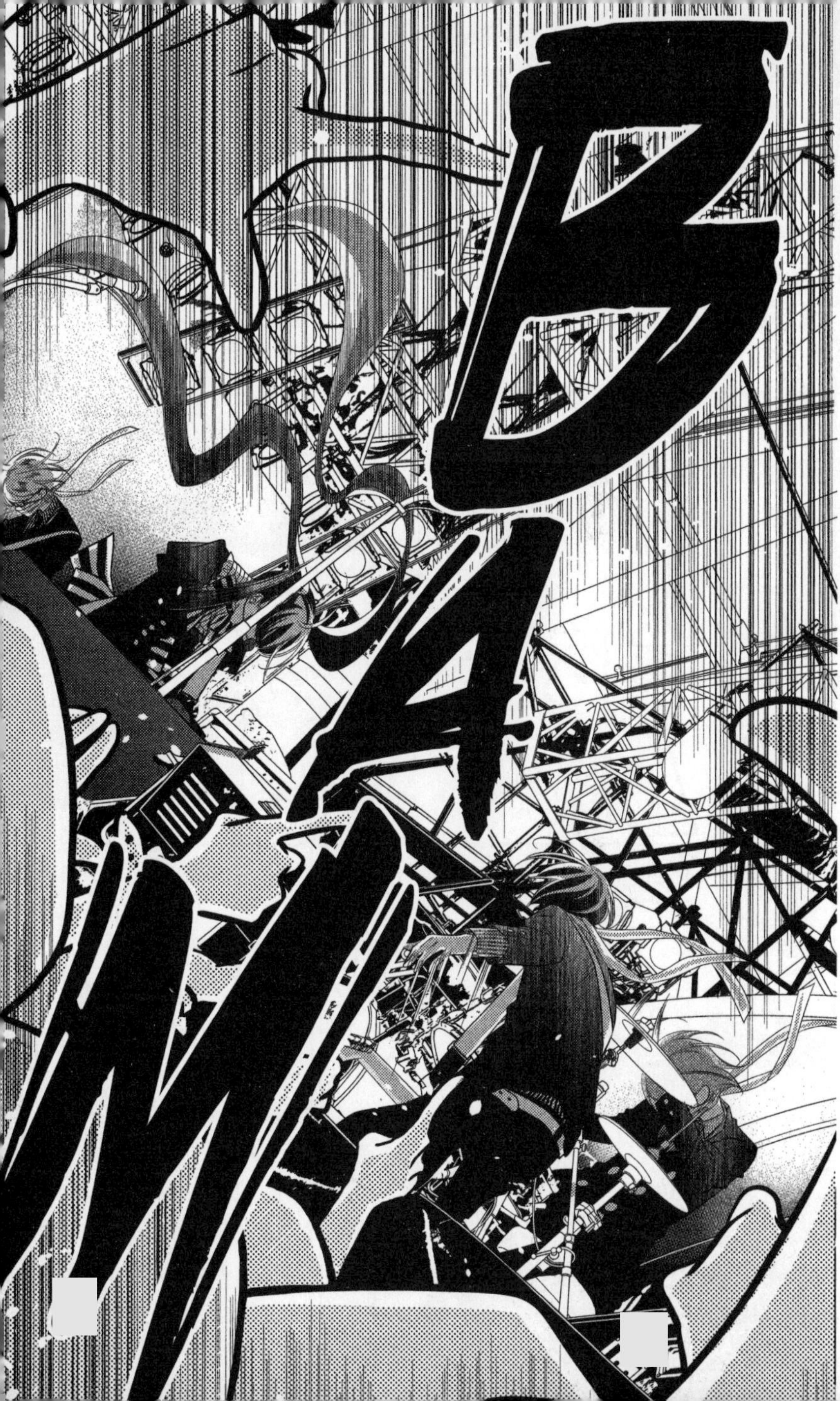
BAM

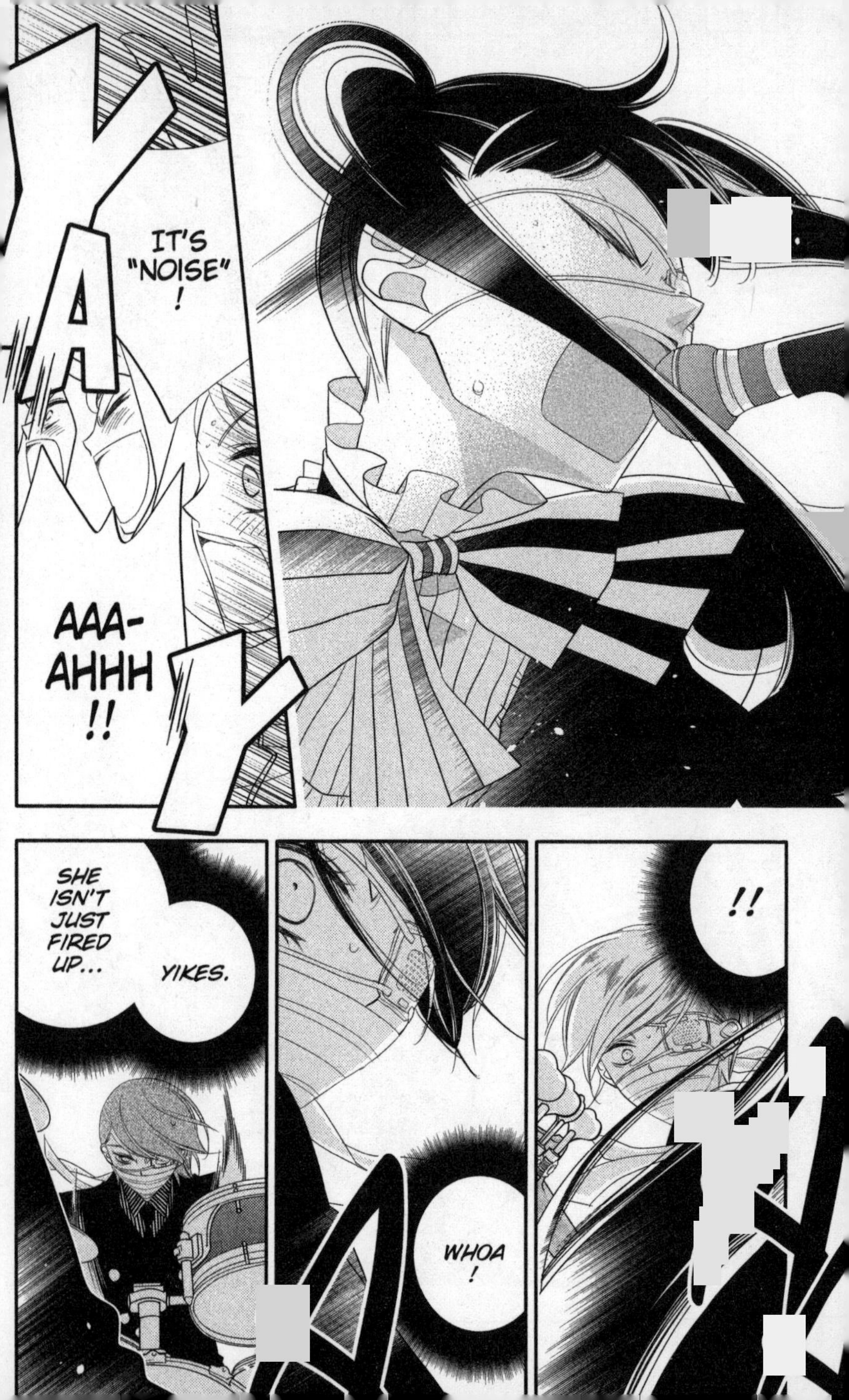
IT'S "NOISE" !
AAA-AHHH !!
!!
WHOA !
SHE ISN'T JUST FIRED UP...
YIKES.

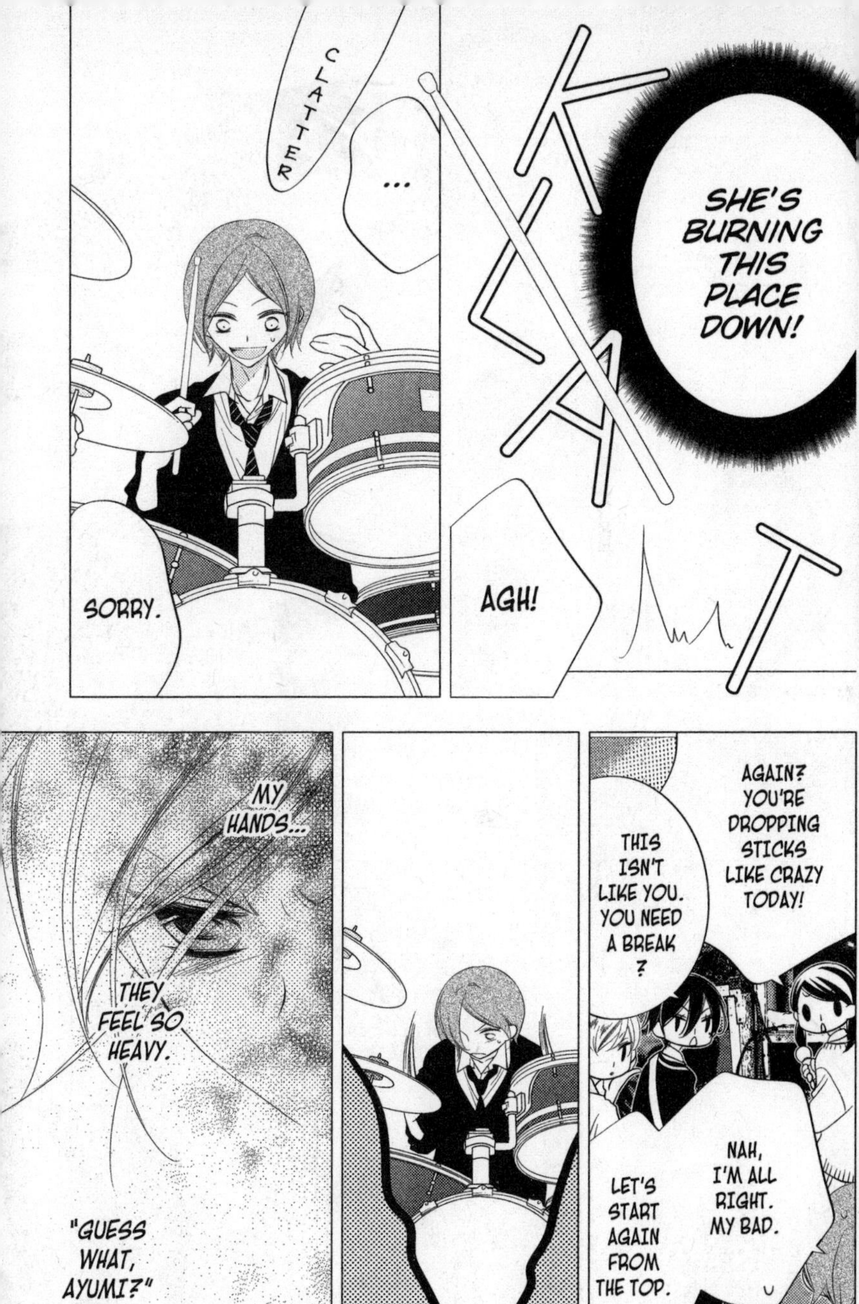
SHE'S BURNING THIS PLACE DOWN!
KLAT
AGH!
CLATTER
...
SORRY.
AGAIN? YOU'RE DROPPING STICKS LIKE CRAZY TODAY!
THIS ISN'T LIKE YOU. YOU NEED A BREAK?
NAH, I'M ALL RIGHT. MY BAD.
LET'S START AGAIN FROM THE TOP.
MY HANDS...
THEY FEEL SO HEAVY.
"GUESS WHAT, AYUMI?"

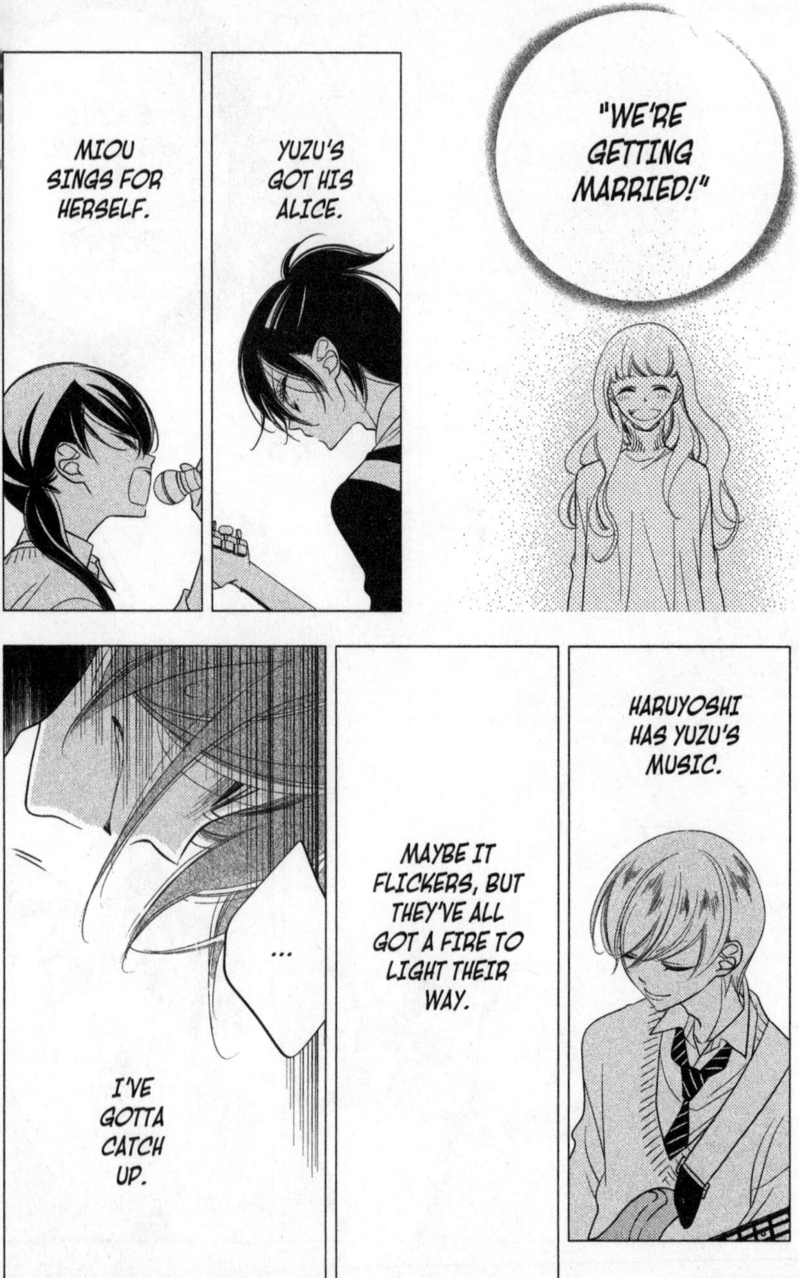
"WE'RE GETTING MARRIED!"
YUZU'S GOT HIS ALICE.
MIOU SINGS FOR HERSELF.
HARUYOSHI HAS YUZU'S MUSIC.
MAYBE IT FLICKERS, BUT THEY'VE ALL GOT A FIRE TO LIGHT THEIR WAY.
...
I'VE GOTTA CATCH UP.

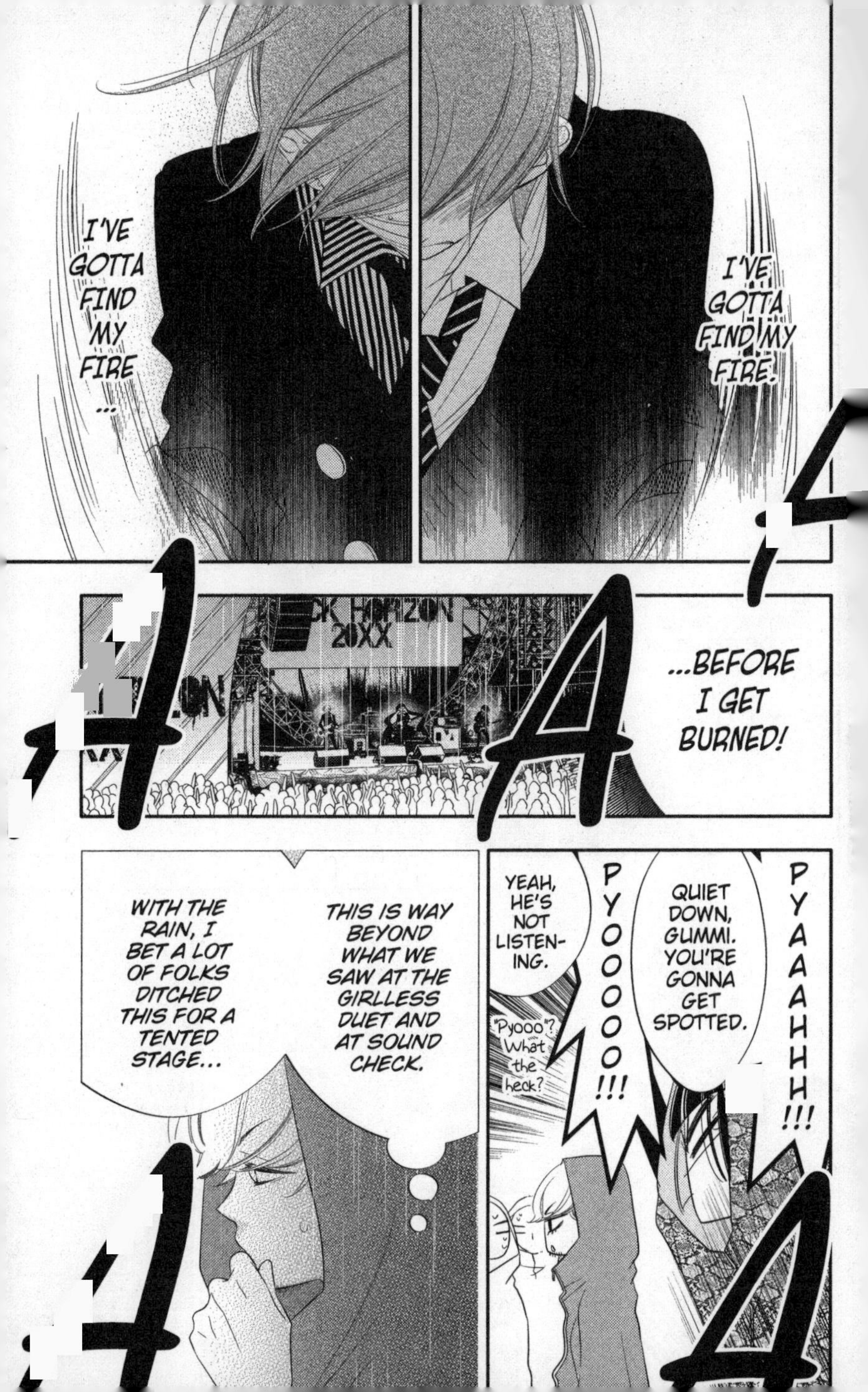
I'VE GOTTA FIND MY FIRE.
I'VE GOTTA FIND MY FIRE...
...BEFORE I GET BURNED!
PYAAAHHH!!!
QUIET DOWN, GUMMI. YOU'RE GONNA GET SPOTTED.
PYOOOOO!!!
YEAH, HE'S NOT LISTEN-ING.
"Pyooo"? What the heck?
THIS IS WAY BEYOND WHAT WE SAW AT THE GIRLLESS DUET AND AT SOUND CHECK.
WITH THE RAIN, I BET A LOT OF FOLKS DITCHED THIS FOR A TENTED STAGE...

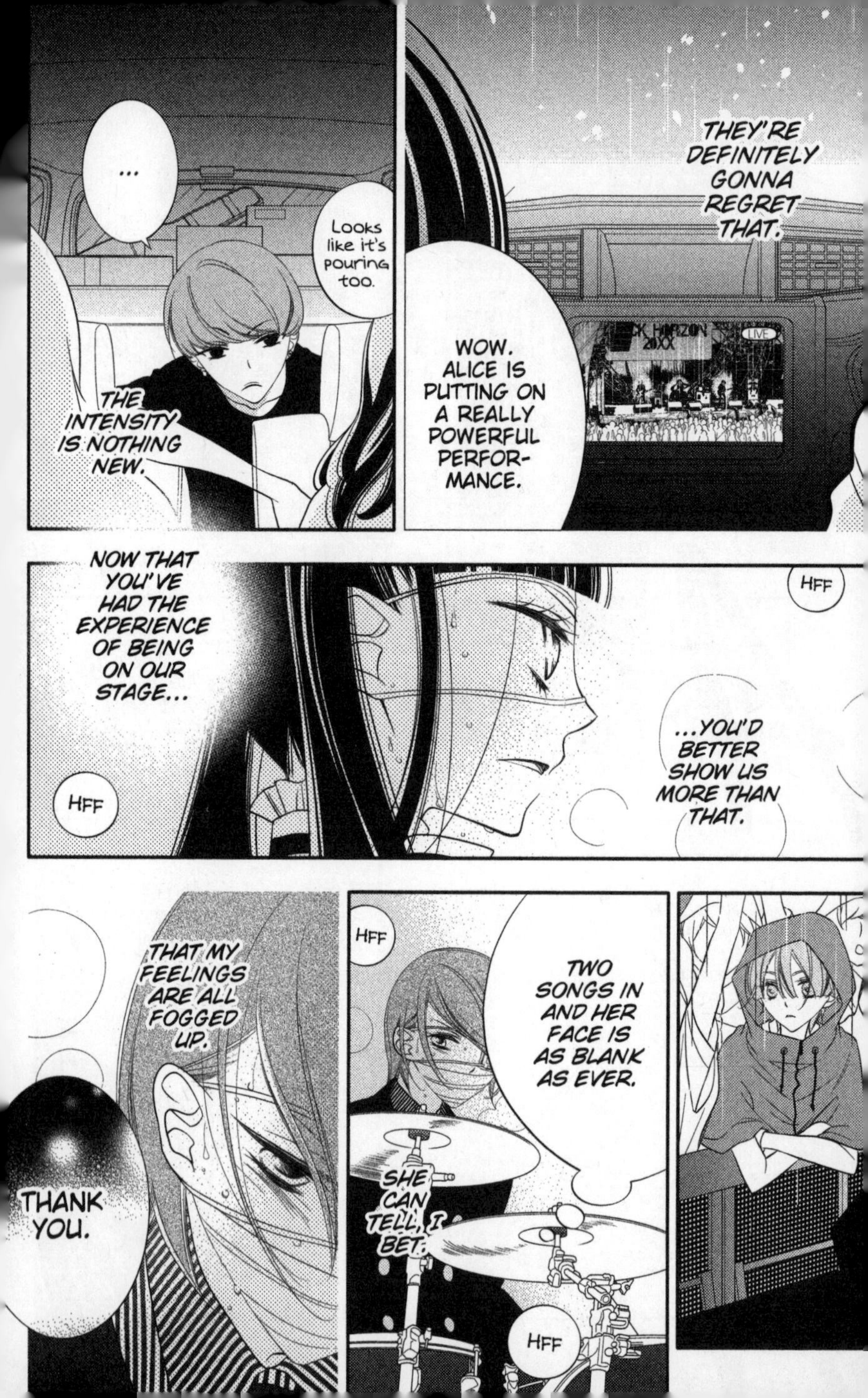
THEY'RE DEFINITELY GONNA REGRET THAT.
LIVE
WOW. ALICE IS PUTTING ON A REALLY POWERFUL PERFORMANCE.
Looks like it's pouring too.
...
THE INTENSITY IS NOTHING NEW.
HFF
NOW THAT YOU'VE HAD THE EXPERIENCE OF BEING ON OUR STAGE...
...YOU'D BETTER SHOW US MORE THAN THAT.
HFF
HFF
TWO SONGS IN AND HER FACE IS AS BLANK AS EVER.
SHE CAN TELL, I BET.
HFF
THAT MY FEELINGS ARE ALL FOGGED UP.
THANK YOU.

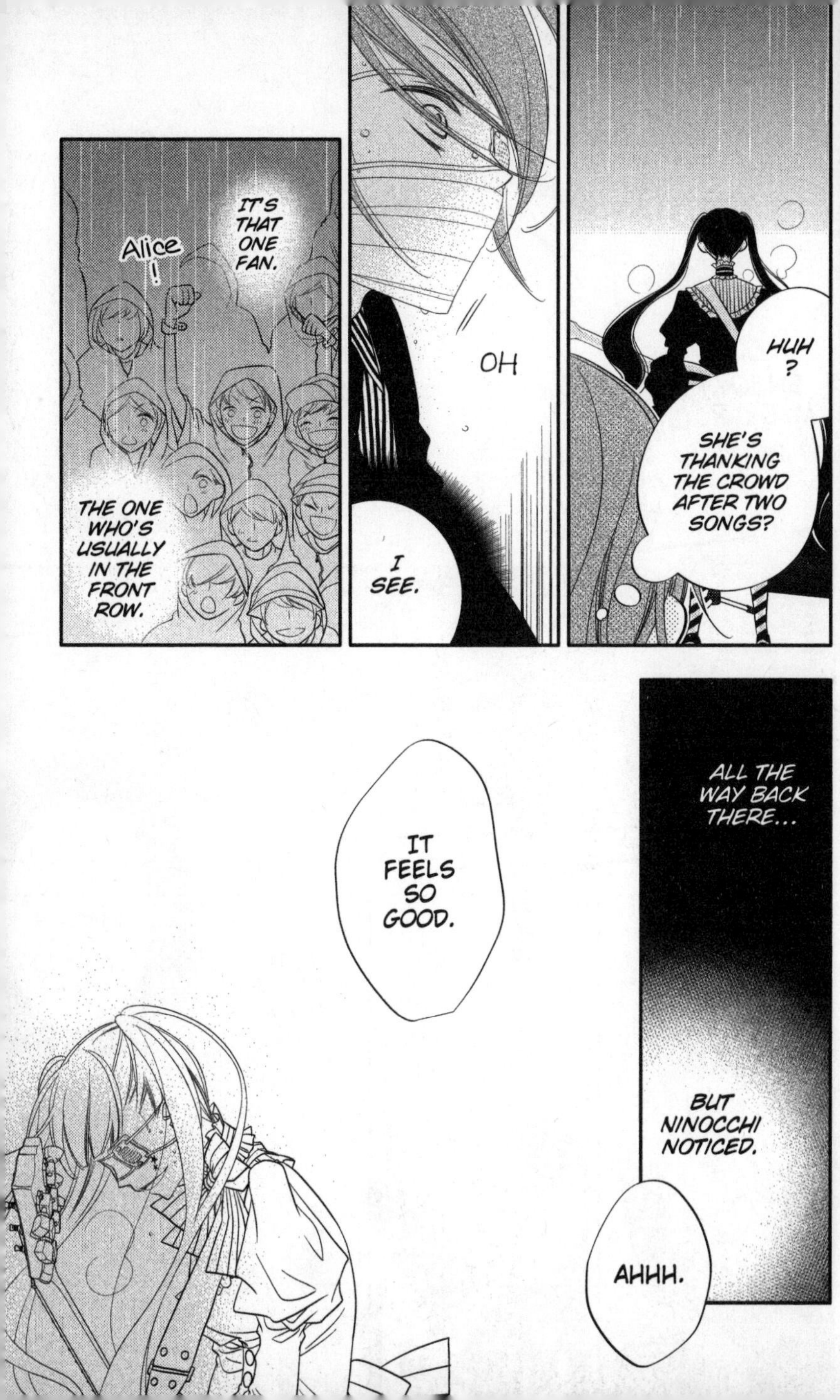
HUH?
SHE'S THANKING THE CROWD AFTER TWO SONGS?
OH
I SEE.
IT'S THAT ONE FAN.
Alice!
THE ONE WHO'S USUALLY IN THE FRONT ROW.
ALL THE WAY BACK THERE...
BUT NINOCCHI NOTICED.
AHHH.
IT FEELS SO GOOD.

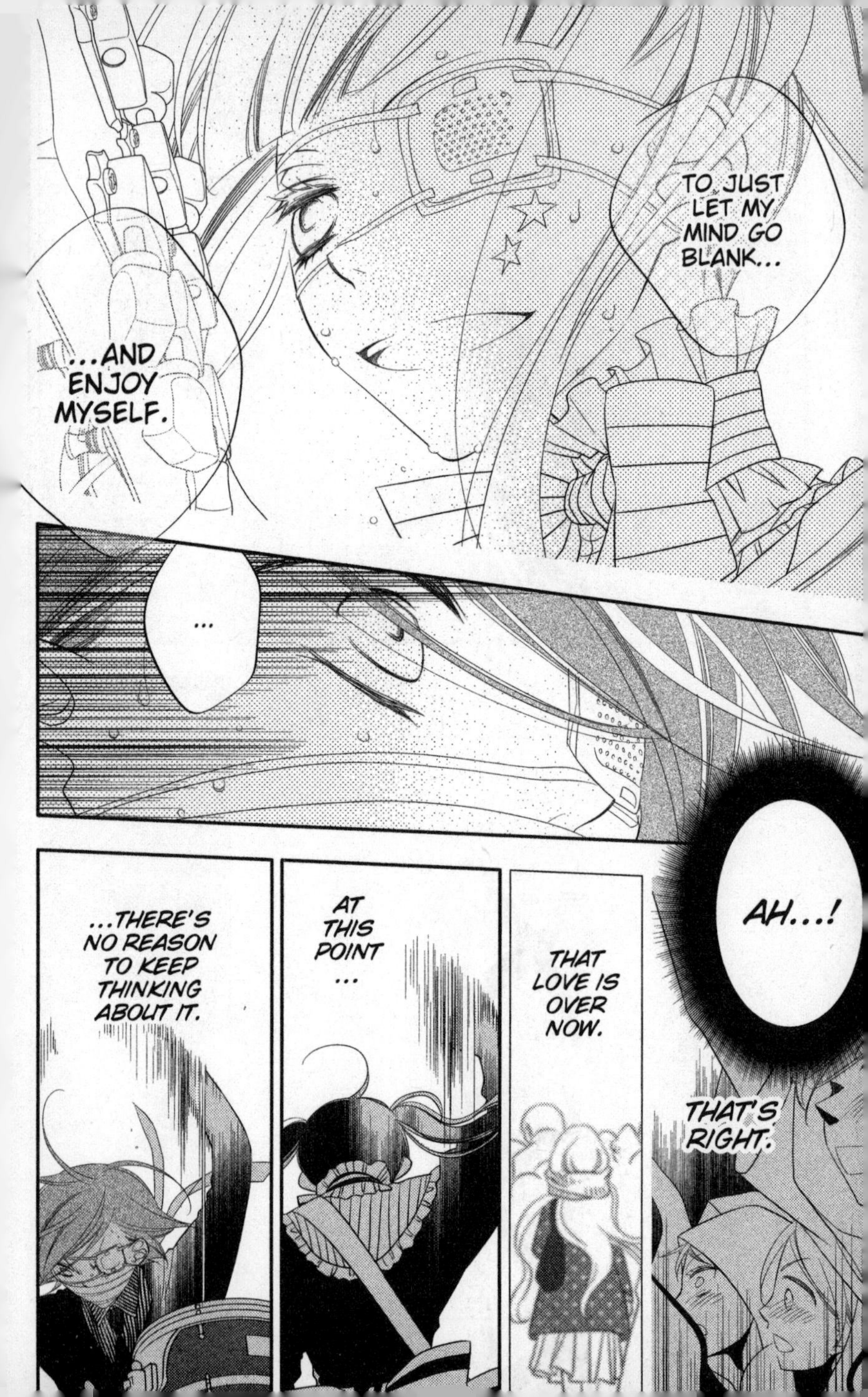
TO JUST LET MY MIND GO BLANK...
...AND ENJOY MYSELF.
...
AH...!
THAT'S RIGHT.
THAT LOVE IS OVER NOW.
AT THIS POINT ...
...THERE'S NO REASON TO KEEP THINKING ABOUT IT.

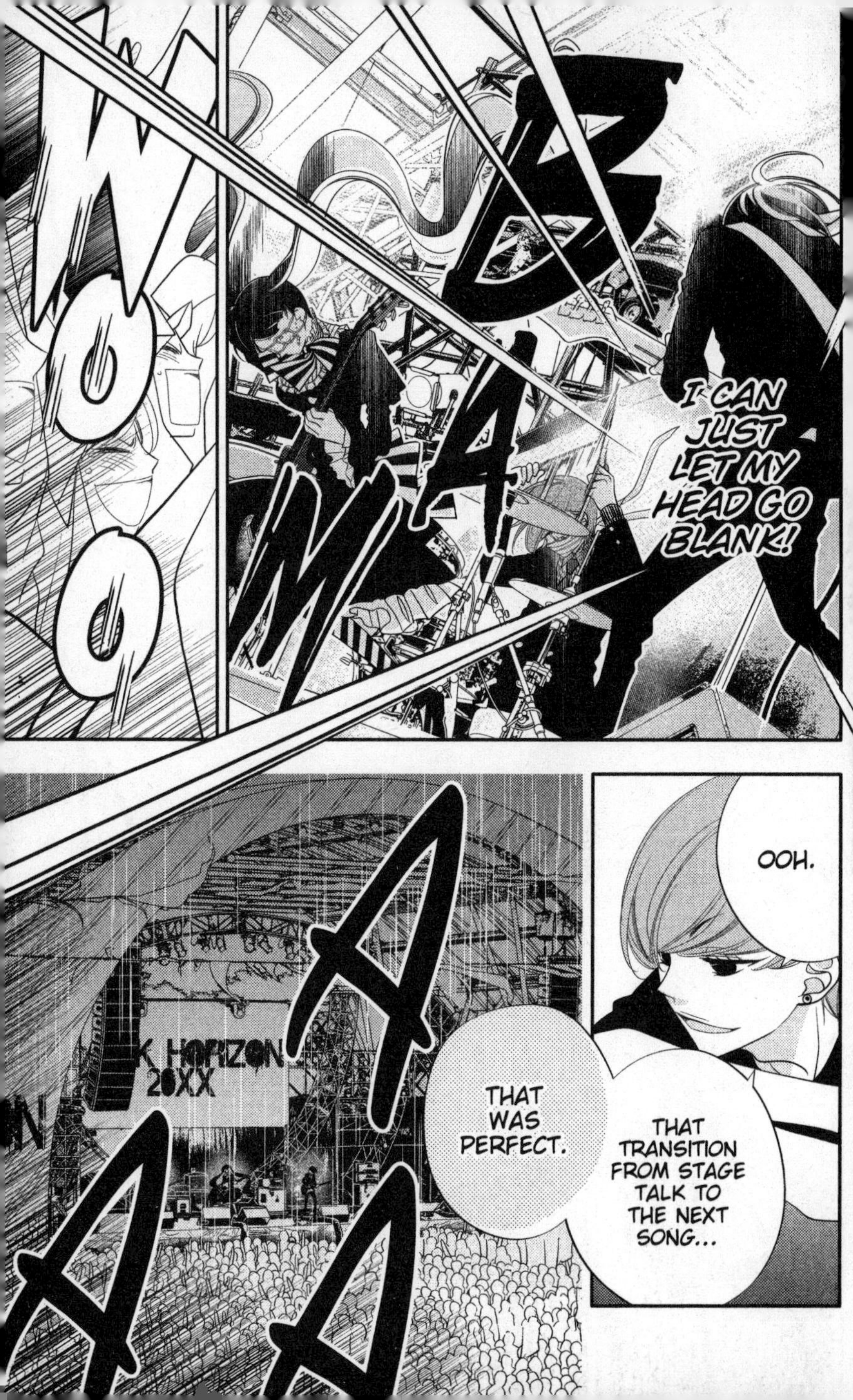
I CAN JUST LET MY HEAD GO BLANK!
OOH.
THAT TRANSITION FROM STAGE TALK TO THE NEXT SONG...
THAT WAS PERFECT.
K HORIZON 20XX

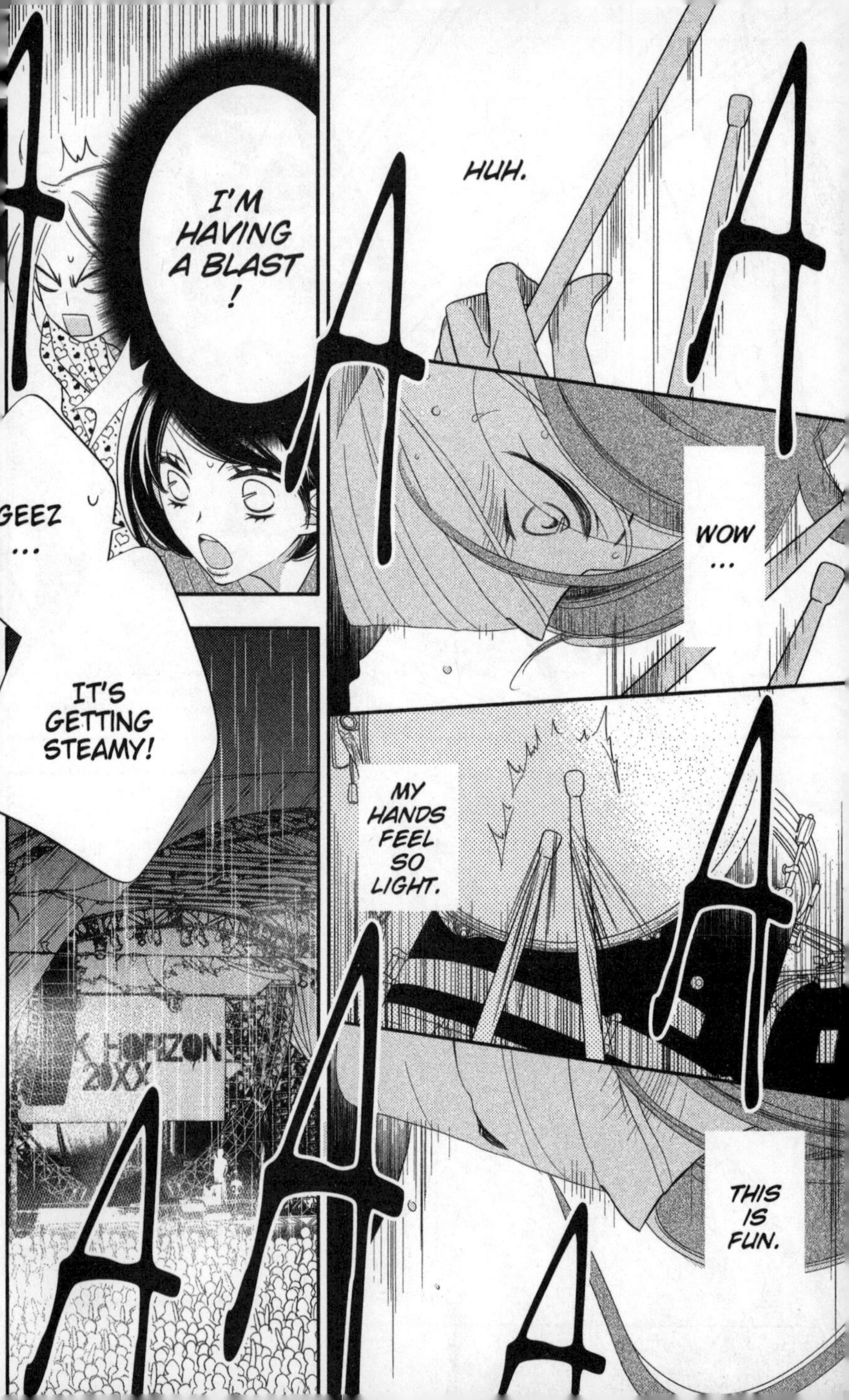
HUH.
WOW...
MY HANDS FEEL SO LIGHT.
THIS IS FUN.
I'M HAVING A BLAST!
GEEZ...
IT'S GETTING STEAMY!
K HORIZON 20XX
HAAAAAA

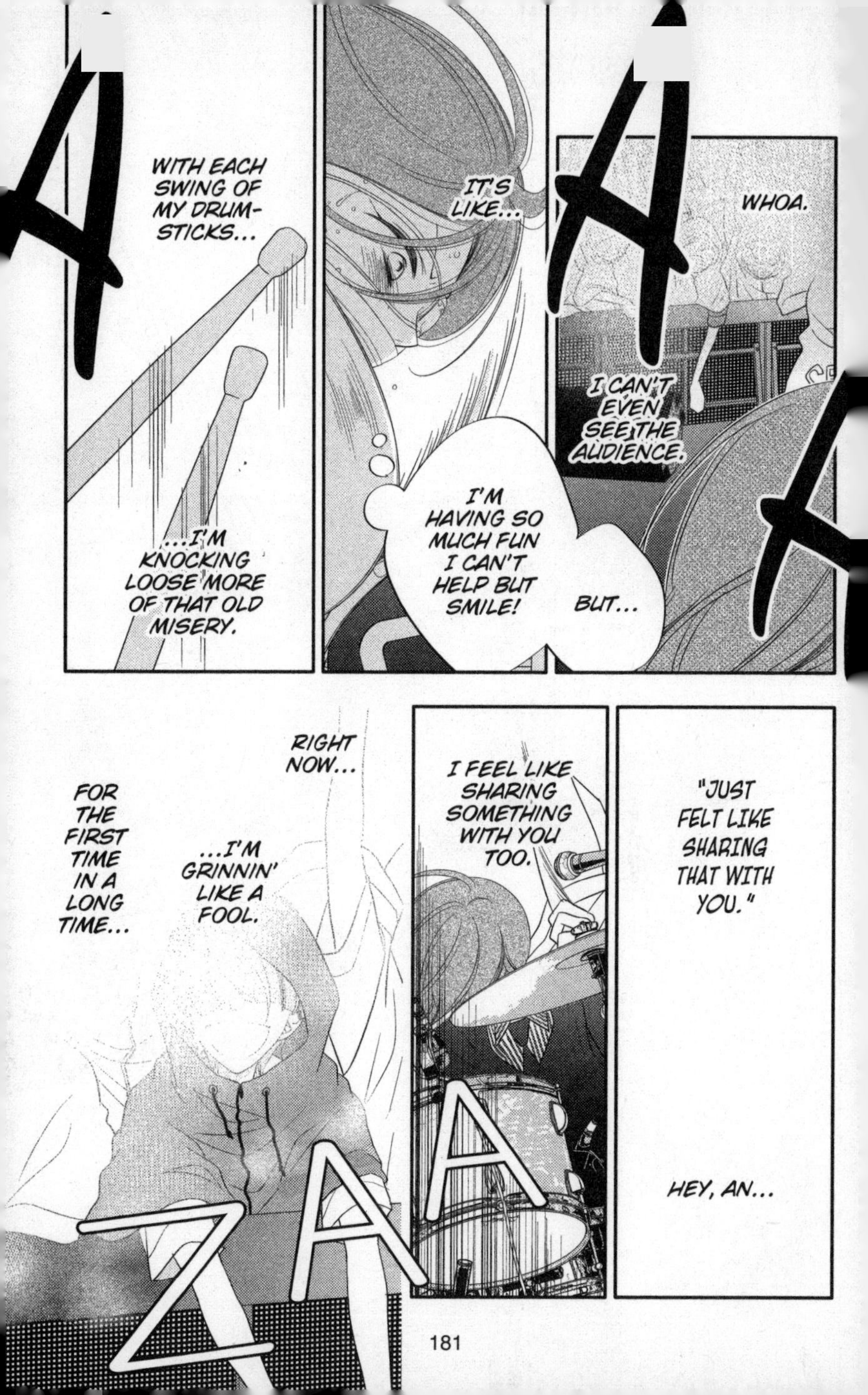

AAAA
WHOA.
I CAN'T EVEN SEE THE AUDIENCE.
BUT...
I'M HAVING SO MUCH FUN I CAN'T HELP BUT SMILE!
IT'S LIKE...
WITH EACH SWING OF MY DRUM-STICKS...
...I'M KNOCKING LOOSE MORE OF THAT OLD MISERY.
"JUST FELT LIKE SHARING THAT WITH YOU."
HEY, AN...
I FEEL LIKE SHARING SOMETHING WITH YOU TOO.
RIGHT NOW...
...I'M GRINNIN' LIKE A FOOL.
FOR THE FIRST TIME IN A LONG TIME...
ZAA

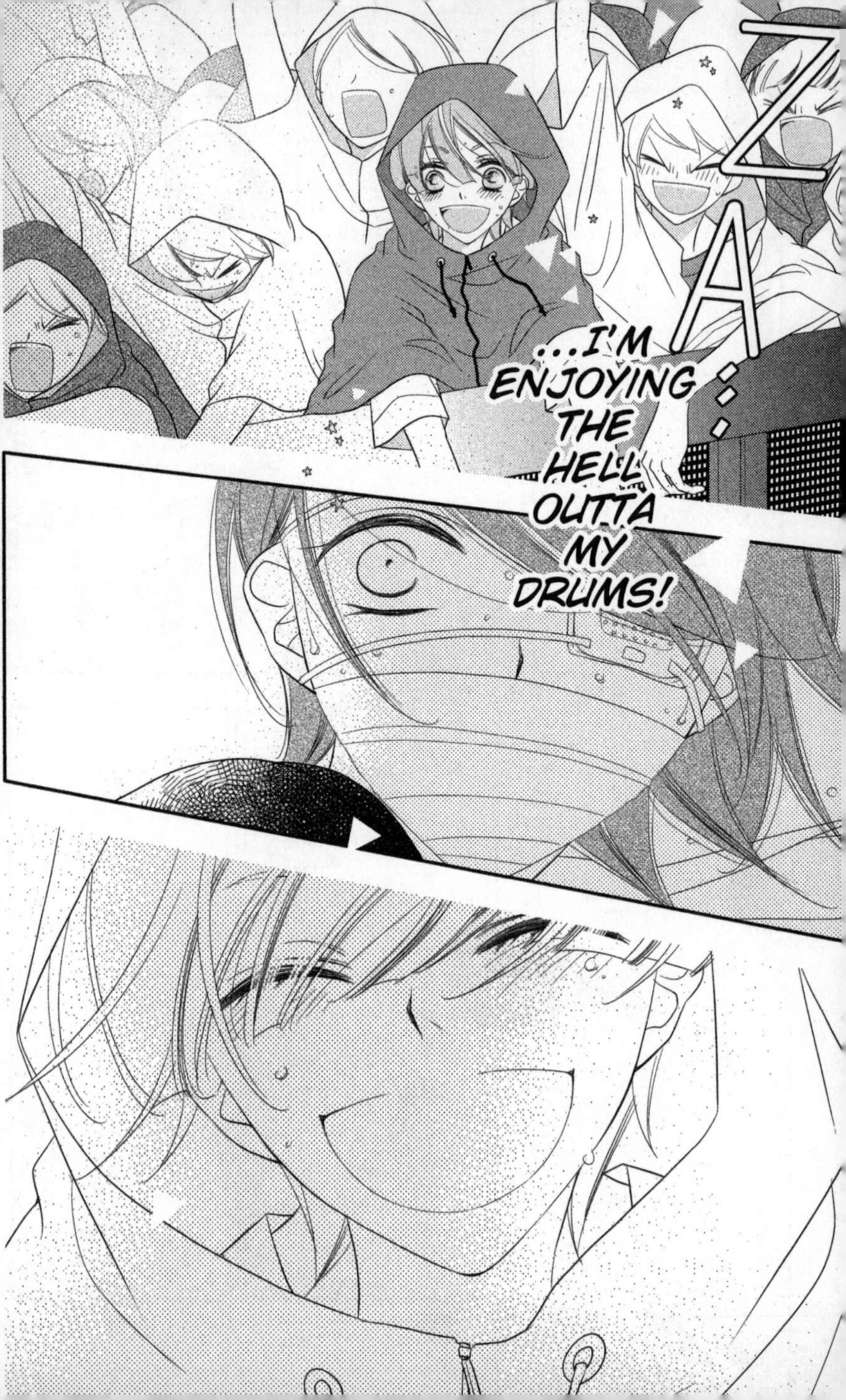
ZA…
...I'M ENJOYING THE HELL OUTTA MY DRUMS!

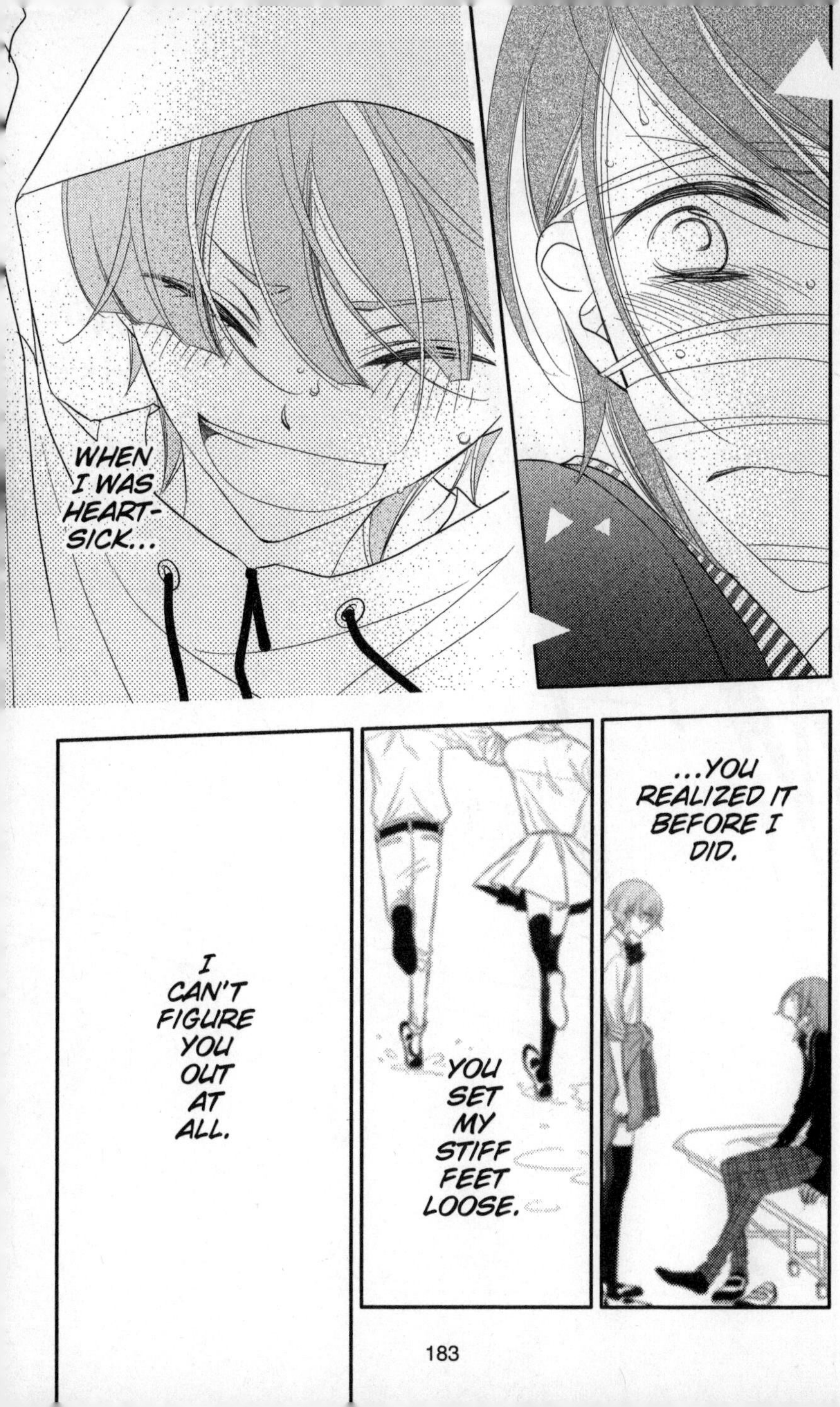
WHEN I WAS HEART-SICK...
...YOU REALIZED IT BEFORE I DID.
YOU SET MY STIFF FEET LOOSE.
I CAN'T FIGURE YOU OUT AT ALL.

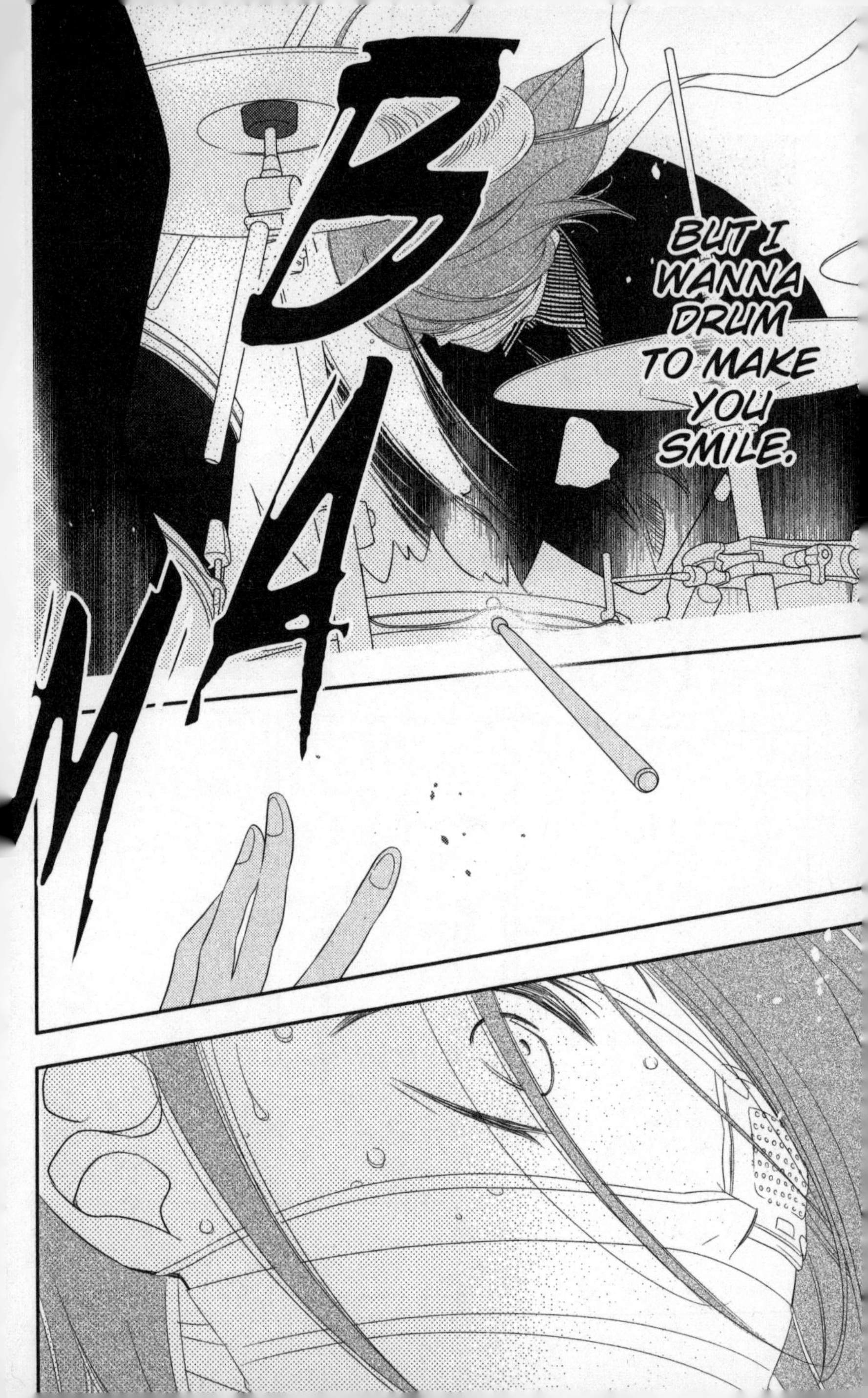
BUT I WANNA DRUM TO MAKE YOU SMILE.
BAM

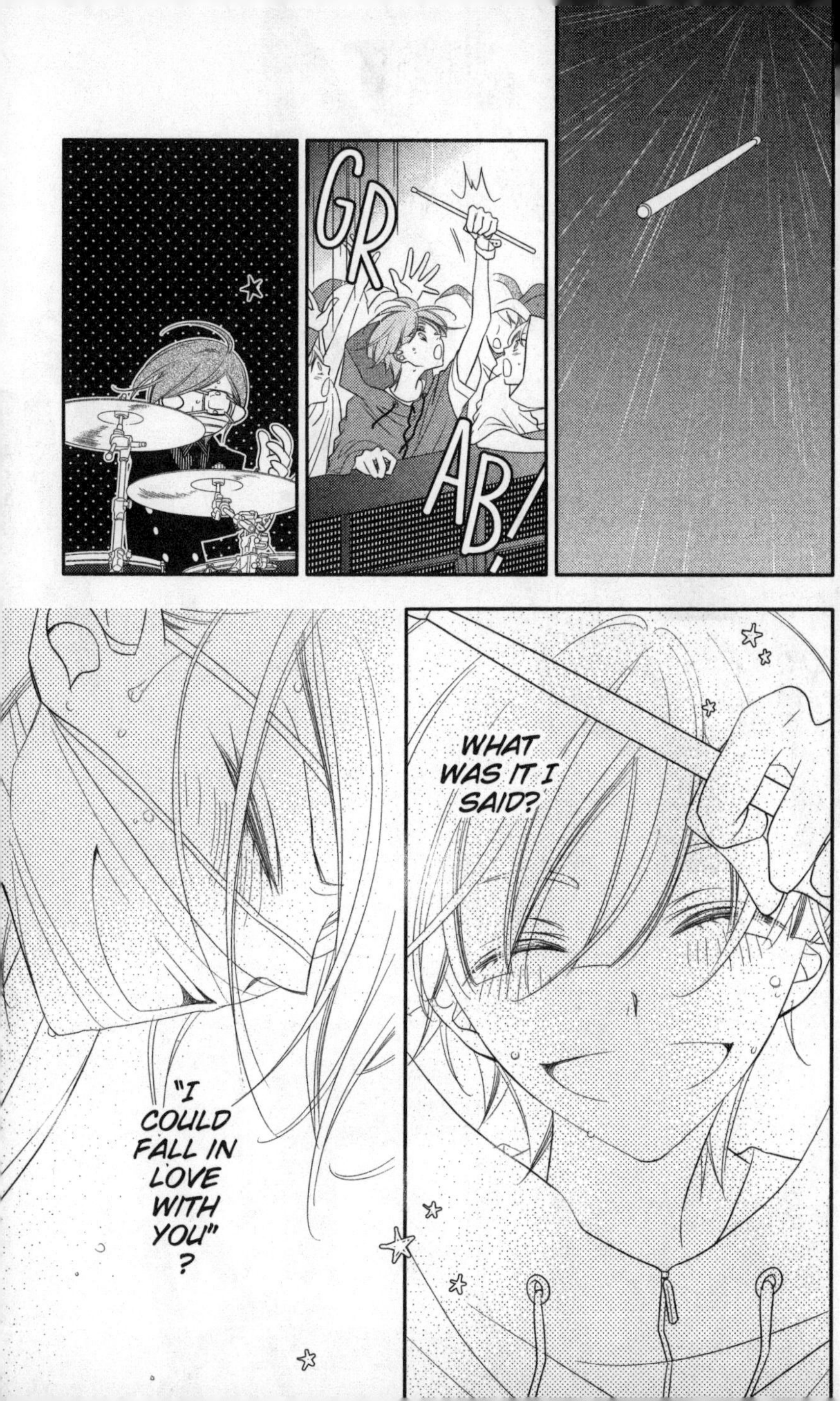
GRAB!
WHAT WAS IT I SAID?
"I COULD FALL IN LOVE WITH YOU"?

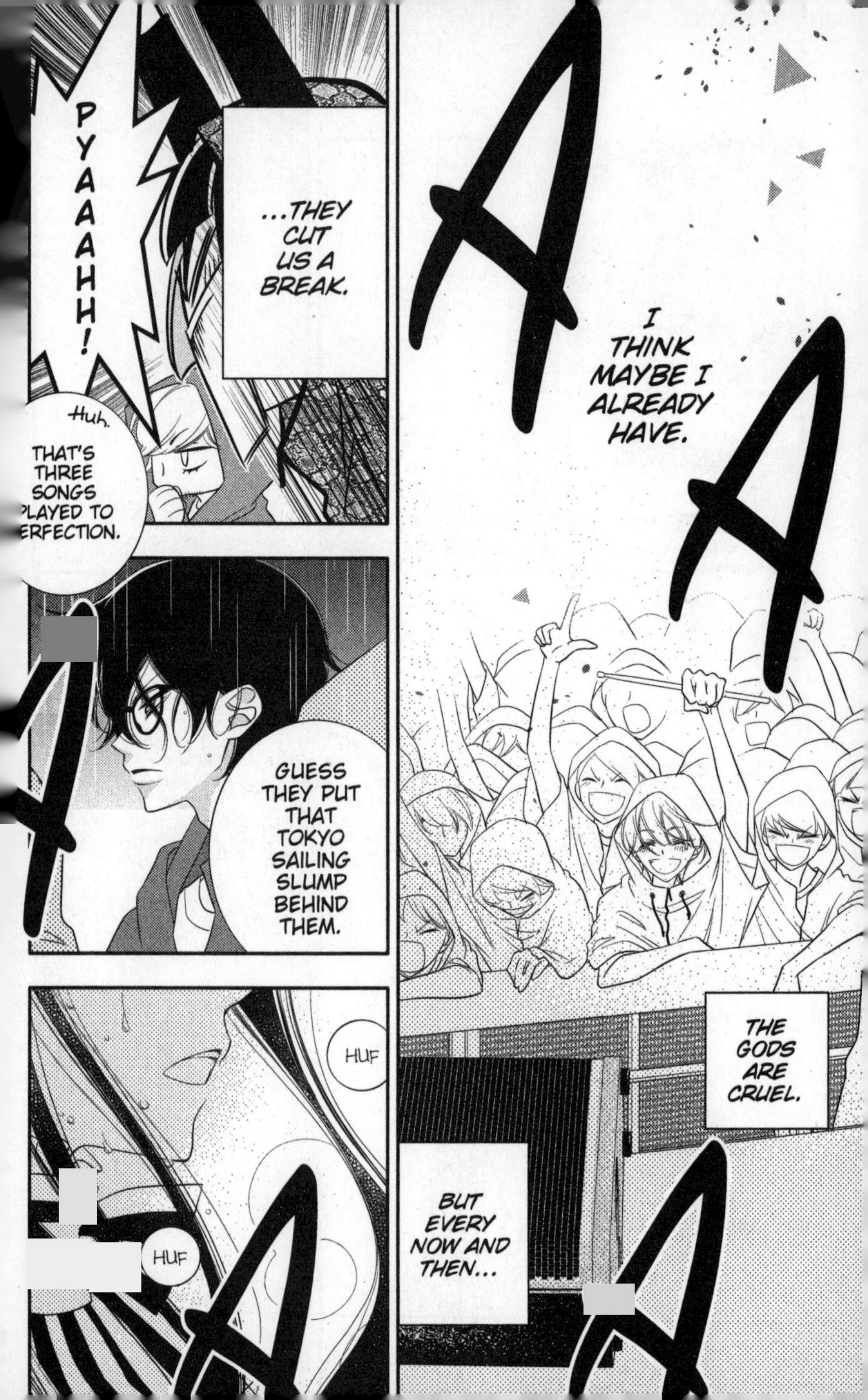
I THINK MAYBE I ALREADY HAVE.
AAAA
THE GODS ARE CRUEL.
BUT EVERY NOW AND THEN...
...THEY CUT US A BREAK.
PYAAAAHH!
Huh.
THAT'S THREE SONGS PLAYED TO ERFECTION.
GUESS THEY PUT THAT TOKYO SAILING SLUMP BEHIND THEM.
HUF
HUF

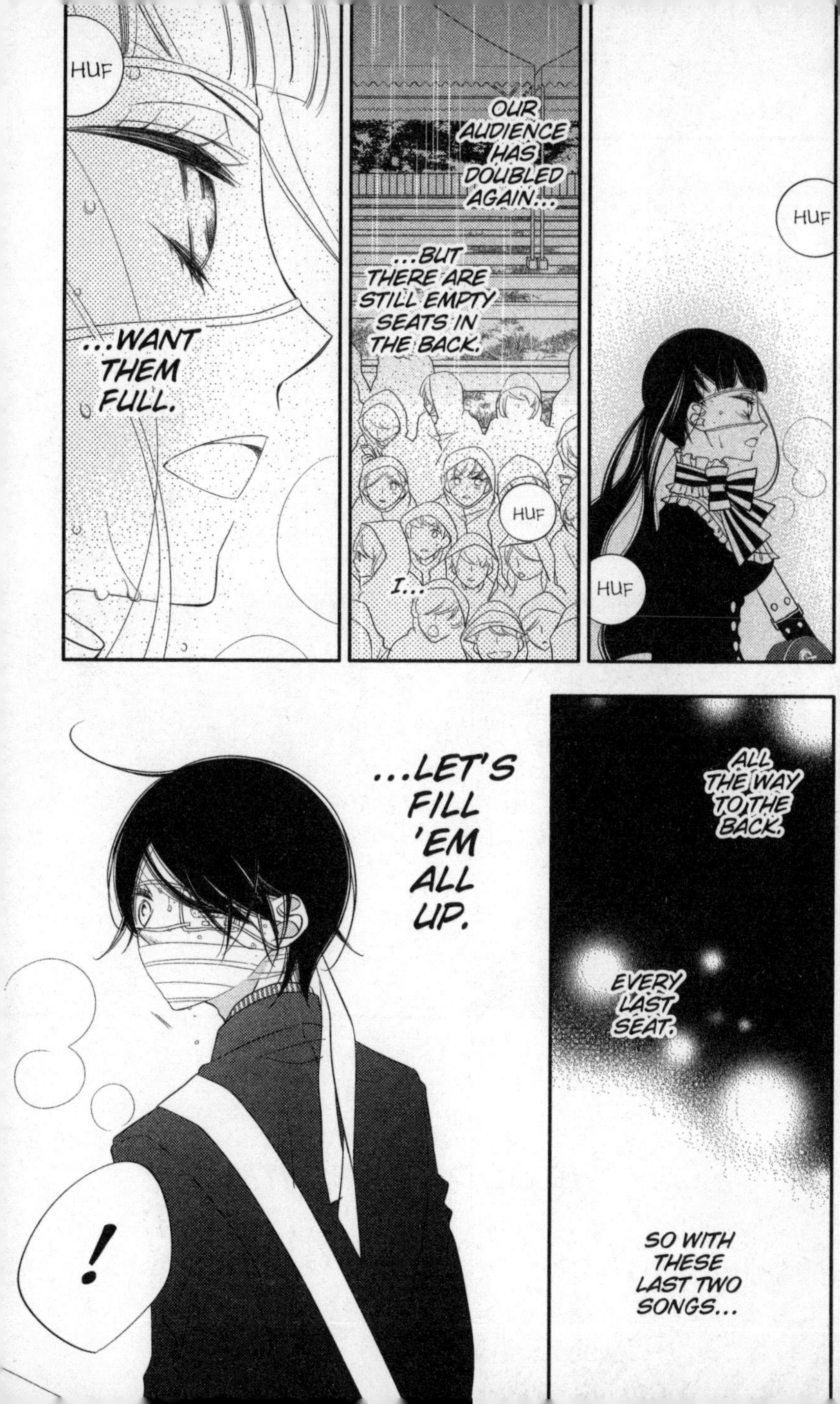
HUF
HUF
OUR AUDIENCE HAS DOUBLED AGAIN...
...BUT THERE ARE STILL EMPTY SEATS IN THE BACK.
HUF
I...
HUF
...WANT THEM FULL.
ALL THE WAY TO THE BACK.
EVERY LAST SEAT.
SO WITH THESE LAST TWO SONGS...
...LET'S FILL 'EM ALL UP.
!

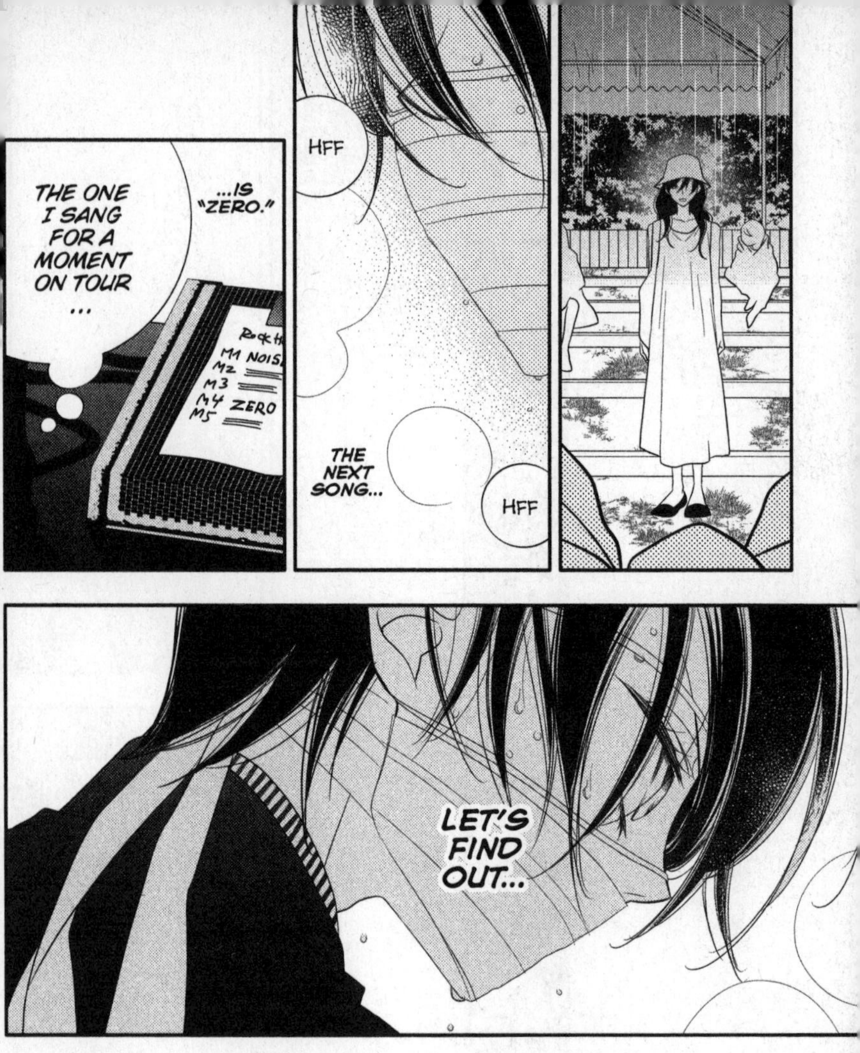
HFF
THE NEXT SONG...
HFF
THE ONE I SANG FOR A MOMENT ON TOUR...
...IS "ZERO."
M1 NOIS
M2
M3
M4 ZERO
M5
LET'S FIND OUT...

...IF THE GODS ARE WITH ME.

TO BE CONTINUED IN ANONYMOUS NOISE 16

For the first time in a long time, I pulled a "Great Luck" fortune during the New Year celebration. That's the best you can get! I'm so happy! *Ha ha*. I'll be throwing myself wholeheartedly into creating manga for what promises to be a fantastic year.

- Ryoko Fukuyama

Born on January 5 in Wakayama Prefecture in Japan, Ryoko Fukuyama debuted as a manga artist after winning the Hakusensha Athena Shinjin Taisho Prize from Hakusensha's *Hana to Yume* magazine. She is also the author of *Nosatsu Junkie*. *Anonymous Noise* was adapted into an anime in 2017.

ANONYMOUS NOISE
Vol. 15
Shojo Beat Edition

STORY AND ART BY
RYOKO FUKUYAMA

English Translation & Adaptation/Casey Loe
Touch-Up Art & Lettering/Joanna Estep
Design/Yukiko Whitley
Editor/Amy Yu

Fukumenkei Noise by Ryoko Fukuyama
© Ryoko Fukuyama 2018
All rights reserved.
First published in Japan in 2018 by HAKUSENSHA, Inc., Tokyo.
English language translation rights arranged with HAKUSENSHA, Inc., Tokyo.

Printed in the U.S.A.

Published by VIZ Media, LLC
P.O. Box 77010
San Francisco, CA 94107

10 9 8 7 6 5 4 3 2 1
First printing, July 2019

viz.com

shojobeat.com

Surprise!

You may be reading the wrong way!

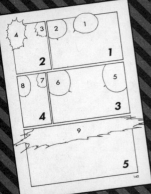

It's true: In keeping with the original Japanese comic format, this book reads from right to left—so action, sound effects and word balloons are completely reversed. This preserves the orientation of the original artwork—plus, it's fun! Check out the diagram shown here to get the hang of things, and then turn to the other side of the book to get started!